Language and Logics

MW00608422

Edinburgh Advanced Textbooks in Linguistics

Series Editors
Peter Ackema, Reader in Linguistics (University of Edinburgh)
Mitsuhiko Ota, Reader in the Phonetics and Phonology of Language
Acquisition (University of Edinburgh)

Editorial Advisory Board
Ricardo Bermudez-Otero (University of Manchester)
Kersti Börjars (University of Manchester)
Greville Corbett (University of Surrey)
Anastasia Giannakidou (University of Chicago)
Caroline Heycock (University of Edinburgh)
Jack Hoeksema (University of Groningen)
Miriam Meyerhoff (University of Edinburgh)
Geoffrey Pullum (University of Edinburgh)
Andrew Spencer (University of Essex)
Donca Steriade (MIT)
Susi Wurmbrand (University of Connecticut)

TITLES IN THE SERIES INCLUDE
Essential Programming for Linguistics
Martin Weisser

Morphology: From Data to Theories
Antonio Fábregas and Sergio Scalise

*Language and Logics: An Introduction to the Logical Foundations
of Language*
Howard Gregory

Visit the Edinburgh Advanced Textbooks in Linguistics website at
www.euppublishing.com/series/EATL

Language and Logics

An Introduction to the Logical Foundations of Language

Howard Gregory

EDINBURGH
University Press

In memory of my parents and first teachers of language
and reasoning
Keith and Margaret Gregory

© Howard Gregory, 2015

Edinburgh University Press Ltd
The Tun – Holyrood Road, 12(2f) Jackson's Entry, Edinburgh EH8 8PJ

www.euppublishing.com

Typeset in 10/12 Minion by
Servis Filmsetting Ltd, Stockport, Cheshire,
and printed and bound in Great Britain by
CPI Group (UK) Ltd, Croydon, CR0 4YY

A CIP record for this book is available from the British Library

ISBN 978 0 7486 9162 3 (hardback)
ISBN 978 0 7486 9164 7 (webready PDF)
ISBN 978 0 7486 9163 0 (paperback)
ISBN 978 0 7486 9165 4 (epub)

The right of Howard Gregory to be identified as author of this work has been asserted in
accordance with the Copyright, Designs and Patents Act 1988, and the Copyright and
Related Rights Regulations 2003 (SI No. 2498)

CONTENTS

PREFACE

This text is intended to take linguistics students beyond the classical logic taught in elementary courses and introduce them to some of the non-classical logics that have found uses in contemporary linguistics. It is based on lectures given at the University of Göttingen between 2002 and 2009.

The book is meant to be flexible enough to be useful for a variety of courses, but it may be useful to know that it was designed as a third course, for students with at least an introductory course and possibly an intermediate course in Formal Semantics already behind them. I was able to teach it as a second course in Göttingen partly because the first course included some Montague semantics – something made possible by the long German winter semesters as well as by the calibre of the students.

Much of the presupposed introductory material is, in fact, recapitulated in the first part of this book. This is intended primarily as revision, and is presented as such, often pointing out the simplified assumptions made and giving the material a slant which will be developed in later chapters. It is not really intended for teaching the basics for the first time, but it is hoped that it can nonetheless be useful in bringing students without much background up to speed. To help this, I have included some material in the early chapters that I would not normally have time to teach in class on a more advanced course. However, the main criterion for inclusion has been usefulness in the rest of the book.

I am grateful to my students for making these courses interesting. As is usually the case, teaching them also helped my own better understanding of the material contained here.

The unusual circumstances in which the book was written have given me less opportunity for interaction than is usual for books of this kind, besides limited access to the bibliography. I would like, however, to thank a number of colleagues and students for valuable feedback, notably Dirk Buschbom, Yuli Feng, Chris Götze, Mingya Liu, Glyn Morrill, Carl Pollard and Linda Wiechetek.

I am also grateful to the editors at EUP, Peter Ackema, Mits Ota, Gillian Leslie and Laura Williamson, for their professionalism, courtesy and encouragement in handling the publication of this book.

CHAPTER 1

MEANING AND LOGIC

Pour le moment, la linguistique générale m' apparaît comme une système de géométrie. On aboutit à des théorèmes qu'il faut démontrer.[1]

Everybody has semantic intuitions. They are part of knowing a language. The following pairs of sentences illustrate two of the most basic of these intuitions, which happen to be also among the most important.

(1.1) Entailment
    1. Chara is a dog.
    2. Chara is an animal.
(1.2) Contradiction
    1. Mary eats meat.
    2. Mary is a vegetarian.

In (1.1), if the first sentence is true then the second sentence must be true. This is **entailment** (the first sentence 'entails' the second, or the second 'follows from' the first). In (1.2), both sentences cannot simultaneously be true. The two sentences together make a **contradiction**.

If we know the meanings of the English words being used, we will probably not argue with any of this. Of course there are certain assumptions here – that the words are being used in their most obvious sense, that the sentences in each pair refer to the same time and the names refer to the same creature. Most of the time, we accommodate these assumptions without thinking.

Note that entailment and contradiction are relations between *sentences*. They involve the notions **true** and **false**, which can generally speaking be applied only to sentences. In these particular examples, however, a crucial role is also played by word meaning. The entailment in (1.1) comes from the fact that a dog is a kind of animal, and the contradiction in (1.2) comes from the fact that 'vegetarian' means somebody who doesn't eat meat. In the language of lexical semantics (the study of word meaning), 'dog' is a **hyponym** of 'animal', while 'vegetarian' and 'meat eater' are **antonyms** (opposites). Entailment and contradiction, however, belong to the language of sentence meaning, not word meaning, and are used to describe relations between sentences, not words.

These semantic intuitions are central not only to understanding language but to reasoning with language. The art of doing this is what the ancient Greeks called **logic**. The trouble is that beyond basic cases like the ones just described, language can mislead. Something seems to follow when it doesn't, or seems to be a contradiction when it isn't, and it may not be obvious where we have gone wrong. Also, the mistake may be sincere, or it may be a deliberate attempt to mislead and manipulate others.

Just to practise, try to put your finger on exactly what is wrong with these lines of argument.

(1.3)   1. If it was sunny, I could go for a swim. But it isn't, so I can't.
   2. That relationship was unhappy. So I can assume that all relationships are unhappy.
   3. Have you stopped beating your wife yet? Whether you answer yes or no, you are guilty of wife beating.
   4. The enemy will come over the hill or through the woods. Here they are coming over the hill. So they won't be coming through the woods.
   5. Most of the troublemakers were students. She's a student, so she was probably one of them.
   6. Everything must have a cause. Therefore there must be something which is the cause of everything.
   7. If there is a clever conspiracy, there won't be any evidence. There isn't any evidence, so that shows there must be a clever conspiracy.

Some of these were probably easier than others, but even in the easy cases, it helps to have methods and a fixed terminology with which to discuss the problem. This can be done relatively informally, or at the other extreme we can aim at mathematical precision. The latter approach is called **formal logic**. Either way, the difference between correct and incorrect (or downright crooked) reasoning is something to care about.[2] Formal approaches share the same concerns but explore them in a more systematic way. There are also degrees of formality. To linguistics students from an 'arts' background, much of this book will probably seem very formal. Mathematical logicians, on the other hand, will see it as rather informal.

What about the plural 'logics' in the title? It is natural to think that either an argument is logical or it isn't, and that there is one logical system that will tell us which. But once we get beyond very basic cases for which our intuitions are clear, we find ourselves in territory where we have to make choices, and it isn't always so obvious that the same choice will be right for all circumstances. Some of these choices will be examined in Chapter 2, and indeed throughout the book. But the general approach will be not so much 'are these the right choices?', but 'what happens if we adopt them?', 'what situations are they useful in?', and 'how are they connected to other choices?' This is, in general, the picture that has emerged in modern logic as it has developed over the past hundred years or more. It was not planned that way; many of the developments were pioneered by people who believed passionately that only one set of choices was correct. However, the fact that they chose differently led to a plurality of systems, and, stepping back a little from the disputes, it seems that use can be made of most of them in different situations.

An analogy from geometry might be useful here.[3] The logic of geometry was first set out by the ancient Greek mathematician Euclid. His method was to put forward principles which seemed to be self-evident, from which all other statements about geometry should be derivable step by step. Such principles are known as **postulates** or **axioms**. The fifth of Euclid's axioms (the 'parallel postulate'), though it seems to hold under everyday conditions, attracted the suspicions of a number of mathematicians, who attempted to reassure themselves by showing that without it we would arrive at a contradiction (and therefore it must be true – an important pattern of reasoning which we will examine in the next chapter). The best known attempt to do this was that of the eighteenth-century mathematician Giovanni Saccheri. Saccheri's version is important because his attempted proof of contradiction was faulty, and the massive structure that he had erected turned out to be a consistent alternative to Euclidean geometry. The implications of this were developed by Lobachevsky, Gauss and others into 'non-Euclidean geometries'. These proved to be more than just a theoretical exercise when it turned out that some of them had real-world applications or models.

So much for geometry; similar situations have arisen many times in logic. Western logic has been dominated by certain postulates which make up what is called 'classical logic' (a term that will be defined more precisely later). Other, non-classical, logics have been developed by people who were dissatisfied with features of classical logic, or had interests for which the choices made by classical logic didn't seem to make sense. These alternative systems, however, are not only consistent but have often proved to have useful applications. So just as we can speak of 'geometries', in the plural, we can speak of 'logics'. Many of these, though devised before the invention of the computer, have turned out to have applications in computing and artificial intelligence. Other applications are possible as well. Linguistics is a particular case in point; none of the logics considered here, with one possible exception, was devised with the interests of linguists in mind. But in every case they have been applied by linguists to phenomena that they wish to reason about.

This pluralistic approach to logics is held by many, though by no means all, modern logicians. It was captured by the title of an influential book, *Philosophy of Logics*, by Susan Haack.[4] This was a conscious reply to Quine's (1978) work, *The Philosophy of Logic* (singular), which rejected most non-classical logics as not being 'real logic'. The title and outlook of Haack's book are both obviously reflected in this one, and the structure of it is as well. Haack distinguished between logics which are *extensions* of classical logic (they are classical logic with additional symbols) and those which are *deviations* from classical logic (the symbols used in classical logic behave in a 'deviant' way). This terminology is rather tongue in cheek, and I will use it here in the same way. The four parts of the book therefore comprise: (i) a revision of classical logic, as standardly taught in introductory semantics courses; (ii) an introduction to modal logic, the main extension of classical logic used in linguistics; (iii) two parts dealing with deviant logics. I have divided deviant logics into partial and substructural, with intuitionistic logic acting as a kind of bridge between the two.

While Haack's interest is philosophical, the purpose of this book is strictly linguistic, and I have tried to stick closely to the linguistic motivation of logics at all times. So this seems a good place to go back to the connection between logic and language.

1.1 LINGUISTIC MEANING

Semantics is the scientific study of meaning, in particular linguistic meaning. To understand where it fits into the architecture of a linguistic theory, it is worth going back to the work of Ferdinand de Saussure,[5] known as 'the father of modern linguistics'. One of Saussure's central ideas was that language is a system of **signs**, each sign being an essentially arbitrary coupling of form and meaning – the **signifier** and **signified** respectively.[6] By form, Saussure meant sound (another main feature of his teaching was insistence on the primacy of spoken language); he therefore spoke of signs as combining 'phonic substance' with some kind of meaning substance. (His term for the latter was 'conceptual substance', but let's not say anything so committal about it just yet.) The nature of this phonic substance and meaning substance, however, was elusive; each could only be understood in terms of oppositions, having no positive building blocks from which it could be built up. For example at the phonic level, there is no such thing as a 'p', only a contrast in voicing between /p/ and /b/, and another contrast (of place) between /p/ and /t/. These particular contrasts are important linguistically because languages fasten on them to distinguish different signs.

This insight proved immensely productive in phonology, where it gave rise to the technical concept of the phoneme and its successors. The nature of the 'meaning substance' – the 'signifieds' – proved more elusive, however. Saussure and his immediate followers were interested in oppositions in lexical meaning, drawing attention to the way that different languages divided up certain conceptual areas (such as colour, or kinship terminology) in different ways, regarding different oppositions and relations as being significant. For example, English has the words green and blue, (classical) Chinese has only one word for both, while Russian has separate words for dark and light blue. In these particular areas, and some others, this insight seems quite clear. However, generalising it beyond a rather limited set of stock examples has proved more difficult. Consequently, the 'meaning' side of Saussure's approach (what he hoped would be a general science of 'semiotics') proved less influential *in linguistics* than his phonological insights. (It has received a great deal more attention in philosophy, especially what is sometimes known as 'continental philosophy'.)

The other distinction that should be drawn here is between lexical signs (roughly speaking, 'words')[7] and the signs corresponding to larger units such as phrases, sentences and whole discourses. The lexical signs link lexical phonology and lexical meaning, and it is here that the arbitrariness of the association between sound and meaning is most apparent. The larger units are built up out of lexical units in ways which may still involve some arbitrariness, but also involve systematic patterns. At the level of form, these combinations are the province of **syntax**. The process by which word meanings combine to form larger units of meaning – or at least that part of the process which is governed by rules and patterns – can be called **compositional semantics**. How these processes work, and how they are related to syntax, are among the main themes of this book.

Although Saussure emphasised the primacy of spoken language, in practice there is often a division of labour in modern linguistics between the analysis of sound into words (the 'speech recognition' problem), and those areas of linguistics which may take written text as their basic data and deal with its structure (syntax) and meaning (semantics). This book falls squarely into the second of these areas, and so we will take 'signifiers' as being written words, which is to say strings of symbols. These can be understood as a stand-in for sound (or for the other forms that 'signifiers' can take, such as sign language). I will refer to signifiers as 'linguistic forms' or 'linguistic expressions', and signifieds as 'semantic content'. This contrast between form and content will often be reinforced by putting the former in inverted commas (in computer languages, a common notation for strings), while the meaning of a word will be represented by a homonymous word in italics.[8]

Syntax came to the forefront of linguistics with Noam Chomsky's 'generative grammar'.[9] Although not the only interest of Chomsky's, part of the significance of that work was that it enlisted techniques from logic and computer language theory to attempt a precise description of natural language syntax. It was not the first such attempt,[10] but it has been by far the most influential, and attracted the interest of, among others, logicians and analytic philosophers.

Generative linguists initially tried to exclude semantics from consideration, on the grounds that the whole idea of meaning was too woolly to allow scientific analysis. Analytic philosophers had long had exactly the opposite problem; they had a lot to say about meaning, but regarded natural language as too vague and nebulous for their sophisticated logical techniques to work on. In the late 1960s some philosophers recognised that Chomsky's syntactic work held out the possibility that this might no longer be true, and proposed that logic could help provide an account of the elusive 'meaning' part of language. The main philosophers concerned were Donald Davidson (1967) and Richard Montague (see Thomason 1974). There are certain important differences between the two, which will be discussed when we get to them.

To motivate the approach we will be using, let's look briefly at how early generative linguists were trying to deal with semantics (those who were trying to deal with it at all). Essentially they would add 'semantic markers' (or features) to the syntactic phrase structure trees. Examples of such markers were NEGATIVE, or CAUSE. There is no denying that these notions play an important role in language. The problem was that they were still being treated at the level of syntax, that is, as **signifiers**, with no account being given of what they signify.

To make this clearer, imagine that I come across the word 'kniga', and want to know what it means. One way I can do that is if somebody translates it for me into English, as 'book'. I can now associate it with the intended meaning *book* – say, a bundle of paper and print markings, or a mental image of them. However, this is only because, as an English speaker, I have a mechanism for associating the English word form 'book' with this word sense. Otherwise the translation would be of no avail. If some well-meaning Japanese friend told me instead that 'kniga' means 'hon', I would be none the wiser. He has just translated from one signifier to another. So it is not just translating that enables me to understand, but translating into something which I can interpret (i.e. match with something non-linguistic, a **signified**).

In the 'book' example, what enabled me to make this match between a signifier and a signified was my knowledge of English. In linguistic semantics, we are looking for an explicit account rather than relying on hunches. So if we are going to use translation, it should be into something whose association with a signified can be explicitly studied. The language of semantic markers, in itself, does not provide this; it simply translates them into another form of signifier, which David Lewis dubbed 'markerese'. He added that they might as well have translated it into Latin![11]

So can we do any better? First, we have to decide what kind of objects the signifieds are. Once we have decided that they are objects outside the linguistic system itself, we are in the territory of 'correspondence theories of meaning', which associate expressions in a language with something non-linguistic.[12] But what exactly? Two major answers to this (though not the only ones) are (i) concepts, and (ii) things in the world. It is also possible that the answer is 'both'; they associate words with concepts, which are in turn associated with things in the world. Generally speaking lexical semanticists (those concerned with word meaning), favour the 'concept' approach, and their work is deeply influenced by cognitive psychology. Logicians, by contrast, have tended to take sentence meaning as basic, because the defining characteristic of sentences is that they and only they can be true or false, and truth and falsity are central in logic. We can take it for now that what makes a sentence true or false is the state of affairs in the world. Consequently logicians tend to take 'things in the world' as basic. This is not a straightforward notion by any means, but we can take as our starting point the statement of Wittgenstein (1922), that to know the meaning of a sentence is to know what the world must be like for it to be true. In other words, we must know the **truth conditions** of a sentence. Consequently semantics done in this way is known as **truth-conditional semantics**.

Analytic philosophy has provided us with two tools we need for this project: (i) a systematic way of representing meaning in an artificial or **formal language**, and (ii) over a century of mathematical reflection on how to relate sentences of this artificial language to truth conditions in the world (or, since the world is a big place, to simplified **models** of it). Our strategy is therefore going to be as follows. First we are going to construct artificial languages into which we can *translate* sentences of English (or some other natural language) in such a way as to bring out their meaningful elements. Then we will provide an *interpretation* of these languages in terms of truth conditions. This latter part has already been done for us, to a great extent, by mathematical logicians, though we still have to spend some effort on understanding what they have done! The creative bit is making sure that the first bit, the translation, does justice to our intuitions about the meaning of language.

1.2 LOGIC AND LANGUAGE: A BIT OF BACKGROUND

The connection between logic and linguistics goes back a very long way – in fact, right back to the beginning of both disciplines, which, as far as the western tradition is concerned, means Ancient Greece.

Independent developments in logic go back to a similar period in India, and to the slightly later 'warring states period' of China. However, the Chinese tradition was dealt a severe blow by the burning of books and persecution of most philosophies by the first emperor, Qin Shi Huang. The replacement of his regime by the Han saw a rehabilitation of philosophy, but this did not extend fully to the followers of Mozi (Mocius), who had been the main pioneers of logic.

Indian logic also developed early and on very independent lines, including some insights that have been adopted by recent western logicians (see Chapter 8 for discussion). In classical Hinduism, logic or Nyaya constituted one of the paths to 'enlightenment', in parallel to other schools such as yoga, the eroticism of the Kama Sutra, or Vedic recitation. (Note that no such claims are made for the contents of this book.) Similar traditions took root in Buddhism, despite the apparent disapproving attitude of the Buddha himself towards speculative thought.

The first systematic western study of logic was that of Aristotle (fourth century BC), and arose out of his interest, and that of his predecessors, in language and argumentation. Shortly afterwards a rival school of philosophy, the Stoa, produced their own school of logic. It was also the Stoics who gave us the first classic study of grammar, that of Dionysius Thrax. This work is the source of our traditional classification of words into different 'parts of speech', based partly on form (morphology), but also partly on the kinds of things described – for example, nouns normally denote 'things', verbs denote actions, adjectives describe properties and so on.[13] The fact that we now take this classification for granted should not obscure the fact that at the time it involved serious linguistic and logical analysis, and reflection on the relationship between language and the world.

When Roman rule in western Europe collapsed in the fifth century AD, the classical literary and philosophical tradition was continued by the Byzantines and later the Arabs. It was transmitted to the Arabs by Syriac and Jewish scholars, and it was through the Arabs that ancient philosophy, especially that of Aristotle, who they greatly admired, was passed on. Traditionally this ancillary role is about as much as western writers have allowed the Arabs, but there is now an increasing appreciation of the vitality of Muslim logic in its own right, for example in modal logic.

Thanks to these scholars, logic was rediscovered by the western Europeans as they got themselves organised again in the High Middle Ages. This prompted a creative concern with language, logic and metaphysics, including a revival of interest in how to relate different types of linguistic expression with different aspects of reality. This led to an approach known as 'speculative grammar',[14] in which the organisation of language was thought to hold clues as to the different categories of things that exist in reality (that is, to **ontology**). This flowering of medieval thought on grammar and logic was codified in the late seventeenth century by the Port-Royal monastery in

France, and this influential version of the classical tradition in logic and grammar came to be known as 'traditional logic' and 'traditional grammar'. In the time of Kant (around 1800), this traditional logic was still regarded as the last word on the subject. Kant himself wrote that Aristotle had said all that needed to be said about logic.

In fact, however, Kant's earlier compatriot Leibniz had already envisioned new departures which would result in the eclipse of traditional logic by modern logic. Leibniz envisaged a calculus for resolving disputes between philosophers in a mechanical way analogous to that of arithmetic. Since the ideas involved in Leibniz' programme play an important part in this book, this is a good place to make them explicit. Following Leibniz' lead, I will take it that a logic requires the following three things:

(1.4) 1. A universal artificial notation, to represent the meaningful elements of language without getting bogged down in the details of particular languages – in Leibniz' terminology, *characteristica universalis*.
2. A system for calculating whether one proposition in this language follows from others – Leibniz called this *calculus ratiocinator*, and we will call it a **proof system**.
3. An *interpretation* of expressions in the artificial language, which is independent of the language itself. Leibniz did not actually appreciate the need for this as a separate element, which only became apparent in the twentieth century. It is usually now called a **model**.

The first of these was provided by Gottlob Frege in his work *Begriffsschrift* or 'Concept Notation' (1879), although the actual notation used by Frege was completely different from the symbols used now. Frege was the first to specify what was involved in constructing such a language, as well as providing technical innovations which made clear the power of the new system (some of these will be discussed in due course). Frege is therefore generally recognised as 'the father of modern logic'. However, his work was not widely known until it was discovered and developed by Russell. Independently of Frege, C. S. Peirce developed a system which is regarded by some historians as a separate origin for modern predicate logic.

The idea of consequence (2 above) has always been central in logic, and it will be discussed in Chapter 2. It is a characteristic of modern logic to be systematic about the way the logical consequences of a statement are calculated (or as it is usually called in logic, **proved**). The oldest method is to pick out certain basic statements which are self-evident or can be agreed upon, and show that other statements follow from them step by step. The statements we use as the basis are called **axioms**. This method goes back to ancient times, and Euclid's use of it in geometry has already been mentioned. While it is still going strong, modern logic has also produced other proof systems. Some of those having important linguistic applications will be discussed in the last part of the book.

The need for the third ingredient was shown in the early twentieth century, when a number of mathematicians sought to prove that arithmetic (and with it, the whole of mathematics) could be derived from logical axioms. The most famous names associated with this were Bertrand Russell and David Hilbert; the latter made this the basis of a huge research programme at the University of Göttingen in Germany. In the process the discovery was made (by Kurt Gödel) that the logic needed to express the truths of arithmetic was **incomplete**; that is, it contained statements which were true but could not be proved. Thus a calculus of consequence could not (contrary to Leibniz' conjecture) prove all statements that were logically true. So a distinction has to be drawn between saying that something must be true and showing that it can be proved. This means we need some way of describing true statements directly. The way to do this was provided by Alfred Tarski's **model theory**, which will be introduced in Chapter 3.

The basic format of the chapters in this book is based on this understanding of the essential ingredients of a logic. The initial discussion of the motivations for each logic will be relatively informal, and is designed to motivate the concepts being used. Then, in the second section of each chapter, an artificial language will be formally defined for the logic, so as to provide the 'concept notation' we need. Some logics share basically the same formal language (in which case the new material will be minimal), others have their own special requirements. Then the semantic interpretation for the logic will be described, also fairly formally. Again, the techniques required for this will be similar for some logics, different for others, and the amount of space needed will vary accordingly. The remainder of each chapter will be devoted to more specialised issues, which may be treated selectively by the instructor, but might interest students in particular lines of research.

Proof theory is distributed through the book as follows. Part I includes some discussion of classical modes of inference (for propositional logic) and syllogisms (for quantifiers), and also introduces the tableau method of verification (though this is not really proof theory). Axioms will feature again in Chapter 6, as they are a convenient and transparent way of comparing modal logics, and then again in Chapter 13. Chapter 10 introduces an important alternative, natural deduction, which is important for the logics in the last part of the book. An important offshoot of natural deduction, the Gentzen Calculus, is introduced in Chapter 12.

Here is a summary of the main systems:

(1.5) **Axiomatic systems**: The oldest approach. Certain statements are picked out as being basic and self-evident, from which all other true statements should follow. These basic statements are known as **axioms** (or 'postulates'). Euclid's use of this approach has been mentioned in the text. This approach has attractive mathematical properties, and is often a concise way of comparing the content of different logics.

Natural deduction: Designed to do justice to the way people in fact construct proofs, using strategies such as **hypothetical reasoning**. See Chapter 10. It is popular because of its intuitive character, and has many applications relevant to linguistics.

Gentzen systems: Similar to natural deduction, but with certain rearrangements which make it easier to compute with. It is thus particularly popular in computational linguistics.

Gottlob Frege

Regarded as the 'father of modern logic' for his invention of the propositional and predicate calculi. Though his primary interest was the logic of mathematics, Frege was also very interested in language, and detailed a number of differences which made his logic unsuitable for dealing with natural language. Besides the mismatches between linguistic forms and those revealed by logical analysis, he was the first to highlight the problem of intensionality in language. Frege worked in relative obscurity for much of his career, until his work was discovered and publicised by Russell. However, he took the discovery of Russell's paradox as proof that his life's work was a failure.

Charles Sanders Peirce

An American scientist and early (late nineteenth century) pioneer of modern logic and semiotics. Peirce's achievements were underrated for a long time because of his failure to hold down an academic position, which seems to have been due to personal opposition from certain established figures. He has been credited with inventing a version of first order logic independently of Frege, along with explorations in relational algebra, many valued logic, and probabilistic and abductive reasoning.

Antoine Arnauld

A theologian and mathematician in seventeenth-century France, chiefly responsible for compiling the Port-Royal grammar and logic. He was associated with the Jansenist movement and, when this was declared heretical, had to go into hiding and finally into exile in the Netherlands. His views on logic and language were strongly influenced by Descartes, and Chomsky's book *Cartesian Linguistics* presents him as an important forerunner of modern ideas on universal grammar.

NOTES

1. Ferdinand de Saussure, quoted in Moot and Retoré (2012).
2. An old but popular book which deals with this in an informal way, with attention to the psychological pitfalls and biases in the way of reasoning with language, is Thouless (1953). A more recent introduction to the psychology of thinking is Kahneman (2011). Early modern logic had to distance itself from 'psychologism' – the idea that logic is just a description of how we do, in fact, tend to reason.
3. Haack (1978).
4. Haack (1978).
5. Saussure (1915).
6. In Saussure's original French, which is often retained for these terms, *signifiant* and *signifié*.
7. We will not be concerned here with signs beneath the level of the word, such as morphemes.

8. Note that many linguistics books use different conventions – some of them even do exactly the opposite!

9. In Chomsky's original work and his subsequent development of his own theory, it is usually known as Transformational Generative Grammar. Other offshoots, such as various forms of Phrase Structure Grammar, have dropped the transformational element; however, they are still generative (that is, they are based on formal languages and rewrite rules, which can be represented by data structures such as trees). Since transformations as such are tangential to the concerns of this book, I will stick to 'generative grammar'. Note that some writers confine the term 'generative' to transformational grammars, a usage which is incorrect but unfortunately widespread.

10. See Chapter 12.

11. Lewis (1970).

12. There is a good introduction in Chierchia and McConnell-Ginet (1990).

13. This is a more modern version of the system. Ancient grammarians regarded nouns and adjectives as the same category (more precisely, 'substantives' and adjectives were both part of the category 'noun').

14. Latin *speculum*, a mirror. The idea was that language is a mirror in which we can see the structure of reality.

PART I

THE CLASSICAL PICTURE

CHAPTER 2

TRUTH TABLE LOGIC

The last chapter introduced the idea of 'meaningful units' of a language, and focused on sentences, whose special characteristic is that they, and only they, can be true or false. From here we can either break sentences down in an attempt to find their meaningful subparts and how they are put together – this will be the approach of the next chapter – or alternatively we can take sentences as basic building blocks and work upwards to how they are combined into larger units, usually by links such as 'and', 'but' or 'if'. This is in some ways the simplest way into logic, and accordingly will be the theme of this chapter. A logic which takes this approach is known as a **propositional logic**,[1] and the links between sentences are known as **connectives**.

2.1 CONNECTIVES

Perhaps the most intuitive examples of connectives join two sentences to form one compound sentence: some of these are so commonly used in logic that they have their own special symbols. Examples are 'and' (& or ∧), 'or' (∨) and 'if. . .then. . .' (→). Because these join *two* sentences together, they are called **binary**. The negation symbol 'not' (¬ or ~) is also a connective, even though it does not join two sentences together (it is a **unary** connective, acting on a single sentence to form its negation). These connectives are chosen because they have useful features. Some of these we will look at now, others later.

As outlined in the first chapter, some of our most basic intuitions about meaning involve patterns of inference. The connectives we have chosen here have intuitively clear patterns of inference, at least up to a point. Here are a few examples:

(2.1) It is cold *and* it is raining. Conclusion: it is raining.
(2.2) *If* it is raining, then the match will be called off. It is raining. Conclusion: the match will be called off.
(2.3) Either Mary ate the cake *or* it disappeared into thin air. It didn't disappear into thin air. Conclusion: Mary ate it.

The important point here is that these inferences depend entirely on the connectives (italicised in the examples). The internal contents of the sentences being joined together are irrelevant. We could replace them by any other sentences, and the inference patterns would still work out. In fact it is usual to replace them by arbitrary letters such as p and q. In the examples below I also replace the English connectives by their logical symbols.

(2.4) p ∧ q. Conclusion: q.
(2.5) p → q, p. Conclusion: q.
(2.6) p ∨ q, ¬ q. Conclusion: p.

In each of these examples, the **conclusion** seems to follow from the other facts listed (the **premises**). It is simply not possible for the premises to be true and the conclusion false. Moreover, this is determined by the connectives used. The logic seems to care about the meaning of the connectives, whereas the content of the individual sentences is so unimportant that we can replace them by any old letters – provided only that we are consistent about using the same letter to stand for the same sentence. For this reason the connectives are known as **logical constants**. The arbitrary letters used to stand in for the 'other stuff' are called **propositional letters**. The principle that they can be replaced by anything as long as we are consistent is called the rule of **uniform substitution**.[2]

Note that the validity of the patterns of reasoning is completely independent of whether we agree with the conclusions. In fact **valid** is a technical word. A pattern of reasoning (or argument schema) is valid if it is not possible for the premises to be true and the conclusion false. (As it is sometimes put, it will never lead you from truth to falsity.) It is possible for the premises to be false, in which case the conclusion may be false as well. The following are instances of the argument schemata we have just used, in which you will probably not be convinced by either the premises or the conclusion; nonetheless, the pattern of argument is still valid as just defined. If you can imagine a world in which the premises are true, then you would have to accept the conclusion as well.

(2.7) The moon is made of green cheese and England will win the World Cup. Conclusion: the moon is made of green cheese.
(2.8) If Scotland is hotter than Saudi Arabia, then the moon is made of green cheese. Scotland is hotter than Saudi Arabia. Conclusion: the moon is made of green cheese.
(2.9) Either the moon is made of green cheese or Paris is the capital of France. Paris is not the capital of France. Conclusion: the moon is made of green cheese.

Validity is not affected by the truth, falsity or even sheer idiocy of the premises; it is simply concerned with whether the correct forms have been followed. To do logic, we have to learn to play by these rules.

In the first chapter it was suggested that a logic requires three components: a formally defined language, a means of interpreting statements in that language, and a method for calculating which statements follow from which. The connectives and the letters p, q and so on give us the basis for a logical language, which we will define more formally in the next section.

What about interpretation? The truth or falsity of a simple sentence is a **contingent** matter – that is to say, it just happens to be true or false, and you have to find out which. For example, to tell whether 'it is raining' is true or false, you have to look out of the window. If you look through a different window, in a different place or at a different time, you may get a different answer. (These windows can be thought of as 'possible worlds'.)

One convenient way of arranging the possible data is to draw a table, known as a **truth table**. Each column is labelled by a different sentence, and each row represents a 'window' telling us whether the sentence is true or false. *True* and *false* are known as **truth values**, so we can say that each row gives a truth value to each sentence. The truth values are normally written as **t** and **f**, or as **1** and **0**. This book will use the latter convention.

This system of truth values may be convenient, but it is not obvious that all sentences really can be classified as 'true' or 'false'. Can you think of any sentences where this is problematic? We will discuss several later, but how about the following, for example:

(2.10) 1. The town is crowded this evening.
       2. Man will reach Mars this millennium.
       3. This coffee pot is sad.
       4. All unicorns are white.
       5. The Pope's wife isn't blond.

If you think there are problems describing any of these as true or false, see if you can put your finger on why.

For the time being, however, we will assume that this can be done for all atomic sentences. What about connectives? One tempting way of interpreting them is to give each of them a column in the truth table, and read their values from the truth values of the smaller sentences that make them up. For example ¬ p takes the truth value of p and simply reverses it, so that it is true when p is false, and false when p is true. Similarly for binary connectives; p ∧ q is true when both p and q are true; if either or both of them are false, then the whole sentence p ∧ q is false.

(2.11)	p	q	p ∧ q	p ∨ q	p → q
	1	1	1	1	1
	1	0	0	1	0
	0	1	0	1	1
	0	0	0	0	1

EXERCISE 2.1.0.1

1. Express these English sentences using propositional logic. Make a key for the propositional letters.
   (a) If it doesn't rain, I will go to the beach, and if it rains I won't.
   (b) I am sad, but if Anna comes and the weather is nice, I will be happy.
   (c) Either he wasn't here, or he was very quiet. (Two versions.)
   (d) Whether they lose or not, the manager will be sacked.
   (e) Mary will not be happy unless somebody gives her an ice cream.

2. Draw the truth tables for these pairs of sentences:
   (a) If it is sunny, Niki is on the beach.
   (b) If Niki isn't on the beach, it isn't sunny.
   (c) It is neither sunny nor cold.
   (d) It isn't sunny and it isn't cold.
   (e) Either the cafe won't be open or the wifi won't be working.
   (f) It won't be the case that the cafe is open and the Wi-Fi is working.
   (g) Pooh will have bread and either honey or cream.
   (h) Either Pooh will have bread and honey or he will have bread and cream.

The last exercise illustrated three important equivalences which are laws of propositional logic.

(2.12) Contraposition
       (a) $\phi \rightarrow \psi$ is equivalent to $\neg \psi \rightarrow \neg \phi$
(2.13) De Morgan's laws
       (a) $\neg (\phi \lor \psi)$ is equivalent to $\neg \phi \land \neg \psi$
       (b) $\neg (\phi \land \psi)$ is equivalent to $\neg \phi \lor \neg \psi$
(2.14) Distributive laws
       (a) $\phi \land (\chi \lor \psi)$ is equivalent to $(\phi \land \chi) \lor (\phi \land \psi)$
       (b) $\phi \lor (\chi \land \psi)$ is equivalent to $(\phi \lor \chi) \land (\phi \lor \psi)$

Contraposition is one of the most basic facts about the relationship between negation and implication, as we will see in Chapter 10. The De Morgan laws show the relationship (called duality) between conjunction and disjunction, and they have the consequence that either can be expressed in terms of the other. The importance of distributivity is not so obvious, but later we will look at some logics which do not have it.

So far we have had the meanings of the connectives defined diagrammatically by means of truth tables. Later in this chapter you will see equivalent definitions given in words and symbols. But let's think for a moment whether these definitions really capture the meaning of the English words we have been using to describe them – 'and', 'or', 'if' and 'not'. If not, this is not the end of the world, as we are trying to make precise technical tools rather than simply trying to describe four English words. But it is a useful question to ask.

The truth table definition of $\land$, first of all, might seem quite natural for 'and'. But consider the following sentences:

(2.15) 1. The dancer left the stage and undressed.
        2. The dancer undressed and left the stage.

One result of the truth table definition is that $p \land q$ always has the same truth value as $q \land p$. Often this is what we want, as in the example we used earlier. 'It is raining and it is cold' seems to mean the same as 'it is cold and it is raining'. However in (2.15) the order of the conjuncts is important. It is natural to understand 'and' in these sentences as something like 'and then'.

Another example comes from syntactic theory, where we might want to say 'a sentence consists of a noun phrase and a verb phrase'. If we are discussing English syntax, we would normally mean by this that it consists of a noun phrase *followed by* a verb phrase. This is not the same as 'a verb phrase followed by a noun phrase', which would not give a grammatical sentence in English. Thus when discussing syntax, as when discussing time, the order of the conjuncts is important.

The other connectives raise further questions. For 'or', one of the most basic is what happens if both alternatives are true. For example does (2.16) entertain the possibility of the lucky child getting both chocolate and ice cream? On the truth table definition we have given, it should do. However, a natural interpretation – and perhaps that intended by the speaker – is to exclude this possibility.

(2.16) I will give you chocolate or I will give you ice cream.

According to the truth table, the disjunction is still true if both disjuncts are true. It *includes* that possibility. But there is an alternative interpretation of 'or' which *excludes* it. These two interpretations are known as **inclusive** and **exclusive** or. The logical symbol ∨ is used for the inclusive version,[3] and has the interpretation already given in the truth tables.

However, we could equally well define a logical connective with the meaning of *exclusive* 'or'. It would have the same truth table as ∨, except that the row where both disjuncts are true would come out as false. We would also need a symbol for exclusive 'or'. Common choices for this are XOR, ∞ and ⊕. This connective is useful for various purposes. However, in logic, including its linguistic applications, 'or' is more often taken as being ∨, even if this is the less intuitive reading. The reasons for this will become apparent in the next chapter. The main thing for now is to be mindful of the difference.

The implication connective has perhaps generated the most controversy of all. The truth table definition (which is known as **material implication**) is an attempt to capture the idea that it is impossible *for the antecedent p to be true and the consequent q false* (compare the definition of entailment, above). This particular combination of truth values (the second row) is the only one that is excluded. In all other cases the implication is satisfied – the implicational formula comes out as true.

This is the least we can expect of an implication connective, and some people would say that it is too easily satisfied. Intuitively we have other expectations of an implication connective. One is that there should be some connection between the antecedent and the consequent. Often in natural language that connection is causal (2.17). At the very least there should be *some* connection. (2.18), for example, sounds very odd; but by the truth table definition it comes out as true. This problem, in general, can be put under the heading of **relevance**.

(2.17) If you put your hand in the fire, you will burn it.
(2.18) If Hitler invaded Poland in 1939, then the square of the hypotenuse equals the sum of the squares of the other two sides.

Another important intuition is that the connection should not be a matter of chance, but a matter of necessity. If you look back at the last paragraph but one, the italicised phrase includes the word *impossible*. But the truth table definition does not convey any idea of possibility or necessity; it is concerned only with what happens to be true.

Once again, the implication connective is a technical tool for logic, and we should not expect it to capture every nuance of the word 'if' in English or other languages. The question is whether these notions of relevance and necessity are important enough to be included, and indeed whether it is possible to do so convincingly. This question will be central in the later parts of the book.

2.2 SYNTACTIC DEFINITIONS

This section gives a formal definition of the syntax of our logical language, which will be our first attempt at a translation language as outlined in the first chapter. The syntax of logical languages is usually given by an **inductive definition**. This is a pattern that will be followed, with variations, throughout the book, so it will be useful to get the hang of it now in the relatively simple context of propositional logic.

First, the ingredients. As already discussed, basic or atomic sentences are represented by propositional letters (p, q, etc.). The connectives are represented by their usual symbols. Propositional letters and connectives together constitute the **vocabulary** of the language. The aim is to give a definition of what constitutes a grammatical sentence or, as it is usually called, a **well-formed formula (wff)** of the language – this notion includes both simple and compound sentences. The Greek letters ϕ (phi) and ψ (psi) are drafted in to stand for any wff (propositional letters can only be used for simple sentences). Finally we have brackets, which are classed as auxiliary symbols.

The inductive definition consists of three parts. First of all the **base**, which specifies the basic wff's of the language. In propositional logic these are simply the propositional letters. Second come the inductive rules, which tell you how to make new wff's from existing ones by means of connectives. It is convenient to divide these into rules for unary and binary connectives, and that is what is done here. Finally, the definition always closes with a clause that 'nothing else is a wff'. It may seem pedantic to insist on this, but it is important to be able to say that a would-be formula is ungrammatical, that is, is not a wff.

So here we go: the inductive definition for a language $\mathcal{L}$ of the propositional calculus.

(2.19) 1. Any propositional letter is a wff in $\mathcal{L}$.
      2. If ϕ is a wff in $\mathcal{L}$, then so is $\neg\, \phi$.
      3. If ϕ and ψ are wff's in $\mathcal{L}$, then so are $(\phi \wedge \psi)$, $(\phi \vee \psi)$ and $(\phi \rightarrow \psi)$.
      4. Nothing else is a wff in $\mathcal{L}$.[4]

There is a convention that the *outermost* brackets in a formula can be removed. This is because the brackets are there to remove ambiguity, and leaving off the

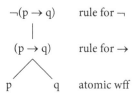

$$\neg(p \rightarrow q) \quad \text{rule for } \neg$$

Figure 2.1   Construction tree for $\neg (p \rightarrow q)$

outermost brackets can never lead to ambiguity. So $(\phi \vee \psi)$, for example, is usually written simply as $\phi \vee \psi$. However, if this formula is negated, then the brackets are no longer outermost, so they must come back: $\neg (\phi \vee \psi)$. Note that the brackets in this example are introduced by the $\vee$, not the negation. According to the rules, only binary connectives introduce brackets. Thus something like $\neg (\phi)$, although you will sometimes see it, is incorrect; it should be $\neg \phi$, without the brackets.

These inductive rules make it possible for us to analyse the structure of any well-formed formula, by tracking the steps by which it is built up. This is usually done by means of a **construction tree** (Figure 2.1). Formulas can be classified as conjunctions, disjunctions, implications, negations, depending on their main connective (or of course simple propositional letters with no connective at all). If the formula is a propositional letter, it is automatically a wff. Otherwise we have to look at the parts of which it is composed. Some useful terminology here: the two formulas joined by a conjunction are known as **conjuncts**. For a disjunction they are **disjuncts**. In an implication $(\phi \rightarrow \psi)$, we have to distinguish between the left and right components, which are known as the **antecedent** and the **consequent** respectively. In a negation, the formula being negated is called the **negand**. So we can say, for example, that a conjunction is a wff if both of its conjuncts are, a negation is a wff if its negand is, and so on.

EXERCISE 2.2.0.1

Are these wff's in $\mathcal{L}$? If so, draw the construction tree. If not, say what is wrong with them.

1. $(p \wedge q) \vee (p \wedge \neg q)$
2. $(p \vee \neg q) \rightarrow r$
3. $p \vee q \vee r$
4. $(p \rightarrow q) \wedge (\neg r)$
5. $\neg (p \rightarrow q) \rightarrow \neg r$

Translate these English sentences into wff's of $\mathcal{L}$. Provide a key for the propositional letters used.

1. If it rains or if the tide is in, we won't lie on the beach.
2. We won't both lie on the beach and go diving.

3. The tide is in, so we will go diving but won't lie on the beach.
4. We will lie on the beach unless the tide is in.
5. Either we will lie on the beach but not go diving, or go diving but if it rains not lie on the beach.

2.3 SEMANTIC DEFINITIONS

We have already discussed how to interpret the propositional connectives and, for classical logic, truth tables are quite a satisfactory way of understanding them. Nonetheless the semantic interpretation of each logic we come to will be given a formal definition, and this cannot always be done using truth tables. This section is an introduction to how the semantics of a logic can be formally described. With other logics it will get a little more complicated and, as with the syntax, we will start getting into good habits now.

The first tool we need is a **valuation**. This is simply a way of determining the truth values of all the propositional letters. In the truth tables, each row gives an array of truth values for the different propositional letters, so we can think of a valuation as a row of the truth table. In propositional logic, where basic sentences have no internal structure, this is really all there is to it.

One important thing to note is that each valuation assigns one and only one truth value to each propositional letter. In mathematical terms, this makes it a **function**. More on these in the next chapter, but we will make use of the mathematical notation for functions to express valuations. Let's say that, according to a valuation V, p is true and q is false. Then we will write $V(p) = 1$, $V(q) = 0$. That is: V assigns to p the value 1, and assigns to q the value 0.

Different valuations are distinguished by subscripts. Thus the valuation corresponding to the first row of a truth table may be called V_1, and so on.

Finally, we have to define the interpretation for compound formulas involving connectives. This is based on the columns in the truth table for each connective; it gives the truth value for the compound formula in terms of the truth value of its component parts and the connective being used.

(2.20) If ϕ and ψ are wffs of $\mathcal{L}$:
1. $V(\neg \phi) = 1$ iff $V(\phi) = 0$
2. $V(\phi \wedge \psi) = 1$ iff $V(\phi) = 1$ *and* $V(\psi) = 1$
3. $V(\phi \vee \psi) = 1$ iff $V(\phi) = 1$ *or* $V(\psi) = 1$
4. $V(\phi \rightarrow \psi) = 1$ iff $V(\phi) = 0$ *or* $V(\psi) = 1$

(iff is an abbreviation for if and only if.)

Unlike the valuation for propositional letters, which gives arbitrary values, this definition gives a constant meaning to the connectives. This is why the connectives are known as **logical constants**. More precisely, the way it is done here, it gives a meaning to expressions *including* the connectives; that is, it defines the interpretation of $\phi \wedge \psi$ rather than simply that of $\wedge$. This indirect way of giving the interpretation is known as a syncategorematic definition. Direct (or categorematic) definitions will be introduced in Chapter 5.

EXERCISE 2.3.0.1

Draw a truth table for $(p \wedge \neg q) \rightarrow r$. Write out the valuations V_1 to V_8 corresponding to the eight rows of the table. Then take one valuation and account for the truth value of each subformula in terms of the valuation and the definitions in the previous example.

2.4 MODES OF INFERENCE

The ideas of propositional logic and connectives go back, in essence, to the Stoics, and they also discovered what are still some of the most important ways of using them to make inferences. Recall (from the beginning of this chapter) that the validity of inferences has to do with patterns of reasoning and the meaning of connectives. For example:

(2.21) 1. If it is below 40 degrees, Maria won't sunbathe.
      2. It is below 40 degrees.
      3. Conclusion: Maria won't sunbathe.

Recall, too, that the validity of this inference depends on the connective *if*, and the fact that the second premise matches its antecedent and the conclusion matches its consequent. The identity of these subformulas does not matter, and nor does it matter whether they are true or false, intelligent or stupid.

This extremely important pattern of inference is known as *modus ponens*, or in full, **modus ponendo ponens**. The verb *ponere*, in philosophical Latin, means to affirm, and this argument schema gets its name because affirming the antecedent of an implication enables us to validly affirm the consequent.

(2.22) 1. $\phi \rightarrow \psi$
      2. ϕ
      3. Conclusion: ψ

Before reading on, consider which of the following similar argument schemata are valid. You may find it helpful to replace the propositional letters by actual sentences. You should try to find an example that shows that the argument schema is *not* valid (a **counter-example**).

(2.23) 1. $\phi \rightarrow \psi$
      2. $\neg \phi$
      3. Conclusion: $\neg \psi$
(2.24) 1. $\phi \rightarrow \psi$
      2. ψ
      3. Conclusion: ϕ
(2.25) 1. $\phi \rightarrow \psi$
      2. $\neg \psi$
      3. Conclusion: $\neg \phi$

The first of these (2.23) looks plausible, and indeed is often used in everyday conversation. However, it is easy to find a counter-example.

(2.26) 1. If Chara is a cat, she has four legs.
     2. Chara is not a cat.
     3. Conclusion: Chara does not have four legs.

Chara could be a dog. The inference would be valid if *only* cats had four legs (in which case the first premise should be stated as $\phi \leftrightarrow \psi$).

A counter-example to (2.24) can be made in a similar way.

(2.27) 1. If Chara is a cat, she has four legs.
     2. Chara has four legs.
     3. Conclusion: Chara is a cat.

What about the last example (2.25)? That one is valid, so you shouldn't be able to find a counter-example to it. It is a very important pattern of reasoning, whose traditional name is **modus tollendo tollens** (sometimes shortened to *modus tollens*). The verb *tollere* means to deny or negate in philosophical Latin, and the argument establishes a negation on the basis of a negation. Readers may have noticed the similarity to the law of contraposition above (2.12).

The invalid argument schemata (2.23) and (2.24) are also important enough to have names: (2.23) is known as **denying the antecedent** and (2.24) is known as **affirming the consequent**. Although they are both invalid, this does not mean that they have no uses. The kind of reasoning we are almost exclusively concerned with in this book is **deductive** reasoning – the art of deriving conclusions from premises by valid reasoning. This is not the only kind of reasoning that can be considered 'rational'. Denying the antecedent, though not deductively valid, is sometimes useful in practical reasoning when a choice has to be made on the basis of whether the antecedent is true. Affirming the consequent, while again not deductively valid, can also be a reasonable thing to do, if we see that the conclusion is true and want to find a set of premises that might account for it.[5]

Although *modus ponens* and *modus tollens* are the most important modes of inference explored by the Stoics, they also discovered some other ones. They are based on other connectives than implication. Have a look at these three and see if you think they are valid.

(2.28) 1. $\phi \lor \psi$
     2. $\neg \phi$
     3. Conclusion: ψ
(2.29) 1. $\phi \lor \psi$
     2. ϕ
     3. Conclusion: $\neg \psi$
(2.30) 1. $\neg (\phi \land \psi)$
     2. ϕ
     3. Conclusion: $\neg \psi$

The first (2.28) is an important valid argument schema, based on disjunction. Because it uses a denial to establish an affirmation, its traditional name is ***modus tollendo ponens***. It is also known as **disjunctive syllogism** (though it is not a syllogism in the better known Aristotelian sense).

An argument schema similar to (2.29) (using the standard Greek word for 'or') was thought by the Stoics to be valid. This depends, however, whether inclusive or exclusive 'or' is meant. Since the example here uses the symbol for inclusive 'or', which allows for both disjuncts to be true, it is invalid. For it to be valid, $\vee$ would have to be replaced by XOR.

The final example is valid. If both conjuncts cannot be true simultaneously, then if one is true the other must be false. This pattern is known as ***modus ponendo tollens***, since it uses an affirmation (of ϕ) to establish a denial (of ψ).

(2.31) As we know, both material implication and conjunction can be defined in terms of disjunction. *Modus tollendo ponens* is already stated using disjunction. Restate the other three valid modes of inference covered in this section in terms of disjunction. Draw the truth tables, and verify that there is no row in which the premises are true and the conclusion false.

(2.32) Restate disjunctive syllogism in terms of (i) implication and (ii) conjunction.

(2.33) Draw the truth tables for denying the antecedent and affirming the consequent, and highlight the row in which the premises are true and the conclusion false.

Chrysippus

The leading light of the Stoic school of logic, who in ancient times was held in equal regard to Aristotle himself. Unfortunately all his work has been lost, apart from snippets preserved in the work of other writers. He also seems to have had a sense of humour. The story goes that one day he made his donkey drink a bucket of wine and died laughing at the results.

2.5 THE DEDUCTION EQUIVALENCE

One of the most important statements of the relationship between conjunction and implication, and between implication and logical consequence, is the equivalence between (2.34) and (2.35). Suppose we know that if we have premises ϕ and χ, a conclusion ψ logically follows (2.34).

(2.34) $\phi \wedge \chi \vdash \psi$

(2.35) $\phi \vdash \chi \rightarrow \psi$

Now suppose we are given not ϕ and χ, but only ϕ (2.35). Now we cannot conclude ψ; however, we know that if we had χ then we could conclude ψ. So from ϕ we can conclude $\chi \rightarrow \psi$.

The following example may make this easy to remember. If I have bread and cheese then I have a sandwich. If I have only bread then I don't have a sandwich, but I know that if I had cheese I could make a sandwich.

Conversely, if I know (2.35) and I do in fact know not only ϕ but also χ (2.34), then I am entitled to conclude ψ.

This equivalence is known as the **deduction equivalence**. It is an equivalence which, conceptually, we would want to hold for any logic containing a form of conjunction and a form of implication. It is easy to check that it holds for truth table logic, if $\wedge$ is classical conjunction and $\rightarrow$ is material implication. In fact, another way of justifying material implication (for classical logic) is that the deduction equivalence holds when material implication is used.

It can also be proved more rigorously, both for classical logic and most other logics mentioned in this book, using the notions of consequence, conjunction and implication appropriate to each. It can thus be referred to as the **deduction theorem** (for each logic).

2.6 TESTING FOR VALIDITY: THE TREE METHOD

As we have seen, a formula ψ is a logical consequence of ϕ iff: whenever ϕ is true, ψ must also be true. If we compare the two columns in the truth table, the rows where ϕ is true must also be rows where ψ is true. If there is any row where ϕ is true and ψ is false, then ϕ does not entail ψ (or equivalently, $\phi \rightarrow \psi$ is not a tautology).

With formulas involving more than two propositional letters, it can be cumbersome to draw and check truth tables, and the following method is a useful shortcut. It is based on the idea of providing a counter-example (a row where ϕ is true and ψ is false. If we are unable to do so, we are entitled to conclude that the implication *is* valid, because it can be shown that if there was a counter-example, this method would find it. It decomposes the formulae concerned using semantic equivalences that we have already seen, until only **literals** (atomic formulae or the negations of atomic formulae) are left.

The first stage is to write the antecedent of the implication, and underneath it the *negation* of the consequent. This represents our counter-example – a row where the antecedent is true and the consequent, false. It will be the root of a tree which we construct by 'unpacking' the formulae into subformulae, according to their main connectives:

Conjunction: Simply write the two conjuncts one under the other. If the conjunction is true in our counter-example, then so are the two conjuncts.

Disjunction: Here we are not entitled to assume that either disjunct on its own is true, so we split the tree into two branches (think of them as possible worlds). Write one disjunct on each branch.

Implication: This is treated as a disjunction. Using the equivalence $\phi \rightarrow \psi = \neg \phi \vee \psi$, we write the negation of the antecedent in one branch and the consequent in the other.

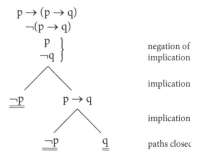

Figure 2.2   Validity of (p → (p → q)) → (p → q) according to the tree method

Negation of a conjunction: This is equivalent to a disjunction by De Morgan's laws;
  write the negation of each conjunct, one in each branch.
Negation of a disjunction: This is equivalent to a conjunction, also by De Morgan's
  laws; write the negations of both disjuncts, one under the other.
Negation of an implication: Write the antecedent and the negation of the consequent one under the other.

The formulae can be unpacked in any order, but it is important that if the tree
branches, any formulas in the trunk that are subsequently unpacked are unpacked
into both branches. As a rule of thumb, it will usually make the process quicker if
formulae that will not result in branching are unpacked first.

If a branch of a tree is found to contain a propositional letter and its negation, then
that branch contains a contradiction and can be closed (by drawing a line underneath
it). When scanning for contradictions, include any literals in the trunk, as they belong
to all subsequent branches.

If any branch remains open when all formulae have been unpacked, that branch
represents our counter-example to the implication we started off with. If all the
branches in the tree are closed, then the tree is said to be closed. This means that the
counter-example we have tried to construct is contradictory, and therefore the implication we started with is valid.

A simple example can be seen in Figure 2.2. Note that there are several ways of
setting out this method, and it is commonly called the tableau method as well as the
tree method.

EXERCISE 2.6.0.1

Check whether the following implicational formulae are valid, using the tree method.
(One of them is not.)

1. $((p \wedge q) \to r) \to (p \to (q \to r))$
2. $((p \to q) \wedge (p \to r)) \to ((p \wedge q) \to r)$
3. $(p \wedge (q \vee \neg r)) \to ((p \wedge q) \vee (p \wedge \neg r))$

4. $((p \wedge q) \vee (r \wedge s)) \rightarrow (p \wedge (q \vee r))$
5. $(p \rightarrow q) \rightarrow ((r \rightarrow p) \rightarrow ((r \wedge s) \rightarrow q))$

2.7 TRUTH FUNCTIONS

The propositional connectives in classical logic have the characteristic that the truth value of a complex formula can be determined from the truth values of its subformulas. Not all English conjunctions have this property. Suppose, for example, we defined a connective Coz corresponding to the English word 'because'. The truth value of (p Coz q) cannot be determined from the truth values of p and q. It might be that *p* and *q* are both true, but *q* is not the cause of *p*, so the complex formula is false.

Another way of putting this is that if a connective is given the truth values of its subformulas, it will give you, on the basis of only that information, the truth value of the complex formula. In other words it is a function from truth values to truth values – or in short a **truth function**.

(2.36)   Earlier in this chapter, we discussed the fact that 'and' in natural language often seems to mean 'and then'. There is nothing to stop us defining a connective in our logical language with this meaning; let's call it T. Would T be a truth function?

Negation, as it combines with just one subformula, is a unary truth function; it computes its value on the basis of just one argument (the truth value of the negand). Whatever truth value you feed it as input, it will give you the opposite truth value as output – this is what you get from this particular truth function.

What other unary truth functions are there? Assuming there are exactly two truth values, 0 and 1, there are four logical possibilities.

(2.37)   1. A function which gives back its input unchanged as its output.
         2. A function which changes its input into the opposite truth value.
         3. A function which gives 1 whatever its input.
         4. A function which gives 0 whatever its input.

Negation is of course the second in this list. The first is an **identity function**. It may not look very useful, but don't jump to that conclusion just yet. There are a number of words in English which work in a similar way, though we have not considered them yet.

The third and fourth functions are the constant true function and the constant false function. They are like a person who gives the answer 'yes' regardless of the question and someone who always gives the answer 'no'.

With binary truth functions, there are more interesting possibilities. If there are two truth values, the number of binary truth functions is $2^{(2^2)}$, giving a total of 16. Three of them are defined in our logical language ($\wedge$, $\vee$, $\rightarrow$). We have also met XOR.

The implication connective gives us two possibilities, as p → q is not the same as q → p. And we can define a connective p ↔ q, which applies if p and q imply each other. This last connective, which we will call bi-implication and read as 'if and only if', is often added to the connectives defined in a logical language. I have not done so here, though I will make use of it occasionally as shorthand. Since it makes *p* and *q* equivalent in terms of truth values, it is also known as the 'equivalence' connective, and written p ≡ q.

A mirror image of implication is **inhibition**, again with two possibilities: p but not q, and q but not p. The common notation for this is p/q or alternatively p − q. Inhibition will be used in the last part of the book.

EXERCISE 2.7.0.1

1. Draw a truth table with columns for p → q, q → p, p ↔ q and p XOR q.
2. Do the same for p − q and q − p. What would the disjunction of these two formulas mean?
3. How can we express each of these in terms of ∧, ∨, → and ¬?

We have already seen that ∧ and ∨ are interdefinable (using negation) by the De Morgan laws, and that implication can be defined in terms of negation and ∨. So the only connectives we really *need* to define in our logical language are negation and *one* out of ∧ and ∨. All the other connectives we use (and in fact all truth functions) can be derived from them. Some logic books do take this approach, in search of conciseness and mathematical elegance. There is often a trade-off, however, between conciseness and transparency.

It is possible to go even further in the direction of conciseness. Two other binary connectives of interest (the last that will be discussed here) are 'neither . . . nor' (written NOR, ↓ or † – the 'Quine dagger'), and 'not both . . . and . . .' (written NAND, or | – the 'Sheffer stroke'). Each of these has the peculiarity that *all* the other truth functions can be defined in terms of it alone, without even using negation. The key to this is that ¬ p can be defined either as p | p or as p † p.

None of the connectives introduced in this section will play a major role in the rest of this book, but it may be worth mentioning a few useful applications.

The property of NOR and NAND just mentioned is useful in electronics. An electronic circuit uses gates to compute truth functions. For example an AND gate takes two inputs and gives the output 1 ('on') iff both inputs are 'on'. It is possible to construct gates individually for ¬, ∨ and the other connectives. However, it is also possible to compute all of these just using one kind of gate (the NAND gate), and in practice this is a cheap and convenient solution.

XOR corresponds to addition modulo 2 (addition in base 2 arithmetic, with only the last digit counting, so that $1 \oplus 1 = 0$). Such modular arithmetic has a long tradition of application in cryptography. Some traditional ciphers involve treating letters as numbers and adding a constant to each letter modulo the number of letters in the alphabet.[6] A later refinement was to vary the number added according to the letters in a key word or phrase.

The modulo 2 version became important with the invention of telegraphy and binary digital encoding. It also has the useful property that if you XOR A with B, and then XOR the result again with B, you end up with A. If A is a stream of binary numbers encoding a message (the plaintext), and B is a stream of binary numbers encoding a key, C is the encrypted message obtained by applying XOR to A and B. If we now apply XOR to the encrypted message C and the key B, we get the original plaintext A back. A toy example is given in the exercise.[7]

EXERCISE 2.7.0.2

1. What is the difference between truth conditions, truth values and truth functions?
2. Define $p \rightarrow q$, $p \vee q$, and p NOR q in terms of only p, q and NAND ($|$).
3. Draw a table applying XOR to the message 1011001110 and the repeated key 0011, and then XOR the resulting ciphertext with the same key to get the original message back. Show with your own examples that:
   (a) If a plaintext is XOR'd with several keys in succession, it can be deciphered by XOR'ing with the same keys in any order.
   (b) If two plaintexts are encrypted with the same key, then XOR'ing the two encrypted texts gives the same result as XOR'ing the two plaintexts.
4. Connectives joining three or more propositions make perfect sense in logic, but are not seen much in linguistic applications, though $\wedge$ and $\vee$ generalise easily to lists of more than two sentences. One other useful ternary connective is the 'if . . . then . . . else . . .' construct, which may be defined as $(p \rightarrow q) \wedge (\neg p \rightarrow r)$. Draw the truth table for this connective, and describe the states of affairs (rows) where it ends up as false.

2.8 NOTATIONS

The syntax given in this chapter is the usual notation for propositional logic, but it is not the only possible one. It was noted in the previous chapter that Frege himself used a very different notation. The present one was developed in the early twentieth century, largely by Peano and Russell. Apart from the symbols chosen for the connectives (and there are some variations on most of these), its main characteristic is that the binary connectives are written *between* the formulas they connect. This is quite close to the syntax of the corresponding words in English (with the exception of 'if'). It is also like the usual syntax for arithmetic operators such as + and ×. It is known as the **infix** notation.

One well-known variant was introduced by the Polish school of logic. The connectives are represented by capital letters, while propositional letters are lower case. The connective is written *before* the formulae being connected (the **prefix** notation).

(2.38) Standard   Polish
     $\neg p$ Np
     $p \wedge q$ Kpq
     $p \vee q$ Apq
     $p \rightarrow q$ Cpq

If one of the juncts is itself complex, then in place of a propositional letter there will be another connective (introducing more subformulae) and so on, until the main connective has had its quota of two complete subformulae. For example, $p \rightarrow (q \vee r)$ will be written as CpAqr.

Note that the bracketing ambiguity in these examples is resolved without any need for brackets. (It is said that Polish notation was invented because Polish typewriters between the wars did not have brackets.)

Readers who are interested in parsing may have noticed that Polish notation corresponds to a top down parsing strategy. It is also possible to do the opposite, to apply a completely bottom up strategy; the propositional letters are listed and then the connective is added to combine them into a complex formula. This is known as 'reverse Polish' notation.

(2.39) Standard   Reverse Polish
     $\neg p$ pN
     $p \wedge q$ pqK
     $p \vee q$ pqA
     $p \rightarrow q$ pqC

This notation is used in some calculators; the numbers are entered first, followed by the operation you wish to perform on them.

EXERCISE 2.8.0.1

1. Write in Polish notation:
   (a) $p \wedge (q \vee r)$
   (b) $(p \wedge q) \vee r$
2. Read these formulae in Polish notation (translate them into infix notation).
   (a) CKpqKqp
   (b) CKpNpCqr
   (c) NAKpNpCNpp
   (d) CCKpqrCCpqr
   (e) CCpCqrCCpqCpr
3. Translate the same formulae into reverse Polish.
4. What parsing strategy does the standard infix notation correspond to? (Hint: think how it traverses the construction tree, from left daughter to mother to right daughter.)

NOTES

1. For now, I will use 'proposition' and 'sentence' as equivalent, but see Chapter 7.
2. They can replaced by other propositional letters or even by more complex expressions, always subject to the same proviso that we do so consistently. A **substitution**, if we want to write it out explicitly, comprises a list of propositional letters in the original formula, each paired with a single expression which is to replace it in all its occurrences.
3. It stands for the Latin *vel*, which is said to have had precisely this meaning, as opposed to the other Latin word for 'or', *aut*.
4. More fully: 'nothing is a wff in $\mathcal{L}$ that cannot be formed from clauses 1–3 in a finite number of steps'.
5. Two major kinds of reasoning besides deductive are **inductive** and **abductive**. The difference is explained as follows by Peirce (1870). Most inferences involve a rule (here the implicational premise), a fact (the antecedent) and a result (the consequent). Deductive reasoning, as in *modus ponens*, starts with a fact and a rule and infers the result. Inductive reasoning starts with facts and results and tries to infer the rule (generally using probabilities). Abductive reasoning starts with the result and a set of rules and tries to infer the most probable fact that might lead to the result.

   It is tempting to add seductive reasoning – the bewitchment of language and rhetoric as described by Thouless (1953).
6. Examples are the 'Caesar shift', in which three was added to each letter, and the Kama Sutra code, where the alphabet was divided into two parts and the offset was therefore half the length of the alphabet.
7. This is the basis of what is usually known as the Vernam cipher (though that name is sometimes applied to a slightly different concept, the 'one time pad'). It was used in the Lorenz cipher, used for high level communication by the Germans in the Second World War. The Colossus, widely regarded as the first computer, was built in order to crack it. The Vernam cipher is also the basis for many implementations of the *crypt* command in Unix. It is not in itself a very secure cipher, though the XOR operation figures as a part of many stronger ciphers.

CHAPTER 3

PREDICATES

The previous chapter looked at the combination of basic sentences into larger sentences. This chapter will concentrate on the internal structure of basic sentences, and the meaningful elements within them. Since the most important of these meaningful elements are predicates, this approach is known as predicate logic. As usual we will first discuss the ideas of predicate logic relatively informally. We will then give more formal definitions of its syntax and semantics, and show how it can be used as a translation language.

Do we really need to analyse the internal structure of basic sentences, or would it be enough to treat them as unanalysable building blocks or 'atoms' as in the previous chapter? Here are two considerations which seem to show that analysis of their internal structure is necessary.

First, consider what the alternative would mean. If sentences are unanalysable, they and their meanings (truth conditions) would have to be stored in our heads as a very long list. But the number of sentences (even basic sentences) is infinite, and our brains cannot store infinite lists. Moreover, we continually encounter or create new sentences, whose meanings we cannot have learnt, but which cause us no problems. It seems that this infinity of sentence meanings can be computed by rearranging smaller building blocks. The meaning of the sentence depends on the building blocks and the way they are put together. This is known as the principle of **compositionality**, normally attributed to Frege.

Second, if sentence meanings were atomic, there should in principle be no relation in meaning between different basic sentences. But, in fact, different sentences are often related in meaning, and we may want to describe that relationship. For example, 'John loves Mary' does not mean the same as 'Mary loves John': the truth of one is not dependent on the truth of the other. Nonetheless there is a relationship between the two sentences; they consist of the same building blocks put together in a different way. We often get at this relationship in ordinary language by using expressions like *vice versa*: 'John loves Mary, but not vice versa'. Such relationships (and many others) can easily be treated using predicate logic.

3.1 PREDICATES

The first task facing us in this chapter is to analyse basic sentences into their main meaningful elements. The following example sentences will start us off.

(3.1) The cat killed the sparrow.
(3.2) Mary is a student.
(3.3) Greece is beautiful.
(3.4) Russia is bigger than England.
(3.5) Vienna is in Austria.

The first sentence illustrates the very common pattern traditionally described as Subject-Verb-Object. This occurs in some form in most languages, though not necessarily in the same order (for example in Japanese it would be Subject-Object-Verb). It is helpful to think of the sentence as describing a situation, in which there are a certain number of participants. In this case the situation can be described as a killing situation. The element which contributes this description is called the **predicate**. In this example, the predicate is the main verb. As the first of several rules of the thumb in this section, you can take it that the main verb, if there is one, will be the predicate.

A killing situation requires two core participants, one to play the role of killer and the other to play the role of victim. As Sherlock Holmes says, a murder requires (at least) a killer and a corpse. In the situation described here, the cat is playing the role of the killer, while the unfortunate sparrow is playing the role of the corpse. In other examples of killing situations, these roles will be played by other participants.

Note that it is the meaning of 'kill' that determines that a killing situation needs two participants, and hence the sentence has both a subject and an object. A snoring situation only requires one participant, and hence a sentence like 'Mary snores' will have a subject but no object. The technical word for participants is **arguments**. So the first sentence in the examples contains a predicate and two arguments. We can represent this using a simple notation which states the predicate first, and then lists the arguments: *Kill(the-cat, the-sparrow)*.

The order in which the arguments appear is arbitrary, but should be consistent. The order I have used here is usual because in many languages the subject precedes the object in syntax. It therefore has some mnemonic value to do things this way. If this course was in Malagasy, which has Verb-Object-Subject word order, it would be natural to do it the other way round. By the way, we should not speak of the role-players in a situation as being subjects and objects, since these are syntactic terms not semantic ones. A number of schemes have been devised for classifying semantic roles (or 'theta' roles as they are sometimes called), but none has become standard. One of the most general and flexible, however, uses the terms 'actor' and 'undergoer' for the two roles in this kind of sentence, and I will sometimes follow this convention; however, this is completely informal (hence the use of inverted commas instead of bold face).

What about the other examples? In each of these, the predicate is not a verb but some other part of speech. The only verb in them is the copula, which I will take for the time being as making no semantic contribution; it happens to fulfil a grammatical requirement in English, though not all languages, to have a verb in every sentence.

In the second and third examples, there is only one participant; Mary, who is a student, and Greece, which is beautiful. The situations here are a bit different from those described by verbs, but nonetheless we will treat them in a similar way. They could be described as the situation of somebody being a student, and the situation of something being beautiful. What kind of role is the single participant playing in each case? We can say that Mary is an instance of studenthood, and Greece is an instance of beauty. The role of both is to instantiate what is expressed by the predicate.

The two sentences can be written in our predicate-argument notation as *Student(mary)* and *Beautiful(greece)*. Notice that the copula, which I described as making no semantic contribution, is simply left out. So is the indefinite article (in this kind of sentence, where a noun phrase is used as a predicate). Notice also the convention that predicates begin with a capital letter, while arguments are written in lower case – even when a proper name is involved.

The last two examples each have two participants, and they each involve a relation between the two; a relation of comparison in the first case, and of location in the second. In neither case is the predicate describing the situation a verb. In the first it is the adjective 'big'; it is also possible to say that the predicate is the combination 'bigger than', which exactly expresses the relation between Russia and England. This can be written *Bigger-than(russia, england)*. In the last sentence the predicate is the preposition 'in', which describes the spatial relation between Vienna and Austria: *In(vienna, austria)*. Again, the copula is ignored.

EXERCISE 3.1.0.1

Translate these sentences into predicate-argument notation. They involve deciding who pronouns refer to (just choose whatever you think is most probable) – and sometimes other paraphrases. Use the connective symbols from the previous chapter where required to join sentences together.

1. Stephen loves Mozart and he plays the piano.
2. Igor is a dog and if William comes he bites him.
3. Arwen is an elf and she loves Aragorn.
4. Romeo and Juliet love each other.
5. Polyphemus loves Galatea but not vice versa.

This gives us a language for representing the meaning of constituents within a sentence (full definitions will be given in the next section). But first, what about its semantic interpretation? In propositional logic, basic sentences (propositional letters) were simply assigned truth values by arbitrary-looking valuation functions. In predicate logic we want them to be built up from the constituent parts of the sentence, as required by the principle of compositionality and discussed above. To do this we will build **models** – simplified reconstructions of possible states of affairs in the world. One of the simplest (but nonetheless very powerful) ways of doing this involves notions from set theory. This is the approach that will be used here and in the rest of this book.

Starting informally, a model starts off with a set of individuals, known as the **universe** or often as the **domain of discourse**. Every name (individual constant) in the language refers to one of these individuals. What counts as an individual is usually quite flexible, so for example fictitious individuals (like Gandalf), languages (like German) and natural phenomena (like the sea) might be included in our universes. There are, of course, philosophical questions here, some of which will be touched on later (see especially Chapters 5 and 7). But it should be borne in mind that our purpose is to build models to interpret natural language, and natural languages tend to treat such things as being parallel to individuals: 'I like Gandalf', 'she doesn't like German' and 'they love the sea' make perfect sense in English, and importantly they seem to make the same kind of sense as 'John likes Mary'. We will follow the lead of natural language here – at least up to a point.

What about predicates? A useful place to start is that predicates are very often used in language for classifying things. To say that Julia is a student is, from this point of view, to divide the world into objects which are students and objects which are not. How exactly we perform this act of classifying is another matter, which will get some attention in Chapter 8. But assume for the moment that we can determine, one way or the other, whether a predicate can apply to an individual. Then we have, in effect, put the individual into a **set**, in this case the set of students. The denotation of a predicate is therefore a set – the set of all the objects in the world to which the predicate can be truthfully applied – in this case, the set of all students.

When the predicate is a verb, it is perhaps most natural to think of it as a classification of situations and their participants. Since our universe, in the simple model we have at the moment, consists of individuals, our focus will be on the individuals who bear the roles in the situations described. So if we say 'Mary snores', we are classifying Mary as the individual bearing the role of snorer in snoring situations. The difference between this kind of classification and the more straightforward classification of individuals effected by nominal or adjectival predicates is a subtle one which will be ignored for the moment, and we will treat predicates like 'snore' simply as denoting a set of snorers.

To generalise: we will be interpreting unary predicates, whatever their part of speech, as **sets**. How does this help us to calculate the truth value of a sentence from the denotations of its constituent parts? If the predicate denotes a set and its argument denotes an individual, then the sentence will be true if the individual is a member of the set. If the individual is outside the set, then the sentence will be false.

We will turn now to predicates with two arguments. Each argument, as before, denotes an individual in the universe. The predicate denotes a particular relation between two individuals, each having a different role in the situation. For example the predicate 'kill' denotes a relation between killers and victims. We can see this relation as classifying not simply individuals, but *pairs* of individuals. It holds, for example, between Brutus and Caesar, between Lee Harvey Oswald and J. F. Kennedy, and between Achilles and Hector – but not, for example, between Brutus and Achilles. It is important to note also that it holds only in one direction between Achilles in the role of killer and Hector in the role of corpse being dragged round the walls of Troy, and not vice versa. The order between them matters, and for this reason we need **ordered pairs**, the order serving to keep the roles separate. If two people kill each other, for example Arthur and Mordred, there are two ordered pairs involved: Arthur-Mordred and Mordred-Arthur (corresponding to the sentences 'Arthur killed

Mordred' and 'Mordred killed Arthur'). We will follow the same convention noted above in connection with the syntax of predicates, of listing the 'agent' role before the 'undergoer' role.

These notions of **relation** and **ordered pair** are precise mathematical terms, though they may be less familiar than plain sets and individuals. They will be discussed further later in this chapter.

In principle the same method is followed for ternary predicates, such as 'give'. A giving situation requires a three-way relation between a giver, a gift and a recipient. Classifying a situation as a giving situation involves identifying an **ordered triple** of individuals cast in these roles. These days the 'gift' role tends not to be played by human individuals, but examples which would be classified as 'giving triples' might be Salieri-poison-Mozart,[1] or Aphrodite-Helen-Paris.

Relations with four or more places are rarely found in language, if at all. If they were needed, the method outlined would deal with them in an analogous way.

EXERCISE 3.1.0.2

1. What roles are required by the following predicates: dance; go; put; teach; buy; rain; near; between; girl; mother; enemy; sad; jealous; fond. Can any of these roles be omitted in English when the predicate is used?
2. Can you think of any English verbs with four arguments? Can any of them be omitted?

3.2 SYNTAX OF PREDICATE LOGIC

This section will extend the inductive definition in the last chapter to give a language of predicate logic suitable to cover the notions explored in the previous section. This is, in fact, only a part of predicate logic, though a very important one. To get the most out of predicate logic we need not only predicates but also functions and quantifiers. These will be discussed in later chapters. The language defined in this section is a quantifier-free predicate logic (QFPL). Here goes.

First, we need to define the alphabet (vocabulary) for the base clause of the definition. This will consist of **predicates** and **individual constants**, the latter representing the arguments. For present purposes, the arguments of predicates are always individual constants. Each predicate comes with a number, its **arity**, which is the number of arguments it requires. The predicate symbol and its arity together constitute the **signature** of the predicate and is usually written P/n where P is the predicate symbol and n is the arity. It is important to note that the same predicate letter may be used with different arities, but is considered to be a *different predicate* in each case. An analogy from natural language would be the verb 'eat', which can be transitive or intransitive. Linguists differ as to whether these are 'two different verbs', but they would definitely be two different predicates according to the logic defined here.[2]

Summarising this, we define the vocabulary of a language $\mathcal{L}$ of QFPL to be (i) a set of predicate symbols of arity n for each value of n (in practice usually 1 to 3), and (ii) a set of individual constants. A common convention, which we will use in this chapter, is to use upper case letters (or whole words beginning with a capital) for the predicate symbols, and lower case letters for the individual constants.

(3.6) 1. If P/n is a predicate and $a_1, \ldots a_n$ are individual constants, then $P(a_1, \ldots a_n)$ is a wff in $\mathcal{L}$.
2. If ϕ is a wff in $\mathcal{L}$, then so is $\neg \phi$.
3. If ϕ and ψ are wff's in $\mathcal{L}$, then so are $(\phi \wedge \psi)$, $(\phi \vee \psi)$ and $(\phi \rightarrow \psi)$.
4. Nothing else is a wff in $\mathcal{L}$.[3]

This is almost identical to the definition given in the previous chapter, except that propositional letters have been replaced in the base clause by formulas formed from predicate symbols and the appropriate number of arguments. Note that predicates with the wrong number of arguments are not well formed, by virtue of the closure clause (the last clause). In effect, this pedantic-looking clause is doing the job of theta theory in syntax: formulae which do not have the right number of arguments for the predicate are ungrammatical.

While in pedantic mode, there are a couple of other small points to make here. One is that the brackets used in the base clause are doing a different job from the brackets introduced by the connective rules (the remaining clauses). The former simply separate the predicate from the arguments, while the latter, as we have seen, play an important role in disambiguating compound sentences. In fact the former are usually omitted by mathematical logicians, along with the commas separating the argument places. (How should the base clause be changed to reflect this?) This is partly because mathematical logicians tend to use simple capital letters as the predicate symbols, while linguists tend to use whole words, and the brackets affect readability (compare Ljm and Love(john, mary)).

3.3 MODELS FOR PREDICATE LOGIC

As with syntax, the semantics for composite sentences is the same as for propositional logic; the connectives are still interpreted using the truth tables. It is with basic sentences that things get a bit more complicated. These are no longer atomic propositional letters but formulas with internal structure, and we want their truth value to be built up from the meanings of the constituent parts, in accordance with the principle of compositionality.

The requirements for a **model** are (i) a universal set or **domain of discourse**, which we will call D, which is assumed to be non-empty, and (ii) (following the correspondence theory of meaning), a link between expressions in the language and things in D. This link is an **interpretation function**, which we will call I. Since I is a function, it links each expression in the vocabulary of the language with one and only one value in D.

Following the discussion in the first part of the chapter, the individual constants will be interpreted by individuals, that is elements of D; unary predicates will be interpreted by sets, and predicates with an arity greater than one will be interpreted by relations. Predicates and individual constants together are known as **non-logical**

constants,[4] because their interpretation depends on the model. Recall that logical constants have their interpretation given by the logic (the examples we have met so far are the propositional connectives).

In the following definitions, recall from basic set theory that individuals are defined as elements of D, and all sets are subsets of D. The set of all possible ordered pairs formed from elements of D is written as $D \times D$, and any binary relation will be a subset of that. Similarly a ternary relation is a subset of $D \times D \times D$, the set of all possible ordered triples formed from elements of D. So let's go:

(3.7) $\mathcal{M} = \langle D, I \rangle$
    1. For any individual constant a in $\mathcal{L}$, $I(a) \in D$.
    2. For any unary predicate P/1 in $\mathcal{L}$, $I(P) \subseteq D$.
    3. For any binary predicate P/2 in $\mathcal{L}$, $I(P) \subseteq D \times D$.
    4. For any ternary predicate P/3 in $\mathcal{L}$, $I(P) \subseteq D \times D \times D$.

We can now calculate the truth value of any basic formula, with respect to the model M, in the way already discussed. A formula with a unary predicate is true if the individual denoted by the argument is an element of the set denoted by the predicate. For predicates with more than one argument, the formula is true if the ordered tuple formed from the arguments in the right order is an element of the relation denoted by the predicate. Otherwise the formula is false. Note that a single individual can be regarded as an ordered tuple of length 1. This enables us to collapse the clauses for predicates of different arity into a single clause.

(3.8) If $P(a_1, \ldots a_n)$ is a wff in $\mathcal{L}$, then $P(a_1, \ldots a_n)$ is true with respect to a model M iff $\langle I(a_1), \ldots I(a_n) \rangle \subseteq I(P)$.

This is known as a Tarskian truth definition, as it follows the simple but influential format laid down by Alfred Tarski for a truth definition in model theory:[5]

(3.9) An expression P in a language L is true with respect to a model M iff N holds in M (where N is a set of conditions).

The interpretation of complex formulae proceeds exactly as in the previous chapter, using the semantic definitions for the connectives. Nothing new here, but they still form part of the semantic rule for the logic, so we reproduce them.

(3.10) 1. $V(\neg \phi) = 1$ iff $V(\phi) = 0$
    2. $V(\phi \wedge \psi) = 1$ iff $V(\phi) = 1$ *and* $V(\psi) = 1$
    3. $V(\phi \vee \psi) = 1$ iff $V(\phi) = 1$ *or* $V(\psi) = 1$
    4. $V(\phi \rightarrow \psi) = 1$ iff $V(\phi) = 0$ *or* $V(\psi) = 1$

Note that the truth values are not given by I but by V, as before. The set of truth values is not part of the model, and I is a function linking the language and the model.

EXERCISE 3.3.0.1

Translate the following sentences into predicate logic giving a key for all predicates. Define a model with respect to which they are all true.

1. Arwen is an elf and Aragorn is not an elf.
2. Aragorn and Arwen love each other, but Aragorn does not love Gollum.
3. Gollum is not an elf or a hobbit.
4. If Arwen leads Frodo to Mordor, she is not an elf.
5. Frodo is a hobbit, and Gollum leads Frodo to Mordor.

3.4 SETS AND LEXICAL SEMANTICS

Thinking in terms of sets gives us a way of capturing lexical semantic relations. Some of these are relations between form and meaning (*signifiant* and *signifié*) or, in lexical semantic terminology, between **word forms** and **word senses**. Such relations include **homonyms** (same word form paired with several different word senses). Others are relations between word senses, and it is those that we are concerned with in this section. Given that word senses can be modelled as sets, it is tempting to try to model word-sense relations such as **synonymy**, **antonymy** and **hyponymy** in terms of set theory.

Some of our most basic intuitions at the level of sentence semantics are **entailment** and **contradiction**. The corresponding lexico-semantic relations are termed **hyponymy** and **antonymy**. A is a hyponym of B if anything that can be described as A can also be described as B. Thus *dog* is a hyponym of *animal*, because anything which is a dog is also animal. It is often useful to think of hyponymy as a 'kind of' relation: a dog is 'a kind of' animal. Similarly A and B are antonyms if nothing can be both A and B. In the examples we used in the first chapter, 'vegetarian' is an antonym of 'meat eater', because nothing can be both a vegetarian and a meat eater.

In set theory, hyponymy corresponds to the subset relation. If *dog* is a hyponym of *animal*, then the set of Dogs is a subset of the set of Animals, and by definition nothing can be in Dogs which is not in Animals. It is easy, and useful, to represent this visually by a Venn diagram.

The antonymy between *vegetarian* and *meat eater* can be captured by saying that the set of Vegetarians and the set of Meat eaters are **disjoint** – they have no members in common, or the intersection between them equals the empty set. Having said that nothing can be a member of both, an important question that arises here is whether something can be a member of neither, or whether everything has to be a member of one or the other. Take for example 'human' and 'not human' (in the literal sense of the word 'human'). It would seem that everything would have to be one or the other. Set-theoretically, this means that the set of Non-humans is the **complement** of the set of Humans (the universal set D minus the set of Humans). However, this is not true of all pairs of antonyms. For example 'happy' and 'unhappy' are antonyms, but it is possible, one might think, to be neither happy nor unhappy. In this case the relation of disjointness is *not* a relation of set complementation.

Another important lexico-semantic relation, **synonymy**, can be treated in terms of mutual hyponymy, as equality of two sets is usually defined as a mutual subset relation. For example, 'honest' might be taken as a synonym of 'truthful', at least in certain core word senses of the two words. We can say that the set of Honest Entities is a subset of the set of Truthful Entities and vice versa – this makes them by definition the same set, and anything that is in either one must be in the other.

With verbal predicates, things may seem to be more complicated, but they can be dealt with in the same way. For example *amble, lurch* and *lope* are all hyponyms of *walk* (though it has been suggested that in this case we should gloss the hyponym relation as 'a way of' rather than 'a kind of'). The set of people who lurch is a subset of the people who walk. The same treatment can be applied to two or three place relations, as relations are sets (of ordered pairs or triples, but still sets). For example, *strangle* is a hyponym of *kill*. This means that the set of ordered pairs $\langle x, y \rangle$ such that x strangles y is a subset of the set of ordered pairs $\langle x, y \rangle$ such that x kills y. If $\langle x, y \rangle$ belongs to the strangling relation then it must belong to the killing relation as well.

- Extend this idea to two-place predicates which are antonyms, such as 'love' and 'hate', or 'bigger-than' and 'smaller-than'.

There are a few more points to be made here about the relationship between lexical semantics and sentence semantics. The first is to reiterate the difference between lexical relations such as hyponymy and sentence-level relations such as entailment, as pointed out at the beginning of this book. While remembering the difference, it was also pointed out that there is often a connection. Entailment between sentences often depends on hyponymy between the predicates, and likewise with contradiction and antonymy.

This connection is captured by the way that models are set up. A sentence is true iff the referent of its argument (or arguments, as an ordered tuple) belongs to the set denoted by the predicate. However, if a predicate P is a hyponym of Q, then any entity which is a member of $||P||$ has to be a member of $||Q||$, and therefore if $P(x)$ is true, $Q(x)$ will be true.

However, there is an important difference between this kind of meaning relation and the logical inferences discussed in the last chapter. The latter were a result of the meanings of the connectives as logical constants (their meaning is given by the semantic definitions in the logic, independent of any valuation or model). The lexico-semantic relations dealt with in this section, by contrast, are not given by the logic (see the semantic definitions given above, in which there is no mention of them). In fact, it was mentioned that we have not (yet) defined any logical constants for our predicate logic. Truths which depend on meaning relations between predicates, should not therefore be called **logical truths**. The correct term for them is **analytic** truths. (Truths which are not analytic are called **synthetic**)

Although these lexical relations are not determined by the logic, they are important facts to capture when reasoning with language. They are additional facts about meaning to take into account alongside purely logical axioms. For this reason, they are often given a status 'alongside' the logical postulates, and are known as **meaning postulates**. To ensure that they are respected by the semantics we are building, it is usual to stipulate that the only suitable models for interpreting a language are those which respect the meaning postulates of the language. For example we will not build a model in which the set of dogs is not a subset of the set of animals, or in which the set of vegetarians and the set of meat eaters have a non-empty intersection.

There is a related type of restriction on models which may help to make this issue clearer. We might want to exclude from our models states of affairs that are impossible for physical reasons, such as the same object being in two places at the same time. This is also not a *logical* requirement, but one which stems from postulates about the physical world. Such restrictions are known as **physical constraints**. Both physical constraints and meaning postulates can be treated as extra axioms, provided it is clear that they do not originate in the logic but have been added to it as a set of supplementary requirements. Model-theoretically, they are dealt with by simply discarding models which do not conform to them.

The relationship between word meaning and real-world information is a delicate one which lexical semantic theories have to deal with. In principle, meaning postulates should be part of the lexicon, whereas real world information belongs rather in the mental encyclopaedia. In practice, it can be difficult to know where to draw the line. However the distinction is made, the encoding of both kinds of information in formal semantic theories is done in a similar way.

3.5 SETS AND CONNECTIVES

There is an important connection between sets and connectives which becomes clear when we look at set-forming operations.

There are several ways of specifying the elements of a set. One is simply to list them, which is practical for small sets, and is sometimes preferable if the set is just a jumble without any particular logic to its membership. The set of objects on my desk at the moment would be a good example. However, if there is some definite criterion for set membership, for example the set of capped Scottish rugby players, then it is more convenient to state that criterion using a **set constructor** (3.12).

(3.11) {computer, coffee cup, keys, candle holder, empty wine glass, ointment for bad shoulder. . .}

(3.12) {x: x has played rugby for Scotland}
(the set of all x such that x has played rugby for Scotland)

An **operation** is a function from elements of a set (or ordered tuples of elements) to elements of the same set. So a set-forming operation is an operation on the set of all sets, a function from sets, pairs of sets and so on, to sets. Informally, it is a way of forming new sets from old. The most important of these in set theory are set union, intersection and complementation. They are set-forming operations because the results are new sets (the sets $A \cup B$, $A \cap B$ and $\sim A$). This should be distinguished from the subset relation, which states a relation between two sets but does not define a new one.

These operations are easy to define in terms of set constructors:

(3.13) 1. $A \cup B = \{x: x \in A \text{ or } x \in B\}$
     2. $A \cap B = \{x: x \in A \text{ and } x \in B\}$
     3. $\sim A = \{x: x \notin A\}$ (x is *not* an element of A)

These definitions make use of the connectives introduced in the previous chapter (italicised). Note that *or* in set union means inclusive or ($\vee$), because set union includes the objects that are in both sets. Note also that the *not* in set complementation behaves like the $\neg$ of the previous chapter. The complement of the complement of A takes you back to A.

This connection between set theory and logic (the 'laws of thought') was elaborated by George Boole in the mid-nineteenth century,[6] and the logic described has since become known as Boolean logic. The classical logic developed by Frege and Russell is Boolean, and for the purposes of this book, classical logic means (is defined as) Boolean logic. Whereas Boole was investigating the mathematics of logic, Frege and Russell were working on the logic of mathematics (especially set theory), and they converged from different angles on the same logic.

3.6 PROPERTIES OF RELATIONS AND FUNCTIONS

3.6.1   MORE ON RELATIONS

Relations were introduced above as the denotations of predicates, primarily of arity ≥ 2 (though one can also think of sets as one-place relations). There are some important properties of binary relations, especially, which will play a major role in the rest of the book.

First some basic definitions. Relations are sets, and like any other sets can be defined by set constructors. For example the denotation of the Love relation can be written as $\{\langle x, y \rangle: x \text{ loves } y\}$ (the set of all ordered pairs $\langle x, y \rangle$ such that x loves y). The set operations discussed above are easily extended to relations. First of all there is the set complement, $\{\langle x, y \rangle: x \text{ does not love } y\}$, the set of all pairs of individuals who do not participate in the Love relation.

Write similar definitions for the following operations:

1. The intersection $L \cap K$ of the Love and Know relations.
2. The union $L \cup H$ of the Love and Hate relations.
3. The difference $K - L$ between the Know and Love relations.

Relations also have other operations which do not apply to ordinary sets. One which is intuitive linguistically is the **converse**[7] of a relation, written as R^{-1}. This is the same set of ordered pairs as R, but with the order of each pair reversed. It can be thought of as a kind of 'passive voice'. Love^{-1} can be defined as $\{\langle x, y \rangle: y \text{ loves } x\}$;

Love^{-1} (j, m) means that John is loved by Mary; we could write it as Loved-by(j, m). It can also be used for certain lexical antonyms. For example, Bigger-than is the converse of Smaller-than, Above is the converse of Below.

Since both the complement and the converse have some claim to be considered the 'opposite' of a relation (both Below(x, y) and ¬Above(x, y) can be considered 'opposites' of Above(x, y)), this gives us some handy terminology for distinguishing between two interpretations of the pre-theoretical word 'opposite'.

Converse, strictly speaking, only applies to binary relations, but similar permutations of the order of arguments can be defined for relations with three or more arguments, to capture, for example, dative shift or dative passive.[8]

Another important operation is **projection**, usually written π (pi). This picks out the left or right argument (if we are considering binary relations). Linguistically, it can be seen as picking out theta roles. For the Kill relation, π_1 (Kill) picks out the killers, and π_2 (Kill) picks out the victims. In terms of the graph representation of relations described above, if the ordered pair is a point, projection picks out its x co-ordinate or y co-ordinate. Projection is easily extended to relations with an arity of more than two.

Thinking of relations graphically as tables, projection picks out columns. We can also pick out rows, tuples which meet some particular criterion. This is known as **selection**,[9] written with the Greek letter σ (sigma). As relations are sets of tuples, this amounts to forming a subset of a relation (usually a subset defined by a particular property). For example, we can pick out the restriction of the Kill relation to those tuples where the killing was intentional, which gives us the denotation of Murder, a hyponym of Kill; since it is a subset of the tuples in Kill, we are being consistent with our earlier treatment of hyponyms as subsets.

Projection and selection are operations on single relations, but we might also want to combine them. The basic operation here is the **cross product** of two relations, R × S. This combines both the rows and the columns of R and S. If R and S do not have any arguments in common, this is usually not a terribly interesting operation. If they do, however, it is often useful and intuitive to confine attention to the tuples which have the same value in the shared argument place. For example, suppose we want to combine the relations Give/3 and Produce/2, where the latter is a relation on places and objects. We can then form a four-place relation combining the 'gift'| argument of Give with the 'product' argument of Produce, and the tuples of the new relation will pick out the events in which objects that were made in Germany were given as gifts. As the last sentence suggests, this corresponds to the use of conjunction in relative clauses, and indeed this particular form of product formation can be thought of as an interpretation of conjunction applied to relations. It is known as the **natural join** of two relations, and is notated by the 'bowtie' symbol: R ⋈ S.

Apart from its linguistic interest, this approach to relations is used in **relational databases**, which have been an important database model for several decades. A database consists of a number of tables (relations), the columns being labelled by **attributes**[10] while the rows (tuples) are usually identified by means of a particular attribute which has a unique value for each tuple and functions as a **key**. (Often some kind of serial number is used for this purpose; names are not always suitable since in many applications, unlike in predicate logic, they cannot be assumed to be unique.) Reasoning about the database is based on relational operations such as those described in this section, which form the basis of **relational algebra**. The set of basic operations varies in different implementations, but one possible basis is the following list: projection; selection; cartesian product; set union; set difference; identity (naming the relation itself); and a renaming operation (notated ρ, the Greek letter 'rho'), which enables us to rename a relation or any of its attributes. Other operations, including natural join and set intersection, can be defined in terms of these.[11]

EXERCISE 3.6.1.1

1. Suppose we have two relations, Read and Speak, between people and languages. We want to define the intersection of the two relations (people who both read and speak a language). Intuitively this calls for an intersection between two relations, but intersection is not one of the primitive operations listed above. Define the intersection using set difference.

3.6.2 PROPERTIES OF BINARY RELATIONS

Certain binary relations have properties which do not apply to relations in general:

Reflexivity: The relation holds between x and itself, whatever x may be.
Symmetry: If the relation holds between x and y, then it must hold between y and x. (Such a relation contains its own converse.)
Transitivity: If the relation holds between x and y and also between y and z, then it must hold between x and z.

It is important to be clear that a relation is reflexive, symmetric or transitive only if these properties hold *necessarily*, regardless of what the arguments are. The fact that many people love themselves does not make Love/2 a reflexive relation. An example would be Same-age-as/2, which holds between *any* object and itself.

Clearly Love/2 is also neither symmetric nor transitive. If x loves y, then it *may* be that y loves x, but of course it may not be. One instance of unrequited love is enough to show that Love/2 is not symmetric. On the other hand Married-to/2 is symmetric. If x is married to y, then y must be married to x. Likewise Love/2 is not transitive. If John loves Mary and Mary loves Peter, it is not a foregone conclusion that John loves Peter. An example of a transitive relation would be Older-than/2. If John is older than Mary and Mary is older than Peter, then necessarily John is older than Peter.

The opposites of these properties can also be important. Again, note that they mean that the relations cannot hold in the specified ways, not just that they do not necessarily hold.

An **irreflexive** relation is one that *cannot* under any circumstances hold between x and itself. An example would be Different-from/2 (or Not-equal-to/2 in mathematics).

The opposite of symmetry is tricky, and happens to be important. The idea is that the relation cannot hold between x and y and between y and x, but there are two cases to be considered, depending whether $x = y$. If $x = y$, then we would also be saying that the relation is irreflexive. This may be what we intend, or it may not. If we do, then the relation is said to be **asymmetric**: if R holds between x and y then it does not hold between y and x, and there can be no case where x = y. If not, then it is **antisymmetric**: if R holds between x and y then it cannot hold between y and x except in the case where x = y. It cannot hold both ways between two *distinct* objects x and y.

The opposite of transitivity holds no such complications (and is generally less important): it means that if R(x,y) and R(y,z), then ¬R(x,z). An example might be Father-of/2.

These properties will be developed further in the next section.

3.6.3 RELATIONS AND FUNCTIONS

Finally, for now, we should discuss functions, which have been introduced and so far used relatively informally. A function is a process which takes one or more arguments and returns a value. Furthermore it usually only makes sense for certain types of argument, and will only return a certain type of value.

One way of formalising functions is as relations. A function with one argument can be seen as a two-place relation, one with certain special properties. The set from which its arguments are drawn is its **domain**, and the set from which its values are drawn is its **range** (or co-domain). The function itself is a set of ordered pairs each consisting of one element of its domain and one element of its range. For example the Square-of function can be viewed as the relation $\{\langle 1,1 \rangle, \langle 4,2 \rangle, \langle 9,3 \rangle, \ldots\}$. Notice that I have written the ordered pairs here with the arguments on the right and the values on the left, to be consistent with the convention in this chapter that the denotation of the subject is written first, so that Square(4, 2) can be read as '4 is the square of 2'. It is equally possible, and more common in other contexts, to write the argument-value pairs the other way round.

More important are the properties that make this relation a function. A function gives one and only one value for every argument in its domain. So when the function is written as a relation, every element of its domain will occur once and only once, on the right of an ordered pair (as written here). The element of the range written with it on the left will give its value.

There is no requirement that all the elements of the range will appear in the function, or that they will be used only once. A function in which they are used only once is known as a **1:1** function; it gives a different value for each argument. A function in which all elements of the range are used is called a function **onto** its range (rather than merely 'into'). If the function is both 1:1 and onto, then its inverse is also a function; it is known as the **inverse** of the original function f, and written f^{-1}. Other terms for 1:1 and onto (respectively) are **injective** and **surjective**.

This treatment of functions as relations is known as the set-theoretic encoding of functions. More precisely it captures the graph of a function (the ordered pairs correspond to points on a graph).

One of the most important operations that will feature in this book is **composition** of functions (and, more generally, of relations). Suppose we want to find the square root of the cube of a number n. These notions of course have their own arithmetical shorthand, but we can write the function as root(cube(n)) – the application of the function (square) root to the *result* of applying the function *cube* to n. The combined procedure being executed on n is the composition of *root* with *cube*, written *root ∘ cube*. (There are a number of other notations, including a semi-colon: *root; cube*.) Note also that the functions are actually applied in the reverse order from that in which they are written (though here, too, notation can vary).

Generally, if we have two functions f and g, and the range of g is in the domain of f, then we have a composed function f ∘ g.

Composition also applies to relations. Suppose R/2 is the *brother-of* relation, and S/2 is the *wife-of* relation. Then R ∘ S is a brother-in-law relation.[12] This is not a function, as you might not have a wife, and if you do your wife may have 0 or more brothers. But the notion of composition is the same: two relational concepts are combined to form a single relational concept which holds between two arguments.

EXERCISE 3.6.3.1

1. Make a model in which Ranevskaya sells the Cherry Orchard to Lopakhin for 1,000 rubles. Define ternary relations Sell/3 (two versions, one with dative shift), the binary relations Buy/2 and Pay/2 and the inverses of all these. Write out the ordered pairs or triples that would be needed in each case for the corresponding sentence to be true.
2. Which of these binary relations have any of the properties discussed in this section? (You will find it convenient to draw up a chart.) Mother-of; Sister-of (careful with this one!); Two-years-older-than; At-least-as-old-as; Same-age-as; Subset-of; Related-to; Entails.

3.7 ALGEBRAIC BACKGROUND I

For this section, the most important properties of binary relations are reflexivity, symmetry, antisymmetry and transitivity. They are used to define the following types of relation:

Equivalence relation: A binary relation that is reflexive, transitive and symmetric.
Partial order: A relation that is reflexive, transitive and anti-symmetric.

A relation that is reflexive and transitive without any stipulations as to symmetry or anti-symmetry is called a **preorder**.

An equivalence relation on a set S partitions S into disjoint subsets. For example, the relation Same-age-as (say in years completed) will partition a group of children into age groups; the relation Equals partitions the set of numerical expressions into numerical values (numbers). The age groups and numbers, defined in this way, are called *equivalence classes*.

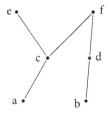

Figure 3.1   A Hasse diagram

Important partial orders include the subset relation, using the definition of subset as ⊆ (subset or equal). A set is always a subset of itself. Also if A ⊆ B and B ⊆ C, then A ⊆ C. Furthermore, if A ⊆ B and B ⊆ A, then A and B are the same set, so this satisfies the definition of antisymmetry.

What about entailment? First of all ϕ entails ϕ. This trivial looking fact is a cornerstone of all the systems of logic explored in this book; it is known as the **axiom of identity**. It is also true that if A entails B and B entails C, then A entails C. This is another important principle known as the **transitivity of entailment**. At any rate you can easily check that both the principles put forward here are true in truth table logic.

The question of symmetry is a difficult one. Is it possible for A and B to entail each other without being the same proposition? An influential answer to this question was provided by Adolf Lindenbaum, who argued that mutually entailing propositions should be treated as a single equivalence class, as defined above. Now it is possible to redefine entailment as a relation between equivalence classes of propositions (rather than simply between propositions). If this is done, then it is clear that entailment is antisymmetric, because any mutually entailing propositions will belong to the same equivalence class. (In truth table logic this can be justified by the fact that they will always have the same truth value.)

This is an example of a trick that is available with any preorder: it can be factorised into an equivalence relation and a partial order, simply by treating instances where R(a, b) and R(b, a) as equivalence classes and defining a new version of the relation accordingly. If we do this with entailment, then the resulting structure is known as a **Lindenbaum algebra**.[13] Note the parallelism that results between entailment and the subset relation. The subset relation is a partial order relation on the set of sets, while entailment is a partial order relation on the set of propositions (strictly speaking the set of equivalence classes of propositions, but this simplification is normal once Lindenbaum's trick has been explained and understood).

It is convenient to represent partial orders by means of Hasse diagrams (Figure 3.1). The points denote the members of the set and the lines denote the relation. The arrows that are normally used for the direction of a relation are unnecessary, as it is assumed to go 'upwards'. The loop that should mark the relation between each element and itself is omitted; it can be assumed, because a partial order is reflexive. The transitivity also does not need to be marked explicitly, as it can again be read off the diagram 'up' the page. To avoid any commitment as to what partially ordered set is being represented, we can refer to the nodes simply as 'points', and the relation as 'precedes' (x precedes y, or in symbols x ≤ y). The term 'partially ordered set' is often abbreviated to **poset**.

In many Hasse diagrams there will be points where lines branch or converge. If lines branch from a point p to several higher points, then p is called a lower bound of those points. If these are the only lines approaching those points from below, then p is the **greatest lower bound** (glb) of those points (anything that precedes them also precedes p). If lines converge from several points to a higher point q, then q is an upper bound of those points; and if these lines are the only ones moving upwards from those points, then q is their **least upper bound** (lub). (The glb and lub are also known as the **meet** and **join** respectively, or infimum and supremum.) An intuitive example from arithmetic is the set of positive integers ordered by divisibility, where the glb represents the highest common factor and the lub represents the lowest common multiple.

It may also be that a poset has a point right at the bottom that precedes all other points, and/or an element right at the top that is preceded by all other points. Not all posets have such points, but if they do exist, they are the glb and lub respectively for the whole poset. The divisibility poset just mentioned has a bottom element – the number 1, which divides all positive integers. It doesn't have an obvious top element, though a point ∞ is sometimes added just to give it one. Bottom elements are written as ⊥, and top elements as ⊤.

These features that posets may or may not have, have been brought in here because they are important features of both the poset of sets under the relation ⊆ and the poset of propositions under the entailment relation. Both of these belong to an important class of posets called **lattices**. There are a number of ways to define a lattice, but let's take for a moment the definition that it is a poset where every two elements have a glb and a lub. (This may be one of the two elements, if one of them precedes the other.) In set theory, any two sets have a largest common subset, which is their intersection; they also have a smallest common superset, which is their set union. (If one is a subset of the other, then their intersection is the smaller set and their union is the larger set.)

Not all lattices have a ⊤ or ⊥ element; those which have both are called bounded lattices. In the lattice of sets, ⊥ is ∅ and ⊤ is D (the universal set).

- Draw the Hasse diagram for the subsets of the set {a, b, c}, and check the glb and lub of each pair of subsets.

The Lindenbaum poset of propositions under entailment constitutes a lattice. Take two propositions, p and q. One proposition that entails both is the proposition p ∧ q, which is their glb. (Any other proposition which entails both p and q must also entail p ∧ q.) In the other direction, both p and q entail p ∨ q, and this is their lub, as it entails any other propositions that both p and q entail. What about the top and bottom elements? According to the truth table, one thing that all propositions will entail is a proposition that is always true. Conversely, a proposition that is always false will entail all propositions. We remarked earlier on the counter-intuitive and possibly unsatisfactory nature of this situation, but let's go with it for now. This means that ⊤ is interpreted as truth and ⊥ as falsity. One way of looking at them, which fits in with the lattice operations, is that ⊤ is the disjunction of all propositions, and ⊥ is the conjunction of all propositions. Since 'all propositions' includes both propositions and their negations,[14] their conjunction will always be a contradiction and their disjunction will always be a tautology.

You will have noticed that no mention has been made so far of negation (or of set complementation). To deal with these we need to introduce further structure to our lattices. A complement of a point p in a bounded lattice is a point p' such that the glb of p and p' is ⊥ and their lub is ⊤. Lattices in general do not have to have such points, and if they do exist they do not have to be unique.

- Look back at the Hasse diagram you drew three paragraphs ago, and find the set complements of the set {a}, which is the set {b,c}. Verify by following the lines that the glb of these two points is ∅ and their lub is the total set {a, b, c}.

In the set-theoretic lattice, as you would expect, every point has a complement. This makes it a **complemented lattice**. It is also true that the complement is unique, though this is not required to be a complemented lattice.

In the lattice of propositions, the natural candidate for the complement of a proposition is its negation. And if we stick to the negation connective of *classical* logic, that is indeed what we find. For any proposition p and its negation $\neg p$, the glb is $p \wedge \neg p$, which is ⊥ (false). And in classical logic the lub $p \vee \neg p$ is always true so it will be ⊤. So in the Lindenbaum algebra for *classical logic*, every element has a complement, and this complement is in fact unique.

Tracing the structure of the set theoretic lattice and the Lindenbaum lattice in parallel, we have seen that their structure is essentially the same. They are both lattices, both bounded, both complemented; furthermore the complement in both cases is unique. (This further feature requires them to be **distributed** lattices, so that they satisfy distributivity as mentioned in the previous chapter. This property will be discussed later in connection with non-classical notions of negation; for now, it simply rules out certain possible configurations of a complemented lattice in which an element can have more than one complement.) Lattices which have these properties (bounded, complemented and distributive) are called **Boolean algebras**, and it is this identity of algebraic structure that Boole was the first to highlight.

(3.14) Draw the Lindenbaum algebra starting with propositions p and q and fill in all the distinct propositions that can be formed from them using ∧, ∨, ⊤, ⊥ and ¬. Check that the points you have marked as ¬p and ¬q obey the definition of complements as given above.

1. How many elements are there in your lattice? (For the Boolean algebra generated by two atomic propositions there should be $2^{(2^2)}$.)

2. Mark on your lattice the points representing $p \mid q$, $p \dagger q$, $p \infty q$, $p \leftrightarrow q$, $p \rightarrow q$ and $q \rightarrow p$. How would you characterise the remaining points?

3. What is the lub of $\neg p \vee q$ and p? What does this represent?

(3.15) Draw the lattice consisting simply of 0 as $\perp$ and 1 as $\top$. Verify that it fulfils the conditions for a Boolean algebra (checking distributivity may be a bit tedious – you may take it that it is in fact distributive). This is known as 'the two-element Boolean algebra' or simply 2.

(3.16) A homomorphism is a function between two structured sets which preserves structure – that is, if its arguments are in a certain structural relationship in the domain of the function, then its values will be in the corresponding structural relationship in the range. The relevant structure for posets is the partial ordering, that for lattices is the glb and lub. For a function h to be a homomorphism between lattices, it is necessary that it preserves $\wedge$ and $\vee$. It does this if $h(a \wedge b) = h(a) \wedge h(b)$, and likewise for $\vee$.

1. Assume in the propositional lattice you drew earlier that p is true and q is false. You can now define a function from your propositional lattice to 2, which we can take as a valuation V whose value is 1 for p and 0 for q. Draw this function, either as a set of ordered pairs or in some other way if you prefer, so that it assigns truth values according to the truth table.

2. Is V a homomorphism?

3. An isomorphism is a homomorphism which is 1:1 and onto, meaning that it has an inverse function h^{-1} which is also a homomorphism. Effectively, its domain and range are then relabellings of the same structure. Is V an isomorphism?

NOTES

1. As with Lee Harvey Oswald, I am merely following one popular version of events; all disclaimers apply.
2. Syntactic arguments for this being the correct *linguistic* analysis for verbs like 'eat' are given by Levin and Rappaport Hovav (1995).
3. More fully: 'nothing is a wff in $\mathcal{L}$ that cannot be formed from clauses 1–3 in a finite number of steps'.
4. Also sometimes as logical variables, though I avoid that terminology here. They should not be confused with variables in the logical language, which will be introduced in the next chapter.
5. Tarski (1935).
6. Boole (1854).
7. Also known as 'inverse'. In this book I use 'converse' for relations and 'inverse' for functions (later in this section), which is fairly common terminology but nothing hinges on it.
8. Exemplified in these sentences:
   1. John gave the triffid to Mary.
   2. John gave Mary the triffid.
   3. Many was given the triffid by John.
9. Also 'restriction'.
10. As attributes give the columns names, this set-up is slightly different from predicate logic where argument places are defined only by their number in the arity of the relation. As has been seen, argument places correspond to theta roles, and attribute names can be thought of as analogous to theta role labels. The set of attributes of a relation is called a **schema**.
11. Relational algebra goes back to Peirce, who, even in the pre-computer age, foresaw its usefulness in handling data. Peirce's ideas were developed into the relational model for databases by Edgar Codd in the 1970s, and were partially implemented (though not to

Codd's satisfaction) in the database management language SQL. Codd used a different set of primitive operations from those listed in the text.

12. Since a brother-in-law can also be the husband of your sister, the brother-in-law relation is, more fully, the union of two composed relations.

13. If we decline to take this step, then we are left with a preorder.

14. For logics which include a negation connective.

CHAPTER 4

QUANTIFIERS

The last chapter introduced some of the basics of predicate logic and its interpretation. One limitation of the approach presented there is that arguments can only be filled by individuals, whether these are described by names or by descriptions such as 'the cat' or 'the cherry orchard'. In fact, however, many noun phrases (NPs) do not denote individuals at all. You probably know the old story in which the Greek hero Odysseus is captured by the one-eyed giant Polyphemus. Odysseus gives his name as Nobody. When he later blinds Polyphemus and the neighbours come running to help, Polyphemus tells them that 'Nobody' is gouging his eye out. So they tell him to stop making such a noise about nothing, and Odysseus escapes. The point, which the other giants as good semanticists have appreciated, is that 'nobody' cannot normally refer to an individual.

This chapter therefore introduces quantifiers.

4.1 SYLLOGISMS

It was observed in the last chapter that, while we had extended our original propositional language to talk about the internal structure of sentences, we did not introduce any new logical constants. Recall that the propositional connectives were described as logical constants because of the pivotal role they play in patterns of logical inference. Ordinary predicates and their arguments do not have this kind of role, although they can give rise to certain patterns of inference which were added to the logic as meaning postulates. If we want to examine *logical* patterns of inference involving units below sentence level, then it is quantifiers that we should look at, in particular the group of quantifiers 'all', 'some', 'none' and 'not all'.

This has been known since ancient times, and was the basis for one of the earliest logical systems, Aristotle's system of **syllogisms**. Aristotle was interested chiefly in patterns of reasoning such as the following.

(4.1) *All* dogs bark; *all* Labradors are dogs; *Conclusion*: *all* Labradors bark.

(4.2) *No* plants have legs; *all* flowers are plants; *Conclusion*: *no* flowers have legs.

(4.3) *All* gems are beautiful; *some* stones are gems; *Conclusion*: *some* stones are beautiful.

You should satisfy yourself that these patterns are valid; that is, if the premises are true, there is no way the conclusion can be false. Moreover, their validity depends only on the quantifiers used (italicised in the examples). The rest of the sentences could be replaced by anything, as long as the substitutions are consistent. Here is an example of the second of these patterns, with 'plants' replaced by 'machines', 'flowers' by 'computers', and 'have legs' by 'can be in love'.

(4.4) *No* machines can be in love; *all* computers are machines; *Conclusion: no* computers can be in love.

This argument is equally valid; if the premises are true, then so is the conclusion. If you think a computer can be in love, then you have to deny at least one of the premises.

As with connectives, it is common to reduce these inference patterns to schemata in which only the quantifiers are kept, the remaining terms being replaced by arbitrary letters. Here are the three patterns given above, and a fourth one thrown in. These are not all the syllogisms considered by Aristotle, but constitute an important subset of them; Aristotle himself proved that all his syllogisms could be reduced to one of these four. The traditional mnemonics for these schemata (not Aristotle's) are given too.[1]

(4.5) All B is A; all C is B; therefore all C is A. 'Barbara'
(4.6) No B is A; all C is B; therefore no C is A. 'Celarent'
(4.7) All B is A; some C is B; therefore some C is A. 'Darii'
(4.8) No B is A; some C is B; therefore not all C is A. 'Ferio'

It is important to notice that the other terms in these arguments (written here as A, B, C) are expressions that can be used as (one-place) predicates; for example *dog*, *gem*, *computer*. And we know from the last chapter that predicates can be treated as sets. This turns out to be a very fruitful hint as to how to deal with quantifiers (and indeed syllogisms).

Perhaps the most satisfactory way of approaching quantified sentences is as relations between sets. Let's look at Aristotle's logical quantifiers first.

All P is Q: This is the subset relation. There is nothing in P which is not also in Q.
Some P is Q: There is something in the intersection P ∩ Q.
No P is Q: There is nothing in the intersection P ∩ Q; the intersection is empty, the two sets are disjoint.
Not all P is Q: There is something in P which is outside Q (P is not a subset of Q).

This is not unlike the lexico-semantic relations discussed in the previous chapter, but they are not confined to them. For example All P is Q is not confined to situations where P is a hyponym of Q (e.g. 'All swans are white'); No P is Q is not confined to cases where P and Q are antonyms (e.g. 'No students are rich'). The relation between sets *may* arise through meaning postulates, but it doesn't have to.

It is possible to use Venn diagrams of these set-theoretic relations to model Aristotle's syllogisms and show their validity (Figure 4.1). For *no*, the intersec-

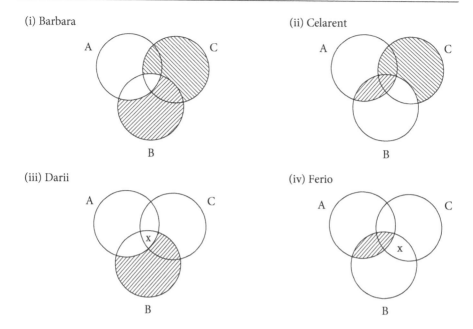

Figure 4.1   Syllogisms of the first figure

tion between two sets should be shaded out. For *some*, a cross should be marked there to show that it is not empty. For *all*, shade out the region of P that is outside Q. For *not all* do the opposite, and put a cross in the same region. (The object represented by the cross is a counter-example to the claim that all P is Q.) When the information from the two premises has been marked on the three sets involved in the syllogism, the conclusion can be read off the Venn diagram without any further additions. This shows that the conclusion is a consequence of the premises.[2]

We now want to be able to express these ideas in our logical language. Here we face a choice, because there are two different approaches to this problem that have become popular in linguistics: first order logic and higher order logic, introduced into linguistics by the programmes of Donald Davidson and Richard Montague respectively. We will be discussing both in due course (section 4.7 and next chapter). This chapter will focus on first order logic, as this offers a fairly straightforward syntax which also fits well with the notation we used in the previous chapter.

For both approaches, we will need two new types of symbol: quantifier symbols and variables.

We have already been using variables informally in the last chapter, and were in effect using them in the discussion of syllogisms just now: the *x* we used to indicate the presence of something in some region of the Venn diagram, for example the *x* we put in P ∩ Q to indicate that there is something that is both P and Q. The claim that there is something there is called **existential quantification**, and the existential quantifier is written ∃x. From the discussion of set operations in the previous chapter, we know that being in an intersection involves a conjunction; the intersection is {x: P(x) *and* Q(x)}. Combining these notions, we can write ∃x(P(x) ∧ Q(x)), which can be read as follows: there is some *x* such that x is P and x is Q.

To represent *all*, we shaded out the part of P that is outside Q, to indicate that P is a subset of Q, blocking anybody from putting an *x* there. It is like saying, 'If anybody wants to put an *x* in P, it will have to be in Q as well'. This implication is used to express the subset relation. The quantifier used here is the **universal quantifier**, which is written ∀x and read 'for every *x*'. Combining these notions, we get ∀x(P(x) → Q(x)).

The other two logical quantifiers can be expressed in terms of ∃ and ∀. For example, 'no P is Q' is the flat denial that you can put anything in P ∩ Q: ¬∃x(P(x) ∧ Q(x)). (Remember ¬ does not introduce an extra set of brackets.) And 'not all P is Q' is the denial of the universally quantified statement in the previous paragraph: ¬∀P(x) → Q(x)). Since we marked it in the Venn diagram by putting an *x* in the part of P that is outside Q – in defiance of the non-negated universally quantified sentence – we can say the same thing by making an existential statement that there *is* something in that area of the diagram: ∃x(P(x)∧¬ Q(x)).

In natural language there is an important asymmetry between the terms that have here been labelled P and Q. Normally the expression denoting P goes closely with the determiner to form an NP. It is actually what syntactians call an N′, and P will be referred to as the N-bar set or the **restriction**. Q on the other hand is the denotation of the main predicate of the sentence (in these cases a verb phrase (VP)), and will be referred to as the **focus set**. You will notice that the syntax we have just introduced does not reflect that distinction. This is something that will be discussed later in this chapter, and in the next one. An alternative approach would be to restrict the variable to a particular set as soon as we introduce it: $∀x_{x∈P}x∈Q$, or $∃x_{x∈P}x∈Q$. This is known as restricted quantification. However, in first order logic variables are not restricted in this way: ∀x(P(x) → Q(x)) envisages that you can put an *x* anywhere you like, but if it is in P then it will be in Q. First order logic uses unrestricted quantification. and the work of restriction is done instead by the implication or conjunction that goes with it.

The syntax and semantics defined in the next two sections are known as first order predicate logic or first order quantification theory. They extend our language of quantifier-free predicate logic from the last chapter by introducing quantifiers and variables.

4.2 SYNTAX OF FIRST ORDER QUANTIFICATION THEORY

For the syntax, we add the quantifier symbols ∀ and ∃, and a set of **individual variables**, normally taken from the end of the alphabet (x, y etc.). If we really need a lot of them, they are sometimes named x_1, x_2 and so on instead. The quantifier symbols are added to the vocabulary of our logical language. Variables are not formally considered part of the vocabulary of the language, but rather auxiliary symbols.

Individual variables and individual constants together make up the set of **terms**, and we modify the definition for basic formulas so that the arguments of a predicate can be any terms – constants, variables, or a mixture of the two. So, for a language $\mathcal{L}$ of first order quantification theory (FOQT):

(4.9) If P/n is a predicate and $a_1, \ldots a_n$ are *terms*, then P $(a_1, \ldots a_n)$ is a wff in $\mathcal{L}$.

The rules for compound sentences remain unchanged:

(4.10) 1. If ϕ is a wff in $\mathcal{L}$, then so is $\neg\phi$.
      2. If ϕ and ψ are wffs in $\mathcal{L}$, then so are $(\phi \wedge \psi)$, $(\phi \vee \psi)$ and $(\phi \rightarrow \psi)$.

Now the rules for introducing quantifier symbols. The rules themselves are simple enough (4.11), but they need a bit of discussion.

(4.11) If ϕ is a wff in $\mathcal{L}$ and x is a variable, then $\forall x\phi$ and $\exists x\phi$ are wffs in $\mathcal{L}$.

Before the discussion, let's not forget to close our inductive definition. This concludes the syntactic rules for this chapter.

(4.12) Nothing else is a wff in $\mathcal{L}$.

The rules for quantifiers introduce expressions with three parts: the quantifier symbol, a variable, and a wff ϕ which is the **scope** of the quantifier.

- Note that there are no brackets introduced around the scope in this rule. However, you are used to seeing expressions like $\forall x(P(x) \rightarrow Q(x))$. Where do the brackets in this expression come from?

You will also notice that there is no mention of occurrences of x inside ϕ. This probably seems strange, as the whole point of this syntax is to link the quantifier with certain arguments within its scope. We can assume that x will occur somewhere inside ϕ. (If it doesn't, then the quantification is said to be **vacuous**. This is discussed in section 4.4 and in subsequent chapters.)

If ϕ itself does not contain quantifiers, any variable that occurs within it is said to be **free**. Free variables can be thought of as the equivalent of personal pronouns – 'he', 'she', 'it', though of course without gender.

A quantifier (quantifier symbol plus variable) is said to **bind** any free occurrence of the same variable within its scope. The quantified sentences we have already met are straightforward examples of this, and being able to read and interpret sentences like these is the main thing at this stage.

One technicality: from now on we should be careful to refer to wffs as formulas, not sentences. Up till now it hasn't mattered (and formulas in propositional logic, for example, are often referred to as sentences). The presence of free variables changes this. A formula which contains a variable, such as Love(x, mary), is not considered a sentence. (We cannot assign it an interpretation until we know who 'he, she or it' is.) On the other hand if all variables are bound, as in ∀x Love(x, mary) – 'Everybody loves Mary' – then it can once again be called a sentence (though it is still a formula).

(4.13)　Translate these sentences into FOQT.
1. All elves love Aragorn, but not all elves love Gimli.
2. Nobody who loves Newcastle loves Sunderland.
3. Some flowers are purple and some are white.
4. If nobody drinks vodka, then nobody is drunk.
5. If anybody understands Greek, Paul does.

(4.14)　Are these wffs in FOQT? If not, why not? If so, draw the construction tree.
1. $\forall (x \rightarrow (P(x) \wedge Q(x)))$
2. $\forall x((P(x) \wedge R(x,y)) \rightarrow Q(y))$
3. $\exists x(\neg(P(x) \vee Q(x)))$
4. $\forall x(P(y) \rightarrow (Q(z))$
5. $\forall x(P(x) \rightarrow \exists y(Q(y) \wedge R(x, y)))$

(4.15)　Which variables in these formulas are free? For those that are not, which quantifiers are they bound by?

4.3 SEMANTICS OF FIRST ORDER QUANTIFICATION THEORY

We have inherited from previous chapters a model $\mathcal{M} = \langle D, I \rangle$ – that is, it consists of a domain D and an interpretation function I – and rules for evaluating atomic formulae using set theory, and rules for the interpretation of compound sentences using classical connectives. These all function exactly as before. We need a mechanism for interpreting variables and quantifiers, in that order.

The first thing is that variables are not interpreted by I, which is to say that their interpretation is not given by the model $\mathcal{M}$. This should be clear if you think of free variables and personal pronouns. A model will not tell me whether 'he loves Mary' is true, or who 'he' in this formula refers to. Even if we could ask I to do this job, it would be useless for our purposes. We don't want to change our model every time we use 'he' to refer to a different person. Moreover, it would be treating variables as names, which is a conceptual mistake; we would be in danger of ending up like Polyphemus.

We therefore introduce a separate function, from variables to individuals in D. This is called an **assignment**. For some reason, an assignment is normally called *g*. We can have an assignment g_1 which assigns *x* to Bob and *y* to Harry, an assignment g_2 which assigns *x* to Harry and *y* to Jill, and so on. In practice, we will never have to specify all possible assignments, but this is how it works.

We have now introduced several functions whose job is to interpret different kinds of expression: valuations, interpretation functions and variable assignments. The distinctions are important, and it would be good at this point to make sure you understand them. Valuations assign truth values to propositions, either out of the blue (as in propositional logic) or with respect to a model. An interpretation function links the vocabulary of the language with elements of a model. An assignment links variables (which, remember, are not part of the vocabulary of the language) with individuals.

Nonetheless it is convenient sometimes to talk about denotation in general regardless of which of these mechanisms is actually involved. To do this, we now define a generalised **denotation function**. This is written with a 'circumfix' notation, as $|| \ldots ||$, with its argument as whatever comes in the middle. When the denotation depends on a model and / or an assignment, we remind ourselves of the fact by putting these as a subscript. For example $||\alpha||_{\mathcal{M},g}$ is read as 'the denotation of some expression α with respect to a model $\mathcal{M}$ and an assignment g'.

This simplifies the semantic definitions for arguments of a predicate – terms which can be either individual constants or variables.

(4.16) If t is a term in $\mathcal{L}$, then
  1. $||t||_{\mathcal{M},g} = I(t) \in D$ if t is an individual constant
  2. $||t||_{\mathcal{M},g} = g(t) \in D$ if t is an individual variable

Thus both get a denotation in D, regardless of which mechanism is doing the work.

We will use the same notation for predicate denotations, although in fact predicates are always interpreted by I. (It is important to note that variables in FOQT range only over individuals, not sets – see section 4.7 below.) The following definition means, in fact, exactly the same as the definition given in the previous chapter for the interpretation of predicates.

(4.17) If P/n is a predicate in $\mathcal{L}$, then $||P||_{\mathcal{M},g} = I(P) \subseteq D^n$.

The denotation will be a subset of D, D × D, or D × D × D, and so on up to n dimensions.

The denotation of an atomic formula is also unchanged, except that arguments may include variables as well as individual constants. I will use the slightly more concise notation just introduced.

(4.18) If $P(t_1, \ldots t_n)$ is a wff in $\mathcal{L}$, then $||P(t_1, \ldots t_n)||_{\mathcal{M},g} = 1$ iff $\langle ||t_1||_{\mathcal{M},g}, \ldots ||t_n||_{\mathcal{M},g} \rangle \in ||P||_{\mathcal{M},g}$.

You are advised to compare these definitions carefully with those given for QFPL in the previous chapter, and to convince yourself that they are indeed the same, apart from the introduction of variables.

The rules for connectives are unchanged, and I will not repeat them here.

Finally, we come to the rules for quantifiers. With quantifiers we are concerned with what different valuations assign to the bound variable (let's call it x). For the universal quantifier, we look at all the individuals in D that can be assigned to x, and see if the resulting formula (the scope of the quantifier) is true. For the existential quantifier, we look at the individuals that can be assigned to x, until we come across just one for which the scope of the quantifier evaluates to true. If this works, then the quantified formula is true. Otherwise it is false.

1. Use a model $\mathcal{M}$ where D = {a, b, c, d} and I(P) = {a, c}. Assume we will use four variables, w, x, y and z. How many assignments are there which assign all variables to different individuals? (Remember a function does not have to return different values for all its arguments.)
2. In the same model, evaluate P(y) for all possible assignments of y. Is $\forall y P(y)$ true or false? How about $\exists y P(y)$?

That is almost all there is to it, but not quite. It would seem from the previous paragraph that when evaluating quantified formulae we are not concerned with any particular assignment g, but looking at all assignments. In this case we are no longer evaluating the formula with respect to $\mathcal{M}$ and g, it would seem. As far as quantification is concerned, that is indeed correct. However, we cannot just forget about g, because there may also be free variables somewhere in the formula, and we need to keep their interpretation consistent. So we consider only assignments that agree with g on other variables, but can assign the bound variable we are interested in (which we are calling x) to any element d in D. The notation we will use for this is $g[x \mapsto d]$ (you will see minor variations in the literature). This allows us to interpret quantifiers and their bound variables as described in the last paragraph, while not changing the denotation of free variables.

Here, then, are the definitions:

(4.19) 1. If $\forall x \varphi$ is a wff in $\mathcal{L}$, then $\|\forall x\ \phi\|_{\mathcal{M},g} = 1$ iff, for every d ∈ D, $\|\phi\|_{\mathcal{M},g[x \mapsto d]} = 1$.
2. If $\exists x \phi$ is a wff in $\mathcal{L}$, then $\|\exists x\ \phi\|_{\mathcal{M},g} = 1$ iff there is some d ∈ D such that $\|\phi\|_{\mathcal{M},g[x \mapsto d]} = 1$.

These last clauses may be a bit of a mouthful, if you are coming to them for the first time. This is a normal reaction.

4.4 RELATIONS BETWEEN QUANTIFIERS

It was noted in the first section of this chapter that the same state of affairs can often be described by more than one quantifier. For example, $\neg \forall x(P(x) \rightarrow Q(x))$ is equivalent to $\exists x(P(x) \wedge \neg Q(x))$. In classical logic, the logical quantifiers are interdefinable by means of negation. They are said to be **duals** of each other.

(4.20) 1. $\forall x \phi \equiv \neg \exists x \neg \phi$
2. $\exists x\ \phi \equiv \neg \forall x \neg \phi$

This is reminiscent of the interdefinability of $\wedge$ and $\vee$ in classical logic through the De Morgan equivalences. In fact the principle is the same, given that we can think of a universal quantification as a big conjunction (ϕ is true of a and b and c . . .), and of existential quantification as being a big disjunction (ϕ is true of a or b or c . . .) – except, of course, that not all individuals in the domain might have a name. (Why is this a possibility?)

In Aristotelian logic, the relation between quantifiers can be depicted using

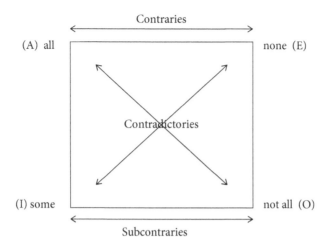

Figure 4.2   The Square of Opposition

the famous Square of Opposition (Figure 4.2). This was not due to Aristotle himself; it was probably invented by Apuleius, was popularised by Boethius, and thereafter became part of the stock in trade of scholastic and traditional logic. The four logical quantifiers sit at the corners of the square, each labelled by a vowel.[3]

The quantifiers at diagonally opposite corners are called **contradictories** – they are the negations of each other, as we have already seen. E is the contradictory of I, and A is the contradictory of O. In each pair, one is true iff the other is false. A and E, on the top edge, are **contraries**: they cannot both be true, but it is quite possible that neither is true. I and O, on the bottom edge, are **subcontraries**; they might both be true, but they cannot both be false.

Beyond this point, modern classical logic and the Aristotelian Square part company. This is because of their treatment of universally quantified sentences where the restriction set is empty, for example 'All unicorns are pink'. (In FOQT, where universal sentences involve an implication, this means when the antecedent of the conditional is false.) Using the truth table definition of implication, such universally quantified sentences are evaluated as true. This strikes many people as unintuitive, and indeed this case is known in the literature as **improper quantification**. Aristotle did not regard such sentences as true, and thus in his logic, A entails I. Similarly on the other side of the square, E entails O in the corner below it. This entailment relationship in traditional logic between the top and bottom corners is known as the **subaltern** relation. In modern classical logic, by contrast, the quantifiers vertically above and below each other in the square are duals.

One major advantage of modern first order logic over traditional logic is its ability to deal with multiple quantification. In Aristotle's syllogisms, each proposition has only one quantifier, and logicians in this tradition were puzzled by inferences involving sentences with more than one quantifier.

(4.21) Behind every powerful man is some powerful woman.
(4.22) There is some powerful woman who is behind every powerful man.

Assuming that (4.21) is true, does it entail (4.22)? Part of the trouble here is that (4.21) is ambiguous. On one reading, it means the same as (4.22) (and therefore does entail it). On another reading of (4.21) there are many separate women involved. Since this second reading is at least plausible (maybe), it might lead people to argue that the reading corresponding to (4.22) also has to be accepted. At least, some medieval logicians found themselves arguing along these lines, even though (4.22) seems less plausible.

One of the triumphs of Frege's logic was its ability to represent this difference in meaning clearly for the first time. To make the logical forms simpler I will refer to men using the variable x and women using y, and omit the predicates Man(x) and Woman(y) (in other words I am using, for the moment, restricted quantification). The full first order representations will be given afterwards.

(4.23) 1. $\forall x \exists y$ Behind(y, x)
          for every man x, there is a woman y such that y is behind x.
     2. $\exists y \forall x$ Behind(y, x)
          there is a woman y such that, for every man x, y is behind x.

What this representation shows is that the ambiguity depends on the relative scope of the two quantifiers. In the first the existential falls within the scope of the universal quantifier, and is evaluated separately for every man. In the second it is the other way round, and the existential quantifier asks us to find one woman for whom the universally quantified sentence in its scope evaluates to true.

As promised, here is the full logical form, including explicitly the predicates Man(x) and Woman(y). As normal, the universal quantifier is associated with an implication and the existential with a conjunction. If these sentences are not immediately transparent to you, you are advised to study them carefully.

(4.24) 1. $\forall x$(Powerful-Man(x) $\rightarrow$ $\exists y$(Powerful-Woman(y) $\wedge$ Behind(y, x)))
     2. $\exists y$(Powerful-Woman(y) $\wedge$ $\forall x$(Powerful-Man(x) $\rightarrow$ Behind(y,x)))
        (a) Draw the construction trees for both these statements.
        (b) Do you think the second sentence follows from the first? If not, what state of affairs in a model would provide a counter-example? Construct such a model.

4.5 MORE QUANTIFIERS

The discussion so far has focused on the logical quantifiers, not unreasonably for a book which is at least partly about logic. However, there are a great many other quantifiers in natural language. To start with, there are the natural numbers. Intuitively, 'three P are Q' means that there are three entities in the intersection P ∩ Q.[4] More formally, the number of entities in a set is called the **cardinality** of the set, and is written using the circumfix function $|\cdots|$. So 'three P are Q' is true iff $|P \cap Q| = 3$. On the other hand, we often use 'three' to mean 'at least three'. If I say 'I have three million pounds', you would probably accept that as true if I in fact have four. (Unless, of course, you are a tax inspector.)

4.6 TRANSLATING INTO FIRST ORDER LOGIC

Combining the ideas from this chapter and the previous one, it is now possible to translate a wide variety of English sentences into our logical language, and thus provide them with a model-theoretic interpretation. We will look at a few of them here.

Adjectives modifying nouns often denote the conjunction of the adjective and the noun; for example a red car is a car and it is red (a red object). Such adjectives are known as intersective adjectives, because the entity denoted will be in the intersection of the sets denoted by the adjective and the modified noun.

Defining relative clauses can easily be handled in the same way. A woman who sings is in the intersection of the set of women and the set of entities that sing. This also elucidates why these structures are called 'defining' relative clauses; they restrict the entity being described from the whole set of women to the part of the set which intersects with the set of singing entities.

These ideas combine with the quantifiers introduced in this chapter to considerably extend the range of sentences we can deal with. Here is some practice.

(4.25) Translate these sentences into first order logic.
1. Every Australian cricketer reveres Don Bradman.
2. No student who knows Greek does not understand philosophy.
3. Every man who possesses some fortune is in want of a wife.
4. Not every student in Germany learns German.
5. Every mountain on the moon is named after a scientist or philosopher on Earth.

4.7 FIRST AND HIGHER ORDER

This section will focus on the difference between first order and higher order logics. Both are predicate logics, with variables (usually) and quantifiers.

When we started using predicates and arguments, it was stipulated that the arguments of predicates had to be individuals, though, following the example of natural language, we would be quite flexible about what we are prepared to count as an individual. How far can we allow this flexibility to go? For example, can a predicate be an argument of a predicate? In first order logic, the answer is an emphatic *no*.[5]

This question goes back to the early history of modern logic and that of set theory, in both of which Frege and Russell played a central role. In set theory, the analogous question is whether a set can be an element of a set (not to be confused with being a subset of a set, which all sets are by definition). If it can, this raises the possibility that a set can be a member of itself. This leads to the famous Russell paradox, which at first seemed to throw the foundations of set theory (and logic) into confusion.[6] Frege was devastated by its discovery. Several ways were found of working round this apparent problem. Russell's own proposal was to organise sets in a system of levels or **orders**. First we start with a universal set of individuals, and consider sets which contain only such individuals. These are first order sets. Then we can allow sets which take first order sets as their members; these are second order sets, and so on. This idea is no longer the preferred way of doing set theory, but it remains influential in logic.

Thus in first order logic, as formally adopted in this and the previous chapter, the only sets are sets of individuals. Arguments of predicates are confined to individual constants or variables, and variables range only over individuals, elements of D. As a result, quantified statements can only be made about individuals. This affects the assumptions made by our model theory about what kind of things exist – its **ontology**. First order logic only commits itself to the existence of individuals. Sets are merely a technical aid, and in fact anything that has been said using sets in these chapters can be expressed in other ways (as we will soon see). We cannot say, in first order logic, 'there is a set S such that . . .' The test of what you (or your theory) accept as existing is that it can be referred to by a variable and quantified over; as Quine famously put it, 'To be is to be the value of a variable.'

To put properties and relations into our ontology would be to claim that they exist as objects, a process known as **reification**. Plato was perhaps the best known exponent of the idea that goodness, beauty, even tableness and chairness, are real objects (more real than the particulars that instantiate them).[7] The debate over this is known as the problem of universals. Bertrand Russell, who was a strong advocate of first order logic (as was Quine), regarded reification as a regrettable tendency of natural language which disappears under proper logical analysis (i.e. using first order logic) – one of many mismatches between language and logic which he termed the problem of 'misleading form' in language. As was mentioned in the introduction, Russell and Frege regarded this mismatch as so glaring that they did not regard their logic as suited to natural language at all. Davidson and Montague, from their different points of view, were among the first to propose that the two could be made to fit, and the question whether the logic used should be first order or higher order soon became part of the debate.

This book is for linguists, so I will try to isolate the linguistic questions involved here.

First of all there is the ontological question. Is it important in natural language to be able to treat properties as arguments of a predicate? Here are a few examples that suggest it is.

(4.26) 1. This car is red. Red is a colour.
        2. Katia is everything that Anna isn't.
        3. Beauty is truth, truth beauty.

In the first example red is used first as a first order predicate, then apparently as the argument of another predicate. If it is being used in the same sense in both sentences, then it would seem that *colour* is a second order predicate, taking a first order predicate as its argument. In the second example, we have explicit quantification over properties, as the sentence seems to mean that Katia has all the properties that Anna doesn't have (perhaps kindness, loyalty . . .). To express this we need second order variables, which can be assigned to sets.

For the third example, we need to note that the idea of two entities being equal is not expressible in first order logic. It is usually interpreted through Leibniz' principle of the **identity of indiscernables** – two entities are the same iff they share all the same properties (there is no means of telling them apart). In the example, if the two nouns are properties, then equality between them is a higher order notion. The two properties share all the same higher order properties, which, as properties of properties, will themselves be second order predicates. But to quantify over second order properties, we need second order variables, which means we are using third order logic!

The second question is the mismatch, which we have noted a few times, between linguistic form and first order logical form. The disparity between the logical form of a quantified sentence and its syntactic structure was referred to earlier. At an even more basic level, there is nothing in a first order formula corresponding to a VP; the construction tree for a predicate and its two arguments is a 'flat' structure, the subject and object arguments being sisters. These mismatches are not necessarily tragic, and it should be noted that many syntacticians have been willing to accept logical forms for sentences which are a long way from the apparent syntactic structure. However, if other methods can achieve a better match, then it would seem to be worth trying.

Finally, it has been argued that first order logic is simply not able to express important things that can be expressed using higher order approaches. Take quantification, since that is the subject of this chapter. The basic concept of a quantifier, it was suggested, is a relation between two sets. That itself is a second order idea; but we have seen that it is possible to approximate it using first order logic, at least for the logical quantifiers. In fact it is possible for many other quantifiers besides. But not all. In a very important paper, Barwise and Cooper (1981) showed that the quantifier *most* cannot be reduced to first order logic.

Finally there is the problem of intensionality. The denotation of expressions in the language is fixed, which is nice in mathematics, but problematic in natural language, where expressions like 'the president of the USA' have different denotations in different contexts. Frege[8] already pointed this out as a major difference between logic (i.e. his logic) and language. There is no obvious way of accommodating intensionality in first order logic. The higher order logic advocated by Montague, on the other hand, can have a good stab at expressing the necessary distinctions, as we will see in Chapter 7.

Important note: many semanticists, including some very eminent ones, would disagree with the last few paragraphs, or at least with any suggestion that first order logic is inadequate. There are a number of programmes which seek to enrich first order logic to capture natural language semantics better. Both first order and higher order logic have their uses, and both will be needed for discussions in later parts of the book. In the next chapter, however, we will look at the powerful and influential higher order approach pioneered by Montague.

We have mentioned second and third order notions in this section. How high do we have to go? Probably no natural language phenomena need more than third order logic. The system we will look at in the next chapter, however, can produce as high an order as we like, without difficulty; it is sometimes termed ω order, meaning orders up to infinity.[9] This might seem like overkill. On the other hand we have already been using a logic which allows us to form predicates with an arbitrary number of arguments, even though in natural language you rarely if ever need more than three.

NOTES

1. See note 3 below.
2. It is also a good example of **visual logic** in which information is read off diagrams rather than from a string of symbols, exploiting our intuitions of space and direction. The Hasse diagrams of the previous chapter were another example. See Chapter 9 for further discussion.
3. These vowels are responsible for the traditional mnemonics for the Aristotelian syllogisms, already mentioned. For example, Barbara has the quantifier All three times, and hence three 'a' vowels.
4. Or graphically 'three x's', but note that these are three entities, not three variables.
5. There are some developments of first order logic, such as property theory, in which this is not so clear-cut.
6. If a set can be a member of itself, then we can divide sets into those which contain themselves as a member, and those which do not. Let's call the former 'abnormal' and the latter 'normal', though nothing hinges on the names. We can then form the set of normal sets and the set of abnormal sets. The paradox arises when we ask if the set of normal sets is itself normal. It can be seen that if it is normal then it is abnormal, and if it is abnormal then it is normal.
7. The Theory of Forms, set forward in the person of Socrates in many of Plato's 'middle' dialogues.
8. Frege (1892).
9. The letter ω, omega, is the last letter of the Greek alphabet. Learning the Greek alphabet is a good investment of time for semantics students.

CHAPTER 5

FUNCTIONS: THE LAMBDA CALCULUS

This chapter introduces one of the main contributions of Richard Montague to linguistics, known as Montague semantics. (It also had an influence on syntax, on which context it is usually called Montague Grammar.) Montague's own presentation of his work (three short papers, published after his early death in 1971) is notoriously and unnecessarily difficult. However, it has been reworked by a number of excellent writers since then into a more digestible form, and it is this tradition that is drawn on here.

The end of the last chapter introduced the distinction between first order and higher order logics. One of the cornerstones of Richard Montague's programme for semantics was the use of higher order logic. Montague semantics in general (and its developments, such as Generalized Quantifier Theory) are not covered by this book. However, this chapter will introduce his influential choice for a logical translation language: the simply typed **lambda calculus**, which is the basis for many of the ideas discussed in the rest of the book.[1]

The lambda calculus is a theory of functions. Functions have been discussed already in earlier chapters; however, from now on they will take centre stage, and it is important to consolidate some basic notions.

A function is a process that acts on an input (the **argument**) to produce an output (the **value**). Feeding an argument to a function to get a value is called **function application** – the function is applied to the argument. If a function **f** is applied to an argument **a** to give a value **v**, then the normal notation for this is **f(a) = v**.

(5.1) 1. capital-of(scotland) = edinburgh
      2. square-of(4) = 16
      3. mother-of(william) = diana

As we also saw in Chapter 3, a function can also be seen – and written – as a binary relation, subject to particular constraints. In this case the same function can be written F(v, a) (5.2). Since the order of arguments in a relation is a matter of convention, it can be reversed as long as everybody is clear what they are talking about. The order used here respects the conventions used in Chapter 3 for natural language predicates. It also observes the usual capitalisation convention for first order predicates, which does not apply in higher order logic.[2]

(5.2) 1. Capital-of(edinburgh, scotland)
       2. Square-of(16, 4)
       3. Mother-of(diana, william)

In this chapter and generally in the rest of the book, the notation in (5.1) will be used for functions. This is usual when the focus is on functions, as is the case in the lambda calculus. It is useful, however, to be able to switch perspectives between the two approaches.

5.1 PREDICATES AS FUNCTIONS

In semantics, we have to deal with several kinds of linguistic expressions, each with their own type of meaning. The two basic types are normally taken to be names (individual constants), which denote individuals, and sentences, which denote truth values. What about a predicate, such as 'is rich'? It does not denote anything specific in the world, and at the same time it cannot (on its own) be classified as true or false as a sentence can. On the other hand if you combine it with an individual – say Bill Gates – the combination will be a sentence and can be judged as true or false. So the predicate denotes neither an individual nor a truth value, but a 'function from individuals to truth values'. If it is applied to the individual Bill Gates, the resulting truth value will be *true* (1). If it is applied to the individual Howard Gregory, the result will be *false* (0).

Let us apply this scheme of things to the top level of a syntactic phrase structure tree – the subtree consisting of the root node S and its two daughters, NP and VP. Let's say that the NP is 'mary' and the VP is 'snores'. We can annotate each node with the appropriate meaning, let's say *m* for the NP and *snore* for the VP. Remember that *snore* is a predicate, a function from individuals to truth values. Applying *snore* to *m* gives us *snore*(*m*), which is the meaning of the whole sentence and can be written at the S node.

The set-up just described is typical, so let's have another look at what we have got there. First of all, there is a local subtree, part of a syntactic tree containing just a mother and its daughters. One of the daughters (called the **functor daughter**) has a function as its semantic content. The other (the **argument daughter**) has something which can serve as the input to that function. The mother is annotated with the value, computed by applying the function to its argument (Figure 5.1).

We also need to keep track of the kind of meanings involved, to make sure that the function gets an argument of the right type and computes a value of the right type. To do this we use what we can think of for the moment as a bookkeeping system. It consists of recording the types of the semantic expressions at the different nodes. At the NP node (the argument daughter) we have an expression which denotes an individual, so we annotate that node with *e* for entity. At the S node (the mother) we have something which denotes a truth value, so we annotate it with *t*. At the VP node we have a one-place predicate, which is a function from individuals to truth values. We can write this as $e \rightarrow t$. All we have to do is make sure that the symbol to the left of the arrow (the input) matches the type on the argument

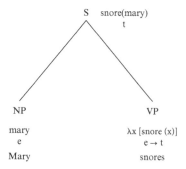

Figure 5.1   Function application in a simple sentence

daughter, and that the symbol to the right of the arrow (the output) matches the type on the mother.

This approach goes back to Frege, who observed that a predicate is a kind of incomplete expression (today we might say 'unsaturated'), which could be interpreted as a function. He speculated that all combinations of semantic expressions proceed in exactly this way, by function application. This idea is known as **Frege's conjecture**.

5.1.1 CHARACTERISTIC FUNCTIONS

In Chapter 3 we said that the denotation of a one-place predicate was a set. In the last few paragraphs, however, I have been treating it as a function (of a particular type, namely from entities to truth values). So what is the story here?

In fact these are two different ways of looking at the same thing. For every set A of individuals, there is a function from individuals to truth values that returns *true* if the individual is in the set A, and *false* if it is not. This function is called the **characteristic function** of the set A, and can be written χ_A (using the Greek letter χ or 'chi'). We can do the same thing the other way round, too. If we have any function from individuals to truth values, we can form the set containing exactly those individuals to whom the function assigns *true*, and excluding those to whom it assigns *false*. So sets of individuals and functions from individuals to truth values are equivalent. Sometimes it is helpful to think in terms of sets (for example in the use we have already made of Venn diagrams), and sometimes it is useful to think in terms of functions. At the moment it is useful to think in terms of functions.

We could draw an analogy with a nightclub, with some rule for admission. A bouncer stands outside with a checklist, or a sheet of instructions, and as each person approaches, he either lets them in or sends them away. The set corresponds to the nightclub and the people who belong in it. The bouncer, though it is probably not written in so many words in his job description, is computing the characteristic function of the set.

Graphically, we can represent the characteristic function of a set as a matrix, with the entities in the domain on the left and the two truth values 1 and 0 on the right. If the domain of our model consists of {a, b, c, d} and the set of snorers is {a, b}, then the characteristic function of the predicate *snore* will take a and b to 1, and will take c and d to 0.

5.1.2 LAMBDA EXPRESSIONS

If we are going to deal seriously with functions, we come up against the question of how to write them. Some functions can be thought of as a list, or lookup table. The *capital city* function we used earlier is an example of such a function; it consists of a list of countries and their capitals, whether in somebody's memory or in an atlas. However, this will not do for complicated functions, or ones which seem to be computed by some rule rather than by lookup. A second approach might be to give each function a name which reminds us of the rule to be used. For example the *square* function refers to the well-known rule of multiplying a number by itself. However, how many names of functions do we need? So many that learning all the names of functions we need becomes impractical. And on top of that, some functions can be complicated. Suppose we want to cube a number and take the square root of the result? It seems cumbersome to call this the cube-then-take-square-root function. And functions can get a lot more complicated than that.

One solution is to develop a way of systematically describing what a function does. The most popular way of doing this is the lambda calculus, developed by Alonzo Church. It consists of two parts. First you separate out the arguments of the function, and write them to one side as variables. Then in the main body of the function, you write what you do to the variable(s) to compute the value of the function. You can think of it as a recipe for finding the value. For example the *square* function has just one argument, for which we can use the variable x; and the recipe for finding the value is to multiply x by itself – x * x. To complete the notation, the variables in the list of arguments are marked by prefixing them with the Greek letter λ (lambda), and the recipe is enclosed in square brackets (not always, but we will follow this practice for the time being). So for the *square* function, we end up with $\lambda x[x*x]$.

The occurrence of λ is said to **bind** the variable x, and the 'recipe box' in square brackets is its **scope** (just like with the quantifiers in the previous chapter).

When the function is used (i.e. applied to an argument), the argument is slotted in in place of the variable x in the scope. Since in this example x occurs twice in the scope, the argument will be written twice, and ends up being multiplied by itself.

(5.3)　1. $\lambda x[x * x]$ (3) – the function is applied to the argument 3.
　　　　2. 3 * 3 – the argument (3) is substituted for both occurrences of x in the scope, the apparatus of lambda and square brackets being removed.
　　　　3. 9 – the value returned by the function.

Let us have a look at some linguistic examples. The predicate *snore* in Figure 5.1 (p. 69) can be rewritten as $\lambda x[snore(x)]$. This is a function that looks for an individual to slot in in place of the x. If the function is applied to m (Mary), then we have $\lambda x[snore(x)](m)$. Substituting m for x in the scope and removing the lambda and square brackets, we get snore(m), which is a sentence (a recipe for a truth value).

In this example, it may not seem that the use of lambda notation buys us very much compared with what we had already. In this particular case it probably doesn't. But remember that this is a very simple example. The lambda system helps us to track exactly what is going on when things get more complicated.

When dealing with unary predicates, it is helpful to think of the λ operator as forming properties; for example $\lambda x[\text{snore}(x)]$ can be thought of as the property of being a snorer, or of 'being an x such that x snores'. We can get some more interesting properties simply by using the propositional connectives:

(5.4) $\lambda x[\neg \text{smoke}(x)]$ – the property of being a non-smoker (an x such that x does not smoke).

(5.5) $\lambda x[\text{scholar}(x) \wedge \text{gentleman}(x)]$ – the property of being a scholar and a gentleman (an x such that x is a scholar and x is a gentleman).

(5.6) $\lambda x[\text{smoke}(x) \wedge \neg \text{drink}(x)]$ – the property of being a smoker but non-drinker (an x such that x smokes and x does not drink).

This is very reminiscent of the set constructors used in Chapter 3. In fact, this section is fulfilling the promissory note made there about the construction of new predicates using connectives. Connectives, as we have defined them, can only be applied to propositions, not predicates. In these examples, the connectives themselves are correctly applied to propositions, but the resulting expression is a predicate.

All of these would be the meanings of quite complex VPs – we will see shortly how these complex meanings can be built up compositionally in the syntax. But first let us see what happens when one of these complex VPs is combined with the NP 'John' to form a sentence.

(5.7) 1. $\lambda x[\text{scholar}(x) \wedge \text{gentleman}(x)]$ (j)
       2. $\text{scholar}(j) \wedge \text{gentleman}(j)$
       3. = true iff John is a scholar and John is a gentleman

When the lambda expression for the complex VP is applied to John, j is substituted for x in both conjuncts inside the recipe box. The resulting formula (a conjunction) gives a recipe for finding the truth value.

5.1.3 CURRY FUNCTIONS

So much for one-place predicates, the denotations of VPs or intransitive verbs. What about the denotations of transitive verbs? In Chapter 3, these were treated as binary relations, sets of ordered pairs. It was also pointed out there that there is a mismatch between this treatment and the syntactic structures favoured by most modern syntacticians, following Chomsky, in which (to simplify a little) the object combines first with the verb to form a VP, and then the subject combines with the VP to form a sentence. Maybe that is the best we can do, and accept the mismatch between logic and language as a fact of life?

Montague was among those who took Chomsky's syntactic arguments seriously, and proposed a solution to this problem, based on a trick with functions that logicians had known for some time. To understand it, let's look first at a very simple mathematical example: addition. This is a function which takes a pair of numbers as its arguments, and returns their sum as its value. By convention, + is written as an 'infix' between its two arguments, but that is only a distraction. We could equally well write 2 + 3 as Plus(2,3), with the function as a prefix. Either way, we have a function with a pair of arguments.

What happens if we only feed it one argument, say the number 1? What we have then is the '+1' function, which can be applied to any number n to give the result $n + 1$ (i.e. it increments n by 1). Going back to the start, if we originally fed in the number 5, the result would be a function that takes a number and increments it by 5. To summarise, instead of feeding two numbers at once to the + function, we feed them one at a time.[3] The result of applying it to the first argument is *another function*, this time a one-place function, which looks for the second argument and increments it by the amount of the first. When both arguments have been consumed, the result is the same as if they had both been fed into the function together at the beginning.

How does this work in the lambda notation? We have two lambdas, one for each argument, and hence two 'layers' round the recipe box. This will be applied to two numbers, first 2, then 3. The first argument will substitute for x, the second argument for y.

(5.8) 1. $\lambda x[\lambda y[x + y]]$ – the 'plus' function, set up to consume its arguments one by one.
2. $\lambda x[\lambda y[x + y]]$ (2) – it is fed with the first argument, 2, which will be substituted for x.
3. $\lambda y[2 + y]$ – the result is the 'increment by 2' function, which will add 2 to any number.
4. $\lambda y[2 + y]$ (3) – this new function is then applied to the second argument, 3.
5. 2 + 3 – the result of substituting 3 for y. This of course then evaluates to 5.

Now let's look at a linguistic example (Figure 5.2), the transitive verb 'speak' (as in 'speak a language'). In syntax the object is inside the VP, and so we want it to combine with the verb first. The verb is first applied to the argument denoting a language, say Russian. The result of this is the property of speaking Russian, which is an appropriate VP meaning (it denotes the set of Russian speakers, or the characteristic function of that set). This then applies to the subject argument, say Anna, to give the value *true* iff Anna is in the set of Russian speakers.

Note carefully that in this approach the 'undergoer', as it is fed to the function first, appears before the 'actor' in the formula. This is unlike the syntax for binary relations used in Chapter 3, and can cause confusion.

(5.9) 1. $\lambda x[\lambda y[(speak(x)(y)]]$ (russian)
2. $\lambda y[(speak(russian)(y)]$
3. $\lambda y[(speak(russian)(y)]$ (anna)
4. (speak(russian)) (anna)

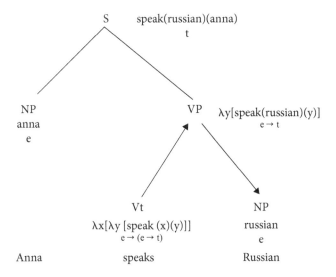

Figure 5.2   Function application in a transitive sentence

It is helpful to look at this in the context of a syntactic tree, and to do our type book-keeping for it. As before, the S node gets type t, the subject NP node gets type e, and the VP node gets type $e \rightarrow t$. Now look at the subtree consisting of the VP and its two daughters, the transitive verb and the object NP. The NP will get type e, because we are assuming at the moment that NPs have this type. Then it follows from the rules that we discussed earlier that the type for the transitive verb must be a function from the type of the argument daughter (e) to the type of the mother ($e \rightarrow t$). So the type for the transitive verb is $e \rightarrow (e \rightarrow t)$. What does this mean in plain English? It is the type of a higher order function from individuals to sets (or characteristic functions of sets). It takes as input the individual supplied by the object NP, and gives as output the set of individuals denoted by the VP.[4]

Let's practise this immediately.

EXERCISE 5.1.3.1

For each of the following sentences: (i) draw a tree, (ii) annotate the nodes with 'type bookkeeping' information, and (iii) write the lambda expression for the transitive verb. Then underneath: (iv) apply the transitive verb to its object argument, (v) reduce it, and copy the result to the VP node, (vi) apply the VP expression to the subject argument, and (vii) reduce it, and copy the result to the S node. Now look again at the expression for the VP, and state what it means.

1. Paul supports Newcastle.
2. Anili cooks curry.
3. Winograd wrote Eliza.

4. Aragorn slays orcs.
5. Margaret teaches maths.

This trick of converting a binary relation into a higher order function is known as currying, and the functions themselves (in this case, the denotations of transitive verbs) are known as **curry functions**, after Haskell Curry. As Curry himself always acknowledged, they were in fact developed by Moses Schönfinkel[5] (and had been known even longer). However, the terminology seems to be more or less fixed, and we will continue to use it here. Since there is a 1:1 correspondence between binary relations and curry functions, the process can also be reversed, which is known as 'uncurrying'.

An uncurried function takes its two arguments together as an ordered pair. This corresponds to a flat syntactic structure, in which the subject and object are sisters of the head. It is similar to the binary relations of Chapter 3, but the notation is, for example, love ($\langle j, m \rangle$) instead of Love(j, m). The uncurried verb is a function from ordered pairs to truth values – the characteristic function of a binary relation (set of ordered pairs).

This concludes our initial look at some basic uses of the lambda calculus in linguistics. In the next sections we will, as usual, formally define the syntax and semantics we are using.

5.2 SYNTAX OF THE LAMBDA CALCULUS

5.2.1 SYNTACTIC DEFINITIONS

The version of the lambda calculus we are using here is the simply typed lambda calculus. The types are those that we introduced for bookkeeping purposes earlier, to make sure that functions get the right type of argument. We will start with an inductive definition of the set of types, to make our bookkeeping language a bit more rigorous.[6]

(5.10) 1. The set of basic types is {e, t}.
        2. If σ and τ are types then so are ($\sigma \rightarrow \tau$) and ($\sigma \times \tau$).
        3. Nothing else is a type.

Types formed with $\rightarrow$ are the types assigned to functions, and are known as **functional types**. Types formed with $\times$ are known as **product types**, and are the type assigned to ordered pairs. The non-basic types are collectively known as 'derived types'. By convention, outermost brackets are usually omitted, as in our previous logical languages.

Other notations in the literature for functional types include $\langle \sigma, \tau \rangle$ (this was Montague's preferred notation), and (σ, τ). In the first of these, the angled brackets should *not* be omitted even when outermost. Do not confuse the ordered-pair notation here for product types.

Now for the definition of the well formed expressions (wfe) of the lambda calculus itself. Note that all expressions are typed, and that the definition of well formedness makes reference to that type – so expressions which are not of the correct type are not well formed (as the inductive closure reminds us).

(5.11) 1. For every type σ, the vocabulary of the lambda calculus includes a set of constants of type σ. There is also a potentially infinite supply of variables of type σ. By convention, constants will be written a, b and so on, while variables will be written x, y and so on.
   2. If α is a wfe of type $(\sigma \rightarrow \tau)$ and β is a wfe of type σ, then $(\sigma(\beta))$ is a wfe of type τ (function application).
   3. If α is a wfe of type τ and x is a variable of type σ, then $\lambda x.\ \alpha$ is a wfe of type $(\sigma \rightarrow \tau)$ (lambda abstraction).
   4. If α is a wfe of type $\sigma \times \tau$, then $\pi_1(\alpha)$ is a wfe of type σ and $\pi_2(\alpha)$ is a wfe of type τ (projection).
   5. If α is a wfe of type σ and β is a wfe of type τ, then $\langle \sigma, \beta \rangle$ is a wfe of type $\sigma \times \tau$ (pairing).
   6. Nothing else is a wfe.

Note, first, the replacement of wffs by wfes. Unlike the predicate calculus, predicates and arguments are now expressions in their own right (rather than just building blocks used to make formulas); but they are not formulas by themselves. Formulas are expressions of type t. This is indicated by using α and β rather than ϕ and ψ for wfes in general. ϕ and ψ will still be used, however, for expressions of type t.

In the rule for lambda abstraction, α is the **scope** of the lambda operator, which binds every *free* occurrence of x in α. This is exactly as we saw with quantifiers in the previous chapter, except that here α can be any expression, not necessarily a formula. Note that, as with quantifiers, there is no actual requirement for x to occur free in α. If it doesn't, this is known as **vacuous abstraction**. Note also that the square brackets used in the previous section to mark off the 'recipe boxes' (scopes of lambda operators) are not part of the language formally defined here. Instead, the scope is marked by a dot (even this is sometimes omitted). The square brackets were introduced for expository purposes, but will be dropped after this chapter.

To say that an expression α is of type σ, I will often write $\alpha{:}\sigma$. This is not part of the definitions, and is used informally for the time being. Its formal significance will become apparent in Chapter 10.

5.2.2 RULES FOR APPLICATION, ABSTRACTION AND REDUCTION

In the introduction to this chapter I assumed a naïve phrase structure grammar as a working syntactic theory, with the nodes of the tree decorated by types and expressions of the lambda calculus. Montague himself did not use phrase structure grammars but a form of categorial grammar. Although the latter will be discussed in the last part of the book, Montague's own treatment of it was not particularly interesting, and I prefer to use a syntactic lingua franca that most linguistics students will be familiar with.[7]

The rules for semantic interpretation can be generalised from the examples we looked at earlier as follows.

(5.12) 1. Annotate each subtree with type information, with a functional type on one of the daughter nodes, the correct input type(s) on the other daughter node(s), and the correct output type on the mother node.
2. Annotate the preterminal nodes with an expression of the lambda calculus of the appropriate type, as the logical translation of the word dominated by the preterminal.
3. Annotate the mother of each subtree with an expression formed from the annotations of the daughters, according to the Rule of Function Application (rule 2 of the inductive definition).
4. Perform function application on this expression as explained informally in section 5.1 and more formally below.
5. The root node should end up annotated with an expression of type t, representing a proposition.

In this process of semantic annotation we are likely to encounter expressions which need to be further processed, or **reduced**. Examples of this were given in the introductory section of what happens when a lambda expression representing a function is applied to an argument. This is one type of reduction (known as β reduction). The reduction rules of the lambda calculus are traditionally named using Greek letters. There are actually eight of them, but the three that play a role in this book are as follows.

α (**alpha**): This allows us to rename any variables bound by a particular lambda expression, to avoid conflicts in variable naming. The catch is that we cannot give them a name which might lead to them being 'captured' by another lambda operator that is already using that variable name. If you make sure the new variable is genuinely 'new' (not already in use), then this danger can be avoided. If you want to use a variable that is already in circulation, you have to check that it is 'free for (substitution for) x in α' – that using it instead of x in the scope α will not lead to it being bound by another lambda operator λy already present in α.

Definition: $\lambda x.\alpha \mapsto_{\alpha} \lambda y.\alpha$ [x/y] – where α [x/y] means that all free occurrences of x in α are replaced by y. Condition: y is free for x in α.

β (**beta**): This is what happens in function application, as already described.

Definition: $\lambda x.\alpha(\beta) \mapsto_{\beta} \alpha[x/\beta]$ – that is, the λx disappears, leaving α with all occurrences of x in α replaced by β.

η (**eta**): You will have noticed that the semantic annotation for an intransitive VP 'snores', for example, is sometimes written as the constant $snore$ of type $e \rightarrow t$, and sometimes as the longer expression $\lambda x.snore(x)$, of the same type. In fact these are equivalent. To reduce the longer form to the shorter one is to perform **eta reduction**:

Definition: $\lambda x.\alpha(x) \mapsto_{\eta} \alpha$

An expression that cannot be reduced any further by β or η reduction is said to be in $\beta\eta$ **normal form**. (Alpha reduction, despite its name, is not a form of reduction in this sense, as the output is not shorter than the input.) The simply typed lambda calculus has the following important properties:[8]

The Church-Rosser property: All expressions will reduce to the same $\beta\eta$ normal form regardless of the order in which the steps of reduction are carried out.

Strong normalisation: All expressions can be reduced to $\beta\eta$ normal form in a finite number of steps.

Abstraction can be seen as the opposite of reduction, specifically β reduction. Suppose we have an expression (in fact a formula) ¬smoke(mary). We can abstract over that to get the property of being a non-smoker. If we then applied that function to *mary*, we would get the original formula back.

(5.13) 1. ¬smoke(mary)
  2. λx[¬smoke(x)]

In this case we are working down the syntactic tree, rather than upwards as we were with function application. Given a sentence, we can obtain the VP by this technique of abstraction. Given a VP, for example λx[speak(german)(x)] – the property of being a German speaker – we can abstract again to get an expression for the transitive verb *speak* (as in 'speak a language'). Again, if we apply this to *german*, we will get the original expression back. For this reason β reduction is also known as λ conversion, the opposite of λ abstraction.

This can be useful in figuring out the logical translations we need for lexical entries.

(5.14) 1. λx[speak(german)(x)]
  2. λy[λx[speak(y)(x)]]

The last example has been written as speak(y)(x) rather than (speak(y))(x). This is because of a convention that function application is 'left associative', so that the extra brackets can be left out. Lambda abstraction, by contrast, is assumed to be right associative, so that I could have left out the outermost square brackets here. These bracketing conventions, which reflect the most common patterns of use, make it possible to write expressions more simply. They will be used frequently later in the book.

Also note once again that the syntactic subject is referenced in these expressions by the last (innermost) lambda operator, and the last argument of the function – because it is the last to be fed to the function.

The other two syntactic rules concern ordered pairs. We have already met projection in Chapter 3. The pairing function is the opposite; it licences the formation of ordered pairs from their component parts, whereas projections break them up. Product types are not the main focus of attention in this chapter; in fact, many treatments omit them completely, assuming that binary relations are always curried.

5.3 SEMANTICS OF THE LAMBDA CALCULUS

The main principle behind models of the lambda calculus is that, just as we have many types of expression, we need many types of object for them to refer to. We define these many types of objects by means of a **frame**, which can be thought of as a map of what kinds of objects there can be in our **ontology** (as discussed at the end of the previous chapter). The set of possible denotations for an expression of a particular type is known as the **domain of denotation** for that type.

For the basic types e and t the domains of denotation are the set of individuals D and (for classical logic) the set $\{0, 1\}$ of truth values, which it is convenient to write as 2. The denotations of functional types will be function spaces (sets of functions from some domain of denotation to another), and the denotations of product types are product spaces. The latter include spaces such as the space $D \times D$ in which the binary relations of Chapter 3 were defined; as such they should cause little difficulty, and the focus here will be on functions. The set of functions from set A to set B is written B^A.

Some basic examples:

1. The domain of denotation for VPs (type $e \rightarrow t$) is the set of functions from D to 2 (i.e. characteristic functions of sets). This is written 2^D.
2. The domain of denotation for ordered pairs of individuals (type $e \times e$) is $D \times D$, as is familiar from Chapter 3.

    The domain of discourse for a type σ is written $\mathbf{D}_\sigma$. Don't confuse this with D, the domain of individuals.

(5.15) 1. The domain of denotation of the basic types, e and t are D and 2 respectively.
  2. If σ and τ are types, then $\mathbf{D}_{\sigma \rightarrow \tau} = \mathbf{D}_\tau{}^{\mathbf{D}_\sigma}$
  3. If σ and τ are types, then $\mathbf{D}_{\sigma \times \tau} = \mathbf{D}_\sigma \times \mathbf{D}_\tau$

As compared to first order logic, the ontology of this system includes not only individuals but functions of different types. Note specifically that sets of individuals are included in the ontology, because there is a domain 2^D for functions of type $e \rightarrow t$, which are the characteristic functions of sets of individuals. Relations are also included in the ontology; there is a domain for curry functions, which correspond to the characteristic functions of binary relations.

This concludes the definitions for the frame, which is the scaffolding for our model of the lambda calculus. The model itself will assign denotations to the expressions in our logical language, in such a way that the system of types and domains of denotation is respected. The model is a generalisation of our first order model $\langle D, I \rangle$. The interpretation function takes expressions of each type to objects in the appropriate domain of denotation for that type. We also need a variable assignment g which will assign variables of each type to the appropriate domain of denotation. Since we now have variables of all types, we can easily perform higher order quantification, though that is not covered in this book. Recall that the variable assignment is not part of the model; as before, however, it is convenient to treat constants and variables together using the generalised denotation function $||\cdots||$.

With these preliminaries out of the way, the definition for basic expressions is very straightforward:

(5.16) 1. If a is a constant of type σ, then $||a||_{M,g} = I(a) \in \mathbf{D}_\sigma$
      2. If a is a variable of type σ, then $||x||_{M,g} = g(x) \in \mathbf{D}_\sigma$

The rules of semantic interpretation for composite expressions also follow from the previous discussion. They will be the result of function application, lambda abstraction (creating new functions), pairing or projection. The first rule, for example, states that the denotation of $\alpha(\beta)$ will be the result of applying the denotation of α (a function) to the denotation of β, and that the result will be in the appropriate domain of denotation for the output of the function.

(5.17) 1. If α is a wfe of type $\sigma \to \tau$, and β is a wfe of type σ then
$$|| \alpha(\beta) ||_{M,g} = ||\alpha||_{M,g}(||\beta||_{M,g}) \in \mathbf{D}_\tau$$
      2. If α is a wfe of type τ, and x is a variable of type σ then
$$||\lambda x[\alpha]||_{M,g} = f \in \mathbf{D}_\tau{}^{\mathbf{D}_\sigma} \text{ such that, for every } d \in \mathbf{D}_\sigma, f(d) = ||\alpha||_{M,g[x \mapsto d]}$$
      3. If $\langle \alpha, \beta \rangle$ is a wfe of type $\sigma \times \tau$, then
$$||\pi_1(\langle \alpha, \beta \rangle)||_{M,g} = ||\alpha||_{M,g} \in \mathbf{D}_\sigma, \text{ and } ||\pi_2(\langle \alpha, \beta \rangle)||_{M,g} = ||\beta||_{M,g} \in \mathbf{D}_\tau$$
      4. If α is a wfe of type σ, and β is a wfe of type τ then
$$||\alpha, \beta||_{M,g} = \langle ||\alpha||_{M,g}, ||\beta||_{M,g} \rangle \in \mathbf{D}_{\sigma \times \tau}$$

The only slightly tricky rule here is the second. It defines the denotation of a lambda abstract as a function which can take any element d of its domain as argument and returns as its value the denotation of its scope α with all free occurrences of x in α assigned to d. This assignment of the lambda variable to the denotation of the argument is the semantic equivalent of what happens in β reduction, where the free occurrences of x in the scope are replaced by the argument.

Since there may be other free variables in α, we retain the assignment g with only reassignments of x being considered. The reasoning here is exactly parallel to the semantic rules for quantifiers in the previous chapter.

5.4 CONNECTIVES AND HIGHER ORDER LOGIC

The reader will have noticed that nothing has been said in these sections about connectives or quantifiers. They were neither defined as part of the logical language, nor given a special semantic interpretation. This is because as far as the lambda calculus is concerned, there is nothing special to say about them. They are simply constants. If we want them to be interpreted as *logical* constants, we have to provide these definitions *on top of* the lambda calculus (they are not part of it). This is very easy for connectives. So far in this chapter I have been using the familiar connective symbols – informally, as the definitions have not been updated to include them – intending them to have the meanings familiar from previous chapters. This kind of abbreviation or **notational convention** is quite common in books of this kind, both for connectives and quantifiers. However, this particular convention can be misleading for students. This section will deal with the higher order translation of connectives.[9] The formal integration of logical constants into the lambda calculus will give us a translation language based on higher order logic, which was our objective.[10]

1. Assume that we have a constant *not*, in the vocabulary of the language defined in this chapter, and we wish to stipulate that it has the interpretation of the connective ¬. Define this constant formally, giving its type and domain of denotation as a unary truth function, and define the function which it denotes.
2. Do the same with the constant *and*, which we want to have the interpretation of the logical connective ∧. Remember that as a binary connective, it will take as its input an ordered pair of truth values.

In this little exercise, you were asked to spell out the truth functions denoted by two of the main connectives from Chapter 2, one unary and one binary. The binary connective was treated as a function taking both its arguments at once as an ordered pair; this implies a flat syntactic structure, with the two conjuncts as sisters of the conjunction. This is a plausible syntactic structure for conjunction in English, and is adopted by some, though not all, syntactic theories. In some other languages, however, such as Japanese (5.18) and Turkish, the first conjunct is made into a subordinate clause, giving a binary branching structure. In English, a binary branching structure is needed for implications, assuming that these correspond to conditional sentences in English (5.19). So it would be useful if we could find a semantic treatment that is closer to binary branching syntactic structures.

(5.18) *Ki-ta-kute sake-wo non-da* (**Japanese**)
        come-Past-Conj wine-Acc drink-Past
        He came and drank the wine.
(5.19) If Mary is unhappy, she drinks wine.

This is parallel to the problem we faced with transitive verbs, and the same solution is available here as well: currying. Let us take the conjunction example first, as the semantics of conjunction are probably more intuitive than material implication. Instead of taking the two arguments together as an ordered pair as above, we curry the function into one of type $t \rightarrow (t \rightarrow t)$. The first conjunct combines to give a unary truth function of type $t \rightarrow t$ at the S-bar node. This S-bar function will then look at the second argument to give the truth value of the whole sentence, as follows:

1. If the first conjunct was false, then we know immediately that the whole conjunction is false. In this case the S-bar function is the constant false function, which returns false without even looking at the second argument.
2. If the first conjunct was true, then the truth value of the whole sentence depends entirely on the second conjunct. The S-bar function will therefore be the identity

function, reading the truth value of the second conjunct and returning the same truth value for the whole sentence.

The second example (5.19) proceeds in the same way, except that the connective is implication. The first argument (the subordinate clause, or antecedent of the conditional) is combined first to give a new function at the S-bar node. This function then combines with the second conjunct to give a truth value for the whole composite sentence.

1. Which unary truth function sits at the S-bar node if the antecedent is true, and which function sits there if the antecedent is false?

Although the connectives defined in this section have the same meaning as in Chapter 2, there is a significant difference in the way they have been defined. The semantic rules in Chapter 2 did not define the interpretation of connectives in themselves, but rather gave the truth conditions for sentences in which the connectives occurred. The higher order functions in this section, by contrast, are the actual interpretation of the connectives (they are constants of a higher order type, namely that of curried binary truth functions). The indirect approach used in Chapter 2 is said to be **syncategorematic**, while that we have just seen is **categorematic**. While both approaches are perfectly viable, it is consistent with the approach of Montague semantics to try to interpret each type of expression directly, as we have just done.

5.5 MORE TYPES

5.5.1 OPERATIONS ON PREDICATES

In the same vein, we saw earlier in this chapter how the lambda operator can be used to define Boolean operations on predicates, despite the fact that connectives, strictly speaking, can only operate on propositions. We will now integrate this more closely into the syntax, starting with predicate negation. It was observed in Chapter 2 that there is a mismatch between the negation operator of propositional logic and the syntax of negation in English and other natural languages. The former is usually read as 'it is not the case that', which is intelligible but is not the usual way of expressing negation in English. The most usual syntax for negating a sentence in English is to attach the negation to an auxiliary verb, which formally negates the VP.

(5.20) It is not the case that [Mary speaks Italian].
(5.21) Mary doesn't [speak Italian].

In discussing the syntax of this last sentence, I will assume that there are two VPs, the lower one headed by the main verb, 'speak', and a higher one headed by the auxiliary 'doesn't'. Some readers may prefer to think of the auxiliary as having a distinct category I, and the higher VP as an I-bar. Either is fine for present purposes.

Annotating the tree with type information, we see that both VP nodes are of type e → t. The auxiliary must therefore be of type (e → t) → (e → t), a function from sets to sets. In the case of the negative auxiliary 'doesn't' (which I will treat as one word, though this is not essential), the semantics of the auxiliary will convert the set denoted by the lower VP (the set of entities that speak Italian) into its complement, which will be the interpretation of the upper VP. The latter is then applied to Mary in the normal way.

(5.22)   1. **doesn't** = $\lambda x[\lambda y[\neg x(y)]]$
         2. $\lambda x[\lambda y[\neg x(y)]]$ (speak(italian)) (mary)
         $\mapsto_\beta \lambda y.[\neg(\text{speak(italian)})(y)]$ (mary)

Note again the distinction between this VP negation and the negation connective defined in Chapter 2. In this case it is made clearer by the attachment of the negation to an auxiliary, though actually even if English did not use auxiliary support (like German or many other languages) the semantics would be virtually the same. It is therefore potentially misleading to write it using the symbol for propositional negation, $\neg$. The latter symbol is used within the scope (recipe box) for the negative auxiliary, but there it is used in its proper sense as it negates something of type t.

The same approach can be applied to conjunction and disjunction of predicates.

(5.23)   1. Peter [[drinks wine] and [eats garlic]]
         2. **and** = $\lambda\langle x, y\rangle [\lambda z[x(z) \wedge y(z)]]$
         3. $\lambda\langle x, y\rangle [\lambda z[x(z) \wedge y(z)]]$ ($\langle\langle$(drink(wine)), (eat(garlic))$\rangle\rangle$) (peter)
         $\mapsto_\beta \lambda z[\text{drink(wine)}(z) \wedge \text{eat(garlic)}(z)]$ (peter)

As in the example with negation, the expression we have defined is an operation on sets (or characteristic functions of sets), and not a connective. However, connectives are used in the definition, applying correctly to expressions of type t. This is a common and convenient approach, which shows the use of the lambda operator as a set-forming operator, and it is the approach that will generally be used here. However, there is a more direct approach, which is to define the semantics of these expressions directly as operations on sets, using the fact that the algebra of sets (the powerset algebra) is Boolean, just like the algebra of truth values in classical logic. We can thus say that the predicate operators discussed in this section are 'versions' of the connectives which apply to predicates rather than propositions (i.e. they are of different types) but implement the same Boolean operations (complementation, glb and lub).

5.5.2 RELATIONAL PREDICATES

The main example of relational predicates is transitive verbs, which have already been discussed. However, relational predicates can be found in many syntactic categories. Check whether you agree that the following denote binary relations, although in some cases (especially most nouns and adjectives) the second argument is syntactically optional.

(5.24)   **Verbs**: kill, eat, love, go (to), rely (on)
         Prepositions: in, above, of
         Adjectives: interested (in), jealous (of), fond of
         Comparisons: bigger than, different (from)
         Nouns: friend (of), husband (of), capital (of)
         Deverbal nouns: destruction (of), student (of), invasion (of)

These can occur in a variety of syntactic roles, but the exercise at the end of this section assumes that they are the main predicate of a sentence. If they are not verbs, they will need a copula (previous section). However, you can treat the prepositions that go with some of them as part of the predicate (e.g. bigger-than).

5.5.3 DEFINITE DESCRIPTIONS

Up till now the arguments of predicates have been either names or variables of type *e*. The variables have generally been part of quantified expressions, which in first order logic, as already discussed, do not contain anything corresponding to an NP constituent. Quantified NPs in higher order logic are the subject of Generalized Quantifier Theory. See Keenan (1996) for an introduction. It is also possible for a free variable to be an argument of a predicate, in which case it is best thought of as the logical translation of a personal pronoun.

There is another kind of individual-denoting expression which can be introduced here – the **definite description**, or NP consisting of 'the' and an N-bar constituent (in the simplest instance, a common noun). It was not possible to define these compositionally in first order logic.[11] Thinking type-theoretically, the determiner has to be a function from sets (the N-bar set) to individuals (the denotation of the NP); so it is of type $(e \rightarrow t) \rightarrow e$. This function will be written with the Greek letter ι (iota), and is known as the iota operator. This notation comes from Russell's (1905) treatment of definite descriptions in first order logic, which will be discussed in Chapter 8.[12]

What we need is a function that will pick out an individual from the N-bar set to be the denotation of the NP. In the case of 'the', the individual concerned is the only member of the N-bar set. (This is simplified and does not include plural definite descriptions.) In other words, the N-bar set must be a singleton set, and the ι function converts a singleton set to its only member.

(5.25)   1. If α is an expression of type $(e \rightarrow t)$ and $||\alpha||_{\mathcal{M},g} = \{d\}$, then $||\iota(\alpha)||_{\mathcal{M},g} = d$

What if the N-bar set is not singleton? It could have more than one member, or could be empty. This means that ι as defined is not a function from 2^D to D, as it is only well defined for those sets in 2^D which happen to be singleton. A function which is only defined for part of its domain is known as a **partial function**. But introducing partial functions into our logic would make it more complicated. Since our concern in this section is just to build up the type theory for different kinds of expressions, we will not pursue it here, but will assume in the examples that ι is applied only to singleton sets. The question of how to deal with other cases is a very important one, which involves the limitations of classical logic, and as such will be discussed in Part III.

5.5.4 ADJUNCTS

The essential syntactic characteristic of adjuncts is that they combine with something of a particular category (as their sister) to give something of the same category as their mother. Type-theoretically, this means that they are functions from a type to itself. An adjective is a function from N-bars to N-bars, while a VP adverbial is a function from VPs to VPs (or V-bar to V-bar in some frameworks). Since both N-bars and VPs are assigned the type $e \to t$, this means that both these adjuncts will be of type $(e \to t) \to (e \to t)$. Sentential adverbs, by contrast, are of type $t \to t$.

Semantically, this means that adjuncts are functions from a domain of denotation into itself. Such functions are known as **automorphisms**.

In Chapter 4 we discussed the treatment of some adjectives as conjunctions (set intersections) of the adjective with the N-bar it modifies, and it was mentioned that this treatment does not work for all adjectives. There are essentially three types, which may be exemplified by 'red', 'big' and 'former'. They can be distinguished by their entailment patterns.

Intersective: If something is a red car, then it is both a red entity and a car. The entity is in the intersection of the two sets, which entails membership of both.

Subsective: If something is a large mouse, then it is a mouse, but we cannot say straightforwardly that it is a large entity. Similarly with a small elephant. The effect of adjectival modification is to restrict the entity to a subset of the N-bar denotation (for which reason these adjectives are sometimes called 'restrictive').

Intensional: If an individual is a former girlfriend, then they are neither a girlfriend, nor a former individual. The individual may still exist, but just no longer stand in the same relationship. The set of former girlfriends is therefore neither a subset of the set of former entities nor of the set of girlfriends.

The thing to note here is that although these modes of assigning denotation are considerably different, they all involve the adjective acting in some way on the N-bar. In the first two cases, they take a subset of the N-bar set (in the first case by forming an intersection, which is a subset of both sets; in the second case, by some other method). In the third case, the adjective could be said to introduce an additional parameter; we are not dealing with the set of girlfriends as such, but with a related set, the set of girlfriends at some other time. So in all cases, the effect of the adjective is that of a function from the denotation of the unmodified N-bar set to a different but related set of the same type. This is the justification for treating adjectival modifiers as functions of type $(e \to t) \to (e \to t)$.

5.6 COMBINATORS

When dealing with predicate negation, we treated the negation element as an auxiliary verb of type $(e \rightarrow t) \rightarrow (e \rightarrow t)$. In this case, the function of the auxiliary was simply to add support for the negation ('*do* support' in Chomskian terminology). Other auxiliaries may add different semantic information, usually of a logical kind (such as tense or modality, to be discussed in Chapter 6).

Similar remarks apply to the copula, which is a syntactic requirement in English sentences when the predicate is non-verbal, but is dispensed with in a number of languages in some or all of these cases. Recall, for example, the translation of 'Greece is beautiful' in Chapter 3 as Beautiful(greece), without a copula in sight. (It is true that the copula in English contributes tense information, which we are ignoring for the time being.)

It is useful to look at what these elements are doing in the sentence *apart from* the extra information that they may be contributing. Primarily, it is taking a predicate of type $e \rightarrow t$, and telling it to combine with something of type e to get a truth value. Of course this is exactly what the predicate, as something of type $e \rightarrow t$ would do anyway, even if the auxiliary (or copula) was not sitting there telling it what to do. We can either write a function as f(x) or alternatively as Apply(f, x), where f is one argument of a higher order function which applies it to its other argument(s).[13] From now on I will call this higher order function the **Apply** combinator, which I will normally write as I^*.[14] Its definition is extremely simple: it says 'take an x, take a y and apply x to y'. The definition of 'doesn't' is repeated here for comparison.

(5.26) $I^* = \lambda x[\lambda y[x(y)]]$
(5.27) **doesn't** $= \lambda x[\lambda y[\neg x(y)]]$

An expression like Apply does not contribute any specific information of its own because it has no constants. Its function is purely to manipulate other expressions, which it references with lambda-bound variables. There are no other variables. Expressions like this have a special place in the lambda calculus.[15]

(5.28) 1. An expression with no constants is called a **pure lambda term**.
      2. An expression with no free variables is called a **closed lambda term**.
      3. An expression which is both pure and closed is called a **combinatorial lambda term**.

By a slight abuse of terminology, combinatorial lambda terms are often simply called **combinators**, which is strictly speaking a term not from the lambda calculus but from combinatorial logic. The precise relation between the two will be discussed later in the book.

Here are some more useful combinators which can be used for manipulating lambda expressions. Many of them correspond to operations that we have already expressed as rules (just as Apply corresponds to function application). The first two enable us to switch between sets of ordered pairs and curry functions.

(5.29) **curry**: $\lambda x[\lambda y[\lambda z[x(\langle y, z \rangle)]]]$
(5.30) **uncurry**: $\lambda x[\lambda \langle y, z \rangle [x(y)(z)]]$

Others enable us to compose functions, to reverse the order of arguments, to duplicate an argument, or conversely to discard an argument. They will play an important role from Chapter 11 onwards.

EXERCISE 5.6.0.1

1. What would you expect to be the result of applying **curry** and then **uncurry** (or the other way round)? Evaluate the expression

   curry(**uncurry**(love(mary)(john))), and check that the result is as anticipated.

2. Draw trees for the following sentences, annotate them with type information, and devise semantic translations (lambda expressions) for the lexical items.
   (a) The Kremlin is in Moscow.
   (b) Mary is jealous of John's former girlfriend.
   (c) The big cat terrorised the small dog.
       Now derive the lambda expressions to annotate the non-terminal nodes.

Richard Montague

An American philosopher and logician, regarded as one of the outstanding students of Tarski. In the 1960s he became interested in the work of Chomsky, and was one of the major figures responsible for introducing logical techniques to linguistics, especially higher order and modal logics. His influence on linguistics derives from three papers, which were published posthumously after his murder at the age of forty.

NOTES

1. It was mentioned in the introduction that semanticists are divided over whether a translation language is really necessary as an intermediary between formally analysed (i.e. parsed and disambiguated) natural language and model-theoretic interpretation. Montague was fairly and squarely with those who believe that it is *not* necessary, and he only uses the lambda calculus in some of his work. However, it is has proved very convenient and influential. Moreover, there are others who argue that some intermediate language is useful or even necessary to capture the dynamics of meaning.
2. Second order predicates are sometimes written with curly letters, $\mathcal{A}$, $\mathcal{B}$ and so on, to distinguish them from first order predicates. But the effort of finding new typefaces every time we go up one order gets tiresome after a while, and in the lambda calculus there are usually no capitals or similar embellishments.
3. In functional programming, applying a binary function to just one argument is called 'partial application'.
4. Note that in Figure 5.2 we could simply specify the verb content as the constant *speak* of

type $e \rightarrow (e \rightarrow t)$ on the analogy of Figure 5.1. As an exercise, you might like to redraw Figure 5.2 in this way.

5. Chapter 13.

6. Other flavours of the lambda calculus are either 'untyped' or involve more complicated constructs such as parametric or polymorphic types. These will play a minimal role in this book.

7. Montague himself said, 'I have never seen any interest in syntax except as a preliminary to semantics.' In this and the next few chapters I will adopt, or pretend to adopt, a similar attitude.

8. The first is true of the lambda calculus in general, the second only for the simply typed version.

9. For quantifiers see Carpenter (1998).

10. Although the lambda calculus includes a formal language and a semantics, it is not, strictly speaking, a logic, as it does not have a consequence relation (see the discussion at the end of Chapter 1). The rewriting (reduction) rules given earlier in this chapter may look superficially like proof systems, but they are not calculating consequences, only equivalences. For this reason, although higher order logic uses the lambda calculus, the two should not be identified.

11. Some basically first order systems, including Frege's, included 'function symbols' for the same purpose. However, functions are not strictly first order, as their definition includes equality, which as we have seen is not a first order notion.

12. Not content with using Greek letters, it is usually written upside down. We will keep it the right way up, since it is easier and the operator we are defining here is not quite the same as Russell's anyway.

13. The name comes from functional programming.

14. Think of I as standing for 'identity'. It is, in fact, one of the family of identity functions (Chapter 13).

15. For the following definitions, note that in the lambda calculus, expressions or wfes are often called 'terms'.

PART II

MODALITY

CHAPTER 6

POSSIBILITY AND NECESSITY

If a coin comes down heads, that means that the possibility of its coming down tails has collapsed. Until that moment the two possibilities were equal. But on another world, it does come down tails. And when that happens, the two worlds split apart.[1]

6.1 MODAL LOGICS

6.1.1 GENERAL IDEAS

The system of truth table logic is concerned with facts – with what happens to be the case. What happens if we want to talk about possibilities? Natural language is full of talk about possibility, and close relatives such as impossibility and necessity. These are modal notions, often conveyed in English by modal verbs such as 'can' and 'must'. They are also the usual intended interpretation of modal logic (though the idea of modality will be given a broader definition).

Moreover statements of this kind support patterns of reasoning, just as the statements we were dealing with before. Aristotle's logic included 'modal syllogisms', in which one or more premises and the conclusion were modal statements, and this idea was developed, and to some extent systematised, by some of his successors. Here are some inferences that we would probably accept as valid and which include modal notions. Check that you agree they are valid (some of them admit of some discussion).

(6.1) 1. It is necessary that I will lose my job, and it is necessary that my wife will leave me; therefore it is necessary that I will be both jobless and wifeless.
2. It is not possible for Mary to be both in London and in New York. Therefore if she is in London, it is impossible for her to be in New York.
3. There is snow on the equator. Therefore it is possible for there to be snow on the equator.
4. It is not possible for you to be telling the truth; therefore necessarily you are not telling the truth.
5. If it is snowing, then it is cold. Possibly it is snowing; therefore it is possible that it is cold.
6. It is not possible that Colonel Mustard was in the dining room and in the

cellar; therefore necessarily either Colonel Mustard was not in the dining room or he was not in the cellar.

Aristotle's syllogistic was a quantificational logic, so that the idea of a *propositional* modal logic was not developed by him or his successors. Treating modality and quantification together led to complications, which will be left to the next chapter. This chapter will be concerned with *propositional* modal logic – that is with statements of the form 'necessarily ϕ' and 'possibly ϕ'. To get a modal propositional logic, it is important that any internal structure of ϕ is fully contained within ϕ, so that we can forget about it. This leads to a preference for syntactic structures like 'possibly ϕ' or 'it is possible that ϕ' which are not the most natural in English, where modality is more commonly expressed by auxiliaries. We saw the same thing earlier with negation and 'it is not the case that ϕ'. In fact we can easily obtain a more natural syntax for sentences with modal auxiliaries in the same way that we did for sentences with negated auxiliaries (p. 81f), and we will not be particularly worried about this here.

As normal, this introductory section will contain an informal discussion of some key concepts, motivating examples and background. Sections 6.2 and 6.3 will give a more formal presentation of the syntax and semantics of modal logic. Section 6.4 is a more detailed discussion of the different modal systems we can obtain with our tools, and some of their applications. The last two subsections of this can be omitted, if time is short, without repercussions later in the book. Section 6.5 introduces the standard translation relating modal logic to classical logic and relation algebra.

To express the inferences discussed above, we need to extend our logic with new logical constants, representing necessity and possibility. As we will see shortly, there are many kinds of necessity and possibility, but let's stick for the moment to the ideas of logical or physical necessity. The most popular symbols for necessary and possibility are $\Box$ and $\Diamond$ repectively. $\Box\phi$ can be read as 'it is necessary that ϕ', or 'necessarily ϕ', and $\Diamond\phi$ as 'it is possible that ϕ' or 'possibly ϕ'.

The last inference in (6.1) can now be expressed as follows:

(6.2) $\neg\Diamond(p \wedge q) \vDash \Box(\neg p \vee \neg q)$

> Key:
> p = 'Col. Mustard was in the dining room'
> q = 'Col. Mustard was in the cellar'

As when we were dealing with propositional connectives, we divide the language into logical constants and 'other stuff', which can be anything as long as it is kept constant. The 'other stuff' has been expressed here, for simplicity, as propositional letters, though it could also consist of first order formulae or lambda expressions of type t (subject to certain provisos).

If you are convinced that the entailments in (6.1) do indeed follow, then we also need to set up a semantics in which inferences with this pattern are valid. A possible semantics will be discussed informally in this introduction, and more formally later in the chapter. First, however, a short historical excursus on the ups and downs of modal logic may be helpful.

6.1.2 THREE ROOTS OF MODAL LOGIC

There are at least three strands of thought underlying the emergence of modern modal logic in the early twentieth century.

The first is the importance of modal reasoning itself, as introduced at the beginning of the chapter. This had been explored by Aristotle, and sporadically by his successors, but fell into neglect, even disrepute, with the emergence of modern classical logic. Mention has already been made of the complications arising from the interweaving of a modal and a quantificational component. As a result, the success of the modal syllogistic is controversial. (Łukasiewicz, for example, described it as 'a failure'.) There is even some uncertainty about how it actually worked. Some interesting treatments, however, are introduced in the next chapter, along with modern explorations in quantified modal logic.

Frege, in particular, dismissed modal logic, and its reintroduction was to provoke strong opposition from advocates of first order logic such as Quine as well as Russell.[2]

The second strand arose from dissatisfaction with the truth table definition of the implication connective. In Chapter 2 we introduced $p \rightarrow q$ as meaning that 'it is not possible for p to be true and q to be false'. In fact I was not being entirely honest there, because in the definition of material implication there is nothing about 'possible': it merely means that it is not the case that p is true and q false. This definition really gives the bare minimum that we can expect from an implication connective (it does not lead from true antecedents to false consequents). It has a number of counterintuitive consequences, sometimes referred to the 'paradoxes of material implication'. For example, any statement p which happens to be false implies anything, while a statement q that happens to be true is implied by anything. Moreover for any two statements p and q, one must materially imply the other, even if there is no connection between them.

It is natural to expect more than this, to feel that implication should reflect a *necessary* connection between p and q. It would be good to be able to express this stronger sense of implication in our logic.

This criticism of material implication was elaborated in the early twentieth century by C. I. Lewis,[3] who introduced a new connective called **strict implication** as an alternative to material implication. This connective, given the notation a (the 'fish-hook'), was intended to capture a more adequate notion of implication as inference or entailment; $p \prec q$ does not simply mean that p∧¬q does not happen to be the case, but that it *couldn't* be the case. In the modal notation introduced above, this can be represented as ¬◊(p∧¬q). Because □ and ◊ are duals (see below), this is equivalent to □¬(p∧¬q); this in turn, by De Morgan's laws, gives us □(¬p∨¬¬q), or □(¬p∨ q) by double negation, and hence by the definition of material implication, □(p → q). In other words, it is simply material implication with the necessity operator stuck in front of it.

Some books call the strict implication connective **entailment**, for which the symbol ⇒ can be used. However, it is not clear that Lewis' connective fully captures the idea of entailment, although it comes closer than material implication (see Chapter 11 for discussion). It will therefore be referred to throughout this book as strict implication, not entailment.

It is not immediately obvious what principles should govern the behaviour of strict implication, and Lewis devised a family of five alternative systems for it, which he labelled S1–S5. Other writers contributed further alternatives. This plurality was at first a problem, as there was no clear semantics to help logicians decide between them.[4] Since strict implication can be defined in modal terms, as we have just seen, it became apparent that a semantics for strict implication was essentially the same as that needed for possibility and necessity. The provision of such a semantics enabled the different systems to be compared more coherently.

The third strand was the distinction between sense and denotation which was so important to Frege. For him, it was one of the fundamental features of natural language which distinguished it from mathematics; and consequently, one major reason why the logic that he helped to develop was not, in his opinion, appropriate for the study of natural language. Recall that the main problem here was that the denotation of an expression can vary according to times or more generally to the state of affairs in the world; nonetheless our grasp of its sense still enables us to pick out its denotation if we have the right facts. A semantic solution to this problem was suggested by Carnap, which happens to also offer a semantics for modality and strict implication – the idea of possible worlds. We will discuss this here with reference to modality; the problem of sense and denotation, or in the terminology of Carnap's theory **intension** and **extension**, will be treated more naturally in the next chapter.

6.1.3 POSSIBLE WORLDS

Let us go back to the loose quotation from the early Wittgenstein used in Chapter 1: that to understand the meaning of a sentence is to know what the world must be like for it to be true.[5] If we can decide which statements are true and which are false, for all statements, then we have a description of the world. We can think of this as a row in the truth table (i.e. a valuation); let's call it V_0, or Row 0. That is, for present purposes, 'the world'. What about the other rows in the truth table? They represent possible states of affairs which don't happen to hold in this world. If Row 0 is a description of the world, then it is natural to think of the other rows as descriptions of other **possible worlds**; they look like Row 0 in all respects except that they do not happen to describe the actual world in which we are sitting and evaluating propositions.

Carnap's suggestion[6] was that a statement is necessarily true if it is true in *all* possible worlds, and it is possibly true if it is true in *some* possible world. In other words, necessity and possibility are *quantifiers over possible worlds*. Recall that a statement that is logically true will be true in all rows of the truth table (necessity). while a statement which is logically false will be true in no rows (impossibility). A statement which is neither necessary nor impossible is called **contingent**.

A special case of possible worlds is states of affairs which hold in the real world but at some past or future time. This is a case that is quite easy to understand intuitively,

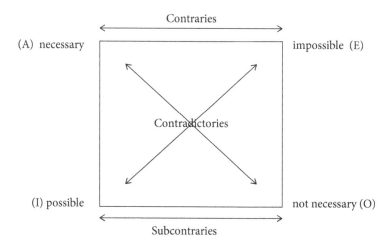

Figure 6.1   The modal Square of Opposition

without the science fiction quality of some other treatments of possible worlds. (This is particularly true of states of affairs in the past, which were at one time actual just as the present is actual; talking about future states of the world brings its own questions.) For this reason times will be used quite a lot in this chapter as examples of possible worlds. Even here, however, we very often wish to contrast what happened with what might have happened, or what people did with what they should have done. So talk about other possible states of affairs, which have never held and maybe never will in the real world, will not go away. We will discuss later how we are going to view them ontologically.

Now it is possible to form a simple Square of Opposition from the modal notions 'necessary', 'possible', 'impossible' and 'not necessary' (Figure 6.1), which in many ways parallels the square of opposition for quantifiers in Chapter 4. If we agree that modal operators are quantifiers over possible worlds, this is not surprising.

As in the quantificational square, the opposite corners of the square are contradictories; the two top corners are contraries (a proposition can be necessary or impossible or neither, but not both); and the two bottom corners are subcontraries (a proposition can be both possible and not necessary, but it cannot be neither). The modal operators on the same side are dual, being interdefinable by negation:

(6.3) 1. $\Box\phi = \neg\Diamond\neg\phi$
      2. $\Diamond\phi = \neg\Box\neg\phi$

In the traditional square there is also a subaltern relation, where each of the top corners implies the one below it. For the (non-modal) square of quantifiers, as we have seen, this relation does not hold in modern classical logic. For modal logic, the analogous question (if a proposition is necessary, does this imply that it is possible?) gets the answer 'it depends'. There is a plurality of modal logics, and it will get a different answer in different cases. But, at least in many logics, it gets the intuitive answer: yes, if a proposition is necessary then it is at least possible.

The basic propositional modal logic we will be using in this chapter includes the following ingredients:[7]

Propositional calculus: The entire contents of classical propositional logic as defined in Chapter 2 – both the syntax and semantics (along with the rule of **uniform substitution** of variables).

Modal operators: Necessity and possibility operators, as just discussed.

Necessitation: A rule that enables us to state that if a formula is logically true, then we can prefix it with the necessity operator: if $\models \phi$ then $\models \Box\phi$. Specifically, this means that if a material implication is a tautology (which, recall, means that the consequent is a logical consequence of the antecedent), then we can introduce the strict implication connective: if $\models \phi \rightarrow \psi$, then $\models \Box(\phi \rightarrow \psi)$, and thus $\models \phi < \psi$.

Modus ponendo ponens: This basic inference rule of propositional logic is carried over into modal logic.

Although this gives us a basic modal logic, it leaves many questions about the intended behaviour and interpretation of the necessity operator. For many years the exact consequences of adopting the different systems proposed by Lewis or others were difficult to evaluate because of the lack of a suitable semantics for them. However, this changed when a very elegant semantic theory was provided by Kripke, which facilitated the comparison of different modal systems.

The next few sections will look at some of the different interpretations of modal operators, and introduce the notion of accessibility relations, which is at the heart of Kripke's semantics.

6.1.4 KINDS OF MODALITY

In English, modal verbs such as 'can' and 'must' cover a variety of different meanings. As we have seen, this was one of the objections brought by Russell against modal logic. We should expect to see the same flexibility in the corresponding modal operators as well.

(6.4)   Before reading on, try to paraphrase the meaning of 'must' or 'can' in each of these sentences.
   1. Nobody can run 100 metres in less than five seconds.
   2. Citizens must pay their taxes.
   3. It can't be a square and a circle at the same time.
   4. I must have a drink; I'm dying of thirst.
   5. He must be home; I can hear his voice.
   6. I thought she was Russian, but actually she must be Ukrainian.

These examples are intended to represent some of the traditionally recognised types of modality, each of which has been studied as a subject in its own right. Try to match the examples with the characterisations in the following list. They are given with their traditional labels, derived from Ancient Greek. Possibly you will debate some of the examples.

(6.5) **Alethic** This is purely logical necessity, sometimes extended to cover meaning postulates and physical constraints (i.e. truth in all models under consideration – see Chapter 3). In this extended sense, it is sometimes referred to as metaphysical necessity (Greek *aletheia*, truth).

Deontic Moral obligation or duty (Greek *deon*, duty).

Epistemic Necessity according to the knowledge of a cognitive agent (Greek *epistamai*, I know).

Doxastic Consistency with the beliefs of a cognitive agent. (Greek *doxa*, belief – cf. 'ortho-doxy', right belief).

Dynamic Necessity in terms of ability, often physical ability (Greek *dynamai*, I am able).[8]

Bouletic Necessity as the definite will of an agent (Greek *boulomai*, I want).

We can expect that some of the rules of modal logic will be different for different kinds of modality, and indeed they are.

For alethic modality, it seems reasonable to require that if ϕ is necessarily true, then ϕ is (actually) true. This requirement, called **veridicality** (truth-telling or truth-implicating), is characteristic of alethic logic. (It is built into the name 'alethic'.) For deontic modality, by contrast, this inference does not hold. Citizens do not always pay their taxes.

A similar contrast distinguishes epistemic from doxastic modality. Epistemic modality is normally taken to involve the same veridical property as alethic modality; if I know that ϕ, then ϕ is true (and if it is not true, then my claim to know it is unjustified). But if I only *believe* that ϕ, then there is no guarantee that ϕ is true. What in practice distinguishes knowledge from belief – under what conditions we can claim to know something as opposed to merely believing it – is the main topic of debate in the branch of philosophy known as **epistemology**. But the logic of the word 'know' seems to require this veridicality, regardless of how we arrive at knowledge, or however sceptical we may be that claims to knowledge can even be made.

In alethic and epistemic logic, we will therefore require this principle of veridicality to hold, while in deontic and doxastic logic we will not.

Another way of classifying the different types of modality is that some involve the notion of necessity relative to some cognitive agent. Alethic logic traditionally does not. Deontic logic also probably does not, or at least is not normally treated that way.[9] The other types of modality listed clearly *do* involve some kind of relativisation to agents. In these cases, we need to introduce some parameter to indicate which agent is under discussion, and this is often written as a subscript. For example, $K_j\phi$ and $K_m\phi$ state that John and Mary, respectively, know ϕ.

Parametrised systems such as these are examples of **multi-modal** logics, where more than one necessity-type operator is used at the same time.

Another example of a multi-modal logic is temporal logic, where it is usual to have different operators, call them P and F, for the past and the future: Pϕ means that ϕ is true at some point in the past, and Fϕ means that ϕ is true at some point in the future. The 'some' in this description indicates that they are the temporal equivalent of $\Diamond$ operators; the corresponding $\Box$-type operators are written H for the past and G for the future ('have done' and 'going to' are useful mnemonics, though they do not correspond to the exact meaning of these operators).

If we mix different types of modality, or modality with tense, then the result is also a multi-modal logic.

EXERCISE 6.1.4.1

1. Do you think that dynamic and bouletic modal logics are veridical?
2. Describe in English the meaning of the possibility operator $\Diamond$ in deontic and doxastic modal logics.
3. Do the same for the H and G operators of temporal logic.
4. Draw Squares of Opposition for deontic and epistemic logic. Unpack in English the meaning of the four corners of each square, and check that the relations of contradictory, contrary and so on hold as explained in the text.

6.1.5 ACCESSIBILITY RELATIONS

Modal operators are interpreted as quantifiers over possible worlds; however, we may want to include only a subset of the possible worlds when evaluating modal statements. For example, in evaluating past statements, we will only be interested in past times. In evaluating doxastic statements about Mary's beliefs, we are only interested in the possibilities that Mary is able to consider. If we want to evaluate a deontic statement about what should happen, we may want to close our eyes to the actual world, where it is quite likely *not* to be true. The subset of worlds we include are said to be **accessible**.

But we also have to say 'accessible from where'. Once again, times provide an intuitive example. If we are using a future operator (F or G), we will want to quantify over only future times. But future relative to when? It may be relative to the present moment, or it may be relative to some other vantage point – for example in the past, as in the sentence 'Mary was going to die'. From the standpoint of the time in the past being referred to, points are still in the future which, relative to the present moment, may already be in the past, and that might include the moment of Mary's death.

Consequently, accessibility has to be treated as a relation – an **accessibility relation** – which specifies which worlds are accessible from where. The accessibility relation S for modal logic is a binary relation on the set of worlds, where S(w, v) means 'world *v* is accessible from world *w*'. Note that the order of worlds in this paraphrase is the other way round from the formal notation, which could be read more literally as 'world *w* can see into world *v*'. If we are in world *w*, then the set of accessible worlds is {v ∈ W|S(w, v)}.

As a matter of notation, note that in most treatments of purely modal logic, the accessibility relation is written as R rather than S. It is called S here because we will later be dealing with other kinds of accessibility relations besides modal ones, and it is convenient to keep a consistent notation throughout the book. We will distinguish it from other relations, when necessary, by calling it a modal or **positive** accessibility relation.[10]

Once we are armed with an accessibility relation, we can prove a fact about modal logic which takes us slightly further than the basic suppositions we made in the first section. Besides ordinary *modus ponens*, we can introduce a principle sometimes known as 'modal *modus ponens*', which is related to *modus ponens* much as strict implication is related to material implication. This says that if we have a strict implication $\phi \prec \psi$ and its antecedent ϕ is itself a necessary truth, then we can deduce ψ as a necessary truth:

K: $\Box(\phi \rightarrow \psi) \rightarrow (\Box\phi \rightarrow \Box\psi)$

To see that this is valid, consider that if the antecedent is true, then the material implication $\phi \rightarrow \psi$ must be true in all accessible worlds. That is, there is no accessible world where ϕ is true but ψ is false. If we now take the consequent, $\Box\phi \rightarrow \Box\psi$, this can only be false if ϕ is true in every accessible world, but ψ is not (it is false in at least one). This, however, would involve a world where ϕ is true but ψ is false, contradicting what we supposed earlier.

This principle of modal *modus ponens* is valid for all logics set up the way just described, with an accessibility relation. It is usually known as **K**, after Kripke, and postulated as an axiom (more on these later). Any modal logic that conforms to it is known as a **normal modal system**. Of Lewis' original systems, S1 to S3 are not normal, which has led to them not being studied so much since the advent of Kripke semantics.[11]

As S is a binary relation, we can also specify its properties (reflexive, symmetric, transitive etc.). These will play an important role in this chapter, and this would be a good time to reread the relevant material in Chapter 3 if you are unsure about them.

Kripke's key insight was that properties of the accessibility relation can give a semantic characterisation of different modal systems. Take, for example, the principle of veridicality, introduced in the last section. It can be expressed as a formula, usually given the label **T**.[12]

T: $\Box\phi \rightarrow \phi$

For **T** to be not valid, we need a set-up where the antecedent $\Box\phi$ is true and the consequent ϕ is false. This means that ϕ is false in the actual world. However, $\Box\phi$ requires that ϕ is true in all worlds or, to be precise, all *accessible* worlds. If ϕ is false in the actual world, then the actual world cannot be one of the accessible worlds.

For alethic logic, we want a necessary proposition to be true in the actual world, and must therefore require that the actual world *is* one of those taken into consideration when evaluating $\Box\phi$. If it is, then it is impossible for **T** to fail.

For **T** to be valid, we therefore require the current world, let's call it w_0, to be accessible. Accessible from where? From the current world, our point of evaluation. So we are in fact requiring that the accessibility relation S be reflexive; that whichever world is our point of evaluation, the same world must be accessible. Imposing this condition of reflexivity on S is the exact semantic correlate of enforcing the principle **T**:

Reflexivity: for every world $w \in W$, $S(w, w)$.
Validity: **T** is valid iff S is reflexive.

In deontic logic, by contrast, when we say that ϕ is morally necessary, we do not mean that it is true in the actual world, but only in worlds which conform to our desired standards. If we wish to maintain the interpretation of necessity as truth in all worlds, then it must be possible to omit the actual world from consideration. Therefore for deontic logic we do not require that the accessibility relation be reflexive.

This is not an isolated example; it is possible to capture many of the axioms in which modal logicians are interested by means of properties of the accessibility relation, including reflexivity (as here), transitivity, symmetry and a number of others. This will be explored further after we have given formal definitions for the syntax and semantics we are using.

For multi-modal logics, an accessibility relation is required for each modal operator used (counting each pair of necessity and possibility operators for this purpose as a single operator, as they are interdefinable and use the same accessibility relation). For epistemic logic, for example, there is an accessibility relation for each agent, which partitions the possible worlds into those which are compatible with the agent's state of knowledge and those which are not. The worlds which are accessible to an agent are his or her **epistemic alternatives**, and we will say $K_m\phi$ (Mary knows ϕ) iff ϕ is true in all Mary's epistemic alternatives. For temporal logic, the future operators G and F quantify over future points in time, while past operators see only past time; the two accessibility relations are **converses** of each other (Chapter 3), working in opposite directions.

6.2 SYNTAX OF MODAL LOGICS

For modal logic we extend the syntax of classical logic (propositional, first order or higher order) with the unary operators $\square$ and $\lozenge$. These operators, together with the other unary propositional operator $\neg$, are termed **modalities**.

Alternative symbols for $\square$ and $\lozenge$ are in common use in older books, and in studies of specialised types of modality such as deontic, as also in temporal logic. Except in temporal logic, however, their use seems to be becoming less common. They will be treated as notational variants, which are not included in the formal definition, but will occasionally be used for convenience (especially the temporal operators).[13]

Because of the duality of $\square$ and $\lozenge$, which applies in all the systems discussed in this chapter, it is not strictly necessary to include both, though we will do so here.

So here is the inductive definition for a language $\mathcal{L}$ of propositional modal logic:

1. All wffs of the propositional calculus are wffs of $\mathcal{L}$.
2. If ϕ is a wff of $\mathcal{L}$, then so are $\square\phi$ and $\lozenge\phi$.
3. Nothing else is a wff of $\mathcal{L}$.

For higher order logic, 'wff' is replaced as usual by 'wfe of type t'.[14]

As usual, ϕ in the second clause of this definition is the **scope** of the modal operator.

Note that the definition allows for the iteration or 'stacking' of modalities (e.g. $\Box\Box\Box\phi$). This has not been important in the discussion up to now, but will be later in this chapter.

It is quite common to also include the connective $\Rightarrow$ for **entailment** or $\prec$ for **strict implication**; as already discussed, many writers regard these as equivalent, and definable as $\Box(\phi \rightarrow \psi)$, where $\rightarrow$ is material implication. I have not included either in the formal definition, but will occasionally use $\prec$ informally to make complex modal formulas more readable. The entailment connective $\Rightarrow$ will reappear in Chapter 11.

This is perhaps a good place to sound a warning about the scope of $\Box$ in the formula $\Box\,(\phi \rightarrow \psi)$. The natural English formulation, 'if ϕ is true then ψ must be true' conceals an ambiguity. In the formula just given, the scope of the necessity operator ('must') is the whole implication; it is the implication that is necessary. However, the English sentence can also be read as saying that ψ is necessary if ϕ happens to be true, which is a completely different proposition ($\phi \rightarrow \Box\psi$). This is an extremely common mistake, and you are advised to watch out for it.

EXERCISE 6.2.0.1

Translate these English sentences into propositional modal logic. Give a key for the propositional letters. If you use $\Box$ and $\Diamond$, specify for each instance what kind of modality you intend it to denote. For temporal notions, use the operators G, F, P and H. Some sentences have more than one reading.

1. The train may have been delayed.
2. It will definitely rain.
3. If Anna knows that it will rain, then Fred ought to believe it.
4. Anna believes that Fred believes it will rain, but it is impossible.
5. Anna did not know that the train had been delayed, but she will know.
6. Fred knew that the train either had been delayed or would be delayed.
7. If it is possible that it will rain, Anna must know that it will.
8. If the train can not be delayed, Fred should know that it will not ever be delayed.

In the introduction to this chapter we saw that the behaviour of the modal operators varies in some respects. However, there are also some properties common to all normal modal logics.

(6.6) In normal modal logics, the operators $\Box$ and $\Diamond$ are:

Dual:$\Box$ and $\Diamond$ are interdefinable by means of negation: $\Box\phi = \neg\Diamond\neg\phi$, and conversely $\Diamond\phi = \neg\Box\neg\phi$. This is the same as the duality of the classical quantifiers $\forall$ and $\exists$.

Normal: $\Box$ and $\Diamond$ are a **normal** pair of modal operators, which means that they interact with the propositional connectives as follows: $\Box\phi \wedge \Box\psi$

implies $\Box(\phi \wedge \psi)$, and $\Diamond(\phi \vee \psi)$ implies $\Diamond\phi \vee \Diamond\psi$. In other words $\Box$ distributes over conjunction, while $\Diamond$ distributes over disjunction.

Positive: If ϕ implies ψ, then $\Box\phi$ implies $\Box\psi$ and also $\Diamond\phi$ implies $\Diamond\psi$. This may be compared to negation, whose entailment pattern operates the other way round: if ϕ implies ψ, then $\neg\psi$ implies $\neg\phi$ (Chapter 2). $\Box$ and $\Diamond$ are therefore termed positive modalities; negation is also a modality, but a negative one.

If you check back with the inferences in (6.1) at the beginning of this chapter, you will see that several of them illustrate these general rules.

6.3 SEMANTICS OF MODAL LOGICS

There are several approaches to the semantics of modal logics. The one used here is **frame semantics**, also known as relational semantics, or Kripke semantics.

The first thing we need for a semantic interpretation of modal logic is a set of worlds. For temporal logic we need a set of times in the actual world; and if we wish to combine modal and temporal logic we may need sets of times in different worlds (or a set of pairs of worlds and times – this approach was popularised by Montague). More generally, we can think of worlds and times alike as being contexts, information states, or points where a proposition is evaluated. We will later develop this into a more general notion than the worlds and times we have been dealing with up to now. However, for now we will simply call them worlds.

The second thing we need is at least one binary positive accessibility relation S on worlds. In the case of a multi-modal logic we need an accessibility relation for each necessity–possibility pair of modal operators; in this case S can be subscripted with the symbol for the operator. In systems like epistemic logics, where the modal operator is itself subscripted for agents, S can simply be subscripted with the name of the agent. The definition given below assumes just one accessibility relation.

The third thing we need, for propositional modal logic, is a valuation, which tells us which basic formulae are true in which worlds. We do not have to worry in this chapter about a domain of discourse.

The first two ingredients together are known as a **modal frame**. They do not actually evaluate any formulae for us, but give us a structure of connections between worlds in which they can be evaluated. The frame plus the valuation constitute a **model** for modal logic.

To summarise:

1. A frame $\mathcal{F}$ for modal logic = $\langle W,S \rangle$, where W is set of worlds and $S \subseteq W \times W$ is an accessibility relation.
2. A model $\mathcal{M}$ for modal logic = $\langle W,S,V \rangle$, where V: $(W \times \mathcal{L}) \rightarrow 2$ is a function from wffs and worlds to truth values, such that:
   (a) if ϕ is a wff, then $V(\Box\phi, w) = 1$ iff, for every world w' such that $S(w, w')$, $V(\phi, w') = 1$.

(b) if ϕ is a wff, then $V(\lozenge\phi, w) = 1$ iff, for some world w' such that $S(w, w')$, $V(\phi, w') = 1$.

(c) for a non-modal wff ϕ, $V(\phi, w)$ gives exactly the result that $V(\phi)$ would give in classical propositional logic (Chapter 2).

The definition of a valuation can be given in another form, which will tie in with later chapters. This is by means of a relation $\Vdash$ between worlds and formulae which are true in those worlds ($w \Vdash \phi$ iff ϕ is true in w). The symbol $\Vdash$ can be read 'supports' or 'satisfies' (or sometimes 'forces').

Formally, the equivalence looks like this:

1. $w \Vdash \phi$ iff $V(\phi, w) = 1$

I will generally use this second form in the remainder of the book when dealing with frame semantics, as many people find it more transparent.

As can be expected from the earlier discussion, most of the semantic interest of this chapter will be in conditions on frames – which amount chiefly to properties of the accessibility relation S. If S is reflexive, we talk about the frame being reflexive. These conditions on frames are independent of which model we are considering; for example the condition that a frame be reflexive has the consequences that we have shown regardless of which propositional letters are true or false in any world (i.e. the valuation). The veridical principle **T**, for example, is valid on *any* reflexive frame, and hence in any model whatsoever whose frame is reflexive.

It is to this relationship between modal principles and modal frames that we will turn next.

EXERCISE 6.3.0.1

1. A news report on a recent earthquake in Italy states that the advice from scientists that they could not be confident that there would be an earthquake was misrepresented in the media as saying that they could be confident that there would not be an earthquake. Translate the highlighted expressions into propositional modal logic. What kind of modality is involved? Show that the second statement does not follow from the first, using a frame.

2. Consider the model $\mathcal{M} = \langle W, S, V \rangle$ where $W = \{w_0, w_1, w_2\}$, $S = \{\langle w_0, w_0 \rangle, \langle w_0, w_1 \rangle, \langle w_0, w_2 \rangle, \langle w_1, w_1 \rangle, \langle w_2, w_2 \rangle\}$, and $V(p, w_0) = 1$, $v(p, w_1) = 0$ and $v(p, w_2) = 0$

   (a) Draw a diagram for the model. Is the frame reflexive?

   (b) Restate V using the relation $\Vdash$.

   (c) For the formula $p \rightarrow \lozenge p$, answer the following:

      i. Is it true (in w_0, the actual world)?

      ii. If it is true, is it also valid on $\mathcal{M}$ (true in all worlds)?

      iii. Is it valid on the frame $\langle W, S \rangle$? (Or can you change its truth value just by changing V, without changing the frame?)

iv. Is it valid on the class of reflexive frames? (Change the accessibility relation but keep it reflexive.)

v. Is it valid on all frames? (Erase the loops in the accessibility relation.)

(d) Answer the same questions for the formulas (i) $\Box p \land \neg p$, (ii) $p \rightarrow \Box \Diamond p$

3. (a) The modal logics studied in this chapter include all the classical connectives, including negation. Show using a frame the equivalences that enable us to interdefine $\Box$ and $\Diamond$ by means of negation, namely $\Box \neg \phi \equiv \neg \Diamond \phi$ and $\Diamond \neg \phi \equiv \neg \Box \phi$.

(b) Show using a frame the following two entailments:

   i. $\Box(\phi \lor \psi) \vDash \Box \phi \lor \Diamond \psi$

   ii. $\Box \phi \land \Diamond \psi \dashv \vDash \Diamond(\phi \land \psi)$

These interaction rules relate the positive modalities without relying on negation (Dunn 1995).

6.4 MODAL SYSTEMS

6.4.1 AXIOMS AND FRAMES

The examples already discussed illustrate how the content of different modal systems can be captured in two ways, which correspond to each other: axioms, and conditions on frames.

Axioms: We have seen that important properties of modal systems can often be simply captured by formulas, as in the case of veridicality and **T**. If we want our modal logic to have a property, then we include the appropriate formula and make it an **axiom**.

Conditions on frames: The content of a modal system can often also be captured semantically by conditions on its frame (properties of its accessibility relation). The example we have seen so far is the correspondence between reflexive frames and veridicality.

Axioms were discussed a little in the introduction, but since they play a more prominent part in this chapter, a brief note may be helpful on how they are used in axiomatic proof systems, or Hilbert systems as they are often known.

In an axiomatic system, the set of theorems (all the provably true statements of a logic) can be derived from a special subset which are stipulated to be true and need not be derived from anything. In a derivation or proof, each statement is derived from a previous one by one of the allowed rules; but axioms can be introduced at any point, without any further justification. Typically, axiomatic systems contain many axioms, and only a few simple rules – often only *modus ponendo ponens* and uniform substitution. (We will meet other proof systems where the main work is done by rules.)

Usually there are many ways of selecting which truths to list as axioms. The main thing is that there are enough of them to derive all theorems, preferably without redundancy. One way is to select many, relatively simple, formulae which somehow illustrate the behaviour of connectives, or relationships between them. For example one pair of axioms in classical logic, $(\phi \wedge \psi) \rightarrow \phi$ and $(\phi \wedge \psi) \rightarrow \psi$, illustrate part of the meaning of conjunction in classical logic: that if a conjunction is true, then either of the conjuncts can be derived as true, as is easily checked in the truth tables. A logic which does not include these truths, or some other axioms from which they can be derived, is not the same logic as the logic of the truth tables.[15]

We will not give the axioms for classical propositional logic here, but concentrate on modal axioms, which describe the behaviour of modal operators. Although it is possible to use other proof systems with modal logics, axioms are a very perspicuous way of characterising the different modal systems.

Here is a very simple example of the use of axiom **T** to prove p $\rightarrow$ q from the premise $\Box$(p$\rightarrow$q):

1. $\Box$(p$\rightarrow$q) (given)
2. $\Box\phi \rightarrow \phi$ (axiom **T**)
3. $\Box$ (p$\rightarrow$q)$\rightarrow$(p$\rightarrow$q) (substituting (p$\rightarrow$q) for ϕ in line 2)
4. p$\rightarrow$q (*modus ponens*, from lines 3 and 1)

(Note that when *modus ponendo ponens* is used in an axiomatic system, it is often referred to as **detachment**: it enables the consequent of the major premise to be detached from that formula and stated in its own right. We will not often use this terminology here, but you will see it in many other books.)

It is useful to think of modal logics as a family of logics, whose content can be engineered or 'tweaked' by modifying the axioms and conditions on frames to give the desired results. Often what looks like a slight 'tweak' can have quite drastic results. This is typical of the kind of logics we will be studying in the rest of this book.

We will now look at some more examples of axioms and frame conditions, starting by revisiting veridical and non-veridical systems.

6.4.2 VERIDICAL AND NON-VERIDICAL

We have already taken a brief look at the axiom of veridicality, **T**, and the reflexivity condition on frames needed for it to be valid. A first basis for an alethic or epistemic modal logic would therefore consist of the axioms **K** and **T** together. This is generally known as system T after its characteristic axiom. Because of the lack of standardisation of modal labels already mentioned, some writers like to specify systems by listing all the axioms they contain, so system T can also referred to as KT. (Note the convention that axioms are labelled in bold type, while systems are not.)

An alternative formulation of T is given as T′ below. This is equivalent because of the duality of $\Box$ and $\Diamond$.

T′ $\phi \rightarrow \Diamond\phi$

Check that you agree that this is as intuitively plausible as **T**, both for alethic and epistemic logic. You have already verified that it must be valid on any reflexive frame, if you have done the exercise in the previous section.

What about non-veridical systems such as deontic and doxastic logic? Clearly we do not want **T** or its equivalents, but this does not mean that 'anything goes'. It is common to add to these logics a weaker requirement, an axiom known as **D** (for deontic, though it also, conveniently, works for doxastic).

D: $\Box\phi \rightarrow \Diamond\phi$

This states that if ϕ is necessary (obligatory), then, while it does not have to be true, it must at least be possible. It is important to be clear that this is the *deontic* possibility operator, so it does not mean that ϕ has to be physically possible, or even logically possible (though doubtless these would be nice). The intended interpretation can be worked out from the duality of the modal operators: $\Diamond\phi$ is equivalent to $\neg\Box\neg\phi$, so it means 'it is not the case that $\neg\phi$ is obligatory', that is, ϕ is permissible. It precludes, in other words, situations of contradictory moral obligations, such as Orestes' dilemma in Greek tragedy when he is obligated to commit the crime of matricide to fulfil his duty of avenging his father. Of course moral dilemmas do nonetheless occur, and how to deal with them is a hot question for deontic logicians.

This works similarly for doxastic logic, as follows: $\Diamond_a\phi$ means that it is not the case that a believes $\neg\phi$, so axiom **D** here requires that a cognitive agent not believe ϕ and $\neg\phi$ at the same time. This is also not self-evident, as some agents are not completely rational. How to deal with conflicts of belief in the same agent is another complicated question.

The requirement that if ϕ is necessary then it is possible it amounts to requiring that at least one world is accessible. If no world is accessible, then $\Box\phi$ is vacuously true and $\Diamond\phi$ is false, and this is the only situation where this can arise. So for a frame where **D** is valid, we require that every world can see into at least one other world (which may or may not be itself). This makes the accessibility relation S a **serial** relation.

Seriality: For every $w \in W$, $S(w, w')$ for some $w' \in W$

Apart from the question of veridicality, doxastic logic patterns in much the same way as epistemic logic, and will not be further treated separately here. However, here are a few more remarks on deontic logic before we leave it.

In deontic logic the set of worlds considered does not generally include the actual world; the worlds that are accessible for quantification are the worlds where what should be the case, is the case. These are sometimes termed 'worlds of perfect obedience'. However, it is sometimes argued that in a world of perfect obedience, $\Box\phi \rightarrow \phi$ should hold, even though it does not hold when evaluated in the actual world. Thus we might want to consider another axiom:

$\Box(\Box\phi \rightarrow \phi)$

This is to capture the intuition that although the real world is not one where obligations are fulfilled, it *should* be the case that obligations which hold in a world are fulfilled in that world. Semantically, it amounts to imposing the reflexivity requirement not on all worlds, but on all worlds of perfect obedience'.

Shift reflexivity: For every world w' ∈ W such that S(w, w'), S(w', w').

Imposing a 'deferred' frame condition, which applies to every accessible world but not the actual world, is something we will see again.

6.4.3 COMPLETE MODALISATION: S4 AND S5

Returning to alethic (and epistemic) modality, we have discussed the importance of **T**, but there are other interesting requirements to put on the behaviour of □ besides that of veridicality. The two that are most often discussed are:

4: $\Box\phi \rightarrow \Box\Box\phi$

B: $\phi \rightarrow \Box\Diamond\phi$

- What would these requirements mean in (i) alethic logic, (ii) epistemic logic?

The first thing to note about these examples is that they both illustrate the possibility of multiple modal operators in front of a formula. This is licensed by the inductive rules for our syntax, as was commented at the time. Strings of modal operators like this are known as stacked or **iterated modalities**. As was also pointed out, negation counts as a modality, so combinations of negation and modal operators also count as iterated modalities; however, the comments in this section will refer to non-negative modalities (sequences of modal operators not including negation).

So how should these iterated modalities be interpreted? It has to be said that strings of modal operators soon become problematic for most people's intuitions. Formulas **4** and **B**, which imvolve sequences of just two modal operators, are probably easy enough for most people (though this may still be deceptive). But expressions like $\Box\Box\Diamond\Box\Diamond\Diamond\Box\phi$ are very difficult for anyone to process.

One of the convenient results of adopting axioms such as **4** and **B** is that iterated modalities can be brought down to a more manageable length. Consider, for example, a system including **4** along with **T**. The presence of **T** makes **4** a bi-implication: $\Box\phi \leftrightarrow \Box\Box\phi$. This means that any sequence of two □s is equivalent to a sequence of just one □. Although the syntactic rules allow us to write as many □s as we like, they can be treated as just plain □. A formula which allows us to do this in a modal system is known as a **reduction thesis**, and a modal system which contains one or more of them is known as a system of **complete modalisation**.

If we add **4** to **T** we get system S4, and if we then further add **B** we get S5. (An alternative formulation of S5 will be introduced shortly.) S4 and S5 are the most important modal systems in discussions of epistemic and alethic logic. They are both systems of complete modalisation; the maximum length of a *distinct* string of modal operators is three in S4, and in S5 it is reduced to just one. The relations between the distinct modalities can be pictured in diagrams (Figure 6.2).[16]

What does axiom **4** mean? In alethic logic, it means that if something is necessary then it is necessarily necessary; necessity does not arise by chance. In epistemic logic,

(i) Entailment between the modalities in S4 (from left to right)

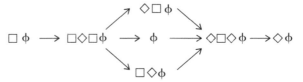

(ii) Entailment between the modalities in S5

$$\Box\, \phi \longrightarrow \quad \phi \quad \longrightarrow \Diamond\, \phi$$

Figure 6.2   Modality graphs of S4 and S5

it means that if I know something, then I know that I know it; I am aware of what I know, a property known as **positive introspection**.

Turning to frame semantics, **4** corresponds to the condition that S is transitive. If $\Box\phi$ is true in w_0, then ϕ is true in every world accessible to w_0. Take w_2 as an arbitrary example of such an accessible world, and now consider all worlds w_2 that are accessible to w_1. Is ϕ true in w_2? If S is transitive then it must be, because then w_2 is accessible to w_0, and we have already established that in all such worlds ϕ is true. So $\Box\Box\phi$ is true. If S were not transitive, we would not be able to show this conclusion; we could simply construct a model in which ϕ is false in w_2, and then the conclusion would be false.

Axiom **4** can also be expressed as **4′** by duality:

4′ $\Diamond\Diamond\phi \rightarrow \Diamond\phi$

In alethic terms, this means that if ϕ is possibly possible, then it is possible. (In epistemic terms it means that if I don't know that I know $\neg\phi$, then I don't know $\neg\phi$ – another formulation of positive introspection.)

If we add **B** to S4, then we get S5. I repeat **B** here for convenience.

B: $\phi \rightarrow \Box\Diamond\phi$

This formula seems to mean that if ϕ is true then it is necessary that it is possible. This is not quite as simple a notion as it might appear, as will be discussed shortly. In epistemic terms, **B** adds what is called **negative introspection**: if ϕ is true, then I know that I do not know $\neg\phi$. Thus agents have full awareness not only of what they know but also of what they do not know.

In terms of frame semantics, **B** corresponds to the condition that S is symmetric, which can be seen as follows. If ϕ is true, then we need to show that $\Box\Diamond\phi$ is true, which means that $\Diamond\phi$ is true in every world w_1 accessible to w_0. This is true if S is symmetric, as then w_1 can look back into w_0, where ϕ is true. If S is not symmetric, we can make a counter-model simply by setting ϕ to be false in all worlds accessible to w_1.

As usual, **B** can be expressed in the alternative form **B′**.

B′ $\Box\Diamond\phi \rightarrow \phi$

- Show that this formula, too, is valid on symmetric frames.
- What does the formula mean in English? Do you think that this is more or less plausible than the original formulation of **B**?

It is possible to reach S5 from system T in one go by adding axiom **5** below (also known as **E**, for Euclidean), which gives us transitivity and symmetry together. This is in fact the usual presentation in logic textbooks, and it is certainly more concise. Once again we have a trade-off between concision and transparency. Using **4** and **B** allows us to see the effects of transitivity and symmetry separately, and tweak our logics accordingly.[17]

5: $\Diamond\phi \rightarrow \Box\Diamond\phi$

With S5 we have reached a frame which is reflexive (remember **T**), transitive (**4**) and symmetric (**B**), which makes it an equivalence relation. In effect this means that every world is accessible to all other worlds. (More precisely, it partitions W into equivalence classes in which each world can see any other world; worlds outside the equivalence class are completely invisible, and do not need to be taken into consideration.) This makes S5 a particularly simple logic to use, as we can, in effect, ignore accessibility relations all together. When we presented necessity and possibility earlier as quantifying over rows of a truth table, we were implicitly using S5: we assumed that all worlds (rows) were accessible all the time. We are also able to ignore iterated modalities, as in S5 all sequences of modal operators are reducible to one (the last in the sequence). It is therefore a popular choice in linguistics, and in particular was selected by Montague as the modal component of his highly influential system.

There is a long-running debate over the relative merits of S4 and S5. Informally, the difference can be put as follows. S4 gives a notion of growth of information; as we proceed along a path in the accessibility relation, propositions which have been established as necessarily true, remain necessarily true. Other necessary truths can be added, but none can be lost. This is guaranteed by the transitivity of S. But this is not a symmetric relation, and this growth of information goes in one direction only. In S5 there is symmetry, and hence no notion of information growth; the whole set of worlds is seen as from a state of complete knowledge.

There are other issues involved as well. One is that axiom **B** allows us to do something which is traditionally considered suspect – to infer a necessity from a contingent proposition. From the fact that ϕ happens to be true, you should not (so the argument goes) be able to deduce anything about necessity. Or in epistemic terms, from the fact that ϕ happens to be true, you should not be able to draw conclusions about an agent's state of knowledge.

On the other hand, it would seem that if ϕ is true, then it must be possible. Thus the formula **B**: $\phi \rightarrow \Box\Diamond\phi$ would seem plausible – but there is a catch.

1. Do you think the first sentence in this last paragraph justifies **B**?
2. If you think that it does, please read over section 6.2 again, and see if you can spot a problem with the argument.

To get to S5 we have been progressively adding axioms. As we do this, each system considered (K, T, S4, S5) includes all the content of the ones before it, and is said to be **stronger** than them. S5 is as strong as a modal system can get. Adding any further axioms either does not add anything (in other words the new axiom was already provable in S5) or results in modal collapse – we are back to classical logic, with no meaningful notion of modality. One way to see this is that once we have an accessibility relation which is an equivalence relation, the next step is reduce the set of worlds to a single world, which can see into itself. Once we do this, then if ϕ is true then $\Box\phi$ and $\Diamond\phi$ are also true, so they are equivalent to ϕ and we have a reduction thesis that gets rid of modalities all together (the maximum distinct sequence of non-negative modal operators is equal to zero). The syntax still licenses us to write as many modal operators as we like, but they contribute nothing. Modal logicians call this system Triv (for trivial). Non-modal logicians just call it classical logic.

We will return to the S4–S5 dilemma several times during the next few chapters, and the whole question of partial versus total knowledge will play an important role in the remainder of this book, in various forms.

EXERCISE 6.4.3.1

1. The text presented S5 as S4 plus the axiom **B** for reflexivity, while most sources present it as T plus the axiom **5** which gives transitivity and reflexivity together. Show that **B** is valid given **5** (easy) and (ii) **5** is valid given **B** in S4. Hint: remember these facts:
   (a) Implication is transitive in classical propositional logic. If $\phi \rightarrow \chi$ and $\chi \rightarrow \psi$, then we have $\phi \rightarrow \psi$.
   (b) We are working in S4, which means that **K, T** and **4** are given.
   (c) You can also use the properties of the modal operators $\Box$ and à as listed in section 6.2.
2. Suppose we reduce the set of worlds to a single world, as in Triv, but this time it cannot see into itself. ϕ may be assigned true or false in that world, as normal, by some valuation V. What does the valuation assign to $\Box\phi$ and $\Diamond\phi$? Do these change if you change the truth value assigned to ϕ? (Hint: reread the discussion of **D**.) The name given to this system is Verum.

6.4.4 TEMPORAL LOGIC

Temporal logic (or tense logic) as a branch of modal logic was developed by Arthur Prior in the 1960s. The system that has become known as 'Priorian tense logic' is a normal modal logic presupposing classical propositional logic as a base (see the definition of the basic normal modal system K, above). The set of worlds is usually referred to as a set T of points of time. This set is structured into a timeline by axioms, and their associated conditions on frames, which we will discuss shortly. It is a multimodal (or 'bimodal') system, with separate pairs of operators for past and future time, and therefore two accessibility relations, one looking to the past and the other looking to the future along the timeline. The operators themselves have already been introduced, but here they are again:

F: true at some point in the future.
P: true at some point in the past.
G: true at all points in the future.
H: true at all points in the past.

The usual rules of duality hold between the necessity- and possibility-type operators in each pair, which are therefore interdefinable. Prior at first used as primitives F and P, which correspond more closely to the meaning of certain English tenses, but later switched to the necessity type operators (many modal axioms look simpler and clearer when expressed using $\square$).

Here are some basic axioms for temporal logic. As the logic is bimodal, each has to be stated as a pair of axioms, one for past and one for future time. The first pair is simply the temporal form of the modal axiom **K**.

1. (a) $H(\phi \rightarrow \psi) \rightarrow (H\phi \rightarrow H\psi)$
   (b) $G(\phi \rightarrow \psi) \rightarrow (G\phi \rightarrow G\psi)$
2. (a) $\phi \rightarrow HF\phi$
   (b) $\phi \rightarrow GP\phi$

The second pair governs the interaction of the past and future modalities. Note the similarity with **B**, except that the necessity and possibility operators are drawn from different pairs. Thus they do not impose symmetry on a single accessibility relation, but instead ensure that the two accessibility relations are converses. They are sometimes known as the 'converse axioms'.

Further axioms may be added to make the set of times behave more like the real timeline – or let's say the timeline implicit in the use of tense in language. These additions depend a lot on people's philosophical assumptions or intended applications, and so they are more or less debatable.

To take one of the less controversial ones, although we do not want time to be symmetric or reflexive, we will presumably want it to be transitive, so axiom **4** will be present in its temporal form. (From this point I normally give only one of each pair of axioms.)

$4_t \ G\phi \rightarrow GG\phi$

We may also want to require that the timeline is unending in both directions, which means seriality.

D$_t$ $G\phi \rightarrow F\phi$

Strictly speaking, this only works if S is not only not reflexive, but actually required to be *irreflexive* – no point of time can see into itself. **D** on its own is consistent with a timeline having an initial or final point, as long as that point can see itself. (Obviously once we get to such a point nothing can ever 'happen', so we would then have a kind of 'freezing' of time, which some writers describe as 'eternity'.)

It is also common to require that between any two points of time there is a third point of time. In modal logic this property, called **density**, is imposed on a modal frame by the converse of axiom **4**, namely $\square\square\phi \rightarrow \square\phi$. The temporal form of this may be included in our tense logic, if we so choose.

C4$_t$ $GG\phi \rightarrow G\phi$

We should bear in mind here that we are not necessarily trying to model all the physical properties of time, but to provide a semantics for tense in natural language. For some applications it may be preferable to treat time as composed of discrete instants. For example, language contains expressions like 'next', or 'the next moment'. If time is dense, then there isn't, strictly speaking, a next moment.

The main thing we are missing so far is an axiom to make the flow of time into a single straight line (to impose a total ordering on the points in T). This is one of the most controversial additions, not because it is difficult, but because it is not clear that that is what we want for all applications. It can be argued that if the future is not yet determined, then the accessibility relation should branch into possible futures. If we further assume that the past is determined and 'linear', this introduces an asymmetry into the picture between the past and future accessibility relations.

Apart from branching time, some ancient cultures had a cyclic model of time. We may ourselves have different ideas of time, which we find more convincing, but as semanticists we might still want to give an interpretation to language about time which does not fit in with our beliefs, rather than to have to treat it as meaningless.

A total ordering on the past can be imposed with (1); and its dual (2) will give us a total ordering on the future if we want it.

1. $FP\phi \rightarrow (P\phi \lor \phi \lor F\phi)$
2. $PF\phi \rightarrow (P\phi \lor \phi \lor F\phi)$

In the next section we will assume a linear time frame, and look at some other questions about Prior's basic tense logic. We will then go on to consider branching time.

6.4.5 MOMENTS OF TIME

The set-up developed in the last section assumes we have some pre-theoretical notion of points in time, and presupposes also that this notion is appropriate to characterise tense in language. Prior was aware that this is not self-evident, and suggested that points in time (the elements of set T) can be characterised by the conjunction of propositions that hold there. We have already seen that worlds can be characterised by the set (or conjunction) of propositions that are true in them.[18] But in natural language we do not normally want to refer to a particular world, whereas there are many expressions – mostly temporal adverbials – which refer to particular times. Sometimes these are vague or require pragmatic explicature to obtain their exact reference (for example specification of a time zone, or resolution of indexical expressions), but in principle it would seem that they can be made to refer to unique points in time. Prior had the idea of introducing into tense logic expressions with exactly this timestamp property, which he called 'instant propositions', but which are now usually known as **nominals**; although they are propositions, and we are still within the framework of a propositional logic, they refer to points of time in much the same way that names in predicate logic refer to individuals. This 'hybrid' between modal logic and predicate logic has proved fruitful, and we will return to it later in this chapter.

A different approach to the problem of isolating points of time is to characterise them as the beginning or end of intervals in which a certain state of affairs holds. Kamp (1968) proposed replacing the Priorian modalities by two binary temporal connectives, **until** and **since**, with the following interpretation:

(6.7) 1. $t \Vdash$ **since** (ϕ, ψ) iff $\exists t' \leq t$ such that $t' \Vdash \phi$ and $\forall t''$ such that $t' \leq t'' \leq t, t'' \Vdash \psi$
2. $t \Vdash$ **until** (ϕ, ψ) iff $\exists t' \geq t$ such that $t' \Vdash \phi$ and $\forall t''$ such that $t' \geq t'' \geq t', t'' \Vdash \psi$

In plain English, **since** (ϕ, ψ) means 'ψ has been true since ϕ'; it is true at t if ϕ holds at some past time t' and ψ holds at every intervening time t''; similarly for **until** and future time.[19] Kamp showed that, perhaps surprisingly, these two operators on their own are able to express the whole of Priorian tense logic and a bit more; in fact they are **functionally complete** (in the sense discussed for NAND in Chapter 2).

It is possible to replace the whole idea of time as an ordered set of points by time as a set of **intervals**. These intervals can be related to each other in various ways,, usually defined in terms of temporal precedence, overlap and containment ('subintervals'). Generally it is possible to define intervals in terms of points and vice versa, so in this sense the two approaches are equivalent. However, it is often suggested that intervals are more intuitive and less philosophically problematic units with which to work, especially when working on tense and aspect. This approach was pioneered by Hamblin (1971), and has since found many applications both in linguistics and in reasoning about computations.

6.4.6 BRANCHING TIME: FROM S4 TO S5

If we assume that the future is not yet determined, we may want to consider a model of time that branches towards the future. We will assume, however, that the past is determinate. Thus every point has a unique **history** (path in the past direction) and one or more **futures** (paths in the future direction). The future temporal operators then become related to modal operators, as Fϕ can now mean either that ϕ may become true (it is in one future) or that it will definitely become true (it is in all futures).

It is interesting to relate this to the epistemic idea of partial and total information, which was introduced in the earlier discussion of S4 and S5; and there is, in fact, a tradition of exploring the territory between S4 and S5 in terms of information growth. Since S4 frames are transitive, the accessibility relation in an S4 frame consists of one or more branches fanning out from each world. Along a branch, once $\Box\phi$ is true, its truth is propagated for the whole length of the branch from that point on, just like $G\phi$ on a temporal frame. Thus information, once it becomes definite (necessary), is never lost or revised in a given future. (Note that because S4 is also reflexive, $\Box\phi$ on this approach means that ϕ is true 'now and forever', unlike $G\phi$ in Prior's basic temporal logic.)

Early explorations of this connection between temporal and modal logics go back to Prior himself. Prior had an interest in ancient philosophy, including the Megarian school, where the notions of time and necessity were among the main objects of study. In particular he was interested in the arguments of one of the Megarians, Diodorus Cronus, a strong advocate of determinism (and one of the teachers of Zeno, the founder of Stoicism). Ancient logicians often conflated time and modality, in that they assumed that any state of affairs that was possible would one day be an actual state of this world.[20] In Diodorus' words, everything in the past is necessary (because it happened), and 'the possible is that which either is or will be'.

Prior believed that Diodorus' determinism corresponded to a linear timeline, whereas a genuinely open future – and the possibility of free will – could be captured by allowing the timeline to branch. The idea of branching time suggests a tree structure, with a linear timeline as a limiting case in which the future is determined, so that there is only one branch. S4 frames, however, are not trees, nor even partial orders (they are preorders, though there are techniques for making them into effective partial orders). Prior and a number of other logicians (notably Dummett and Lemmon) therefore explored various logics which were strengthenings of S4 but fell short of S5, which, as already discussed, does not allow a notion of information growth. This territory between the two logics is described by Zeman[21] as 'the S4-S5 spectrum'. Only a few points on this spectrum will be introduced here.

Prior believed that a linearly ordered frame such as that used in his basic tense logic corresponded to Diodorus' view on determinism. Such a frame can be produced in modal logic by adding to S4 the 'Diodorean' axiom .3,[22] which gives an S4 frame the additional property of **connexity**. The combination of this with S4 gives us the system S4.3, sometimes known as the Diodorean system.[23]

.3: $(\Box\phi < \psi) \vee (\Box\psi < \phi)$

The intuition here is that for any two accessible worlds, call them u and v, either u can see v or v can see u; together with transitivity, this implies that the accessibility relation is linear.

Alternatively we might want not to go as far as this, but to impose some consistency on different futures, so that if ϕ becomes necessary in one branch, then other branches should be consistent with this information at least to the extent of not ruling it out. The axiom that effects this is .2,[24] which, when added to S4, gives the system S4.2.

.2: $\Diamond\Box\phi \rightarrow \Box\Diamond\phi$

The frame condition corresponding to this axiom is **convergence**: if w_0 can see two worlds, w_1 and w_2, then both of these must be able to see a common world, w_0. This puts limits on the ability of different futures to diverge. Intuitively, it captures the idea that we are modelling partial information about the real world, and although following different paths of enquiry may give us different pieces of the jigsaw, they will all fit together in the end.

S4.2 also occupies an important step in the ladder of systems of complete modalisation, discussed above. The maximum number for a distinct sequence of modal operators is two (compare three for S4 and one for S5).

The other system that is sometimes considered in this context is S4.4, which is almost S5; the accessibility relation is made symmetric over all worlds except the actual world, a property that can be called **shift symmetry** (compare shift reflexivity, introduced earlier). S5 does not hold in w_0, but as soon as we move to an accessible world, w_1, symmetry kicks in and S5 logic applies. If S5 is taken as corresponding to 'eternity' (i.e. complete knowledge), S4.4 is called by Zeman 'the logic of the end of time'.

A frame for S4.4 is produced by adding the following axiom, which we will call **.4**.

.4: $\Box(\phi < (\Diamond\Box\phi < \Box\phi))$

Although we started this section talking about temporal logic, the discussion has ended up being much more about epistemic logic, and this is indeed the usual context for discussion of the S4–S5 spectrum. All the systems mentioned here, from S4 to S4.4, have been proposed by scholars over the past fifty years as being the best logic for epistemic modality.[25] S5, by contrast, is widely used for alethic modality.[26]

EXERCISE 6.4.6.1

1. Show the correspondence between the axioms and frame conditions given for systems S4.2, S4.3 and S4.4. Proceed, as we did for **4** and **B**, by constructing a counter-model in which the axiom does not hold, and showing how it depends on the absence of the frame condition. Note that the connective in **.3** and **.4** is $<$, not $\rightarrow$. (This exercise is quite challenging.)

As an appendix to this section, here is a table of some of the modal systems discussed in this chapter, summarising their axioms and frame conditions.

Table 6.1: Some popular modal systems

System	Axioms	Frame conditions
K	**K**	
D	**K, D**	serial
T	**K, T**	reflexive
S4	**K, T, 4**	preorder
S4.2	**K, T, 4, .2**	directed set
S4.3	**K, T, 4, .3**	total preorder
S5	**K, T, 4, B**	equivalence relation

6.5 MODAL REALISM AND FIRST ORDER LOGIC

In modal logic, to say whether a sentence is true or false we have to specify a world at which it is evaluated (or in the case of necessitive or possible statements, to quantify over such worlds). This introduces a parameter into a sentence, without which it cannot be evaluated as true or false. This parameter is not expressed in the logical language itself; it is part of the model. But it may have reminded the reader of the way in which, in predicate logic, predicates combine with arguments before they can get a truth value. Instead of saying that ϕ is true in w, we could almost say that ϕ (w) is true. However, the language of modal logic as we defined it does not allow us to say this.

There is also a conceptual difference between individuals, which we can name and point to, and worlds, whose ontological status is more elusive. We have used them as constructs for our semantics, but do we really think of them as things we can point to like Mars or Pluto? Some modal logicians, notably David Lewis, have adopted a position of 'modal realism', in which other worlds are as real as ours except that we do not happen to be in them – but most are more reticent.[27] However, the similarity between worlds and arguments is an important one, and in this section we will explore it by means of a useful tool: a logical translation which shows the correspondence between modal logic and a subset of first order logic.

This translation algorithm is known as the **standard translation** (from modal logics to first order logic). In outline: a basic proposition in modal logic is translated as a predicate letter of FOQT,[28] taking as its argument the world x in which the proposition is true. The clauses for propositional connectives are straightforward, and only negation and conjunction are given here. Finally, the clauses for necessities and possibilities involve the binary predicate S, representing the accessibility relation, and the modal operators are then translated into quantifiers on variables representing the accessible worlds. In the notation given here, T_x represents the translation function itself, from formulas of modal logic evaluated at x, to wffs of FOQT.

(6.8) 1. $T_x(p) = P(x)$
      2. $T_x(\neg\phi) = \neg T_x(\phi)$
      3. $T_x(\phi \wedge \psi) = T_x(\phi) \wedge T(\psi)$
      4. $T_x(\Diamond\phi) = \exists y(S(x,y) \wedge T_y(\phi))$
      5. $T_x(\Box\phi) = \forall y(S(x,y) \rightarrow T_y(\phi))$

In the translation into FOQT, the accessibility relation, which in modal logic is part of the model, is represented in the logical language itself (as the binary predicate S). It is thus possible to express facts about frames, and hence conditions on frames, as formulas in the logical language. For example, the condition of reflexivity (for axiom **T**) can be written as $\forall x S(x, x)$.[29] Similar formulae can straightforwardly be provided for symmetry, transitivity, seriality, convergence and linearity.

There are some conditions on frames which cannot be expressed as any first order formula, however. One well-known one is the condition of irreflexivity – that $S(x, x)$ does not hold for any x. This was mentioned as a condition which has been proposed for temporal logic. Another example is continuity, a property similar to density that, again, is often postulated for temporal logics.[30] There are also properties proposed for non-temporal modal logics which, similarly, cannot be expressed as first order formulas. A class of frames that can be defined by first order formulas is called **elementary**; most of the modal logics of interest to linguists are characterised by elementary frames, though this is not true of modal logics in general.

The standard translation also enables us to better understand the relationship between axioms and frame conditions. Many of the axioms discussed in this chapter involve iterated modalities, which in turn involve worlds that are several 'hops' or steps in the accessibility relation from w_0. In terms of the standard translation, iterated modalities correspond to **composition** of the S relation (Chapter 3). For a formula $\Box\Box\phi$, for example, we have to consider the current world w_0, an accessible world w_1, and a further world w_2 that is accessible to w_1. We can describe the relationship of w_2 to w_0 as being $S{\circ}S(w_0, w_2)$ – S composed with itself.[31]

Since relation composition can be expressed in first order logic, this composed relation needed for the standard translation of **4** can be restated in the logical language as follows:

(6.9) $T_x(\Box\Box\phi) = \forall y \, \forall z(S(x, y) \rightarrow (S(y, z) \rightarrow T_z(\phi)))$
       $= \forall z(S{\circ}S(x, z) \rightarrow T_z(\phi))$

In S4, this composition $S{\circ}S$ is reduced to S by transitivity, so the translation of $\Box\Box\phi$ reduces to the translation of $\Box\phi$.

We can generalise this composition of the S relation from two steps to any number of steps, and write S'' for $S_1{\circ}S_2{\circ}\ldots\ldots S_n$. In this scheme of things, S^1 will be the plain old accessibility relation S, and we can define S^0 as the identity relation on worlds. (Note that this is not the same as a reflexive accessibility relation.)[32]

We can now use this apparatus to throw some light on the relationship between modal axioms and conditions on frames. Up to now we have been treating this in a piecemeal fashion – introducing axioms and then producing out of nowhere a frame condition which validates them – and the reader may have been wondering if there is some more general principle behind this.

Let us first revisit some of the modal axioms used in this chapter. Generally speaking, they have the following format. The superscripts indicate the number of occurrences, which may be zero.

(6.10) $\Diamond^h\Box^i\phi \rightarrow \Box^j\Diamond^k\phi$

That is to say, the diamonds, if any, occur on the outside of the boxes, if any.[33]

For axioms of the form in (6.10), there is an elegant rule connecting them to their corresponding frame conditions – the **general axiom**, formulated by Lemmon and Scott (1977).[34] The frame conditions can be stated in the following form, where each superscript represents the degree of composition of S, as just described. Again the superscript may be zero, indicating the identity relation.

(6.11) $(S^h(w, x) \land S^i(w, y)) \rightarrow (S^i(x, y) \land S^k(y, z))$

Note, first, that if we set all the superscripts to 1, then (6.10) is exactly the convergence axiom **C** (or **.2**, p. 114), and (6.11) gives exactly the frame condition of convergence corresponding to S4.2.

Let us now check how the system works with S4. In this case, in (6.10), both h and k are set to 0. In terms of (6.11), this means that w = x and y = z, so we are dealing with just two worlds, for which we can use the metasymbols wx and yz. Now $i = 1$ and $j = 2$, so on the left side of (6.11) wx is related to yz by S^2 or S∘S, while on the right side the same worlds are related simply by S. This gives us exactly the condition for a transitive relation: S∘S reduces to S.

The reader might like to play with the corresponding results for **T**, **D** and **B**.

Finally, let us go back to the question of referring to particular worlds. It has already been mentioned that pure modal logic does not have the expressivity to do this, and it is not clear that we would necessarily want to for modality in natural language. However, the case is different with time expressions and, as was discussed in section 6.4.5, it is possible to enrich the language of temporal logic with **nominals**, propositions which hold in exactly one world. One can think of nominals as timestamps or, since they are propositions, perhaps something more like a universal talking clock: 'The time is now exactly . . .', with all relevant co-ordinates explicitly specified. Nominals are usually written using the letters i, j and so on, to distinguish them from ordinary propositional letters. An expression such as $i \rightarrow p$ can be used to mean that p holds at the point in time referenced by i (i.e. it holds when i does, though not necessary only then, as it is not a bi-implication).

This facility for referring to particular times (or worlds, if desired) leads to this being termed a **hybrid logic**: it combines characteristics of predicate logic, where elements of the model can be directly referenced by an expression in the formal language, with pure modal logic, where worlds or times only appear in the metalanguage.

It is common to exploit this bridge between language and model by introducing at least two further operators. The first is the satisfaction operator @ , where $@_i \phi$ means that ϕ holds at the world referenced by i: or in the metalanguage introduced in this chapter, $w_i \Vdash \phi$.

The second, ↓, treats nominals as variables rather than constants. The expression ↓x binds x to the current world (informally, it creates a nominal x which references the current world). We can then find our way back to this world at a later stage simply by repeating the same variable x.

It is possible to enrich hybrid logics with further operators, but we will not explore these here.

The greater expressive power of hybrid logics compared to pure modal logics becomes clear when we use the standard translation. While modal logic translates into a subset of pure first order logic, hybrid logic translates into first order logic with equality. (Recall that pure first order logic cannot express equality.) This is because the @ operator can be used to express the equality of worlds. If i and j are nominals, then $@_i j$ means that the world referenced by i is the same world that is referenced by j.

Here are the clauses that need to be added to the standard translation for modal logic to give the standard translation for a hybrid logic with @ and ↓:

(6.12) 1. $T_w(@, \phi) = T_w(\phi)[i/w]$
        2. $T_w(\downarrow i \phi) = T_w(\phi)[w/i]$

These clauses are interesting because they show how the two operators complement each other. @ uses an expression in the language to pick out a point in the model, while ↓ starts with a point in the model and uses it to define an expression in the language. In the translation into first order logic, where worlds are represented by terms in the logical language, the translations of @ and ↓ simply flip between the variable representing the world w and the variable representing the nominal i.

Furthermore, the translation of a hybrid logic is able to express conditions for non-elementary frames. For example the condition for an irreflexive frame can be expressed by the formula $i \rightarrow \Box \neg i$, where i is a nominal. It states that if w_i is the reference of i, then any world accessible to w_i satisfies $\neg i$, and is therefore not w_i.

Although the focus here has been on the usefulness of hybrid logic for tense logic, it is not particularly linked to tense logic and is applicable to modal logic in general, with many other applications. Another one that is of interest to linguists is its used in knowledge representation formalisms. It can, for example, be used to describe the feature structures used in unification-based frameworks such as Head-driven Phrase Structure Grammar (HPSG), with the ↓ operator enabling structure sharing.

It should be clear from this last section that the connection between modal logics and predicate logic provided by the standard translation is a very useful one; it enables us to treat the frame semantics of modal logic with the same tools used for predicate logic and relation algebra (see Chapter 3). It is the purpose of this book to provide not only an overview of different families of logics, such as the modal family in this chapter, but also to explore relationships between them, and this method of translation is often a useful tool for doing so. Later we will see how modal logics can be related by similar translations to some non-classical logics (Chapter 10).

Arthur Prior

A philosopher and pioneer of modal logic. Prior is best known for his temporal logic, but his importance in the development of possible worlds semantics in general is now acknowledged. One point of interest, for such a major figure, is the extent to which he learnt logic from his own reading, in the relative isolation of his native New Zealand, though he eventually settled in Oxford. He was a very popular teacher, who was a major influence on philosophical logic in New Zealand, the UK and the United States.

EXERCISE 6.5.0.1

1. Translate axioms **4** and **B** into first order logic using the standard translation. Check that they combine with the first order expression of the corresponding frame conditions to give a tautology.
2. Consider the unary $@_i$ operator in hybrid logic as a modality. Is it (i) normal, and (ii) positive?

NOTES

1. Philip Pullman, *The Golden Compass*.
2. 'There is no one logical notion of necessity, nor consequently of possibility. If this conclusion is valid, the subject of modality ought to be banished from logic, since propositions are simply true or false . . .' (from a paper read by Russell to the Oxford Philosophical Society in 1905). Russell's observation about the variety of modal notions will be discussed shortly.
3. There are several Lewises associated with modal logic and possible worlds. In particular, C. I. Lewis should not be confused with David Lewis, whose views will be discussed later; still less with the writer C. S. Lewis, an important figure in what is sometimes called 'possible worlds fiction'.
4. This apparent weakness was one reason why the whole idea of modal logic continued to come under attack, notably from Quine.
5. Wittgenstein's (1922) actual words in the Tractatus: 'To understand a proposition is to know what is the case if it is true' [4.024]; and 'The world is everything that is the case' [1].
6. Carnap (1947). There were some precursors, notably Leibniz.
7. This presentation of modal logic as classical logic with a modal component 'added' was developed by Lemmon.
8. Not to be confused with other senses of 'dynamic logic'!
9. Obligations can be relative to agents (in most countries, for example, citizens and non-citizens have different rights and obligations), but this can be handled by conditionals. For example, $\forall x(\text{Citizen}(x) \rightarrow \Box\text{Pay}(x, \text{tax}))$.
10. The notation S comes from the literature on substructural logics; I believe it is in honour of the Lewis systems, S1–5.
11. Lewis himself favoured the systems S2 and S3, but modern study has focused much more on S4 and S5.
12. This is for obscure historical reasons, though the connection with 'truth' is a useful mnemonic. In some books it is also called **M**, for equally obscure reasons. This is part of the fun of modal logic, guessing what all the abbreviations mean. **T** seems to be more usual in recent work.
13. $\Box$ and $\Diamond$ are often written L and M respectively, for example in Hughes and Cresswell (1996) and Zeman (1973). In deontic logic (Von Wright 1951) they are often written O and P (for obligatory and permissible), sometimes with F (forbidden) added for ¬P. Epistemic and doxastic logics (see especially Hintikka 1962) often use K (knows) and B (believes), subscripted with the name of a cognitive agent. (These are the 'necessity operators'; the dual possibility operators are denoted P and C respectively.) The usual notation for temporal operators, derived from Prior, has already been given.
14. In propositional modal logic, the scope of modal operators normally consists of propositional formulas, and that is what will be done in this chapter. We can replace the propositional formulas by formulas of first order logic or lambda expressions of type *tt provided that* ϕ has no free variables – that is, the formulas are closed sentences and any variables are bound within ϕ. Otherwise our modal logic is no longer propositional, and the com-

plications mentioned in the introduction will come into play. See the next chapter for discussion of these.

15. Not all logicians approach axiomatisation in this way; one branch of enquiry aims at the most concise formulation of a system, using as few axioms as possible. Meredith (see Haack (1978)) showed that it is possible to formulate the whole content of classical logic with one long formula as its only axiom. However, it is not a formula that gives most of us much insight into the classical connectives. There is often a trade-off between mathematical concision and intuitive clarity, and we will normally opt for the latter.

16. The weakest system of complete modalisation is S3, which has a maximum length of five non-negative modal operators. Although originally Lewis' favourite system, it is not normal and also does not include **T**, and it is not so often encountered for these reasons. S4 reduces the count to three; we will shortly see a logic which reduces it to two; and S5 reduces it to one. It can be shown that any further additions to S5 result in 'modal collapse' – in effect, reducing the number of modal operators that actually contribute anything to zero.

17. There is also a modal system including **B** but not **4**; it is known, not surprisingly, as B. As a historical note, the label is derived from Brouwer, the founder of intuitionism (Chapter 10).

18. In Kripke semantics this does not completely enable us to identify worlds, as two distinct worlds may have exactly the same true propositions.

19. There is an asymmetry in English and other languages between 'since' and 'until': the end condition ϕ of 'until' may never hold, in which case ψ can presumably hold forever.

20. See Bobzien (2014).

21. Zeman (1973).

22. Also called **H**, and, even more confusingly, **D** after Diodorus.

23. There is a complication here, which is that in S4.3 time is dense. A Diodorean system with discrete time, which is what Prior was actually after, requires further 'tweaking'; consequently, the name Diodorean is often given to systems slightly stronger than S4.3. See Zeman (op. cit.) for details.

24. Also known as **C**, for convergence.

25. Namely Hintikka (S4), Lenzen (S4.2), Van der Hoek (S4.3), Kutschera (S4.4). See Hendricks and Symons (2014) for references.

26. This contrast has been present since early explorations of S4 and S5. Carnap, who was interested chiefly in alethic modality, strongly advocated S5, while Gödel, for example, who was interested in the idea of truth as provability, was responsible for much of the early interest in S4. (More on this in Chapter 10.) However, the contrast should not be thought of as too absolute, as there are epistemic logicians who advocate S5 and alethic logicians who support S4.

27. At the opposite extreme from Lewis, one may regard a possible world as simply the set of propositions which are given the value true by a particular valuation. Kripke (1980) himself regards the language of possible worlds as conceptually useful, but adds that they are postulated as a technical tool, not 'discovered with telescopes'.

28. You will notice that it is capitalised in the process.

29. It is quite common to see frame conditions expressed using first order logic in expositions of the semantics of modal logic, though in the earlier part of the chapter we have not done so, to make it clear that we were using metalanguage.

30. The difference is that between the rational and real numbers. The rational numbers are dense, while the real numbers are also continuous.

31. Recall the definition of composition of relations: for two relations R and S, $\langle x, y \rangle \in$ R∘S iff $\exists z \, \varepsilon \, D$ such that $R(x,z) \wedge S(z,y)$.

32. In the algebra of binary relations under the operation of composition, the identity relation is an identity in the algebraic sense: $id \circ R = R \circ id = R$.

33. This is true of all the logics considered in this chapter, though not of all modal logics in general. The family of modal logics conforming to the opposite pattern, with boxes on the outside, are known as the Sobocinsky systems. I do not know of any applications of these to linguistics.

34. See Garson (2013).

CHAPTER 7

WORLDS AND INDIVIDUALS

I dwell in Possibility -
A fairer House than Prose[1]

7.1 INTRODUCTION

The previous chapter explored a number of different modal systems, but only for propositional logic, without reference to individuals or quantification. This enabled us to explore ideas of modality and temporality in relative isolation. In this chapter, we reintroduce the logic of individuals, predicates and quantifiers and combine it with the modal operators. We will see that the interactions between the two can be important, both in logic and in language.

We will, however, continue to assume that we are dealing with normal modal logics, defined on top of a non-modal 'base' (last chapter), and that furthermore this non-modal base will be classical. We are, therefore, still dealing with 'extensions' of classical logic. However, instead of classical propositional logic, this will be classical predicate logic – primarily first order, though we will also discuss some ideas from Montague, whose system combined modal logic with the higher order logic of Chapter 5.

Quantified modal logic has a long history. As already remarked, Aristotle's treatment of modality was bound up with quantification; he did not make use of purely propositional logic. Some issues arising from this were taken up by his successors and interpreters in the Middle Ages, with important contributions made by Abelard and Buridan. Medieval logic has a reputation for being boring – 'scholastic' in the worst sense – but both of these seem to have been highly charismatic individuals who liked to live dangerously: Abelard is known for his romance with his student Heloïse, while Buridan seems to have preferred risky liaisons with the wives of powerful people.

The modern rediscovery of quantified modal logic was pioneered by Carnap and Barcan in the 1940s.[2] Later, the widespread acceptance of Kripke's frame semantics led to a flurry of developments on the semantic side, for quantified as for propositional modal logic.

As usual, we will begin with an informal discussion of some of the issues that arise.

Peter Abelard

One of the most brilliant and colourful figures in the medieval revival of logic in western Europe associated with scholastic theology, a combination that got him into trouble several times with the church. Abelard is best known, however, for his romance with his young student Heloïse, whose guardian took drastic measures to stop the relationship. The subsequent correspondence between the two lovers is one of the most famous literary works from the period.

7.1.1 POSSIBLE INDIVIDUALS

We start by revisiting the universe of discourse, or set of all individuals. What individuals are admissible for inclusion? In the early days of modern logic, there was much debate about the status of historical figures, now dead, such as Socrates, and of mythical figures such as Pegasus. The examples came from ancient discussions of the same issue – in what sense, if any, can these figures be said to exist, and if not, how can we meaningfully speak about them?

One prominent figure in these early debates was the Austrian philosopher Alexius Meinong. Meinong developed a theory of 'objects of thought', and maintained that this class should take into consideration objects which do not exist as empirical data in the world. His treatment suggested that we need to keep in balance at least two ideas – a universe of things that actually exist in the straightforward sense of the term, and things which do not but which we can conceive and, importantly for linguists, might wish to talk about. The first set is a subset of the second set, and the two are sometimes referred to as the 'inner' and 'outer' sets of objects.

This leads immediately to a question about the meaning of quantifiers. Recall Quine's insistence that what things could be quantified over (i.e. could be the value of a variable) is the acid test of ontological commitment. This is particularly apparent in the name of the existential quantifier (though by duality it should apply to the universal quantifier as well). If we allow the quantifiers to range over the outer set, then we seem to be asserting existence of something which might not, intuitively, exist. One can then divide the universal set into objects which exist (in the actual world) and those which do not. This gives us formulas such as $\exists x.\text{Exist}(x)$ and, even more puzzlingly, $\exists x.\neg\text{Exist}(x)$. A further problem here is that many philosophers, including Hume, Kant and Russell, have denied that existence can be used as a predicate, in the same way that blueness or snoring can; in fact one of the merits of the existential quantifier, according to this school of thought, is that we can express existence without making it a predicate, and thus avoid precisely these puzzles. It reduces sentences like 'Pegasus does not exist' to a mismatch between linguistic form and logical form.

But it is also possible that part of this problem is due to ambiguities in our use of the English verb 'exist'. To say that the quantifiers range over all possible individuals is an intelligible notion, and to say of some of these objects that they are actual in some world and at some time is also an intelligible notion. We could gloss the existential quantifier as 'for some possible entity', and in place of the predicate Exist/1 we could use something like Actual/1. Then the problematic formulae would state that some possible entities are actual and some are not. It is common to say of elements that are not actual, that they 'subsist' rather than exist.[3]

We will label this position as **possibilist**, though this terminology would be anachronistic as applied to Meinong himself. Since the existence predicate, if we are going to use one, is considered a rather special kind of predicate, it is normally given the special notation E!. (The exclamation mark is part of the notation, not my comment on the idea. It is omitted by many writers.) Thus the possibilist position as described above can be encoded $\exists x E!(x) \land \exists x \neg E!(x)$.

Meinong's approach was opposed by Russell, after some initial hesitation, and fell out of favour in the mainstream of classical predicate logic. This leaves us with the problem of how we can meaningfully talk about entities such as Pegasus or Socrates at all. Russell's highly influential proposal on this matter, along with some of its rivals, will be discussed in the next chapter.

There is also, however, a modal approach to the problem. If we have different worlds, it makes sense to say that the only individuals available in our world are those that actually exist in it, but that we have access to other worlds which, maybe, contain different individuals. This would seem straightforward enough when the worlds concerned are points of time; this deals with the 'Socrates' problem. Socrates is not part of the domain of individuals at the present time, but he was at a previous time, so at least past tense statements about him should be possible. And the 'Pegasus' problem is not very different, if some possible world allows for horses to have wings and to be used for rescuing maidens from sea monsters.

We can then ask whether a quantified formula ranges over the same individuals in our world and in other accessible worlds that we might talk about. If I make a statement about all Greeks in the present tense, that will presumably[4] not include Socrates, but if I make a similar statement in the past tense, it may do.

If this approach makes sense, then we allow for all kinds of objects, but, in any given sentence, we quantify only over objects which are actual in the world in which the sentence is to be evaluated. This is what we will call an **actualist** position.

7.1.2 OPAQUE CONTEXTS AND INTENSIONALITY

In previous chapters we have been taking denotation or reference[5] as the main ingredient of the interpretation of an expression. This works better for some types of expression than others. The interpretation of pronouns, for example, is little more than their denotation (him, her etc.). The same might seem to be true of proper names, and we will asssume this for the present. However, it is not true for many kinds of expression, such as Frege's famous example, 'the morning star' and 'the evening star'.

(7.1) 1. The morning star is the morning star.
      2. The morning star is the evening star.

The two definite descriptions have the same denotation, namely the planet Venus. The first sentence simply tells us that an object is identical to itself. The second, by contrast, is a piece of empirical information. The meanings of the morning star and the evening star do not give us this information, although it becomes evident once we have established the true denotation of the two expressions. It follows from this that the meaning of such an expression is not simply its denotation.

For Frege, the 'something missing' in a purely denotational account of meaning is what he labelled **sense** (*Sinn* in German), which he describes as a way of presenting the denotation, or that which enables us to determine the denotation. The sense of a definite description (like 'the morning star') is what enables us to pick out the right object if we have the necessary knowledge of the world. It can also be that we understand the sense of the expression without knowing its denotation (for example 'the most beautiful woman in the world'), or even that it might not have a denotation in the actual world ('the Lord of the Nazgul', or 'the wife of the Pope'). But if a denotation is available in the actual world, then the sense of the expression will point us to it.

The terminology employed here may give the impression that sense is something more subjective than denotation, but this was not how Frege conceived it. The fact that natural language expressions have subjective connotations, which are not part of their objective, descriptive meaning, is something that he was aware of, as were many of his predecessors,[6] but he called that *Färbung* (colouring), or *Vorstellung* (representation or presentation) – something distinct from *Sinn*. Another component of meaning that he discussed was the pragmatic effect of an utterance, or what we might call its illocutionary force, which he termed *Kraft* (force). These are all important, but by sense, Frege meant something objective rather than psychological, and cognitive rather than performative; to use his own metaphor, it has the same kind of reality as the real image of an object formed by a lens, which is something objective and public, however much it may give rise to the private visual (retinal) images of different observers.

Sentences too have a sense as well as a denotation. Frege was the first to argue that the denotation of a sentence is its truth value, a view which we have been assuming. The sense of a sentence is the content of the thought (*Gedanke*) it expresses, by grasping which we can determine the truth value if we are in possession of the necessary facts. The traditional term in English for this conceptual content of a sentence is **proposition**, and it will be so called here.

The importance of the distinction between sense and reference in linguistics is largely to do with substitutability and compositionality. Let us have a look first at the way the denotations of individual terms and sentences fit together.

(7.2) The most powerful man in the world has two children.

If we assume that the most powerful man in the world is the President of the United States, then at the time of writing, the truth value of this sentence is 1 (true). If we substitute another expression with the same denotation, such as 'Barack Obama', the truth value will be unchanged. On the other hand, if we change the denotation of 'the most powerful man in the world' – for example we decide that it is in fact the Pope – then the truth value will change accordingly.

This substitutability of expressions with the same denotation without change in truth value is what we expect in mathematics. If we have the expression 121 in an formula, and substitute it by 11^2, the value of the formula does not change. And this is how it normally works in English if we substitute expressions with the same denotation. However, as Frege observed, it is not always the case.

(7.3) 1. Anna wants to meet the most powerful man in the world.
       2. Anna wants to meet the President of the United States.
       3. Rudolf knows that 121 is greater than 100.
       4. Rudolf knows that the square of 11 is greater than 100.

In these examples, this principle of substitutability or **extensionality** does not hold. In the first pair, Anna may not be aware that the two expressions denote the same individual – and even if she is, one or the other might be a very misleading way of describing her desire, which may be entirely focused on powerful people, or entirely focused on Americans. Either way, one sentence might be judged true and the other false. Similarly the truth value of the second pair depends on the state of Rudolf's mathematical knowledge, not just on the truth value of the embedded mathematical statement. Thus in these examples the principle of extensionality fails, in the first case for two individual concepts, in the second case for two propositions. Contexts such as these were isolated by Frege – especially the second, in which a sentence is the complement of a verb of **propositional attitude** – as being exceptional, in that the component parts could only be substituted if their sense, not just their denotation, was identical. These contexts were later labelled **opaque** (by Quine) or **intensional** by Carnap, who was responsible for the next major step forward in analysing them – using possible worlds semantics.

In Carnap's terminology denotations are called **extensions**, and senses are modelled by a formal construct which he calls **intensions**. To understand Carnap's proposal, it may useful to think first of times. Consider the denotation (extension) of the expression 'the President of the United States'. Clearly this depends on the year being referred to. If you name a year (from 1789, when the presidency of the United States was inaugurated), and if I have the necessary knowledge of American history, I can give you the name of the president. Thus the individual concept is a function from times to individuals. However, we can extend the same notion to 'what if' states of affairs, which might have turned up presidents who never in fact occupied the White House. Some of them would be close to the real world, differing only in a few votes going the other way. Others might be more far-fetched. In each of these possible worlds, however, some member of the domain of individuals is picked out as being the American president. In other words intensions are *functions from possible worlds to extensions*.

An expression like 'the President of the United States' is a **definite description** – it picks out an individual, but indirectly, as 'president' is really a common noun, not a name. However, the situation is different with proper names (individual constants). Currently, most logicians follow Kripke's suggestion that a name, once applied to an individual, always designates the same individual regardless of worlds and times. This captures certain differences in the semantic behaviour of names and definite descriptions, notably in opaque contexts (to be discussed shortly).

With predicate logic we have to consider expressions which are not sentences. For first order quantified modal logic, which is our main concern here, the other expressions we need are predicates. If we are using a type-theoretic language, the same principle can be applied to the many other types of expression that type theory provides.

The extension of a predicate is a set; but what set it picks out depends on the world or time. Take the set of Germans as an example. If we take 950 as the time, the set of Germans will be the set including, among others, Otto the Great; if we take 1500 it will be a set including Martin Luther; in 1800 it will include Beethoven. The intension of the predicate German/1 is thus a function from times to sets – or more generally worlds to sets, as we might want to include worlds where J. F. Kennedy really was a Berliner.

It may be convenient to summarise here these common types of expression and the names given to their intensions. The intension of a sentence is called a **proposition**. The words 'sentence' and 'proposition' are often used as synonyms in classical logic (for example what we called 'propositional logic' only involves sentences); but when we are dealing with modal logic and intensions, the distinction becomes important. The intension of a one-place predicate is a **property**. The intension of a relation (with two or more places) is known as a **relation in intension**. Relations in intension work in essentially the same way as properties, as you will see in the exercises. The intension of a definite description is an **individual concept**. Names, which do not have distinct intensions at all, are known as **rigid designators**.

This stock of concepts is enough for first order formulas and even for the most commonly used expressions considered in the chapter on higher order logic. In Montague's intensional logic (IL), a higher order modal logic, there is a greater variety of types, including generalised quantifiers and modifiers of various kinds. Montague introduced intension and extension operators, $^\wedge$ and $^\vee$ respectively, so that $^\wedge\alpha$ is the intension of an expression α, and $^\vee\alpha$ is the extension of an expression α, of any type. In Montague these operators are stipulated for particular types of expression, but the ideas can be incorporated into a more principled approach to intensional and extensional expressions in grammar.[7]

EXERCISE 7.1.2.1

1. Describe the intensions of (i) the unary predicate 'is an All Black', (ii) the binary relation 'is bigger than', as applied to countries, (iii) the generalised quantifier 'most Greeks'. Give examples of how the extensions of these expressions have varied historically with time.

2. You would possibly agree that the sentence, 'As the sun set, the morning star lit the sky', sounds anomalous. If so, why might this be considered an intensional context?

3. Account for the expression 'intensional adjective' used to describe the adjective 'former' (Chapter 5).

The Vienna Circle

A group of academics at the university of Vienna in the late 1920s and 30s, gathered around Moritz Schlick. They were science-oriented philosophers who combined empiricism with the logical analysis made possible by the then new development of modern logic. They are best known for logical positivism, an extreme version of Wittgenstein's realism which states that a (non-analytic) proposition is meaningless unless you can verify it. (By contrast, Karl Popper argued that scientific method is based on falsifying statements.) In particular, this was considered to rule out most traditional metaphysics as merely aesthetic. The most important member of the school who figures in this book is Carnap, who was particularly trenchant in using metaphysical almost as a synonym for meaningless. He once described metaphysicians as would-be musicians who happened not to be musical. The interests of the Vienna Circle were shared by a small group in Berlin, notably Hans Reichenbach; this is known as the Berlin Circle. Both circles were disrupted by the Nazi rise to power; Schlick was shot dead by a student, possibly a Nazi sympathiser, while Carnap, Reichenbach and others moved to the United States.

7.1.3 PUZZLES WITH QUANTIFICATION

Ampliation

When talking about other times and other possible worlds, there is often an ambiguity in the intended reference of an NP. Consider the following examples.

(7.4) 1. A thousand years ago, everybody believed that there were exactly seven planets.
   2. In Middle Earth, some people are very little and live in holes in the ground.
   3. Most Russians were very young when the Soviet Union collapsed.

The reference of the subject NPs 'everybody' and 'some people' is in principle ambiguous. In the first sentence, 'everybody' is naturally taken as referring to people alive in the eleventh century. In the second, too, the people referred to are presumably hobbits, not people from our world taking a break in the Shire. These interpretations are clear from the context; the adjustment of the NP reference is done automatically and nobody other than semanticists would probably notice the ambiguity. In the third sentence, however, it is the other way round: the noun 'Russians' has to refer to the set of Russians alive at the present time for the sentence to have its natural meaning, concerned with the passage of time. If we shifted the reference to the Russians alive in 1991, we seem to be painting a very different picture, of a country which at that time happened to have very young demographic profile.

This problem was discussed by medieval logicians, who pointed out that this ambiguity was responsible for some complications in modal and temporal reasoning. The shift of reference of the subject NP to its denotation at the time the sentence is talking about was called **ampliation**, as it can be thought of as an extension of the domain under discussion. The examples show that sometimes ampliation is desirable, while at other times, as in the third example, it is not. Often only the intended sense of the sentence can tell us whether to ampliate or not.

De dicto and de re

During the group stages of the last rugby world cup, the following expression in a news report caused me to do a double take.

(7.5) All three teams could qualify.

The reason was that, as in many competitions, the rules state that exactly two teams qualify from each group, and I wondered for a moment if the rules had been changed. In fact there was just an ambiguity in the sentence, and the usual rules applied, Scotland being the unfortunate team to miss out. The two possible meanings can be paraphrased as follows, the intended meaning being the second one.

(7.6) 1. It could end up that all three teams qualify.
       2. Each of the three teams has it in them to qualify.

This kind of ambiguity is very common when modality and quantification meet. The first paraphrase is meant to suggest that we are talking about the possibility that a particular state of affairs could materialise. It is like taking a sentence (describing the state of affairs) and putting a possibility operator in front of it, much as in the previous chapter. The second is more difficult, but it is clear that what we are talking about is the three teams, and what we say about them is that they all have a certain potential property: that of being a participant in the knock-out phases. In other words, in the first paraphrase the modal operator modifies the content of a non-modal sentence, while in the second at has to do with things and their properties. For this reason, the two readings are called *de dicto* and *de re*, respectively.[8]

The idea that an object can have possible properties (potentiality), or necessary qualities which somehow define the 'essence' of the object, has had a long history in philosophy. It has also come under attack, however, in modern philosophy. Quine, in particular, used the whole phenomenon of *de re* readings – which he regarded as incoherent – as part of his attack on modal logic. Whether he is right or not, they do lead to complications both in linguistic semantics and logical inference. For example, it seems likely that Aristotle took quantified modal sentences as fundamentally *de re* (we will return to this question below). At least, he is interpreted this way by Richard of Campsall, one of his most systematic medieval followers, whose attempts to construct a system of modal syllogisms on this basis ran into problems.

The whole issue of *de dicto* and *de re* will be discussed further after the formal definitions have been introduced in the next section.

The Barcan formula and its relatives

Given that $\square$ and $\lozenge$ are really quantifiers too, they should distribute with $\forall$ and $\exists$ respectively; that is, it should be the case that $\square\forall x\phi \leftrightarrow \forall x\square\phi$ (and similarly for the existential quantifier and $\lozenge$). This is what happens with ordinary quantifiers: $\forall x\forall y\phi \leftrightarrow \forall y\forall x\phi$, and so on. However, there is a complication here, which was discovered by Ruth Barcan (1946).

To see this problem, look at the following pairs of sentences, which involve quantifiers and modal operators – in this case, temporal.

(7.7) 1. (a) Somebody will one day land on the moons of Jupiter.
       (b) There is somebody who will one day land on the moons of Jupiter.
     2. (a) Everybody will always remember the Beijing Olympics.
       (b) It will always be the case that everybody remembers the Beijing Olympics.

In each pair, the second represents a reading which is not the most natural, and raises questions. The second sentence in the first pair suggests that the person described is already born, which at the date of writing is unlikely. In the second pair, the sentence extends to generations who are not yet born and never even witnessed the Beijing Olympics.

- Write formulae representing the two readings for each pair.

Clearly, this involves the question of ampliation, discussed in a previous subsection. However, there is another problem involved here. If the first reading of each pair implies the second, then the first example implies that any subject of a future sentence is already present in the current world. The second example implies that future time will not introduce any individuals beyond those who exist now, and who remember the Beijing Olympics.

The problem noted by Barcan is that these implications are valid by the normal quantifier rules, if modal operators are treated as quantifiers. To be precise, the implications in (7.8) are valid. They are two different ways of expressing the same formula (by duality); in either form, it is known as the **Barcan formula**.

(7.8) 1. $\lozenge\exists x\phi \rightarrow \exists x\lozenge\phi$
     2. $\forall x\square\phi \rightarrow \square\forall x\phi$

In the examples given the operators were temporal, but this phenomenon extends to modality in general:

(7.9) 1. All men are necessarily error-prone / necessarily all men are error-prone.
     2. There could be somebody four metres tall with three heads / there is somebody who could be four metres tall with three heads.
       (a) Write formulae for these sentences and check that they are examples of the same problem.

(b) As we pass from the current world to any accessible world, what does this imply about the set of individuals available in that world? Is it bigger or smaller than the set of individuals in the current world, or is there no correlation?

(c) Write out the converse of the Barcan formula (which is known as the **converse Barcan formula**). Answer the last question in relation to the converse Barcan formula.

The issues arising from this section will also be discussed further after the formal definitions for quantified modal logic have been stated.

EXERCISE 7.1.3.1

1. Is the following argument valid? (From Buridan, see Klima (2001).)
   (a) Nothing that is dead is an animal
   (b) Some men are dead
   (c) Therefore some men are not animals.

Find a term in the argument which is ampliated in one place where it occurs, and not in the other. Why does this matter?

7.2 SYNTAX OF QUANTIFIED MODAL LOGIC

As this chapter simply combines the modal logic of the previous chapter with the predicate logic described in the first part of the book, there is not a lot of syntax here that is actually new. Most of the complications come in the semantics. I will give the syntax for first order modal logic, and then discuss some of the additions that are needed for the higher order case.

The inductive definition for a language $\mathcal{L}$ of first order quantified modal logic is as follows. The non-logical vocabulary of the language consists of a set of individual constants, and a set of predicates P/n for each arity n. We also assume an infinite set of individual variables. Individual constants and variables together are known as **terms**.

(7.10) 1. If P/n is a predicate and $a_1, \ldots a_n$ are *terms*, then $P(a_1, \ldots a_n)$ is a wff in $\mathcal{L}$.
        2. If ϕ is a wff in $\mathcal{L}$ then so is $\neg\phi$.
        3. If ϕ and ψ are wffs in $\mathcal{L}$, then so are $(\phi \wedge \psi)$, $(\phi \vee \psi)$ and $(\phi \rightarrow \psi)$.
        4. If ϕ is a wff in $\mathcal{L}$ and x is a variable, then $\forall x\phi$ and $\exists x\phi$ are wffs in $\mathcal{L}$.
        5. If ϕ is a wff in $\mathcal{L}$, then $\Box\phi$ and $\Diamond\phi$ are wffs in $\mathcal{L}$.
        6. Nothing else is a wff in $\mathcal{L}$.

In clause 4, ϕ is the scope of the quantifier, which binds all free occurences of x in ϕ. In clause 5, ϕ is the scope of the modal operator. Note that these clauses together allow quantifiers to occur in the scope of modal operators and also vice versa. This is the most important thing to notice from this inductive definition.

For higher order quantified modal logic, the first clause is replaced by the standard definitions for well formed expressions of appropriate types; the remaining clauses are unchanged, except that 'wff' is replaced by 'wfe of type t'.

We may also wish to insert a clause for intension and extension operators, following Montague. Since intensions are functions from possible worlds to extensions, we need a new type s, which we can think of as standing for possible worlds. Intensional expressions are then of type $s\to\sigma$, where σ is the type of the corresponding extensional expression.

(7.11) 1. If α is a wfe of type σ, then $\wedge\,\alpha$ is a wfe of type $s\to\sigma$.
      2. If α is a wfe of type $s\to\sigma$, then $\vee\,\alpha$ is a wfe of type σ.

Notice that these clauses do not license expressions of type s, which would actually denote a world. As discussed in the previous chapter, this is not possible in pure modal logic. We will return to this in section 7.5.1.

It is also worth comparing the types in these definitions with those in the Rule of Function Application and rule of λ abstraction in Chapter 5. The similarity is not surprising as the intension operator involves creating a function, while the extension operator involves applying one (finding its value at the current world).

The new types require new domains of denotation. This is semantics rather than syntax, but it is convenient to deal with it here. The domains of denotation for the new types involve the set of worlds W. The domain for intensional types is then the set of functions from W to the domain of denotation of the normal type σ of the expression.

(7.12) 1. $D_{s\to\sigma} = D_\sigma^{\,w}$

7.3 SEMANTICS OF QUANTIFIED MODAL LOGIC

Again, this section consists mainly of combining ideas from modal logic with ideas from predicate logic. However, the interaction between the two is more complicated.

The simplest way to combine individuals with worlds is to combine a modal frame $\langle W, S\rangle$ with a domain of discourse D and an interpretation function I:

(7.13) A simple model $\mathcal{M}$ for a language $\mathcal{L}$ of first order quantified modal logic is a tuple $\langle W, S, D, I\rangle$, where
    1. W is a set of worlds
    2. $S \subseteq W \times W$ is a positive accessibility relation
    3. D is a set of individuals
    4. I is a function mapping individual constants in $\mathcal{L}$ to elements of D and predicates P/n of $\mathcal{L}$ to subsets of $D_1 \times D_2 \ldots \ldots \times D_n$.

In this semantics there is a single domain, so the same individuals are available for quantification regardless of which world we are in. This is known as the **constant domain** semantics, and corresponds to the possibilist approach discussed in the introduction to this chapter.

The (main) alternative to the constant domain semantics is to let the domain of individuals vary according to worlds; in principle, we can have a different universe of individuals for each world. We have seen that this is quite intuitive when worlds are interpreted as times. When talking about possible worlds without restriction, the idea of a set of universes can take on more of a science fiction quality. Instead of a universe, we are talking about several universes, which we could call the 'multiverse'.[9] This multiverse is modelled by a function δ from the set of worlds W to the powerset of D (the set of subsets of D). The subset of D which is the value of δ at a world w is the universe for w. The technical name for the multiverse interpretation of modal logic is the **varying domain** semantics. Since quantification is only over individuals that are actual in w, this corresponds to the actualist position in the introduction.[10]

We can therefore amend the definition of the model as follows:

(7.14) A model $\mathcal{M}$ for a language $\mathcal{L}$ of first order quantified modal logic = $\langle$W, S, D, δ, I$\rangle$

This coincides with a constant domain model if δ is a constant function whose value is D.

It is usual to write the domain which is the value of δ at w as D_w rather than $\delta(w)$.

There are some alternatives between the constant domain and varying domain semantics, which involve letting the domain vary but only within limits. Normally the constraints imposed are associated with the accessibility relation, so that the universes available at two connected worlds are in some sense similar. For example, if w can see another world v, we may want to require that all objects at w are also available in v (possibly along with others): D_w is a subset of D_v. Or we might require the opposite, that v contain no new objects that are not already present in w: this time, D_v is a subset of D_w.

(7.15) **Increasing domain model**: If S(w, v), then $D_w \subseteq D_v$.
        Decreasing domain model: If S(w, v), then $D_v \subseteq D_w$.

Whichever semantics we choose, formulae are evaluated with respect to a model $\mathcal{M}$ and a variable assignment g, as in first order logic, and also with respect to a distinguished world $w \in$ W, which we can take as the actual world. Thus the truth definition for basic formulae can be stated as follows. It differs from the first order definition in Chapter 4 only by the addition of w, as you might like to check.

(7.16) If $P(t_1, \ldots t_n)$ is a wff in $\mathcal{L}$,
        then $||P(t_1, \ldots t_n)||_{\mathcal{M},w,g} = 1$ iff $\langle I(t_1), \ldots I(t_n)\rangle_{\mathcal{M},w,g} \subseteq ||P||_{\mathcal{M},w,g}$

However, from now on we will prefer the notation introduced in the last chapter for frame semantics, which is easier to read and also brings out some important points. First the base case:

(7.17) If $P(t_1, \ldots t_n)$ is a wff in $\mathcal{L}$, then $w \Vdash_{\mathcal{M},g} P(t_1, \ldots t_n)$ iff $\langle I(t_1), \ldots I(t_n)\rangle \in ||P||_{\mathcal{M},w,g}$

Then the recursive truth definition proceeds as follows. The subscript on the ⊩ symbol keeps track of M and the variable assignment g, which is needed for interpreting the quantifiers (which are treated in exactly the same way as in Chapter 4).

(7.18) 1. If ϕ is a wff in $\mathcal{L}$, then $w \Vdash_{M,g} \neg\phi$ iff $w \nVdash_{M,g} \phi$
    2. If ϕ and ψ are wffs in $\mathcal{L}$, then
      (a) $w \Vdash_{M,g} \phi \wedge \psi$ iff $w \Vdash_{M,g} \phi$ and $w \Vdash_{M,g} \psi$.
      (b) $w \Vdash_{M,g} \phi \vee \psi$ iff $w \Vdash_{M,g} \phi$ or $w \Vdash_{M,g} \psi$.
      (c) $w \Vdash_{M,g} \phi \rightarrow \psi$ iff $w \nVdash_{M,g} \phi$ or $w \Vdash_{M,g} \psi$.
    3. If ϕ is a wff in $\mathcal{L}$ and x is a variable,
      then $w \Vdash_{M,g} \forall x\phi$ iff for every d in D_w, $w \Vdash_{M,g[x \to d]} \phi$.
    4. If ϕ is a wff in $\mathcal{L}$ and x is a variable,
      then $w \Vdash_{M,g} \exists x\phi$ iff for some d in D_w, $w \Vdash_{M,g[x \to d]} \phi$.
    5. If ϕ is a wff in $\mathcal{L}$, $w \Vdash_{M,g} \Box\phi$ iff for every v ∈ W such that S(w,v), $v \Vdash_{M,g} \phi$.
    6. If ϕ is a wff in $\mathcal{L}$, $w \Vdash_{M,g} \Diamond\phi$ iff for some v ∈ W such that S(w,v), $v \Vdash_{M,g} \phi$.

Apart from the modal operators at the end, these rules simply replicate those for the propositional connectives and first order quantifiers that we have seen before, with the addition of the ⊩ relation which tells us that the evaluation is taking place in the current world w. When the modal operators are involved, the evaluation involves other worlds v, accessible to w, just as in the previous chapter.

The notation brings out an important difference between the modal operators, whose evaluation involves more than one world, and the other connectives and quantifiers, where everything takes place in just one world. This is what makes the modal operators **intensional**, while the others are **extensional**. Recall that we are dealing here only with classical connectives, so implication is material implication and negation is Boolean negation. Both of these are truth functions (Chapter 2), which are purely extensional. We will later get to logics in which negation and implication (in particular) are intensional connectives, involving more than one point of evaluation.

7.4 SCOPE INTERACTION IN QUANTIFIED MODAL LOGIC

This section revisits some the problems of scopal interaction between modal operators and quantifiers.

Since the modal and intensional operators have scope (see the syntactic definitions above), one might expect scope ambiguities to arise between these operators, negation and quantifiers, and indeed this is what happens. Describe the ambiguities in the following sentences, and see if you can find a scopal ambiguity to account for them.

(7.19) She can not be serious.
(7.20) Somebody must lose his life.
(7.21) Somebody will walk on Mars.

The first involves scope interaction between a modal operator and negation, the other two between a quantifier and a modal operator (temporal in the last example).

- Translate the sentences into quantified modal logic. Try to find two different translations for each sentence, to bring out the ambiguities.
- What happens to the ambiguity in the first sentence if 'can not' is replaced by 'can't'?

The second type of scopal ambiguity – between a modal operator and a quantifier – is responsible for *de re* and *de dicto* readings.

In a *de re* reading the quantifier has widest scope, and the proposition is therefore read as a (modal) formula about individuals. The individuals are understood to have some potential, or to be under some necessity. In the second sentence, there is somebody who is marked out by fate as the victim in whatever situation is being described. In the final example, there is somebody whose destiny is to walk on Mars.

The *de dicto* readings, by contrast, give modally qualified statements about situations which may or must obtain, without saying anything in particular about their participants. The second sentence describes a situation necessarily involving a fatality, but it is not determined who that will be. In the final example a manned space flight to Mars is predicted, but says nothing about the flight crew (who may not even be born yet).

- Write the two readings of each sentence as formula of quantified modal logic, marking each as *de re* or *de dicto*.

Note that on a *de re* reading, the modal operator has scope over an open formula (a formula with a free variable), and therefore the modal formula is making an assertion about the referent of the free variable – the x of which it is true that x may qualify, or x must die. The free variable is only bound once we get outside the scope of the modal operator. On a *de dicto* reading, on the other hand, there is no free variable, as the variable is bound within the scope of the modal operator. The modal operator therefore scopes over a complete sentence.

Given that the distinction between *de re* and *de dicto* readings involves modality, one would expect it to crop up in 'opaque contexts', and indeed it does.

(7.22) 1. Bond knows that somebody is selling secrets to the Russians.
        2. Somebody is known by Bond to be selling secrets to the Russians.
        3. Bond is looking for the double agent.
        4. Bond is looking for a man with a blue raincoat.

On a *de dicto* reading, the first example does not imply that Bond has any idea of the identity of the person selling the secrets; he just knows that secrets are somehow being passed on. On the *de re* reading, which is naturally paraphrased by the second sentence,[11] there is a person x about whom Bond knows that he or she is in the pay of the Russians.

The last two examples concern the substitutability of two NPs in an opaque context. On a *de re* reading there is an individual, who can be described by either NP, for whom Bond is looking. In this case, the NPs are substitutable, and do not form part of the opaque context. On the *de dicto* reading, Bond is looking for somebody satisfying the appropriate description, and the two searches are not known (by Bond) to be equivalent.

Finally, note that the elements creating the opaque contexts in these sentences, 'knows' and 'is looking for' (= 'wants to find') can both be treated as modal operators (epistemic and bouletic respectively, as was seen in the previous chapter). The scopal interaction is therefore very similar to those described in the previous set of examples.

A final wrap-up on *de dicto* and *de re* readings. They have been characterised in this chapter in three different ways. As they are treated here, the three coincide, but it is worth keeping them conceptually distinct.

(7.23) **Scope**: A *de re* reading occurs when a modal operator falls within the scope of a quantifier. Otherwise the reading is *de dicto*.

      Substitutability: In opaque contexts, two expressions with the same denotation can only be substituted if the reading is *de re*.

      Predication: A *de re* reading predicates a potential or essential property of some entity.

7.4.1 MODAL SYLLOGISMS

Chapter 4 introduced non-modal (or **assertoric**) syllogisms and the associated square of quantification. The previous chapter introduced modal squares of quantification. What happens when the two are combined?

The issue is complicated by the difference between ***de dicto*** and ***de re*** readings, as was recognised by Aristotle's medieval commentators. While the interpretation of Aristotle is not certain, it seems that he may have taken ***de re*** readings as basic. Given the subject-predicate structure of Aristotle's logic, this is natural. It is also suggested by the contrast between the following two syllogisms.[12] Each of them is a version of Barbara in which just one of the premises, and the conclusion, are modalised.

(7.24) 1. All B is necessarily A
        2. All C is A
        3. Therefore all C is necessarily A

(7.25) 1. All B is A
        2. All C is necessarily B
        3. Therefore all C is necessarily A

Perhaps surprisingly, Aristotle regarded (7.24), in which the major premise is modalised, as valid, and (7.25), in which the minor premise is modalised, as invalid. However, if the modality is taken as a predicate modifier (i.e. *de re*), it is easy to see why Aristotle regarded the first as valid. The predicates [necessarily A] match up, making the schema a valid instance of Barbara. In (7.25), by contrast, the predicates [necessarily A] and [necessarily B] do not match up.

At any rate, most medieval logicians interpreted Aristotle's modal syllogisms as involving ***de re*** modality (see Lagerlund 2012). The fullest treatment of modal syllogisms is that of Buridan near the end of the period. For ***de re*** statements, Buridan combined the non-modal (assertoric) Square of Opposition with the modal one to

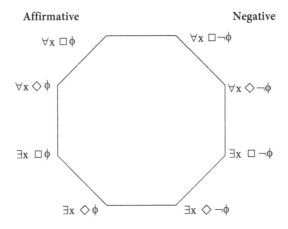

Figure 7.1   Buridan's Octagon of Opposition

get an octagon, which is inscribed ornately in some manuscripts of his work. It is depicted less aesthetically in Figure 7.1. The subject terms are assumed to be ampliated to include all possible referents.

As in Squares of Opposition, all the formulas diagonally opposite each other are contradictories. The top line formulae are contraries, as in the square, but in the octagon each of them has *three* contraries – the formulae in the first three lines on the opposite side. Similarly each formula in line 4 has three subcontraries – the formulae in the last three lines on the opposite side. (Recall that for contraries both statements cannot be simultaneously true, while for subcontraries they cannot be simultaneously false.) There are no named relationships between the two formulas on line 2, nor between those on line 3.

- Mark the contradictory, contrary and subcontrary relations on the diagram.
- In Figure 7.1 the negative statements on the right are written with the negation on the far right, next to ϕ. Rewrite them with the negation on the far left, so that they mean the same thing.
- In the traditional Squares of Opposition, each corner implies the corner below it (the subaltern relation). In the octagon, each corner implies all the nodes below it on the same side, with one exception on each side. What are the exceptions?

Jean Buridan

One of the major late scholastic philosophers, based in Paris, whose major interests were logic, physics and, apparently, the wives of powerful people. His work has been remarkably neglected for someone so influential at the time, and most of it was not published until the beginning of the twenty-first century.

7.5 HIGHER ORDER MODAL LOGIC

7.5.1 TY2

Montague's system[13] was a combination of the typed lambda calculus (Chapter 5); a system of world-time pairs incorporating S5 modality and temporal operators (Chapter 6); and the intension and extension operators introduced earlier in this chapter.

It is useful to discuss here an important variant, introduced shortly after the publication of Montague's work by Gallin (1975). It makes certain things more transparent than Montague's approach, and a number of linguists use it by preference.

It was noted that the type definition in section 7.2 did not allow for expressions of type s in isolation, only 'intensional' expressions of type $s \rightarrow \sigma$ for some extensional type σ. Similarly in the semantics, though the set of possible worlds W is present, it is not added as a basic domain of denotation; only function domains of the form $\mathbf{D}_\sigma{}^W$ are allowed.

Gallin's alternative was to allow worlds into the ontology on the same basis as individuals, and make s a basic type on the same basis as e. We thus have two radically different sets, D and W, in the ontology. This is known as a 'two-sorted logic'.

In discussing predicate logic in Chapter 3, we often came up against predicates whose roles could only be filled by certain types of entities, such as animate entities, or places; in other words they cannot be appropriately filled by any random element of D, but only by entities drawn from certain subsets. If this kind of division of the universe (e.g. into animate versus inanimate, or things versus places) is built into the model, then the subsets are known as **sorts**; we then have a **many-sorted logic**, and the restrictions on theta roles that it is intended to model are known as 'sortal restrictions'. The problem with applying this approach to theta roles in linguistics is that the number of sorts needed proliferates quickly;[14] but the difference between D and W seems to offer a better motivation for a two-sorted logic, as the difference between individuals and worlds is clearly motivated. Sorts in this context are also commonly known as types, hence the name Ty2 for Gallin's two-sorted variant. In this book they will always be referred to as sorts, while 'types' means the typing system used for the lambda calculus.

Once we have our two sorts, we can simply add s to our inventory of basic types, and W to the basic domains of denotation.

(7.26) 1. The basic types for a two-sorted higher order intensional logic are e, s and t.
　　　　2. $\mathbf{D}^e = D$, $\mathbf{D}^s = W$, and $\mathbf{D}^t = \{0, 1\}$.

The existence of intensional types, and the specification of their domains of denotation, do not now require any special rule, but follow from the normal rules for functional types set out in Chapter 5. Note that there is nothing now to prohibit expressions referring directly to worlds, or to functions from something into W. Whether the latter expressions exist in natural language is left as an empirical question.

In Ty2 the intension and extension operators used in Montague's IL also become unnecessary as distinct symbols. Recall from the introduction to this chapter that the modal operators $\Box$ and $\Diamond$ can be thought of in terms of quantification over possible worlds, and indeed this is expressed in the semantic definitions. Now that we have variables of type s, which refer directly to possible worlds, this can be expressed directly, as $\forall w$ and $\exists w$. We now have a more transparent match between the logical syntax and the semantics.

What about the intension and extension operators? Recall that the extension operator takes an expression of an intensional type (which is a kind of functional type), and gives its extension in a world (by default the actual world) as the value of the function. The extension operator can thus be thought of as an instance of function application, using a world ('the' world) as its argument. This too can be made explicit in Ty2 by applying an intensional expression to an extra argument of type s, in a simple case of function application.

The intension operator is the reverse of this; it takes an extensional expression, and designates a function from worlds to the denotation of this expression. But in higher order logic functions are made by lambda abstraction. In fact, the intension operator applied to an expression α is simply lambda abstraction over α, on a variable w ranging over worlds. This creates a function which, given any world, will give the denotation of α at that world.

The following summary of the correspondences discussed in the last few paragraphs may be useful. The expressions from IL introduced in section 7.2 are on the left, their equivalents in Ty2 on the right.

(7.27) 1. $\Box\phi = \forall w\phi$
        2. $\Diamond\phi = \exists w\phi$
        3. $\lor\alpha = \alpha(w_0)$
        4. $\land\alpha = \lambda w\alpha$

It should be mentioned here that Ty2 is not simply a notational variant of Montague's IL, as having expressions of type s increases the expressive power of the language.

Of course Montague could have set up his logic in this way, and it is worth pausing to ask why he decided not to. There is a conceptual price to be paid for treating worlds on a par with entities, and that is in the area of ontological commitment. This works two ways. The first is that possible worlds are being treated as things that actually exist, a position which has been taken by some philosophers (Chapter 6) but which not everybody finds appealing.

The other disadvantage in the parallelism between worlds and things is that ultimately intensions boil down to the same thing as most extensional types, namely functions from one type of 'thing' to another; in other words, they do not seem to be a radically different kind of thing from extensions! This is a long way from Frege, and could be seen as undermining Carnap's treatment of Frege's 'sense' as 'intension'.

However, these comments should not be pushed too far; the ontology of Ty2 does not really take us further in these directions than that of Montague's IL, which equally relies on a set of worlds and equally treats intensions as functions with that set as its domain. But it could be said that Ty2 makes this more explicit, while Montague's treatment makes some attempt not to push things to these conclusions.

7.6 EPILOGUE TO PART II

These two chapters have explored modal systems, first in isolation from quantification and then (this chapter) in interaction with it. In both cases the logic extends classical logic by adding modal operators, but does not change the behaviour of the classical connectives and quantifiers themselves. The next chapter will begin to look at systems in which the connectives themselves deviate considerably from their behaviour in classical logic. In Haack's terminology, they are not extensions of classical logic but deviations from it. In Part III negation is the main deviant, while in Part IV the miscreant we will be most concerned with is implication.

NOTES

1. Emily Dickenson, *I Dwell in Possibility*.
2. Barcan (1946), Carnap (1947).
3. The usual translation of Meinong's term *bestehen*. However, some modal logicians, notably David Lewis, defend the idea that non-actual objects *exist*.
4. The complication here is that the present tense in English does not always refer to present time.
5. Denotation and reference are nearly synonymous, and Frege's classic work 'Über Sinn und Bedeutung' (1892) is commonly translated as *On Sense and Reference*. Those writers who draw a distinction between them (for example Lyons 1981) use 'reference' for what is picked out by an expression on a particular occasion of utterance. Since I think Frege was talking about the meaning of expressions rather than meanings intended by speakers, I use the alternative translation of *Bedeutung* as 'denotation'. Another term that is also used in this context is 'designation'.
6. The distinction between denotation and connotation goes back at least to Mill.
7. Morrill (1994).
8. Latin: 'about the sentence' (*dictum* in medieval logic meant what was asserted by a sentence) and 'about the thing'. This terminology is due to Abelard. The distinction was already known to medieval logicians, but usually termed 'divided sentences' (*de re*) and 'composite sentences' (*de dicto*). Abelard himself analysed the *de dicto* reading as a modal predicate over a whole sentence, for example 'it is necessary [that Socrates runs]', while the *de re* reading corresponds to adverbial modification, 'Socrates [runs necessarily]', where the constituent 'runs necessarily' is predicated of Socrates.
9. However, this is not standard terminology in semantics. The term goes back to William James, but is used more by fantasy writers than logicians.
10. This is slightly simplified. Actualism and possibilism are philosophical positions, while constant domain and varying domain semantics are technical set-ups. The correspondences indicated generally hold, but it is not clear that they do always.
11. Though note that either English sentence can, with suitable intonation, have either scopal reading.
12. Aristotle, *Prior Analytics*, I.9.
13. Montague suggested more than one approach; the comments here apply to Proper Treatment of Quantification (PTQ).

14. The problem is analogous to the treatment of sortal restrictions by features. While ±
    ANIMATE or ± LOCATION seem to have a good motivation, the inventory of features
    needed soon begins to look unconvincing. For example there is a verb 'devein' that is only
    used of prawns, but few people would argue for a universal linguistic feature ± PRAWN
    (Pinker 1989). Similarly, we would not want to give the set of prawns a distinguished
    status in our models.

PART III

NEGATION AND PARTIALITY

CHAPTER 8

MANY VALUED LOGICS

We step and do not step into the same river; we are and are not.[1]

That which is not is the means of apprehending that which is.[2]

8.1 INTRODUCTION

8.1.1 BIVALENCE

All the logics discussed up to now are based on an important assumption: that a proposition must be either true or false, and not both. This is known as the principle of **bivalence**. While the limits of this principle were mentioned in Chapter 2, the subsequent chapters, up till now, have assumed its validity. In this part of the book, however, we look at what happens if we abandon this assumption.

The dominance of bivalence in western logic goes back to Aristotle, who discussed it and made it very clear that, in his opinion, it was essential to logic. Even he, however, did discuss certain possible exceptions. The first involved semantic anomalies which meant that the whole sentence, though grammatical, did not make sense. A famous modern example would be Chomsky's (1957) 'Colourless green ideas sleep furiously'. Is this true? Or if it isn't true, does it make sense to say that they *don't* sleep furiously?

His second reservation concerned gradable predicates, which are true or false 'to a degree' rather than having a clear cut-off point between truth and falsity. Take the example 'This place is beautiful'. While there are instances where people could assent to this judgement very quickly (Greece, for example), and perhaps other places where they would immediately reject it, there are a lot of intermediate points where a judgement of truth or falsity would be difficult to make. Or if a beach is still beautiful with a few beer cans on it, how many beer cans would it take before we would say that it is not beautiful? Many Greek philosophers had already discussed problems like this, which was known as the 'sorites paradox'. Today we would call these predicates 'vague' or 'fuzzy', and one logic designed to deal with them is **fuzzy logic**.

The third problem occurs when an argument of a predicate (especially the subject) does not have anything to refer to. Aristotle and many subsequent philosophers discussed this in connection with names of characters who had died (such as Socrates) or who existed only in myth (like Pegasus). In modern logic, models are usually extended to accommodate such cases, often by invoking possible worlds and possible individuals. In this chapter, however, we set possible worlds aside and look at other approaches to the problem.

In classical predicate logic, models are assumed to provide referents for all individual constants in the logical language (otherwise the interpretation function I would not be a function); such models are said to be 'suitable' for the language, and unsuitable models are not considered. However, the same problem arises with other expressions, notably definite descriptions. As discussed in Chapter 5, these involve a predicate expression (the N-bar), and there is no requirement in models that the interpretations of predicates (i.e. sets) be non-empty. So expressions like 'the unicorn', 'the Emperor of China' or 'the first human on Mars' give rise to the same questions in another form. These expressions may fail to refer, and, if so, it is problematic to evaluate sentences containing them as true or false.

(8.1)   1. The unicorn is sleeping.
        2. The first human on Mars is a Russian.
        3. The present King of France is bald.

(The last of these is a famous example from Russell (1905).)

Note that the negations of these sentences are equally problematic. In classical logic, if the sentences are simply false, then we would expect that their negations should be true, but the negations of these sentences (e.g. 'The unicorn is not sleeping.') seem to be almost as difficult to assign a truth value as the affirmative versions.

The other example that made Aristotle hesitate is what is known as the problem of **future contingents**. His own example was 'There will be a sea battle tomorrow.' Tomorrow, no doubt, we will know whether there is a sea battle or not, but does it make any sense to judge the future sentence true or false today? One view would be that this depends whether the matter is already determined, or whether the relevant decisions are still genuinely 'open'. There is some debate about what exactly Aristotle's view is in this passage, but it was taken in the way I have just described by his influential follower Boethius.[3] The Stoics, who were strict determinists about the future, were quick to denounce it and insist on strict bivalence for future contingents. However, the idea that the openness of the future and therefore human freedom is at stake in such examples was picked up in the twentieth century by the Polish logician Jan Łukasiewicz, who made it the launchpad for the first modern logic rejecting bivalence.

Whatever his doubts, Aristotle not only established the importance of bivalence but formulated two logical laws expressing its consequences for the behaviour of negation. The first was the **Law of Contradiction** (LC), which states that $p \land \neg p$ is always false. The second is the **Law of the Excluded Middle** (LEM), which states that $p \lor \neg p$ is always true; either a proposition or its negation is always true (there is no third or middle way – *tertium non datur*). The latter is precisely what is called into question by the sea battle example, and was denied by Łukasiewicz. It is also questioned by many modern logicians for different reasons. Many of them are interested in epistemological problems relating to the limits of our knowledge and inability to decide all propositions one way or the other.

Logics which do not obey LEM are known as **partial logics**. The LC has rarely been questioned in the western tradition, until recently. Traditional Indian logic is more open on this point.[4] Logics which deny LC will be termed **paraconsistent logics** (not to be confused with *inconsistent* logics).[5]

This part of the book, then, will be about partial and paraconsistent logics. Whereas the modal logics discussed in the previous two chapters are all *extensions* of classical logic, partial and paraconsistent logics are a radical departure from it. In modal logic the logical constants retain their classical meaning, but other devices (the modal operators) are added. The rejection of bivalence, however, means that the behaviour of the familiar connectives and quantifiers will be different. Therefore the logics described in this and subsequent chapters are not 'extensions' but 'deviations'.

Boethius

The leading scholar in fifth century western Europe, as West Roman society was collapsing under the Germanic invasions. In particular, he was one of the most important exponents of Aristotle's logic for several centuries before or after. He had an equally distinguished career in public service, rising to be the chief minister of the Ostrogothic king Theodoric. However, he got on the wrong side of political and religious infighting, and wrote his masterpiece, the *Consolation of Philosophy*, while awaiting execution in prison.

8.1.2 *TERTIUM NON DATUR?*

LEM is an important principle of classical logic. If there are situations where we do not want LEM, then it is natural to look at logics which dispense with this principle. As usual, there is more than one approach to doing this. One of these is to directly contradict Aristotle's dictum that there is no third alternative between truth and falsity, and to claim that actually there is. If we refuse to say that a proposition is true, or that it is false, then it is presumably something else. And that 'something else' can be taken as a third truth value.

Note, however, that it need not be. It is possible, instead, to say that the proposition does not have a truth value, that it does 'not yet' have a truth value, or that the truth value is 'unknown'. It is not clear that these are the same, conceptually, as asserting that it has a third truth value which is neither true nor false, and in fact many writers have expressed philosophical problems with the latter idea. To go back to Frege, saying that something is true has a significance (in his terminology *Kraft* or 'force') beyond merely denoting one member of the set $\{0, 1\}$ rather than the other, rather as winning a game of chess is more than just being able to distinguish between winning or losing positions and classifying your position as one of the 'winning' variety.[6] This is not the end of the argument, and even in chess there are many ways of not winning, not all of which involve losing, and some chess tournament rules count a draw as half a point, while others ignore them.

In many valued logic, the special status of truth can be maintained by declaring 1 to be special or **designated**. Sometimes it can also make sense to include other values besides 1 in a set of designated truth values.

The important thing that intermediate truth values share with the classical idea of truth is that they should be preserved by logical consequence. Classical logic preserves truth, in the sense that its rules will not yield false conclusions from true premises, and this is reflected in the definition of material implication. If we have a logic with a third truth value, then that too should be preserved by the rules of the logic. This 'third truth value' option was pioneered by Łukasiewicz and simultaneously by Post and other logicians, leading to many valued logic. 'Many' in this context means more than two: in the first instance three, but once we have abandoned bivalence, there is no obvious reason why we should stop at three.

Intermediate truth values are a technical device for dealing with non-bivalence. Their interpretation is a more complicated matter. A contrast that will recur in this chapter is that between (i) a view that propositions are ultimately true or false, but it is not known which, and (ii) that some propositions cannot ultimately be judged true or false because that is what reality is like. The first can be called an **epistemic** view of partiality, and the second **ontological**.

The Polish School

The Polish school of logic originated in the Austro-Hungarian Empire before the First World War, when an offshoot of the 'School' of Brentano in Vienna (not to be confused with the later 'Vienna Circle') formed in the Galician city of Lemberg (Lwow). When Lwow became part of newly independent Poland in 1918, the school's activities continued, but its centre moved to Warsaw. Here, under the direction of Lesniewski, it saw an amazing flourishing of creativity over a wide range of areas, several of which are discussed in the text. It was also distinguished by a sense of mission – the belief that logic could make the world a more rational place. As Łukasziewicz (1920) said, 'Logic is morality of thought and speech.' The school was disrupted by the German occupation, which led to the emigration, marginalisation or death of many of its leading figures, many of whom were Jews. Adolf Lindenbaum and Janina Hosiasson-Lindenbaum were murdered as part of the Nazi policy of destroying the intellectual leadership of the Jewish community. After the war many emigrated to the West, including Ł ukasiewicz, but the school's work continued, though initially outside Warsaw, which had been destroyed. Its association with the philosophical ideals of the Lwow school brought ideological pressure from the Soviet Academy of Sciences and restrictions on its activities. Nonetheless it was able to maintain a rich research tradition throughout the communist era.

8.1.3 PARACONSISTENCY AND INCONSISTENCY

The usefulness of a logic that rejects LC – and thus accepts contradictions – is perhaps not immediately obvious. It might seem that such a logic is inconsistent – that it adopts a position of 'anything goes', and is no use to anybody. However, the two should be clearly distinguished.

An inconsistent logic is sometimes defined as one that allows contradictions. However, there is a more fundamental definition of an inconsistent logic as one in which any statement follows from any other statement, collapsing the distinction between truth and falsity. The stock example of this is the **trivial logic**, in which all statements are true. If the logic includes negation, that means that every statement and its negation are both true, so all contradictions are true.

The idea behind paraconsistent logic is very different; it allows contradictions because we may want or need to reason about contradictions, in order to arrive at the truth. Perhaps surprisingly, this is not possible in classical logic precisely because it treats contradictions as meaningless; and it is difficult to reason about things which have no meaning. More precisely, it treats all contradictions as the same proposition (often written as a constant $\perp$, read as the **falsum**), which makes it impossible to distinguish between them.

Moreover, an important principle of classical logic (and some other logics) is that from a contradiction, anything follows (*e contradictione quodlibet* or ECQ). The validity of ECQ in classical logic can easily be checked from a truth table. Since a contradiction $\phi \wedge \neg\phi$ is false in all rows, then for any arbitrary formula ψ, $(\phi \wedge \neg\phi) \rightarrow \psi$ is a tautology. This effect is sometimes known as **explosion**. If you think of $\perp$ as the bottom element of a Boolean lattice of propositions ordered by entailment (Chapter 3), then clearly it will entail all propositions in the entire lattice.[7]

It is easy to think of situations where we want to be more discriminating about contradictory information and what conclusions follow from it. There have been several occasions in the history of science when researchers have come across contradictions, but have not drawn the conclusion that anything goes. Examples include the use of infinitesimals in the development of calculus, the wave / particle duality in physics, and Russell's paradox in set theory.

One common practical application is in error handling in computing. Suppose we want to reason about a program whose execution has led to a contradictory state. Using classical logic, if there is a contradiction then the system can only crash (or, even worse, do something arbitrary and unpredictable). However, if we can distinguish different kinds of contradictory state, the program can return at least an error message saying what is wrong and perhaps giving a way to put it right. Alternatively, we might have a smart database which makes inferences from the data it contains. If some of this information is contradictory, we would want our application to be able to deal with the anomaly in a controlled way rather than generate arbitrary and unpredictable answers to our queries.

Another situation where contradictory information naturally arises is in interaction between two or more agents, with differing opinions. This could be in the course of dialogue modelling, or reasoning about information on the web from multiple sources. This situation has parallels with the doxastic modality discussed in Chapter 6. But in modal logic, we imposed a requirement that the information available to each agent at least be consistent (modal axiom **D**). We might want to waive even that assumption and allow the information state of individual agents to contain contradictions.

A related scenario is fiction. Chapter 7 looked at the idea of possible worlds, including worlds of myth or fantasy, providing discourse about individuals that do not exist. However, possible worlds obey the rules of classical logic. We may want to allow writers a bit of poetic licence, to create worlds which are not completely consistent. They may even contain individuals and scenes which are considered impossible on scientific or metaphysical grounds.[8]

Finally, in language we have the problem of intensional contexts. If we cannot distinguish between contradictions, then we have the unhappy situation that if an agent believes one contradiction, then he or she believes every contradiction, even contradictions that they may never have thought of. Note too that because contradictions have the same truth value in all possible worlds, the situation is not saved by the approach to intensionality outlined in the previous chapters; in a modal logic which is built on classical logic, contradictions have the same intension as well as the same extension. Problems like this are known as **hyperintensional**; they are a known problem for modal approaches to intensionality, and paraconsistency is one possible way of addressing them.[9]

Thus a paraconsistent logic is not one where anything goes; on the contrary, we will define it as a logic that does not include ECQ. (The latter can be considered a version of 'anything goes', since it leads to explosion whenever it encounters a contradiction.) The question is whether it is possible to formalise a logic which is paraconsistent but not inconsistent. It is not self-evident that one can, and a degree of scepticism is understandable. However, there are various ways of approaching this, some of which involve multiple truth values and are therefore included in this chapter.

Formally, paraconsistent logics can be seen as the mirror image of partial logics. Where partial logics allow truth values to be undefined (a truth **gap**), paraconsistent logics allow them to be 'overdefined' as both true and false (a truth **glut**) (Figure 8.1). Because of this symmetry it is convenient to discuss them here along with partial logics. However, the main emphasis in this part of the book is on partiality; paraconsistency will get further scrutiny in the last part of the book, as many of the substructural logics treated there are paraconsistent.

As with partiality, interpretations of paraconsistent many valued logics come in two flavours: epistemic and ontological. In the first, contradictions are apparent

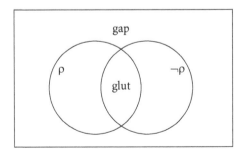

Figure 8.1   Truth gaps and gluts

rather than real, the result of imperfect knowledge. The second claims that reality itself contains paradoxes and the presence of contradictions is not something to be reasoned away. This view is known as **dialethism** (Greek – 'two truths').[10]

As usual the next sections give some formal definitions for many valued logic, with some relevant discussion. The remainder of the chapter discusses some applications in more detail. In general the reader can be selective about these, but note that the definitions in section 8.7 will be important later in the book.

8.2 SYNTAX OF MANY VALUED LOGIC

The adoption of a three valued logic, or any of the other logics mentioned in this chapter, does not involve changing the syntax of the logical language, whether propositional, first order or higher order. This makes for a nice short syntax section. All the 'deviations' arise in the semantics. (However, variant symbols are optionally used for some connectives, to distinguish different behaviours. These will be occasionally used later in the chapter, but not in the formal definitions in the next section.)

8.3 SEMANTICS OF MANY VALUED LOGIC

This section is a great deal more complicated, partly because there are many different ways of approaching the semantics of many valued logic. For a start, we have to decide what we mean by 'many'. Are three truth values enough, or is there motivation for more? And this is related to the fundamental question of what the truth values are intended to mean.

On the other hand, this chapter is concerned almost entirely with propositional logic. And this section will be restricted to two basic approaches to modelling many valued logic, out of the many that are available.

Let's start with Łukasiewicz's three valued logic, $Ł_3$. The three truth values are the classical values *true* and *false*, which we will write as usual as 1 and 0, plus a third value which we can think of as 'maybe', or 'neither true nor false'. This can be written in many ways (common symbols are $*$ or $\#$), but here it will be given the numeric value $\frac{1}{2}$, which will be useful for later developments. Together with the set V of truth values, we also specify a subset $D \subset V$ as **designated** values. For now we assume that $D = \{1\}$; that is, only 1 is designated.

If a statement is neither true nor false, then its negation will also be neither true nor false, so if $V(\phi) = \frac{1}{2}$ then $V(\neg\phi) = \frac{1}{2}$. More generally, we can say that the negation of any truth value can be obtained by subtracting it from 1. The negation of 1 is 0, the negation of 0 is 1, and the negation of $\frac{1}{2}$ is $\frac{1}{2}$.

Conjunction and disjunction can be handled in a similar way. We can assume that they will have their classical values whenever both juncts have classical values. Presumably they should also be $\frac{1}{2}$ if both the juncts are $\frac{1}{2}$. However, suppose we have a disjunction whose disjuncts are 1 and $\frac{1}{2}$. The true disjunct is enough to make a disjunction true, and so we can perhaps ignore the other disjunct. Similarly for a conjunction whose conjuncts are 0 and $\frac{1}{2}$. The false conjunct is enough to falsify the conjunction, without worrying about the other conjunct. However, if it is the other way round, say a conjunction of 1 and $\frac{1}{2}$, the truth value of the conjunction depends crucially on the second conjunct; and since this is neither true nor false, we cannot make the conjunction true or false either; it will get the value $\frac{1}{2}$. By dual reasoning, a disjunction of 0 and $\frac{1}{2}$ will also get the value $\frac{1}{2}$.

The generalisation here is that the value of disjunction is always the maximum of the values of the disjuncts, and the value of a conjunction is always the minimum of the two conjuncts. I will call this the **minimum** interpretation of conjunction, though it goes under many names in the literature. (It should be understood that it goes together with a *maximum* interpretation of disjunction.) Classical logic also obeys the minimum interpretation, restricted to two truth values, as can easily be checked.

Although these evaluations seem reasonable, they are certainly not the only possible approach. Another would be to say that the presence of an indefinite value anywhere in a formula is enough to infect the whole formula. Imagine, for example, a sentence in which one subpart is ungrammatical or nonsensical. This might induce us to throw away the whole sentence, so we could say that the whole sentence is undefined for truth value if any part of it is. This variant of three valued logic is known as Bochvar's logic (sometimes described as the 'logic of nonsense'!).

Implication presents a dilemma. One approach might be to keep it as close to material implication as possible: to take the classical definition of $\phi \rightarrow \psi$ as $\neg\phi \vee \psi$, and read the resulting truth values from the tables for negation and disjunction. This approach was taken by Kleene – together with the 'minimum' interpretation of conjunction, it is known as the 'strong Kleene interpretation'.

However, this was not the approach taken by Łukasiewicz. Implication is meant to correspond to the relation of logical consequence, which will be different in these logics from classical logic. The first requirement is that implication should be true iff the consequent is at least as true as the antecedent. (Material implication fulfils this requirement in classical logic.) What if the antecedent is truer than the consequent? If the antecedent is true and the consequent is false then the implication is false, as in classical logic. But what if one of the two is undefined? We cannot make the implication true, but if we are interpreting $\frac{1}{2}$ as 'maybe', then we might not want to state categorically that it is false either. So Łukasiewicz's solution was to give the implication the value $\frac{1}{2}$.

(8.2) p $\rightarrow$ q	0	$\frac{1}{2}$	1
0	1	1	1
$\frac{1}{2}$	$\frac{1}{2}$	1	1
1	0	$\frac{1}{2}$	1

This can be expressed mathematically by calculating the difference between the truth of the antecedent and the truth of the consequent. This tells us how much 'truer' one proposition is than the other. If the antecedent is truer than the consequent, then the truth value of the implication is this difference subtracted from 1 – a measure of the amount by which the implication fails to be true (the amount by which it fails to 'preserve truth'). If the consequent is at least as true as the antecedent, then we simply give the implication the value 1 (true).

In the exercises you are asked to compare the results of Kleene and Łukasiewicz's interpretations.

We can now give the semantic definitions for Łukasiewicz's three valued logic, $Ł_3$. The valuation V is a function which gives atomic formulas values in the set $\{0, \frac{1}{2}, 1\}$ and which furthermore respects the following conditions.

(8.3) 1. If ϕ is a wff in $Ł_3$, then $V(\neg\phi) = 1 - V(\phi)$.
2. If ϕ and ψ are wffs in $Ł_3$, then $V(\phi \wedge \psi) = \min(V(\phi), V(\psi))$.
3. If ϕ and ψ are wffs in $Ł_3$, then $V(\phi \vee \psi) = \max(V(\phi), V(\psi))$.
4. If ϕ and ψ are wffs in $Ł_3$, then $V(\phi \rightarrow \psi) = \min(1, 1 - (V(\phi) - V(\psi)))$.

This mathematical formulation of Ł generalises to any number of truth values. For example, suppose we want to have four truth values. There are many ways of doing this, but one way is to set the truth values as $\{0, \frac{1}{3}, \frac{2}{3}, 1\}$. Observing that $\frac{2}{3}$ is somehow closer to truth than $\frac{1}{3}$, we could perhaps interpret them as something like {no, probably not, probably, yes}. However we interpret them, these truth values give us Łukasiewicz's four valued logic $Ł_4$, and the recursive truth definition just given is equally valid for it.

Generally, for any number n, the n-valued Łukasiewicz logic $Ł_n$ will have the truth values $\{0, \frac{1}{n-1}, \frac{2}{n-1}, \ldots \frac{n-2}{n-1}, 1\}$. The truth definition in (8.3) applies for any value of n. When the intermediate truth values are strung out in order like this between 0 and 1 they are usually known as **truth degrees**. We can even generalise further and say that a truth degree can be any fraction between 0 and 1 inclusive. This gives the rational valued Łukasiewicz logic $Ł_Q$, which has as many truth degrees as the set of rational numbers. Going even further we can take the truth degrees as the real numbers between 0 and 1 inclusive (the closed unit interval, usually written $[0, 1]$), giving us the real valued Łukasiewicz logic $Ł_R$.

What use are such extensions? One application was hinted at in the discussion of $Ł_4$ – the values between 0 and 1 behave rather like probabilities. It would also seem natural to use truth degrees to model sentences with vague or gradable predicates.

We will come back to these applications below, but first we should look at another, at first sight very different, approach to multiple truth values. It is usually known as Belnap's logic, from the influential paper Belnap (1977).[11]

Suppose we take two truth values, 0 and 1, and keep the classical definition of the connectives, but evaluate truth separately from falsity. In classical logic, truth and falsity depend on each other; if a proposition is true then it is not false, and if it is not true then it is false (bivalence). Now, however, all of the following four possibilities will be allowed. A proposition may be:

1. true and not false (we will abbreviate this as true, or T).
2. false and not true (false, or F).
3. not true and not false (neither, or N).
4. both true and false (both, or B).

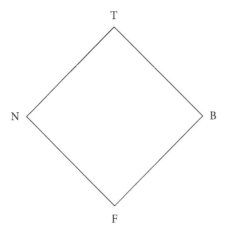

Figure 8.2   The logical lattice BN4

This logic is therefore both **partial** and **paraconsistent**. Although it is built on the two truth values, it has four possible *combinations* of truth values, which gives us a four valued logic. The four 'values' are often referred to as **truth combinations**;[12] they are, in fact, the four possible subsets of the set $\{0, 1\}$ of classical truth values. These four values can be arranged in a lattice, with T at the top and F at the bottom, and N and B as the two intermediate possibilities (Figure 8.2).

For negation, the conditions for truth and falsity are evaluated separately, as follows:

(8.4) If ϕ is a wff in BN4, then
    1. $V(\neg\phi) = 1$ iff $V(\phi) = 0$
    2 $V(\neg\phi) = 0$ iff $V(\phi) = 1$

So far so good; if the value of ϕ is T or F, then we have the classical conditions. What if ϕ is N? Then neither of the clauses come into effect, so the value of $\neg\phi$ will also be N. On the other hand, if the value of ϕ is B, then both the clauses apply, so that the value of $\neg\phi$ will also be B. So both N and B are their own negations.

Now let's apply the same reasoning to conjunction and disjunction.

(8.5) If ϕ and ψ are wffs in BN4, then
    1. $V(\phi \wedge \psi) = 1$ iff $V(\phi) = 1$ and $V(\psi) = 1$.
    2. $V(\phi \wedge \psi) = 0$ iff $V(\phi) = 0$ or $V(\psi) = 0$.
    3. $V(\phi \vee \psi) = 1$ iff $V(\phi) = 1$ or $V(\psi) = 1$.
    4. $V(\phi \vee \psi) = 0$ iff $V(\phi) = 0$ and $V(\psi) = 0$.

This gives the following picture for conjunction, and you will be asked to draw up the truth table for disjunction in the exercises. If the conjuncts have classical values, then the rules for conjunction give the classical results. If the conjuncts are T and N then the conjunction is N, because neither clause is triggered; if they are T and B then the result is B, because both clauses are triggered. If they are F and N then the result is F, and if they are F and B then the result is again F. Finally, if the conjuncts are B and N only the second clause is triggered and the result is F. Notice that in the lattice structure, the result of conjunction is always the greatest lower bound of the conjuncts, as in the propositional lattices we saw in Chapter 2. However, this lattice is not Boolean (why not?).

This leaves implication. Once again we *could* simply define $\phi \rightarrow \psi$ as $\neg\phi \vee \psi$. Instead, we will base it directly on the notion of logical consequence – but with truth and falsity, once again, defined separately. For the implication to be true, we want the antecedent to be true only if the consequent is, and the consequent to be false only if the antecedent is. If the antecedent is true and the consequent is false, then the implication is, as usual, false. Here is the definition in symbols.

(8.6) If ϕ and ψ are wffs in BN4, then
    1. $V(\phi \rightarrow \psi) = 1$ iff
       (a) if $V(\phi) = 1$ then $V(\psi) = 1$ and
       (b) if $V(\psi) = 0$ then $V(\phi) = 0$.
    2. $V(\phi \rightarrow \psi) = 0$ iff $V(\phi) = 1$ and $V(\psi) = 0$.

The truth table for implication in BN4 is given in (8.7), but you might like to work it out yourself first on the basis of the definitions just given.

(8.7) $p \rightarrow q$	T	B	N	F
T	T	F	N	F
B	T	B	N	F
N	T	N	T	N
F	T	T	T	T

This section concludes with two things you can do with BN4, each of which has many ramifications.

First, it was mentioned that the four values of BN4 are taken from the powerset lattice of $\{1, 2\}$. Suppose we treat it as literally this powerset lattice, so that the four elements are ordered not by consequence but by the natural $\subseteq$ relation on the powerset. This involves rotating the lattice through 90 degrees, so that B is at the top, N at the bottom, and T and F between them (Figure 8.3). The original lattice ordered by consequence is known as the **logical lattice**, while the powerset lattice is known as the **approximation lattice**.

BN4 is thus a special kind of structure – a set with two distinct partial orders defined on it, both of which are lattices. This is known as a **bilattice**.

The ordering in Figure 8.3 can be interpreted in terms of information growth, reading it from bottom to top. Instead of truth degrees, we can think in terms of increasing degrees of knowledge. At the bottom we have no information. At the

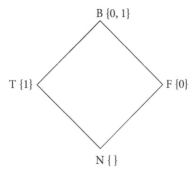

Figure 8.3   The approximation lattice on BN4

next level we have specific information about the truth or falsity of propositions. At the top we have 'too much' information, namely contradictory information. We will call this ordering of increasing information **subsumption**, notated ⊑. An information state *s* subsumes an information state *t* iff *s* has a subset of the information in *t*.

This subsumption ordering can be thought of as a logic of **partial objects**, objects assembled from partial information (total objects being objects about which we have complete information). This will be the subject of Chapter 9. It has found many applications in artificial intelligence (AI), and in linguistic formalisms based on AI, such as HPSG. The bottom element is the empty feature structure, where no information is present. At the second level, information is added to the feature structure by unification. However, the unification of inconsistent feature structures will result in the impossible feature structure, represented by the top element.[13]

Another thing one can do with BN4 is to treat it as a **product logic**. In this the four values are written as ordered pairs, recording the values for truth and falsity separately in that order – thus T is $\langle 1, 0 \rangle$, B is $\langle 1, 1 \rangle$, N is $\langle 0, 0 \rangle$ and F is $\langle 0, 1 \rangle$. In the terminology of product logic, truth and falsity are the two **dimensions**, and the argument places of the ordered pairs are **co-ordinates**. Each co-ordinate is 1 if information from that dimension is present and 0 if it is absent.

This generalises easily to systems of more than two dimensions, or more than two primitive values. Moreover, it can combine a system of truth values with a system representing something else. For example, the two dimensions can be used to separate logic from other semantic aspects a proposition might have, such as factuality. The logic can be kept classical (or whatever other system is preferred), while the combination with the other factors may lead to the whole combination having a non-classical appearance. One particular application, to be taken up in the next section, is to pair the truth or falsity of a sentence with a record of whether its presuppositions are satisfied.

EXERCISE 8.3.0.1

1. (a) Draw the truth table for implication in $Ł_3$ according to the strong Kleene interpretation, and compare it with the table for Łukasiewicz implication as given in the text. In which cases does $\phi \rightarrow \phi$ not get the truth value 1?
   (b) Do the De Morgan laws hold for $Ł_3$, given the definitions of $\wedge$, $\vee$ and $\neg$ in the text?
   (c) Draw the truth table for disjunction in BN4 on the basis of the rules given for the valuation. Draw a truth table for implication defined as $\neg\phi\vee\psi$. In which cases does $\phi \rightarrow \phi$ not hold?
   (d) Compare the truth values for $\phi \rightarrow \psi$ in $Ł_3$ with those for $\neg\psi \rightarrow \neg\phi$. Does the law of contraposition hold?
2. Take the logical lattice and truth conditions for BN4 and remove B, leaving a system with T, N and F. If we rename these 1, $\frac{1}{2}$ and 0, we have what looks like $Ł_3$.
   (a) Check that the tables for $\neg$, $\wedge$ and $\rightarrow$ from BN4, with this substitution, give us precisely the semantics of $Ł_3$.
   (b) Now omit N from BN4, leaving T, B and F. Draw the truth tables on the basis of BN4. Which table differs from the one for $Ł_3$?

Note: the structure in the second part of this question is known as RM3, and we will return to it in the last part of the book as it is a model for a form of relevance logic. Like Łukasiewicz logic, it can be generalised to any number of truth values; for the three valued one, the values are written as -1 (F), 0 (B) and 1 (T). These are known as Sugihara models.

8.4 PRESUPPOSITIONS

For the first sentence in (8.8) to be true, then it must be the case that I have a wife. We could say that it *entails* that I have a wife, by virtue of the lexical semantics of 'my'.

(8.8) 1. My wife is Japanese.
      2. My wife isn't Japanese.
      3. I have a wife.

However, the unusual thing in this case is the second sentence, the negation of the first, also seems to entail that I have a wife. Do you agree with these intuitions? If so, the third sentence is entailed by the first sentence and its negation. It is true whether the first sentence is true or false. (If you do not agree, we will look at some possible reasons for this a bit later.)

This is an unusual kind of entailment, however. In classical logic, the only thing that is entailed by a proposition and also by its negation is a tautology – a statement which is logically true, and therefore entailed by anything. However, statement 3 is not a tautology; it is perfectly possible that I am not married. It is said to be a **presupposition** of sentence 1.

A presupposition is necessary for sentence 1 to be judged true or false; in a sense it is necessary for it to be semantically coherent at all. The listener is not given the option of rejecting the presupposition by negating the sentence; typically, the presupposition comes in 'under the radar' and is not critically evaluated in the process of interpreting the sentence. Usually, we simply accommodate the presuppositions without noticing them, unless there is a glaring problem with them. Because of this they can often be used dishonestly to smuggle in propositions which we would not assent to if they were presented as straightforward assertions. This is the basis of the well-known lawyer's trick in (8.9).

(8.9)   Have you stopped beating your wife? Answer yes or no!

Either an affirmative or negative answer admits the truth of the presupposition, that the addressee has been beating his wife. Note that questions can have presuppositions, whereas they would not normally be said to have entailments. (The answers, whether positive or negative, both entail the presupposition.)

Sentences may have many presuppositions at the same time. Another presupposition of (8.9), for example, is that the addressee has a wife, though this is not normally such a damaging admission.

Before proceeding further, let's classify some common types of presupposition. That in (8.8) is a kind of **existential** presupposition (there is an x such that I am married to x). Another example of an existential presupposition is definite descriptions, which will be discussed shortly.[14] The example in (8.9) is a **factive** presupposition. It often occurs when an event is an argument of attitude verbs like 'regret', or, as in the example, certain temporal or aspectual verbs like 'stop'.

More generally, most sentences include some information that is old or assumed, and other information which is offered as new; the old or topical information is in many cases presupposed. This information structure of the sentence is sensitive to features like focus, whether signalled by intonation or syntactic devices such as clefting. For example, 'Mary ate the cake' does not normally presuppose that somebody ate the cake, because its negation, 'Mary didn't eat the cake' would not entail this. However, 'It was Mary that ate the cake' does presuppose that somebody ate it, as this is also implied by the negation, 'It wasn't Mary that ate the cake'.

Then there are presuppositions which are not so much necessary for the semantic coherence of the sentence in isolation as for its interpretation in context. These generally come under the heading of pragmatics. In fact the whole issue of presuppositions is very close to the no man's land between semantics and pragmatics, and many writers argue that the whole topic is better dealt with under pragmatics – that presuppositions belong to the background assumptions made by speakers and addressees as sentences are *used*, rather than the semantic content of sentences in themselves.[15] Others think that the examples listed up to now, at least, involve phenomena about which semantics may have something to say. They are therefore classified (by them) as **semantic presuppositions**. This section is confined to many valued logics and semantic presuppositions – presupposing that the latter exist.

8.4.1 TRUTH GAPS

Following Frege, the denotation of a predicate is a function from individuals to truth values. This creates a problem if there is no individual to serve as the argument of the function. If there is no argument, then there would seem to be no way of computing the value. This is perhaps not true of constant functions, and there is also the possibility of assigning a value at random; but most predicates are not constant functions, and the random assignment of values is not very satisfactory. In his discussion of the problems of Pegasus and Socrates (Chapter 7), Frege suggested that the interpretation of these names was not defined, and therefore the truth value of sentences containing them was also not defined. One interpretation of this would be to have a special member of the domain of discourse marked as 'undefined'. Predicates taking this abnormal individual as an argument do not get a normal truth value.

The absence of an individual to serve as an argument is a form of presupposition failure (in this case an existential presupposition), and the non-assignment of a regular truth value to the sentence is called a **truth gap**. In the case of proper names, classical predicate logic generally stipulates that all models include individuals to serve as the referents for all individual constants; models that do not satisfy the requirement are omitted from consideration as not suitable for the logical language. (An approach to predicate logic that omits this arrangement is **free logic**.) There is also the option of using modal logic, as in the previous chapter, with a varying domain of individuals (actualist) or a domain including any individuals you could possibly want (possibilist). (Note that when modal logic is given an actualist semantics, the quantificational component is a form of free logic rather than classical predicate logic.)

If we do not avail ourselves of such devices, then truth gaps can arise and are prime candidates for a three valued logic.

However, the problem is not confined to proper names. Another type of expression that refers to individuals is definite descriptions, comprising a definite article or some equivalent and a predicate expression denoting a set. The formal equivalent of the definite article is the ι operator, which was treated in Chapter 5 as a function from sets to individuals which picks out a unique individual satisfying the description in the predicate. But what if there is no such unique individual? We will focus here on the case where there is no individual at all satisfying the description (the predicate denotes the empty set), though there is also a problem if there are too many. Let's take Russell's famous example (8.10); (8.11) is Russell's translation of the iota operator into first order logic with equality.

(8.10) The present King of France is bald.

(8.11) $\exists x((\text{KofF}(x) \wedge \forall y(\text{KofF}(y) \rightarrow x = y)) \wedge \text{Bald}(x))$

There are three parts to this translation. The first is an existential statement that there is (at least) one object satisfying the N' description. The second states that there is *at most* one such object. (This formulation is the standard way of expressing 'only one' in first order logic.) The third is the main predicate of the sentence, in this case the attribution of baldness.

The first part requires there to be at least one King of France. However, as recast by Russell, there is nothing presuppositional about this existential requirement: it asserts the fact that there is one with a flourish of trumpets. If there is not a King of France (or for that matter if there is more than one of them), then the sentence is simply false. This is one way of dealing with the problem of presuppositions: to say that when sentences are analysed properly, the problem does not exist. The only problem is the misleading form of the statement in English, which does not match the logical analysis.

This means that the negation of (8.10) is straightforwardly true, contrary to the intuition suggested at the beginning of this section. Actually, intuitions about this vary considerably. In some contexts, the negation can seem quite unproblematic:

(8.12) The present King of France is *not* bald, because there isn't a King of France.

However, the intuition that in neutral contexts (8.10) and its negation are both equally anomalous finds an echo with a number of people, and was argued strongly, in opposition to Russell, by Strawson (1950). His position is reminiscent of Frege's suggestion about proper names, in the new context of definite descriptions. He also argues that the variation in intuitions owes much to contextual factors, including the topicality of the King of France in the sentence. (When it occurs in non-subject positions, it is much easier to absorb it into the predicate and judge the statement false.)

By contrast, Russell's analysis distinguishes two possible meanings of the negation of (8.10). In his logical translation, the negation can either scope over the whole sentence or only over the claim about baldness. On the former reading, the sentence is true, and on the latter reading, false. The second of these involves the existence of the King of France, and is therefore false according to Russell, problematic according to Strawson. The first is closer to (8.12), in which the whole statement is simply rejected.

However, this rejection may be something different from negation in the usual logical sense of reversing the truth value. Negation is also sometimes used as a rejection of the way the sentence is put (what is often referred to as **metalinguistic negation**). Ths can often be captured by embedding the original proposition in a metalinguistic judgement such as 'I wouldn't say ϕ', or 'ϕ doesn't make sense'. Horn (1989) suggests that this might be what is going on in (8.12).

Another important ambiguity in definite descriptions is that they are not always used with the intention of referring. Sometimes they simply describe the attributes of an individual, making an inference on the basis of these attributes. For example, (8.13) draws an inference from the description of the individual rather than relying on the identity of the referent. By contrast (8.14) relies on the identity of the individual to provide information which is not based on the description (assuming that it is not a characteristic of famous linguists to dress in a particular way).

(8.13) The man with the yellow shirt and pink tie has interesting dress sense.
(8.14) The man with the yellow shirt and pink tie is a famous linguist.

It is with the referential use of definite descriptions that the problem of reference failure becomes acute. With the attributive use it can be interpreted along the lines of a quantifier: 'anybody who wears clothes like that'. It is possible that on this reading, a definite description can make sense even if there is nobody to refer to. Take, for example, the sentence 'Elena's husband is a lucky man'. If it turns out that the person seen with Elena is not her husband, and she is actually divorced, the sentence is still meaningful and can perhaps still be given a truth value (and its negation given the opposite truth value).[16]

8.4.2 INHERITANCE OF PRESUPPOSITIONS

If there is such a thing as semantic presuppositions, what happens when these are embedded in more complex expressions? A first attempt to answer this might be that if presupposition failure affects one part of a statement, then this problem is inherited by the whole statement. As it is often put, the set of presuppositions of a sentence is the union of the sets of presuppositions of its subparts. On this basis the following sentence should inherit the existential presupposition in its second conjunct, leaving the whole conjunction with an unsatisfied presupposition.

(8.15) The moon is made of green cheese and the King of France is bald.

There are two main alternatives here. One is that the falsity of the first conjunct is sufficient to evaluate the whole conjunction as false. This would conform to the strong Kleene tables given above. On the one hand, one might say that the presupposition failure in the second conjunct makes the whole conjunction impossible to assign a truth value. This would be consistent with the weak Kleene tables, and was the idea behind Bochvar's 'logic of nonsense'. The unsatisfied presupposition has **projected** from a part of the tree to the whole tree.

However, some embedding words have the opposite effect, of cancelling the presuppositions in part of the sentence and making any presupposition failure harmless.

(8.16) Mary said that the King of France is bald.

This may be an odd thing for Mary to say, but if she said it, the sentence is true (and if she didn't, it is false). The presupposition problems of the complement clause do not affect the evaluation of the sentence: they are removed from the set of presuppositions inherited by the matrix clause.

Items which have the effect of cancelling presuppositions are known as **plugs**, while those which permit them to propagate are known as **holes**.[17] There are also **filters**, which cancel presuppositions under some circumstances and let them leak through in others.

This suggests that presupposition failure is not merely a matter of 'nonsense', but something more subtle, and it turns out that the *strong* Kleene tables are more promising in the attempt to shed light on it.

The main examples of filters are the logical connectives. In general, the binary connectives do not plug an outbreak of presupposition failure in one of their arguments. However, there are exceptions, conspicuously the following.

(8.17) 1. Either the King of France is bald or there is no King of France.
           2. The King of France is bald if there is a King of France.

These sentences are equivalent, given that in the Kleene tables, whether strong or weak, implication is definable as $\neg\phi \vee \psi$. In both of them, the problematic presupposition failure has vanished.

What is happening here? The second subformula explicitly states, or else denies, the presupposition of the first subformula, and in doing so has the effect of stopping it infecting the whole sentence. It seems that if the antecedent of an implication contains a proposition that is presupposed in the consequent, then that presupposition is cancelled. With disjunction, a presupposition in one disjunct can be cancelled if the other disjunct contains its negation.

Presupposition can also be cancelled using conjunction. In this case the resulting sentence will be false, but at least there is no presupposition failure. (Compare Russell's strategy as outlined above.)

(8.18) There is a King of France and the King of France is bald.

Note that these subformulae do not have to be identical to the presupposition being cancelled but only to entail it, as illustrated by the following examples. The first contains an existential presupposition, but this is cancelled when it is embedded in the other sentences. It is entailed by Harry being married.

(8.19) 1. Harry's wife no longer lives with him.
           2. If Harry is married, his wife no longer lives with him.
           3. Either Harry isn't married or his wife no longer lives with him.
           4. Harry is married and his wife no longer lives with him.

Here is a list of the filtering conditions for connectives.[18] It will be seen that negation, as defined here, does not allow filtering. For all the binary connectives, the conditions allow for possibilities of cancellation. They state what is required, if ϕ has an unsatisfied proposition π, for this presupposition to be satisfied (plugged) at the level of the composite formula.

(8.20) If ϕ presupposes π, then:
           1. $\neg\,\phi$ presupposes π.
           2. $\phi \wedge \psi$ presupposes $\psi \rightarrow \pi$.
           3. $\phi \vee \psi$ presupposes $\neg\,\psi \rightarrow \pi$.
           4. $\phi \rightarrow \psi$ presupposes $\neg\,\psi \rightarrow \pi$.
           5. $\psi \rightarrow \phi$ presupposes $\psi \rightarrow \pi$.

8.4.3 ASSERTION AND PRESUPPOSITION

It seems as if tracking the projection of presuppositions from subformulae may be largely independent of the truth or falsity of the subformulae themselves. If so, it should be possible to keep track of truth value and presupposition side by side in a **product logic** like that introduced in the semantics section. The values would be pairs of binary digits, the first representing the truth value and the second, the satisfaction of presuppositions. We can call the two dimensions, following Beaver (op. cit.), 'assertion' and 'presupposition' respectively. (The terminology varies in the litarature.) Assertion is calculated for each connective by the normal truth-functional connective rules, while presupposition is calculated on the basis of inheritance principles, including the filtering conditions in (8.20).

Note that this is not the same product system as the one in the semantics section. That was equivalent to Belnap's four valued logic, with the two co-ordinates being used to keeping track of truth and falsity independently. The one we are talking about now combines the classical logic of truth values (1 for true, 0 for false) with a calculus of presuppositions such as that outlined in this section. If the possible combinations are translated into a many valued logic, they give the *three* valued logic of the strong Kleene tables, the overall result being the 'undefined' middle value whenever the pre-supposition co-ordinate is 0.[19]

8.5 GOING HIGHER ORDER

It is possible to incorporate quantified logic, whether first order or higher order, into a many valued logic. An influential example of this is Muskens' (1996) higher order partial (and paraconsistent) logic Ty4, which he describes as 'partialized Montague semantics'. This combines Ty2 (Chapter 7) with a form of Belnap's four valued logic BN4 (this chapter, above).[20]

The basic technical problem that reference failure gives rise to is how to give a truth value to a predicate when its argument has an undefined value. In a higher order classical or modal logic the predicate is a function whose range is the set $\{0, 1\}$. If a determinate value in that set cannot be found for every argument, then the denotation of the predicate is no longer a function. So the question arises, whether to abandon the requirement that it should be a function, and if so how exactly.

One alternative would be to treat predicate denotations as **partial functions**. These are like functions except for the requirement that every argument be assigned a value. (On the other hand if there is a value, that still has to be unique.) This apparently simple solution, unfortunately, makes the logic more complicated, as it has to deal not only with predicates but expressions of higher order types, so that we can end up with partial functions from partial functions to partial functions.

Another approach, which was foreshadowed by Frege, is to add to the domain of individuals a special entity to be the denotation of all individual expressions that do not have a normal reference – a kind of 'undefined individual'. This is analogous to using a third truth value for propositions whose classical truth value is undefined. Frege's suggestion was not taken up in the development of classical first order logic, but has been rediscovered in some later developments. Helman (1992) proposes a higher order partial logic constructed in essentially this way. The domain of denotation for each type σ is the union of its normal domain D_σ with the singleton set $\{*_\sigma\}$, where $*_\sigma$ is an undefined element appropriate to type σ. For truth values, $*_t$ will be the 'undefined' truth value. The rule then says simply that a function maps the undefined argument of its domain to the undefined argument of its range.

Muskens opts for yet another approach, which is to replace functions by relations. Recall that in Chapter 5 relations were converted into functions by 'currying'. Muskens proposes to revert to relations, 'reversing Schönfinkel's trick'.[21] However, unlike first order logic, these are higher order relations which can take arguments of different types. As a predicate relating an individual to a truth value is now a relation rather than a function, it can take more than one value from {0, 1}, or none at all. This is another way of expressing Belnap's logic of truth combinations.

8.6 PROBABILITY AND FUZZINESS

In the semantics section above, the non-classical truth values were given, for some systems, a numerical value between 0 and 1, with the higher degrees being somehow 'closer to truth' than the lower ones. In this section we will look at some of the ways in which this 'truer than' relation can be understood.

One way to interpret a third truth value is 'maybe'. When there are many intermediate truth degrees, they can be thought of as probabilities, with values closer to 1 indicating greater probability. This was, in fact, one of Łukasiewicz's original intuitions. However, interpreting his many valued logics in terms of probability theory proved not to be straightforward, as the differences between the two are considerable. Nonetheless it is an application which has recently had a revival of interest.

There are also situations where judgements of truth or falsity are problematic for a different reason: there is no clear cut-off point between the two. This is a common phenomenon in linguistics, notably with the gradable predicates discussed in the introduction to this chapter. It also plays an important part in robotics, where it has led to an approach known as **fuzzy logic**.

Despite their similarity, it is important to appreciate the difference between probability and fuzziness. The following contrast will serve as an example.[22]

(8.21) 1. The patient should survive the next week.
        2. The patient is young.

The first statement is probabilistic. Whether the patient survives or not is ultimately a two valued affair, which will be decided one way or the other. The uncertainty is epistemic. The second statement, however, is by nature only true to a certain degree. Finding out the exact age of the patient to the day and month is not going to make it any easier to judge true or false; it is the kind of judgement that is intrinsically fuzzy.

It should be admitted that this characterisation of probability as epistemic and fuzziness as ontological may not be as cut and dried as it has just been presented. One way of viewing probability is as epistemic uncertainty, but it has also been argued to be a matter of inherent randomness in the phenomena, at least in some cases. Fuzziness, for its part, has also been argued to be a matter of imperfect knowledge. It has also been pointed out many times that 'probable' is itself a good example of a fuzzy predicate!

In any case, both fuzziness and probability, as applications of 'reasoning about uncertainty', will be the subject of this section.

8.6.1 FUZZY LOGIC

Fuzzy logic was developed by Lotfi Zadeh[23] in the context of robotics and automated reasoning. The basic intuition can be motivated as follows. Imagine a robotic train approaching a station, with the rule that if it is in the station it should stop. If this instruction is interpreted in classical logic, it should approach the station at full speed, and then when it decides, on whatever basis, that it is in the station, slam the brakes on. Very logical, but not very comfortable. Fuzzy logic tries to model the knowledge of most human train drivers, that it is better to treat approaching and braking as gradual processes. A 'fuzzy controller' might interpret the rule as saying that if the train is 10 per cent in the station, then the brakes are on 10 per cent, and if it is 50 per cent in the station then the brakes are on 50 per cent. When it is 99 per cent in the station, it should be almost stationary. The classification of the train as 'being in the station' and of the brakes as 'on' are known as **fuzzy predicates**.

This idea has proved very fruitful in robotics and smart gadgets. However, there is a distinction to be drawn between its widespread use as a paradigm guiding an approach to engineering and its formal study as logic, which is a specialised and generally speaking more recent undertaking. The second of these enterprises is sometimes termed formal or deductive fuzzy logic. Łukasiewicz's many valued logic, in which a numerical or quasi-numerical truth degree between 0 and 1 can be assigned to propositions, is the natural place to start, and occupies an important place in deductive fuzzy logic. (Percentages, as used informally in the last paragraph, are normalised in fuzzy logic to values between 0 and 1.)

In natural language it has been argued that most concepts, and not just the obviously gradable ones, are in fact fuzzy. Some objects are **prototypical** examples of the concept, while others are marginal – for example a penguin as an example of a bird, a tomato as an example of a fruit, or boron as an example of a metal. This argument has been used to call into question the idea that predicates like 'bird', 'fruit' or 'metal' pick out sets, as sets are classically considered to have definite boundaries, and one element is not 'more' a member than others. However, this depends on the definition of 'set'. In classical set theory, the characteristic function of a set (Chapter 5) is a function from the set of individuals to the set $\{0, 1\}$ of truth values; if the value for an element d is 1, then it is in the set, and if it is 0 it is out of the set. In a many valued logic we can have many valued characteristic functions, so that the question 'Is this object an element of the set?' can get answers like $\frac{1}{2}$ or 0.99. This formalises the idea of a **fuzzy set**, which is the denotation of a fuzzy predicate. The opposite of 'fuzzy' is 'crisp', and the limiting case of a set whose membership criteria (characteristic function) is a clear-cut yes or no is known as a **crisp set**.

(8.22) 1. Classical (crisp) set: $\chi_s: D \rightarrow \{0,1\}$
     2. Fuzzy set: $\chi_s: D \rightarrow [0, 1]$[24] (other ranges are possible)

Fuzzy characteristic functions are known as membership functions, and their values are called membership degrees.

In deductive fuzzy logic, as in deductive logic in general, a rule takes the form of an inference from a collection of premises to a conclusion. It will first take values for the individual premises (perhaps from the readings of a sensor or from a database, or they might simply be assigned by an expert), aggregate them to calculate a value for the whole set, and then calculate a value for the conclusion which preserves the truth degree of the combined premises. Aggregation is written here as $\odot$; it can be thought of as a form of conjunction. In *deductive* fuzzy logic, the type of conjunction used is constrained by the need for the rule to obey the fuzzy form of the deduction equivalence (Chapter 2):

(8.23) $\phi_1 \odot \phi_2 \odot \ldots \odot \phi_n \leq \psi$ iff $\phi_1 \odot \phi_2 \odot \ldots \odot \phi_{n-1} \leq \phi_n \rightarrow \psi$

The $\leq$ relation is the natural ordering on the truth degrees. The presence of an implication connective enables the truth-preserving property to be extended to embedded rules (which are often not needed in traditional fuzzy logic).

The next question is what properties the aggregation or conjunction operator must have in order to satisfy these conditions.

It was noted in the semantics section that using the **minimum** definition, conjunction and disjunction are not interdefinable with Łukasiewicz implication. However, we can also define conjunction and disjunction connectives which *are*. The definitions will be given shortly. These are sometimes known as 'strong' Łukasiewicz connectives, while the truth tables given in the semantics section are 'weak'.[25]

The requirement for a conjunction in fuzzy logic is that it should be a continuous **t-norm**, an operation on points in a set which captures the idea of distance. A **t-norm** is an operator T which satisfies the following four conditions:

(8.24) **Associativity**: $T(a, T(b, c)) = T(T(a, b), c)$
Commutativity: $T(a, b) = T(b, a)$
Order-preservation: if $a \leq b$ and $c \leq d$ then $T(a, c) \leq T(b, d)$
Unit law: $T(a, 1) = a$

There is more than one way of defining a conjunction so as to satisfy these laws. The minimum conjunction operator of section 8.3 satisfies them; however, we will need a new definition of implication to interact with it, as it does not interact with Łukasiewicz implication in the way demanded by the deduction equivalence. The implication connective we need is known as Gödel implication; the minimum conjunction operator is known in this context as the Gödel t-norm, and the whole combination is known as Gödel or Gödel–Dummett logic. (Strong) Łukasiewicz conjunction is the t-norm which is interdefinable with Łukasiewicz implication; it is known as the Łukasiewicz t-norm, and its definition will be given shortly. Ordinary multiplication is also a t-norm (the Product t-norm), provided that the set of truth degrees is infinite; the corresponding implication connective is known as Goguen implication.[26] There are others as well, not listed here, but these three are the most common set-ups for fuzzy logic.

(8.25)

Logic	t-norm	Implication
G – Gödel–Dummett	minimum	Gödel implication
Ł – Łukasiewicz	strong Łukasiewicz	Łukasiewicz implication
Π– Product or Goguen	multiplication	Goguen implication

Here are the definitions (valuations) for the connectives. Note the different nota-tions for conjunction.[27]

(8.26) Continuous t-norms
Łukasiewicz t-norm (Ł): $V(\phi \,\&\, \psi) = \max(0, V(\phi) + V(\psi) - 1)$
Minimum or Gödel t-norm (G): $V(\phi \wedge \psi) = \min(V(\phi), V(\psi))$
Product t-norm (Π): $V(\phi \cdot \psi) = V(\phi) \cdot V(\psi)$

(8.27) Fuzzy implications
Łukasiewicz logic: $V(\phi \rightarrow_{\text{Ł}} \psi) = \min(1, 1 - (V(\phi) + V(\psi)))$
Gödel–Dummett logic: $V(\phi \rightarrow_{G} \psi) = 1$ iff $V(\phi) \le V(\psi)$, otherwise $= V(\psi)$
Product or Goguen logic: $V(\phi \rightarrow_{\pi} \psi) = 1$ iff $V(\phi) \le V(\psi)$, otherwise $= V(\psi)/V(\phi)$

The t-norms given here with their related implications constitute a 'family' of deductive fuzzy logics. One can, for example, arrange them in order of strength, so that the conjunction of two propositions according to a 'weaker' definition is less than or equal to the conjunction according to a 'stronger' one. (This is included in the exercises.) The t-norm logics have been studied as a family by Hájek (1998), who defined a logic called BL – for 'basic (fuzzy) logic' – of which they are all extensions. The relationships between these logics are summarised in Figure 11.7 (p. 256).

8.6.2 VAGUENESS

This section began with the question of how we can make semantic sense of vague predicates, specifically those whose vagueness is linked to gradability. It was suggested that fuzzy logic, with its graded notions of truth and set membership, was a promising approach. The fraction notation, of course, suggests precision; however, it can be ques-tioned whether our basic intuitions about gradability can really be pinned down and given numerical values. Assigning an exact numerical value for them ('precisification' in fuzzy terminology) threatens to undermine the whole idea of vagueness.

One way of handling this (and there are many in the literature) is in the spirit of meaning postulates. Recall that these are constraints associated with a lexical entry such that only models which respect those constraints will be taken into consid-eration in semantic interpretation. In this way we are not bound to the truth values assigned by a particular model, but can make generalisations about what we expect to be true in any acceptable models.

To take the example in (8.21), 'The patient is young', we have a vague predicate which we might want to capture using fuzzy logic. But how young is young? Supposing the patient is 16, do we want to give the sentence a truth degree of 0.6, 0.7, 0.8 . . .? Different valuations might be plausible in different contexts, but the meaning of 'young' should not be tied to any of them. The crucial properties that need to be captured are listed and then partially formalised (the notion 'close to' is not formalised here).

(8.28) 1. If the age of *a* is less than the age of *b*, then Young(a) will be truer than Young(b).
      2. Some people (real or imaginary) can be characterised as definitely young, or as definitely not young.
      3. Small differences in age result in small differences in 'youngness'.

(8.29) 1. If age(x) $\leq$ age(y), then Young(y) $\rightarrow$ Young(x)
      2. For some x, Young(x) and for some x, $\neg$ Young(x)
      3. If age(x) is close to age(y), then Young(x) $\leftrightarrow$ Young(y)

Fuzzy logic has been applied to the most famous problem of vague predicates, the *sorites* paradox. This has taken various forms over its 2,500-year history, but in one classic form it goes as follows. A large number, call it *k*, of grains of sand constitutes a heap (Greek *soros*). If you remove one grain, you still have a heap of sand. If you continue this process *k* – 1 times, there will be one grain of sand. If you do not accept that this is still a heap, then you are saying that, at some point in the procedure, removing one grain of sand changed the heap into being not a heap.

The form of this argument is that of an **inductive proof**. This is constituted by a **base case**, which says that an object *x* has a property P, and an **inductive step**, which says that if you derive *x'* from *x* by a rule R, then *x'* also has P (in other words P is preserved by R). Then you can show (by a repeated steps of *modus ponens*) that any object derived from *x* by successive applications of R will have property P.

(8.30) **Base case** Heap(k)
      Inductive step Heap(n) $\rightarrow$ Heap(n – 1)
      First conclusion Heap(k – 1)
      . . .
      (k – 1)th conclusion Heap(1)

The consequence relation assumed in this description is bivalent: each inductive step preserves the truth value of 1 intact from antecedent to consequent. Eventually a situation is reached where the value of 1 is clearly implausible, and then the problem kicks in. However, this changes if we use truth degrees and a many valued implication such as Łukasiewicz implication. The truth degree of Heap(n) will change for values of *n* (in this case, the truth degree will decrease as *n* decreases). The implication in the inductive step will therefore not have the truth degree 1, but 1 minus the slight difference in truth degree between the antecedent and the consequent. By the time we reach the last step of the proof, the truth degree will be considerably smaller, perhaps close to 0, but there is no particular point at which we have claimed that removing one grain has turned a heap into a non-heap.[28]

8.6.3 PROBABILITY

During the past few decades, probability theory has come to play an important role in linguistics, especially but not exclusively computational linguistics. It is far beyond the scope of this book to introduce probability theory in general; this section will just look at some connections with many valued logic. As with fuzziness, the treatment of probability as formal logic is best regarded as a different enterprise from probability theory in general, and is less mature as a field of study, though pioneers included Hosiasson, Reichenbach, Carnap and Kolmogorov.

The probability of an event is normalised as a number between 0 and 1, like the truth degrees of a proposition. (The function assigning probabilities is analogous to a valuation.) **Events** are modelled as sets, whose elements are **outcomes**; the whole universal set of outcomes is called the sample space, and notated as Ω. The probability of A is the number of outcomes in A as a proportion of the number of outcomes in Ω. The probability that an event will not occur is the probability of the complement of an event. The probability $P(\sim A)$ of A not happening is simply $1 - P(A)$, just as in many valued logic $V(\neg P) = 1 - V(P)$.

The tables for conjunction and disjunction are more complicated, for at least two reasons, chiefly because we have to take into account whether or not the probability of two events is independent. If it is not, then the probability of the conjunction or disjunction cannot be calculated purely from the individual probabilities of the juncts. In other words conjunction and disjunction of probabilities are, in general, *not truth functions*. By contrast the logics treated in this chapter, though non-classical, are still truth-functional.

The probability of a conjunction of independent events A and B is the product $P(A) \cdot P(B)$, and that of a disjunction is the **probabilistic sum** $P(A) + P(B) - P(A) \cdot P(B)$. In other words, for independent events the Product t-norm $\prod$ is appropriate. What about the minimum or Gödel t-norm? The intersection of two sets is equal to the smaller of the two in just one case, which is when the smaller set is a subset of the larger one. In other words, the minimum t-norm applies when one of the two events is completely dependent on the other (the two are in a subset relationship). Similarly, the probability of a disjunction of the two events, in this case only, will be the maximum of the two events.[29]

Events with some degree of positive correlation are intermediate between the two cases, so that these two t-norms will put a lower and upper bound on the probability of a conjunction or disjunction.

Another notion is the **conditional probability** of one event given another event. It is a measure of the likely connection between two events. The conditional probability of A given B is written $P(A|B)$, and it is defined as the probability of A and B over the probability of B (the proportion of the probability mass in B that is also in A).

(8.31) $P(A \mid B) = \dfrac{P(A \cap B)}{P(B)}$ (where $P(B) \neq 0$)

(8.32) $P(A \cap B) = P(B|A) \cdot P(A)$

Conditional probability can be used to measure the degree of confirmation of a hypothesis by observations. It can be conveniently calculated using the following formula, which is equivalent by Bayes' theorem.

$$(8.33) \quad P(A|B) = \frac{P(B|A) \cdot P(A)}{P(B)}$$

In this arrangement, P(B | A) is known as the likelihood, P(A) is the prior probability (of the hypothesis) and P(B) the probability of the observation. In many cases P(B) can be taken as 1, as it is kept constant while the hypotheses are varied.

Conditional probability looks very much like an implication operator, and the natural question is whether it can be treated as a real logical implication, and if so which one. The claim that it can amounts to 'the hypothesis that *probabilities of conditionals* are *conditional probabilities*'.[30]

Given the relationship to the logic of sets, one option would be to use the definition of material implication and define P(A | B) as P(~B) ∪ P(A). However, the counter-intuitive properties of material implication would kick in badly here. We can ask which instances (outcomes) confirm the implication and which are counterexamples. The expected answer, from the discussion of conditional probability, would be that only those in B ∩ A can be confirming instances and those in ~B ∩ A are falsifying instances or counterexamples. All other outcomes – that is, all those in ~A – should be irrelevant to the probability of the conditional. If we are looking for the probability that if something is a swan then it is black, we should not need to count things that are not swans, like dogs or cats. However, the definition of material implication would treat the latter as confirming instances, in the same way as material implication is judged true in rows of truth table where the antecedent is false. Figure 8.4 shows five such dogs or cats sitting at the bottom of the diagram. While the probability of a black swan in the diagram ought to be .4 (two out of five outcomes in the set of swans), the treatment of dogs and cats as confirming instances makes it .7 (seven out of ten outcomes in the total sample space).

In classical logic material implication gives serviceable results for many applications, but in probabilistic logic it would appear not to be satisfactory. Conditional probability is an estimate of a connection between two events, whereas one of the

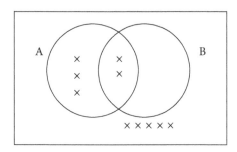

Figure 8.4   Conditional probability and material implication

problems with material implication is that it does not suppose any connection between its antecedent and consequent (the problem of relevance). A satisfactory probabilistic implication should not take account of the irrelevant cases where the antecedent is false, when counting the confirming instances and the counterexamples. This is the case in Bayesian inference, as (8.31) makes no reference to P(~B). A number of proposals for probabilistic implications have been made in the literature; these overlap partly with those used in fuzzy logic, including Gödel implication and Goguen implication.[31]

8.7 ALGEBRAIC BACKGROUND II

The discussion in the last few sections has introduced some concepts from **group theory**, which it will be useful to summarise in this final section in the chapter. These definitions are important for the algebraic treatment of logic in general, not just for the many valued logics of this chapter.

Group theory studies the behaviour of **operators**, which are defined as binary functions from a set onto itself. The operator is usually written as a dot, $\cdot$, and called **multiplication**, as it is a generalisation of multiplication in arithmetic. There is a hierarchy of group-like objects which obey weaker or stronger axioms. For present purposes, we are interested mainly in weaker structures called **monoids**.

Minimally, multiplication is required to be associative, so that $a \cdot (b \cdot c) = (a \cdot b) \cdot c$. Such a structure is called a **semigroup**.

To get a monoid, we add an **identity** element, a special member of the set conventionally written e. It has the property that it multiplies with any element a to give a. One prototypical example of a monoid is composition of functions, which is associative and has the identity function as the identity element. Another is concatenation of strings – the operator is concatenation, and the identity element is the empty string.

In logic, the identity element is taken as *truth* (the constant true proposition, or simply the truth value 1). Its combination with any proposition p gives p. In classical logic the multiplication operator is conjunction, for which the identity is 1, as in arithmetical multiplication. For disjunction the identity is 0, which in arithmetic is the identity when $\cdot$ is interpreted as addition. This is part of the rationale behind the use of multiplication symbols for conjunction and addition symbols for disjunction.

Further requirements can be placed on particular types of monoids. For example they can be **commutative** or **idempotent**.

Commutative: $a \cdot b = b \cdot a$
Idempotent: $a \cdot a = a$

If we take multiplication as modelling conjunction, then in the logics in this chapter it is always commutative, though this is not true for all logics. Minimum or Gödel conjunction is idempotent ($\phi \wedge \phi = \phi$), as is classical conjunction, but strong Łukasiewicz conjunction is not.

In Chapter 3, partially ordered sets (posets) were used to interpret logics. Orders and groups are different kinds of algebraic structures; however, orders – especially lattices – contain a similar notion of binary operator, in the form of **glb** and its dual, **lub**. With these operations, lattices can be given a group-theoretic definition alongside the order-theoretic definition. The operators are required to be commutative and to obey the law of absorption: a $\vee$ (a $\wedge$ b) = a and a $\wedge$ (a $\vee$ b) = a (from which idempotency follows).

In classical logic, conjunction is the **glb** operation, so it can be defined equivalently as **glb** of a lattice or as the multiplication operator of a monoid. This is also the case for Gödel conjunction. This does not work for all notions of conjunction, including strong Łukasiewicz conjunction. So we need a more general way of relating the group and order operations, when they are not the same. This is found in the notion of an **ordered monoid**. An ordered monoid is a set ordered by a partial order $\leq$, which is also a monoid with multiplication operator $\cdot$. In this case multiplication is required to be compatible with the partial ordering, or **isotonic**:

(8.34) If a $\leq$ b, then for all c, a $\cdot$ c $\leq$ b $\cdot$ c.

It is useful to have a name for this more general notion of conjunction which is modelled by the monoid operator $\cdot$ but is not necessarily a **glb** operation. It is called **fusion**, and will be looked at in more detail in Chapter 11.

If the partial order is a lattice, then the ordered monoid is a lattice-ordered monoid. The multiplication operator of the monoid need not be the same as the **glb** or **lub** operations of the lattice, though multiplication must at least respect the ordering in the way just defined. If the order is a linear order, then the ordered monoid is said to be linearly ordered monoid.

Looking back at the conditions for a t-norm, you can see that it corresponds precisely to the operator of a commutative ordered monoid (remember a monoid is automatically associative and has an identity element, in this case 1).

A **group** is a monoid in which every element a has an inverse, sometimes written a^{-1}, such that $a \cdot a^{-1} = e$. In ordinary multiplication, this is of course the reciprocal of a, namely $1/a$.

The logics discussed here do not involve groups or inverses, but ordered monoids do involve the related notion of **residuation**.

(8.35) For any elements a and b there is a greatest element c such that c $\cdot$ b = a. This element c is called the **residual** of a by b, and is written a/b.

While a residual is not an inverse (reciprocal), it can still be thought of as a fraction: if you multiply a/b by b, you get a. In terms of logic, residuation models the implication connective: if a is the interpretation of ϕ and b is the interpretation of ψ, then b/a is the interpretation of $\phi \rightarrow \psi$ (if you combine it with ϕ, you get ψ).

It follows from these definitions that a $\cdot$ b $\leq$ c iff a $\leq$ c/b. Interpreting multiplication as conjunction and residuation as implication, this is the same condition as the deduction equivalence. Because of this correspondence. the deduction equivalence is also known as the principle of residuation. It is one of the most fundamental principles of logic, and there will be many applications of it in the remaining chapters.

EXERCISE 8.7.0.1

1. (a) Which of the following items trigger semantic presuppositions, and what are they? (i) know, (ii) since, (iii) also, (iv) because, (v) continue, (vi) for this reason, (vii) that's why, (viii) try to, (ix) manage to, (x) again.
   (b) Classify the following items as holes, plugs or filters, with examples. (i) maybe, (ii) dream, (iii) of course, (iv) either . . . or . . ., (v) accuse, (vi) hesitate, (vii) it is false that (viii) is it the case that . . .?

2. Look again at the table of filtering conditions for presupposiitons (8.20). Define an operator P such that $P(\phi) = 1$ iff the presuppositions of ϕ are satisfied. Using the strong Kleene tables, we then have the following conditions for projection:
   - $P(\neg\phi) = P(\phi)$
   - $P(\phi \wedge \psi) = ((\neg\phi \wedge P(\phi)) \vee P(\psi)) \wedge ((\neg\psi \wedge P(\psi)) \wedge P(\phi))$
   - $P(\phi \vee \psi) = ((\phi \wedge P(\phi)) \vee P(\psi)) \wedge ((\psi \wedge P(\psi)) \wedge P(\phi))$
     - (a) State the conditions for $P(\phi \rightarrow \psi)$.
     - (b) Evaluate: (i) $P(P(\phi \rightarrow \phi))$, (ii) $P(\neg P(\phi) \vee \phi)$, (iii) $P(P(\phi \wedge \phi))$.
     - (c) Explain why the list in (8.20) is valid.
     - (This exercise is based on Gamut (1990), Vol. I, Ch. 5.)

3. Historically, Łukasiewicz developed his logics taking only negation and implication as connectives, without dealing with weak conjunction or disjunction at all. However, they are definable in his logic as follows:
   - $\phi \wedge \psi = \phi \otimes (\phi \rightarrow \psi)$
   - $\phi \vee \psi = (\phi \rightarrow \psi) \rightarrow \psi$
   (The implication connective in these definitions is Łukasiewicz implication, and $\otimes$ is strong conjunction.)
   (a) Check that this definition does indeed give weak conjunction.
   (b) Does the same definition also work if $\otimes$ is the product norm and $\rightarrow$ is Goguen implication? (See p. 167.)

4. (a) Given two propositions ϕ and ψ, arrange the t-norm operations on ϕ and ψ (G, Ł and Π) in increasing order. Does it matter what examples of ϕ and ψ are taken?
   (b) Do the same for the three versions of strong disjunction (these are also known as t-conorms), which are given by: $\max(V(\phi), V(\psi))$ (the G co-norm); $\min(1, V(\phi)+V(\psi))$ (the Łukasiewicz t-conorm or bounded sum); and $V(\phi) + V(\psi) - (V(\phi) + V(\psi))$ (the probabilistic sum or Π t-conorm).

5. (a) Consider the account of the sorites problem given in section 8.6.2. Of the two premises in example (8.30), which of the premises (or both) do you think should, intuitively, change its truth degree as grains of sand are removed?
   (b) Assume that a million grains is definitely a heap and ten grains is definitely not a heap. Evaluate the two premises for $k = 100,000$ and $k = 10$, according to each of the three t-norm systems described in this chapter.
   (c) Which of the three systems best fits your answer to the first part of this question?

NOTES

1. Attributed to Heraclitus (c. 500 BC).
2. Vātsāyana, see Horn (1989) p. 86.
3. According to another interpretation, which goes back to the medieval Arabic commentator Al-Farabi, Aristotle may have been getting at the need to shift the point of evaluation, thus anticipating modal or temporal logic. There is a good discussion of this in Horn (1989).
4. See Horn (op. cit.) for more details.
5. Some writers refer to both partial and paraconsistent logics as 'partial logics'.
6. Historically, this is one reason for the word 'value' in the term 'truth value'. Frege was influenced by the teaching of the Göttingen philosopher Hermann Lotze that that truth as the object or 'value' of logic, as goodness is of ethics and beauty of aesthetics.
7. Although Aristotle is known for his advocacy of bivalence, he did not state ECQ; in fact, he seems to have denied it. Many medieval logicians, however, believed that it could be proved, and modern classical logic follows them in this. One such proof will be examined in Chapter 10.
8. Meinong's ontology, introduced in Chapter 7, allowed for a domain of impossible entities beyond the layer of possible but not actual entities that 'subsist'. He allows them a mode of being which is usually translated 'absistence'.
9. For other approaches, see Fox and Lappin (2005), Pollard (2008b, 2008c). Since part of the problem arises from the identification of mutually entailing propositions in a Lindenbaum algebra (Chapter 3), one solution is to avoid doing this and make entailment a preorder instead of a partial order.
10. For the ideas discussed in this section, see Priest et al. (2013).
11. Another important figure in its development was Dunn, and it is sometimes referred to as Belnap–Dunn logic. It was used by Muskens (1996) in his TY4 system.
12. Another term is 'generalised truth values'.
13. In AI, and consequently much of the HPSG literature, this subsumption relation is read from top to bottom, so that the empty feature structure is called Top, and the inconsistent feature structure, if it is included, is Bottom. Often this element of the lattice is omitted, and inconsistent feature structures simply 'crash'.
14. Possessives can be thought of as a kind of definite description. In many languages possessive constructions include the definite article, though that is not the case with the English 's construction.
15. Kempson (1975), Stalnaker (1984).
16. This and other issues raised by Strawson about definite descriptions will be discussed further in the next chapter.
17. This terminology was introduced by Karttunen (1973).
18. Beaver (1997).
19. For a short critique of this approach, see Gamut (1990), Vol. I, pp. 186–187.
20. As Ty2 is a two-sorted logic and also bivalent, the 2 in its name can stand for either the number of sorts or the number of truth values. Ty4 refers primarily to the number of truth values. Systems like this can be distinguished by subscripting the number of sorts and superscripting the number of truth values, so that Muskens' logic would be written Ty_2^4.
21. As already mentioned, 'Curry functions' go back at least to Schönfinkel (see also Chapter 13).
22. Hájek (1998).
23. Zadeh (1965).
24. The real numbers from 0 to 1 inclusive.
25. The terminology may be confusing here. As far as disjunction and conjunction are concerned, the weak Łukasiewicz interpretation is the same as the strong Kleene interpretation (while the weak Kleene interpretation is the same as Bochvar's interpretation). Such is life.

26. After Joseph Goguen, a computer scientist and major contributor to fuzzy logic.
27. In the tradition of many valued logic, other symbols are common, notably & for strong conjunction and $\underline{\vee}$ for strong disjunction. The symbol ⊙ is also often used for conjunction or aggregation.
28. Essentially this account was proposed by Goguen, using the Product logic Π.
29. Gaines (1978).
30. Hájek (2001).
31. A survey of the conditions required for a probabilistic implication is provided in Nguyen et al. (2002).

CHAPTER 9

SITUATIONS AND INFORMATION

We believe linguistic meaning should be seen within a general picture of a world teeming with meaning, a world full of information for organisms appropriately attuned to that meaning.[1]

This chapter is unusual, for this book, in that it is about a semantic theory which is not based on logic. Situation semantics is a theory of information, and of how the world gives rise to information. It was introduced by Barwise and Perry (1983), taking as its starting point a semantics for perception complements and attitude reports in language. The framework they developed became very influential in linguistics, reaching the height of its popularity in the early 1990s. In a more general mathematical form known as situation theory, this influence extended beyond linguistics into many other fields.

9.1 AN OUTLINE OF SITUATION SEMANTICS

9.1.1 SITUATIONS

To motivate situation semantics, let's start with perception complements.

(9.1) The reporter saw the planes return to the carrier.
(9.2) The camera caught Katja not stopping at the red light.

Seeing is a binary relation. One role in the relation is for the see-er, filled in (9.1) by a reporter. But what exactly is the other one, that which is seen? It is natural to take [the planes return to the carrier] as denoting a proposition, but what does it mean to see a proposition? Presumably truth values are not visible objects. Barwise and Perry's answer is a simple one: the perception complement is a **situation**, a piece of reality which can be characterised, in this case, as one with planes landing on an aircraft carrier.

Example (9.2) raises the question of what it would mean to see a negative proposition. According to situation semantics, what is seen is again a situation, this time one characterised by a piece of negative information. We still have to discuss what negative information is – and will do so later in the chapter – but at least it seems intuitive that the image caught on camera is that of a recognisable (and possibly expensive) situation.

The first part of this book treated the denotations of sentences as truth values, and in the second part the senses of sentences were treated using the apparatus of possible worlds. So what is the difference between a situation and a world? There are two main ones.

The first is that a situation is small. A world, following Wittgenstein and Carnap, has to be large enough to decide all propositions, to divide them into true and false. Remember that (as Chomsky emphasises) serious languages can generate an infinite number of sentences. And to do possible worlds semantics, we need not only worlds but *sets* of worlds (the denotation of propositions) and in some treatments we end up with sets of sets of worlds.[2] A situation, by contrast, can be arbitrarily small. For example, we can narrow it down to what is going on on the flight deck of an aircraft carrier, and indeed to only one part of what is going on there (ignoring any passing seagulls, or navy personnel scurrying to prepare other planes for take-off). This situation will have nothing to say about the football results, the weather on the other side of the world, or the latest discovery of an exoplanet, or any of the other propositions that we could reasonably express in the same language.

This is to say that situations model **partial information**. In a situation some things are true and some things are false, but for a great many things it will give no information whatsoever. There can also be larger situations which offer a lot more information, but none will give information about everything, unless we define the whole universe as one big situation (a limiting case).[3]

Partiality was introduced in the previous chapter, and will continue to be the theme of this and the next one, only here it will not be modelled by many valued logics. Instead of saying that a statement has a third truth value other than 0 or 1, we will simply say that there is no information about it; it is not **supported** by a given situation. This different strategy leads to a different kind of logic.

The other difference is that situations are *real*. The role of the situation in the example is as something that can be seen. However, situations can enter into a variety of relations with each other, or with individuals. For example, a situation can cause a person to react in a particular way, or it can trigger another situation, either nearby or at a distance.

(9.3) 1. The final whistle brought celebrations in Bucharest and groans of despair in London.
2. Mary contacting her lawyer persuaded John to fly to Australia.
3. Think of a telephone as a very elongated cat: treading on its tail in London makes it miaow in New York.

9.1.2 INFORMATION IN SITUATION THEORY

This approach, in which semantics takes the world as its starting point, is known as **ecological realism**. The world gives rise to information because it contains certain regular patterns, or **uniformities**, to which some agents (themselves part of the same reality) may be sensitive, or **attuned**. A situation, as a slice of this reality, will exhibit some of these uniformities. Let's proceed immediately to some of the examples of uniformities that are relevant to language. Properties, relations, events are examples of things that situations can have in common; we are attuned to situations where it is raining, or something has the property of being broken, or two entities do not like each other. One can characterise situations by these recurring features. In situation semantics, such properties and relations are taken as primitive uniformities (not constructed out of sets and ordered pairs, as in previous chapters).

Individuals can be thought of as a particular case of uniformities which persist across many situations. Place and time are also important uniformities; situations can be characterised as overlapping or successive in time, or near or far in space. These features, just like individuals, are picked up by language and by our cognitive systems.

Using these uniformities to characterise situations involves a degree of abstraction away from irrelevant details, like the passing seagulls in the previous section. When a situation is reduced to a list of features and their values, it is called an **abstract situation**. In effect, the information in it is *digitalised*.[4] These abstract situations are the building blocks of communication. For example, the information in (9.1) enables me to reconstruct the abstract situation on the carrier deck, but I am not able to smell the sea or hear the birds. In situation semantics, an abstract situation is known as a state of affairs or **soa**. Since soas serve as the basic units of information, they have also become known as **infons**,[5] and this is what they will usually be called in the remainder of the chapter.

Distinguishing between situations and infons means that we can deal with infons which are not necessarily factual. As well as saying that an infon corresponds to a situation, we can also say that it does *not* correspond. The infon either is factual or is not factual, with respect to the situation which it is intended to describe. We can say that the situation makes the infon factual or fails to do so. This relation between situations and infons is usually described as **support**; a situation supports an infon iff it makes the infon factual.

Just a few more remarks about the anatomy of infons will be made here, to be formalised in the next section. The core of an infon can be taken as a description of a situation, which as such can apply to more than one situation. This core is therefore known as a **situation type**. It excludes the information about location in space and time which would anchor it to a particular situation. For example, the situation type of Romania beating England in a football match is a situation type which accurately describes more than one situation. If we add a slot for location and set it either to France, 1998, or to Belgium, 2000, we get two different infons, each of which is made factual by one situation.

The other information we need to add is the relationship between an infon and its negation. What does it mean for an infon to be non-factual in a situation? One obvious instance would be if the situation gave us the information that the event described did not occur. In other words the situation supports information which is incompatible with that in the infon. But this incompatible information is itself an infon. So it would seem that we have to split infons into pairs, one giving positive information and the other negative. In other words, each infon has a **polarity**, along with its relation, individual and location arguments.

Does this polarity information belong inside the situation type (like the relation) or outside it (like the location)? Since we can classify a situation as the type of situation where a relation does not hold of one or more individuals, as easily as one where the relation does hold, it seems that polarity belongs inside the situation type. A situation type without a polarity is known as an **issue**. When the issue is resolved by the addition of a polarity, we have a complete situation type.

So we can think of a series of shells: an innermost shell containing the relation and its arguments (the issue), a second shell (the situation type) which also contains the polarity, and an outer shell (the infon) where the location information is also included.

Another way in which an infon can be not factual is for the situation to offer no information about it, neither supporting it nor ruling it out. We can think of this as a different form of negation. The flipping of the polarity of an infon, discussed above, is called **infonic negation**. However, when a situation offers no information one way or the other, this is a different kind of negation: it is the support relation that is negated. It does not hold between the situation and the infon; however, it does not have to hold between the situation and the *negation* of the infon either. Situation semantics offers a variety of resources for talking about negation, as we will see during the chapter.

9.1.3 LANGUAGE AND INFORMATION

This is the basic scheme of things in situation semantics, though there is much to be added; but how does all this relate to language? A language is just one example of uniformities in the world to which certain cognitive agents (namely language users) are attuned. If a speaker utters a declarative sentence in a language I am attuned to, then I am being offered information about a situation. If the information is factual, then the situation described will support it.

The situation where the utterance takes place is the **utterance situation**. Besides the utterance itself, and any body language that goes along with it, it includes the speaker and listener. It can therefore anchor indexicals such as 'I' or 'you' as well as 'now' and 'here'. The situation about which it offers information is the **described situation**. The constraints linking the two situations – as provided by language – constitute the semantic **content** of the sentence uttered.

Let's take a series of situations. The first is an impending change of weather. Because of regularities in the environment, this may be signalled by some subtle physical changes. We can say there is a **constraint** that these changes in situation s involve a change of weather in situation t (where s precedes t in time). Unfortunately I am not attuned to these constraints. However, cows are; moreover, they react to this information by exhibiting a particular behaviour, say lying down on the grass. So there is a constraint linking the behaviour of cows in a situation v to the physical changes in situation s, and hence ultimately the change of weather in situation t. As constraints are transitive (more on this later, but it is known in information theory as the 'xerox effect'), we can see this as a direct constraint betweeen v and t. A cognitive agent who is knowledgeable about cows – say a farmer – might be attuned to this constraint, whether or not she knows about the intermediate business of the changes in air pressure at s.

Suppose I meet this farmer, and she utters the sentence (9.4).

(9.4) It will rain soon.

If I am an agent attuned to the English language, the constraints of this language tell me that somebody's uttering (9.4) in situation u involves a situation t, located shortly after the time of u, where rain is falling. The situation u is the **utterance situation**, t is the **described situation**, and language provides a set of constraints allowing me to construct the information that is offered about t. So although I am neither a cow nor a farmer, I finally get the information that it is going to rain, by means of language.[6]

This view of linguistic information is very simple, but can be elaborated much more richly. On the purely linguistic side, it has become the basis for an approach to grammatical theory known as **information-based syntax**, in which each part of the sentence contributes to a pool of constraints that is built up as the sentence is parsed. The semantic content of the whole sentence, combined with further constraints arising from the utterance situation (in the example gven, the deictic information that will anchor the word 'soon'), provides information about the described situation. The sentence is true iff this information is factual. This schema was first developed using Lexical Functional Grammar,[7] but soon became the basis of a new framework, Head-driven Phrase Structure Grammar.[8]

As a footnote to this section, situation semantics is often described as a theory of information, and work in within this framework often uses the words 'information-based'; it should be distinguished, however, from 'information theory', which usually refers to the tradition of work deriving from Shannon (1948). The latter plays an important role in natural language processing (as also in telecommunications and cryptology), but does not come into the area covered by this book. Note also that 'situation semantics' is usually used only for applications to natural language semantics, while the more general mathematical treatment is known as 'situation theory'.

9.2 THE NOTATION OF SITUATION THEORY

As situation theory was not conceived as a formal logic, it is against its spirit to give its syntax in the same way as the inductive definitions of the other chapters of this book. Nonetheless there is a systematic notation for its main concepts, and the main features of this will be set out in this relatively short section.

The standard notation for basic infons uses angled brackets to mark off the successive layers as described in section 9.1, while the component parts are separated using commas or semi-colons. The slots for the arguments of the relation are not identified by position as in predicate logic, but by labels indicating the **role**. In the schematic examples used here, their values are filled by place holders called **parameters** (marked by the dot over the letter). Roles and parameters will be discussed further in the semantics section. The inner pair of angled brackets includes the relation and a list of its roles (the issue) and the polarity, separated by a semi-colon. (Some writers use 0 and 1 or *yes* and *no* rather than + and − for polarity. In the first case, don't confuse polarities with truth values.)

Issue: $\langle$give, giver: $\dot{x}$, gift: $\dot{y}$, recipient: $\dot{z}\rangle$
Situation type: $\langle$give, giver: $\dot{x}$, gift: $\dot{y}$, recipient: $\dot{z}$; $\pm\rangle$
Infon/soa: $\langle\langle$give, giver: $\dot{x}$, gift: $\dot{y}$, recipient: $\dot{z}$; $\pm\rangle$ location: $\dot{l}\rangle$

Within the outer pair of angled brackets, the slots for time and place are treated in the same way. In the linguistic literature they are often reduced to one slot for 'location' – which, perhaps confusingly, refers to time and aspect[9] – or often just suppressed, along with polarity:

- $\langle\langle$ give, giver: $\dot{x}$, gift: $\dot{y}$, recipient: $\dot{z}\rangle\rangle$.

Parameters are used to track the identity of individuals referred to. To take a linguistic example, the sentence 'Mary snores' will contribute (at least) two infons to the constraint pool feeding semantic interpretation:

1. $\langle\langle$ snore, snorer: $\dot{x}$; $+\rangle$ location: $\dot{l}\rangle$
2. $\langle\langle$ naming, name: /m∈:ri/, named: $\dot{x}$; $+\rangle$ location: $\dot{l}\rangle$

The occurrence of the same parameter in both infons (effected by unification in HPSG) forces the entity described by the NP 'Mary' to be the same entity that plays the *snorer* role in the relation described by the predicate 'snores'. (A full account should also deal with the location parameter.)

The information provided by the VP in this example is not complete in itself, as it contains unidentified parameters, and the same is true of the information offered by the NP. Each of these is therefore not a full infon but a parametrised infon, or parametrised state of affairs. This is often abbreviated to **psoa**.

Infons are often notated by σ and τ and other letters from that area of the Greek alphabet. Two infons with opposite polarities, but otherwise the same, are written σ and σ^-.

Basic infons can be connected by conjunction and disjunction to form compound infons. Here we are very nearly back to symbolic logic.[10] The notions involved are not quite the same as logical connectives, because the latter join propositions, and infons are not propositions. However, we will use the familiar logical connective *symbols* (and will discuss their interpretation in the semantics section). It is also possible to have quantified infons, which involve quantification over parameters.

Infons should not be confused with their notation, but here are some definitions for well-formed *notation for infons* in the style of the inductive definitions used in other chapters. (If you do this at a situation semantics conference, it is at your own risk.)

1. A basic infon is an infon.
2. If σ and τ are infons, then $\sigma \wedge \tau$ and $\sigma \vee \tau$ are compound infons.
3. If σ is an infon, $\dot{x}$ a parameter and S a set, then $(\exists \dot{x} \in S)\,\sigma$ and $(\forall \dot{x} \in S)\,\sigma$ are quantified infons.
4. Nothing else is an infon.

These are the main notational devices standardly used for situation-semantic objects and constructs. Among the more common alternatives: in HPSG they are usually represented using attribute value matrices (AVMs); and they can also be drawn using an extension of Kamp's notation for Discourse Representation Theory.[11] It is not accidental that these are graphical rather than based on strings of symbols. One preoccupation of situation semanticists has been to free discussion of semantic content from dependence on logical notations, and in particular there has been much interest in the semantics of diagrams as an alternative. Some of these developments will be mentioned at the end of the chapter.

EXERCISE 9.2.0.1

Using the notation of this section, write out the infons supported by the described situations of the following sentences.

1. David visited London yesterday.
2. Jenny was given *War and Peace* by her mother.
3. Paul waved to Helen but she didn't wave back.
4. Either she is a ghost or she isn't here.
5. Mariam saw Abdullah before he saw her.

Underline all the information in your answer which was provided by the utterance situation.

9.3 SITUATION SEMANTICS

The notation in the previous section should be considered an optional shorthand for the semantic objects described in this section. This section is therefore somewhat more detailed.

The basic ontology of situation semantics consists of different kinds of **uniformities** – situations, individuals, n-ary relations, locations (temporal and spatial). These together constitute a **scheme of individuation** with which human-like agents dissect the world. Classical situation semantics insists that these uniformities arise from the real world – the philosophy of **ecological realism** described in the introductory section.

States of affairs or infons are formed from these objects as described in the previous section. An infon σ is said to be made factual by a situation s – or, equivalently, s supports σ. This relation – which can be expressed in several ways in English – is called the **supports** relation, and is written $\models$ in the situation semantics literature. There are reasons for this, but for compatibility with the rest of this book I will use the notation $\Vdash$. You should be aware that this is non-standard, and that it implies an analogy with notions from formal logic (the relation between worlds and propositions) which many situation semanticists would not be comfortable with.

(9.5) Given a set of S of situations and a set Σ of infons, $\Vdash$ is a binary relation on $\text{Sit} \times \Sigma$

(9.6) If σ consists of an n-ary relation R, arguments $a_1 \ldots a_n$, polarity + and location l, then $s \Vdash \sigma$ iff $a_1 \ldots a_n$ stand in the relation R at l in s.

Note that situations may also appear as arguments of a relation. This is the point of the discussion of perception complements in the introduction.

As already noted, arguments may also be **parameters**, which are not yet associated with objects. It is natural to think of these as analogous to variables. However, there is an important difference. Variables are syntactic objects, defined as part of a logical language. In situation semantics there is no logical language, just a notation for semantic objects, and so we have to ask what kind of semantic object a parameter represents. This is not easy to answer. If an infon is part of reality, then a parametrised infon should be a part of reality which contains an information gap. It is challenging to think of good examples of these, and some people find this part of the ontology of situation semantics exotic and unclear. One approach is to bear in mind that their main function (as exemplified in the previous section) is to track individuals or instances across situations even when their identity is not known. This is an important cognitive ability, and to that extent seems to correspond to something in the regularities to which an agent is attuned.

When a parameter is identified with an actual object it is said to be **anchored** to that object. An **anchor** is a function from the parameters in an infon to objects. It can be thought of as analogous to an assignment of variables.

Another use of parameters is the formation of non-basic **types**. As used in situation semantics, types are a way of classifying the regularities in the world. The basic types were listed in the description of the ontology at the beginning of the section. Non-basic types are formed by combining a parameter with a statement of the form $s \Vdash \sigma$. For example the type of an individual who is in a photograph of situation s in Barcelona can be formed as

(9.7). $[\dot{x} \mid s \Vdash \langle\langle \text{photograph, subject: } \dot{x}; 1 \rangle, b \rangle]$.

Formally the parameter on the left denotes the possible anchors of the parameter that occurs within the infon. This is known as **absorption** of the parameter. Both the notation and the concept, however, are reminiscent of λ abstraction, and if it is helpful to think of parameters as the situation-theoretic analogue of variables, then absorption can be thought of as the analogue of λ-abstraction, and types as the analogues of λ-abstracts.

Types are used to state constraints. Perhaps the easiest example is constraints on situation types, for example that any smoky type of situation is a fiery type of situation.

(9.8). $[\dot{s} \mid \dot{s} \Vdash \langle\langle \text{smoke, } + \rangle \dot{t} \rangle] \Rightarrow [\dot{s} \mid \dot{s} \Vdash \langle\langle \text{fire, } + \rangle \dot{t} \rangle]$

This is the basic theory of types and constraints. Note the assumption that constraints apply to single situations (the same parameter occurs in both the situation types). Possibly more interesting constraints govern connections between different situations. These more general ideas of constraints will be discussed in sections 9.5 and 9.6.

Finally, parameters are used for quantification. Again, they look very much like variables, but with the proviso that they are automatically restricted, so that quantification in situation semantics is automatically restricted quantification, the restriction being provided implicitly (if not explicitly) by some situation. For example, 'Somebody is tired' may be assumed to refer to somebody in a particular situation (otherwise it is uninformative), while in 'Everybody is happy', the restriction to a given situation is probably necessary if the statement is to be true. This is discussed further in section 9.4.1.

(9.9)   1. $s \Vdash (\exists \dot{x} \in S)\, \sigma$ iff there is some anchor f of $\dot{x}$ to S such that $s \Vdash \sigma\, [\dot{x} \mapsto f(\dot{x})]$
      2. $s \Vdash (\forall \dot{x} \in S)\, \sigma$ iff, for every anchor f of $\dot{x}$ to S, $s \Vdash \sigma\, [\dot{x} \mapsto f(\dot{x})]$.

As indicated in the notation section, infons can be combined into compound infons (besides quantified infons, and the operation of polarity reversal, which is considered to create new basic infons). Although these combinations look very much like the familiar logical connectives of conjunction and disjunction, remember that infons are not propositions, and these operations are therefore not propositional connectives. They are defined as the informational **meet** and **join** of infons.

Meet and join are order-theoretic notions and therefore presuppose an ordering. This is given by informational **involvement**: σ involves τ iff, when σ is factual in s, then so is τ. The meaning of informational meet and join can be best understood using this relation. Meets combine information, joins present alternatives.

(9.10)   1. σ involves τ iff, if $s \Vdash \sigma$ then $s \Vdash \tau$.
      2. $s \Vdash \sigma \wedge \tau$ iff $s \Vdash \sigma$ and $s \Vdash \tau$.
      3. $s \Vdash \sigma \vee \tau$ iff $s \Vdash \sigma$ or $s \Vdash \tau$ (or both).

Conjunctive infons are perhaps easier to understand than disjunctive infons. An example of a disjunctive infon given in the literature[12] is the constraint that in a marriage situation between two people x and y, either x is male and y is female, or y is male and x is female. (This is also inadvertently an example of another important fact about constraints, which will be taken up in section 9.6.)

Note that involvement is a relation on infons, not an operator for forming compound infons. However, it is often written $\Rightarrow$, suggesting the entailment connective in propositional logic.

This set-up – situations, basic infons, the supports relation and the involvement ordering – form an algebraic structure, known as a constraint algebra. This suggests the possibility of using it for a logic, an idea which will be taken up in section 9.5.

Situations are ordered by a 'part of' relation, which we will write, by analogy with logical notions which will be explored later in the book, as $\sqsubseteq$. (The usual symbol is $\leq$, and, once again, some situation semanticists may be uneasy with this co-opting of logical symbols.) In other words, situations are part of larger situations which contain more information (support more infons). It is possible, though not necessary, to posit a maximal situation – the whole world – which includes all situations. This will decide all issues – that is, for every infon σ it will either support σ or σ^{-}, the same infon with opposite polarity, in the same way that a world in previous chapters assigns a truth value to all propositions. It is also possible to consider possible situations, which are subparts of other possible worlds, thus combining situation semantics with possible worlds semantics (known as possibilistic situation semantics). This is an intuitively attractive move, but since situations are not abstract but real, it does not sit easily with the philosophy of ecological realism. We will not discuss this further here, but will return to the combination of modality and partiality in the last part of the book.

Another natural but problematic claim is that if an infon is factual in any situation, it remains factual in any larger situation. (This is called **persistence**.)

(9.11) if s $\Vdash$ σ and s $\sqsubseteq$ s', then s' $\Vdash$ σ.

The first problem is with universally quantified infons: if every swan is white in one situation, it may not be the case that every swan is white in a larger situation as we may have added a black swan. The second problem is with modal statements. Perhaps a limited situation supports the information that Mary might be asleep (it doesn't exclude that possibility); if a larger situation then shows her clearly leaping around in a nightclub, then the addition of information has closed a possibility that was originally open. The problem of persistence is discussed by Richard Cooper (1990).

It is assumed in situation semantics that no situation can support both σ and σ^-. That is, there is partiality but no paraconsistency (Chapter 8).

Finally, you have probably noticed that this section has used terms like content and denotation, but not **meaning**. In situation semantics meaning has a precise definition as a *relation* between situations. In the case of linguistic meaning, this is the relation between the utterance situation and the described situation, constrained by the content of the utterance, and possibly information from other situations (as will be seen in section 9.4.1). For example the meaning of 'It will rain tomorrow' is a relation which includes the ordered pairs of an utterance situation on Monday and a rainy situation on Tuesday, an utterance situation on Tuesday and a rainy situation on Wednesday, and so on.

This relational approach allows situation semantics to account for some subtleties in meaning which are more difficult to describe using standard model theory. For example, part of the meaning of the utterance can consist in conveying information about the utterance situation, not just the described situation. For example, if the speaker says, 'That is my husband', pointing at the President of the United States, this conveys information not only about the described situation but also about the speaker (or at least claims to do so). One of the attractions of situation semantics is this flexibility in incorporating contextual information into the core notion of meaning.

9.4 SOME LINGUISTIC ISSUES

9.4.1 RESOURCE SITUATIONS

In the last section, the meaning of an utterance was described as a relation involving the utterance situation and described situation, and 'possibly others'. This is because we invoke a variety of situations to restrict the meanings of words and phrases. Most of the time we do this unconsciously, and the listener is able to accommodate the intended situation without difficulty. Here are a few examples. What situations do we have to suppose for the phrases in italics to refer successfully?

(9.12) *The car* has broken down again.
(9.13) *Francesca* has gone to Milan.
(9.14) *Every plane* returned to the carrier.
(9.15) *Everything* is on the table.

The first sentence presupposes, strictly speaking, that there is one and only one car (Chapter 8). If we take the actual world, or most imaginable worlds, this is implausible. But there is nothing unusual about the sentence. The second sentence similarly presupposes that a proper name has a unique referent. In logic this is built into the model theory. But if we can imagine that the second sentence is uttered in Italy, there are likely to be many Francescas. What makes the sentences natural and usually easy to interpret, according to situation semantics, is that these NPs are interpreted with respect to a situation, a small enough part of the world for there to be only one car or only one Francesca.

The remaining sentences show that this also applies to quantified NPs. Much literature on quantification[13] has stressed that the N' restriction of an NP has the effect of narrowing down the part of the world that has to be searched. The third sentence can be verified just by searching the set of planes; we do not verify it by searching the set of all things that are not on the carrier and check that none of them are planes. But situation theory goes further: it is not all the planes in the world that are involved but only the set of planes in a particular situation (those planes which had taken off from this particular carrier on a particular occasion).

The fourth sentence (from Cooper 1996) shows neatly that the situation used to give reference to an NP need not be the same as the situation described by the whole sentence. Clearly, the described situation includes the table, but we do not want to include the table in 'everything' (the things that are on the table).

So reference is assigned to an NP by means of a situation which is not necessarily the same as the described situation nor the utterance situation. It is called a **resource situation** – a situation which is assumed to be 'available to be used' for this purpose. For the speaker to use it, it must have some connection with the speaker, and for the listener to understand it correctly, it must also have some connection with the listener. If the speaker's connections and the listener's connections do not coincide, then we get a misunderstanding.

Resource situations have also been applied to the problem of referential and attributive uses of NPs (9.16, 9.17, repeated from Chapter 8).

(9.16) The man with the yellow shirt and pink tie has interesting dress sense.
(9.17) The man with the yellow shirt and pink tie is a famous linguist.

In (9.16) the assignment of reference to the NP is closely connected to the statement about him; anybody who the NP might refer to also qualifies for the comment on dress sense. The situation used to assign reference is part of the situation described by the whole sentence. In (9.17), by contrast, the visual impact of the man's clothes is the situation used to pick out the individual, but the statement about him describes situations which have nothing to do with yellow shirts and pink ties. (He could do his linguistic work wearing a loincloth in the Amazon forest.) In situation semantics we can capture the difference by saying that the resource situation for an attributive NP (8.13) has to be part of the described situation,[14] while the resource situation for a referential NP (9.17) need have nothing to do with the described situation; it is simply some connection available to the speaker and listener which serves to establish reference.

The relational theory of meaning can therefore be extended from a binary relation between the utterance situation and the described situation to include as many resource situations as are necessary to establish the reference of NPs.

9.5 BACK TO LOGIC?

9.5.1 INFON ALGEBRAS

Although situation semanticists reject logic as a starting point for semantics, it is interesting to ask whether relations between infons show a structure which *could* be represented by a logic. Barwise and Etchemendy (1990) argue that infons do have an algebraic structure. This does not mean that reasoning about information should be confined to logical languages; in fact the authors were interested in unifying reasoning about information from heterogeneous sources. (We will look at one of these at the end of this chapter.)

An **infon algebra** $\langle S, I, \Rightarrow, \Vdash \rangle$ contains a lattice $\langle I, \Rightarrow \rangle$ (that is, the set I of infons is partially ordered by the involvement relation $\Rightarrow$, and this poset is a lattice). Note an important assumption here – that $\Rightarrow$ is antisymmetric. Any set of infons has an informational meet and join (the latter can be thought of as alternative cases which jointly exhaust the possibilities in the information given by the set). We can also define the incoherent infon 0 (inconsistent information) and the null infon 1 (no information). Two infons σ and τ are said to be compatible iff $\sigma \wedge \tau \neq 0$, and σ and σ^- are always incompatible ($\sigma \wedge \sigma^- = 0$).

The supports relation $\Vdash$ on $S \times \Sigma$ obeys the following rules:

1. If $s \Vdash \sigma$ and $\sigma \Rightarrow \tau$, then $s \Vdash \tau$.
2. For all s, $s \nVdash 0$ and $s \Vdash 1$.
3. For any set of infons Σ, $s \Vdash \wedge \Sigma$ iff $s \Vdash \sigma$ for every $\sigma \in \Sigma$.
4. For any set of infons Σ, $s \Vdash \vee \Sigma$ iff $s \Vdash \sigma$ for some $\sigma \in \Sigma$.

This is close to several algebraic structures which are models for well-known logics. To complete the picture (as far as this very introductory discussion is concerned), we need an operation on infons corresponding to implication. So we define a new infon $[\sigma \rightarrow \tau]$, which will have the following implication-like properties: (i) if you combine it with σ you have τ, and (ii) if we have any third infon υ which combined with σ involves τ, then υ involves the infon $[\sigma \rightarrow \tau]$.

1. $\sigma \wedge [\sigma \rightarrow \tau] \Rightarrow \tau$
2. if $\upsilon \wedge \sigma \Rightarrow \tau$, then $\upsilon \Rightarrow [\sigma \rightarrow \tau]$.

The infon algebra is now a Heyting algebra (Chapter 10), and the rules just given define a **relative pseudocomplement**. For each infon σ, the infonic negation σ^- is a pseudocomplement, definable as $[s \rightarrow 0]$. Heyting algebras are an algebraic model for the logic discussed in the next chapter – **intuitionistic logic**. So on the interpretation of situation semantics discussed in this section,[15] situation semantics is close to the semantics of intuitionistic logic.

How does this logic relate to classical logic? The relation $s \Vdash \sigma$ can be regarded as a proposition, written as $(s : \sigma)$. (Such a proposition, offering information about particular situations rather than timeless truths, is known as an Austinian proposition.) The negation of the supports relation, $s \nVdash \sigma$, can be written as the same proposition with a negation sign in front of it: $\neg(s : \sigma)$. The behaviour of *this* negation, however, is the same as classical (Boolean) negation: either s supports σ or it does not, there is no 'neither' and no 'both'. In this way we can get back to classical logic, by defining conjunction and disjunction operators for these Austinian propositions and the usual constants (or nullary operators) 1 and 0.

- Check that these operators (negation, conjunction and disjunction of Austinian propositions), obey the zero and unit laws.

These ideas enable us to change perspective between classical and partial views of truth and negation. On the one hand, situations are partial, and may neither support an infon nor its infonic negation, giving a truth gap. On the other hand, seeing things from an external perspective we can say that either it supports an infon or it doesn't, which is a classical proposition.

9.6 CHANNEL THEORY

Section 9.3 introduced the idea of **constraints** as a kind of conditional information about a situation; for example if a situation supports the presence of smoke then it supports the presence of fire. This idea is basic to a situation-theoretic account of inference and information flow, but it gives rise to a number of questions.

First of all, the idea of a situation supporting conditional information is not as straightfoward as the idea of a situation supporting a basic infon or even a conjunction of infons. The constraint about smoke and fire would seem to hold equally whether I am watching an ominous line of smoke coming over the hilltops on a Greek island, or am quietly sitting by the sea with no smoke in sight. For a basic infon σ it is possible to pick out a set of situations where σ is factual. But what is the set of situations where a constraint holds?

Barwise (1993) proposed, first, that constraints are regularities governing *pairs* of situations. If I see flames coming over the hilltops in a situation s, that conveys the information that something is burning in situation t on the other side. The constraint $\sigma \Rightarrow \tau$ tells us about a connection between s and t. It states that if $s \Vdash \sigma$ then $t \Vdash \tau$: the connection between the two situations makes smoke in *s* information about fire in *t*. Examples given by Barwise include: (i) the level of mercury in a thermometer giving information about the ambient temperature (or the health of a patient), and (ii) the markings on a map giving information about the region being mapped.

This connection between situations is called a **channel**. So the answer to the question posed a couple of paragraphs ago is that constraints hold with respect to channels (or channels support constraints). Does this mean that a channel can be thought of as a particular kind of situation? If we think of constraints as being a particular kind of infon (on the analogy of an implication being a particular kind of proposition), then there is a conceptual advantage to reifying the channel as being itself a kind of situation. The relation between channels and constraints is then just like any other instance of a situation supporting an infon. If *c* is a channel between *s* and *t*, which Barwise would write s $\xrightarrow{c}$ t, then we can also see this as a triple $\langle c, s, t \rangle$ of situations, or more generally of 'sites' where information may hold. The constraint holds at *c*, the antecedent at *s* and the consequent at *t*. This ternary relation on situations will be important in the last part of the book, especially Chapter 11.

Another important intuition that the idea of channels is intended to capture is that constraints do not hold everywhere; they depend on the reliability of the connections. For example the robustness of the information conveyed by mercury about temperature assumes that the thermometer has been accurately calibrated, and similarly with the map and the terrain it is supposed to represent. Physical and semantic constraints, similarly, may be limited to parts of the world. Physical constraints which hold under everyday conditions might not in extreme conditions. Similarly meaning constraints which are assumed to be valid in one context may not be universal. An example of this was given in section 9.3, with the constraint that marriage is between people of opposite sexes. At the time when Barwise was writing, that was probably an accurate assumption. Twenty years later, the constraint still applies in some jurisdictions but not all.

To summarise, a channel represents connections in the world which allow information to flow from one situation to another. The channel supports information in the form of an implicational constraint. If a channel exists between *s* and *t* which supports $\sigma \Rightarrow \tau$, then if *s* supports σ, *t* will support τ (and if *t* does not support τ, then something has gone wrong with the channel between *s* and *t* so that they do not in fact stand in the required relation).

9.7 VISUAL LOGIC

Although situation semantics can be said to have a logic, as we have just seen, a major emphasis in it has been to get away from the idea of logic as we know it – a symbolic language whose strings are manipulated by a system of deductive rules. This change of perspective has led to a growth of interest in the semantics of systems which are not based on language at all – in particular, diagrams.[16]

Two good illustrations of this were encountered in the first part of this book: Hasse diagrams, used for partial orders (Chapter 3), and Venn diagrams, which we used to illustrate syllogisms and quantification (Chapter 4).

Recall, first, how Venn diagrams were used in the discussion of syllogisms such as Barbara and Celarent. The three circles were arranged to represent all possible relations of the three terms (N' denotations or sets) involved in the syllogism. Then parts of this space were either shaded out (for the universal quantifiers *all* and *no*) to mark them as empty, or marked with a cross (for the particular quantifiers *some* and *not all*) to mark them as non-empty. The conclusion then corresponded to the situation represented in the diagram, and was therefore taken to be valid, because there was no way that it could be otherwise.

Note, first, the use of our intuitions about space to validate the rules of the syllogisms. By implication, the configuration of the diagrams has a greater immediacy to it than the manipulation of strings of symbols. We can shift perspective and, instead of treating it as a supporting justification for the validity of an argument, use the diagram as itself a proof of the argument. This requires a set of rigorous rules for the construction and interpretation of diagrams, which, as we will see, is not as straightforward as it might seem.

Using diagrams, once the premises have been set out in the appropriate way, the conclusion is already there on the page. Using sentential logic, the conclusion would have to be stated separately, licensed by a rewriting rule. But with visual logic there is no need for this additional step. It could be said, therefore, that visual logic comes closer to the idea of the conclusion of a deduction being already inherent in its premises (or as situation semanticists would say, the information in the premises **involves** the information in the conclusion).

EXERCISE 9.7.0.1

Hasse diagrams were used in Chapter 3 to represent partial orders. As compared with general binary relations, which can be represented by directed graphs, they take advantage of the properties of partial orders to present a simpler and more readable diagram. They also take advantage of certain features of the spatial representation.

What spatial feature encodes:

1. the directionality of the relation?
2. the antisymmetry of the partial order?
3. the transitivity of the partial order?

Another intuitive representation of transitivity is provided by Euler circles (Figure 9.1). The first diagram shows the validity of Barbara, which relies on the transitivity of the subset relation (the interpretation of the universal quantifier). The second shows the transitivity of entailment, thinking of propositions as sets of possible worlds, and entailment as the subset relation on these sets.

These diagrams rely on the transitivity (and acyclicity) of the spatial inclusion relation between convex regions in a plane. These structural properties are shared between spatial relations and the target structure,[17] in this case logical entailment. We can also use the symmetry of the overlap relation to mirror the symmetry of the

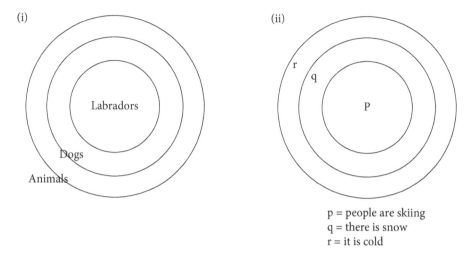

p = people are skiing
q = there is snow
r = it is cold

Figure 9.1   Euler circles showing transitivity

quantifier *some*. The direct exploitation of spatial relations can make Euler diagrams seem a more directly accessible representation than Venn diagrams, which require additional marking (crosses and shaded regions).

Although graphical representations can represent things which cannot be directly represented in one-dimensional strings, care is still needed in specifying the rules for their construction and for reading off valid inferences. A number of examples of potential pitfalls are discussed by Lemon and Pratt (1998), including the fallacious deduction in (9.18). We have three premises and a putative conclusion.

(9.18) 1. Some A is B and C.
        2. Some B is C and D.
        3. Some C is D and A.
        Some A is B and C and D.

Each of the premises asserts a non-empty intersection between three sets.

• Try to think of an intuitive counter-model to the deduction in (9.18).

As a matter of set theory, the putative conclusion does not follow. There may be no entity that is simultaneously A, B, C and D.

Suppose, however, that we tried to diagram this situation with Euler circles. As a matter of *geometry*, it is impossible to enclose four convex regions of a plane in such a way that any three triples of them have non-empty intersections but all four taken together do not. Suppose you have three intersecting circles: call the pairwise intersections a, b and c, and the intersection of all three d. It is impossible to add a fourth circle which intersects a, b and c without it also overlapping d, giving a non-empty intersection of all four circles.[18] A naive application of the Euler diagram method for syllogisms would therefore lead us to regard the deduction, wrongly, as valid.

What has gone wrong here? The rules of topology have introduced extra non-logical constraints, and this has led to a deduction which is not sound on purely logical principles. (Note that Venn diagrams would not have this problem; the intersection of all four sets can be shaded out as empty.)

Visual approaches have aroused interest from time to time throughout the history of logic, although situation semantics seems a good context in which to discuss them. Charles Peirce, who has a claim to be one of the founders of modern logic, believed it was the best approach, and Frege's own notation included graphical elements. Since then, however, symbolic logic has been the mainstream. Situation semantics was responsible for a revival of interest, and another impulse has come through the growth in popularity of substructural logics, some of which can be evaluated through a graphic system called proof nets. These logics will be discussed in Chapter 12.

9.8 EPILOGUE

Situation semantics enjoyed great popularity in the 1990s because of its emphasis on partiality, with intuitive linguistic applications, and in some circles because of its realistic philosophy of information. The emergence of HPSG during this period also contributed greatly to its popularity among linguists. However, not everybody was either convinced by its unusual ontology or prepared to forego the technical convenience of the mainstream logical techniques described in the earlier part of this book.

A natural reaction was a growth of interest in partial *logics*, when it became clear that partiality could be captured within the framework of a Montague-style logical approach. A classic example was Muskens' (1996) TY4, described in Chapter 8. Logics whose basic inspiration came from proof theory also began to become popular; these will be described in the last part of this book. As a result, some linguists have abandoned situation semantics and reverted to logic; another group remain convinced by the informational philosophy of ecological realism; there is also a broad intermediate spectrum of people who use techniques from situation semantics while being agnostic about its philosophical complications.

NOTES

1. Barwise and Perry (1983).
2. In some Montague-style treatments the denotation of a complementiser phrase is, by type lifting, a set of properties of propositions – a set of sets of sets of worlds. See Keenan and Faltz (1985).
3. Perry (1986).
4. Devlin (1991).
5. Devlin, op. cit.
6. Despite the term **described situation**, it is not quite correct to describe the semantic content of the sentence as a description of the situation, especially if a description is thought of as an expression in a language; an infon as we have defined it is a state of affairs in the world, not a linguistic object. However, for any infon a corresponding situation description can be generated (for example a paraphrase of the features in the infon), and

the situation can be *described* as a situation of such a kind that the infon holds there. In other words there is a one-to-one correspondence between infons and descriptions of situations. See Zalta (1990) for discussion.

7. Fenstad et al. (1985)

8. Pollard and Sag (1987, 1994)

9. If aspectual information is complex, that is, the event has internal structure, then it is correct to talk of a **course of events** or **coe** rather than a state of affairs.

10. Barwise and Seligman (1997), however, develop a completely different interpretation of these concepts.

11. For example Cooper (1996).

12. Barwise and Etchemendy (1990).

13. See especially Barwise and Cooper (1981).

14. One way of looking at this is that the sentence expresses a constraint on situations with yellow shirts and pink ties, that they provoke attention.

15. Note that going from standard models of situation semantics to the infon algebras of this section requires certain additional assumptions, only some of which have been mentioned here.

16. Barwise and Etchemendy (1995).

17. Stenning and Lemon (2001).

18. Helly's theorem.

CHAPTER 10

INTUITIONISM AND CONSTRUCTIVE PROOF

Space and time are its pure forms, sensation in general its matter. We can cognize only the former a priori, i.e., prior to all actual perception, and they are therefore called pure intuition; the latter, however, is that in our cognition that is responsible for its being called a posteriori cognition, i.e., empirical intuition. The former adheres to our sensibility absolutely necessarily, whatever sort of sensations we may have; the latter can be very different.[1]

Chapter 8 looked at one natural way of treating non-bivalence: the introduction of three or more truth values. The last chapter introduced another approach, that of situation semantics. The latter is different from most of the theories described in this book, in that it was not conceived as a logic (based on symbols), but rather as a theory of information. Nonetheless it can be treated as a logic, and despite the reservations of its founders, this has proved a popular and fruitful approach in linguistics, enabling the linguistic insights of situation semantics to be combined with familiar and well-explored logical techniques.

In this it has something in common with another system: intuitionism. This was originally a philosophy of mathematics,[2] conceived (by L. E. J. Brouwer) in conscious opposition to the domination of mathematics in the early twentieth century by the then new logic of Frege and Russell. In particular, Brouwer rejected the Law of the Excluded Middle (**LEM**) from classical logic; this seemed to assume that every mathematical question can be answered one way or the other, and led to proof methods which Brouwer did not regard as justified.[3] Nonetheless, intuitionism turned out to have a logic of its own. This was formalised by Heyting (1930), and intuitionistic logic soon became a productive field of enquiry in its own right, whose relation to classical and modal logics has been extensively explored. It represents an important alternative to multiple truth values in giving a semantics for non-classical logic.[4]

This chapter will look at some of the main features of intuitionistic logic. In particular it will focus on the notion of proof, which is central to intuitionism. This will also enable the chapter to serve as a bridge to the systems in the last part of the book, which are proof-theoretic in inspiration.

10.1 INTUITIONISM AND NATURAL DEDUCTION

Natural deduction (ND) was invented by the Göttingen logician Gerhard Gentzen in the 1930s, as an alternative to the proofs from axioms favoured up to that time.[5] As the name suggests, it was intended to capture a more intuitive way of thinking about logical deduction. But there was another motive as well, which was to examine the nature of proofs as objects in their own right, rather than simply a means of getting from A to B (from premises to conclusions). In a similar way, we have emphasised the importance of seeing functions as objects in their own right, rather than simply ways of pairing arguments and values. Just as we can reason about functions, so we can also (thanks to ND) reason about proofs. Although one can do ND with classical logic too, it was originally devised for intuitionistic logic, and this is the most natural context for it.

Not content with ND, Gentzen proceeded to invent yet another proof system, which has desirable computational properties that ND does not have, though it is in certain respects less 'intuitive'. This is known in his honour as the Gentzen Calculus, and will be introduced in Chapter 12.

Like other proof systems, ND is a system of rewriting formulas, according to certain rules. The **derivation**, as it is called, starts with certain formulas that are given (the **premises**), and continues until you reach a final formula which is called the **conclusion**. Each rewritten formula occupies a new line, which is normally numbered, and a note is made on the right of the rule that sanctions the rewriting.[6]

The distinguishing feature of ND is the nature of the rules, which bring out certain important features of the logic with great clarity. They are of two kinds: structural rules and connective rules. In this chapter we will focus on connective rules, leaving the structural rules for now implicit (they will get their share of attention later). Connective rules reflect the meaning of the connectives, the important logical constants.

Each connective has an **introduction rule** which licenses its introduction (thus building a complex formula), and an **elimination rule** which allows us to remove it (thus breaking up a complex formula). We can think of the introduction rule as expressing under what circumstances we are allowed to state a conjunction, disjunction, implication or negation. An elimination rule tells us what we get if we 'cash in' the connective. For example if we cash in a conjunction, we can get either of the conjuncts (because if a conjunction is true, both of its conjuncts are true – this is what it meant to state the conjunction in the first place).[7]

Perhaps the simplest connective rule is conjunction elimination:

(10.1) Conjunction elimination
    1. $p \wedge q$
    2. p $\wedge$ Elim, 1
(10.2) $p \wedge q \vdash p$

The first example here is the derivation itself, which is very simple. We are licensed to write p in line 2 by $\wedge$ elimination from line 1, and this justification (including the line number 1) is written to the right of the new formula.

The consecution I have written below the proof (10.2) summarises what is proved by this derivation; from the premise $p \wedge q$, we have proved p. (Note that we could have equally well proved q instead of p, because we can obtain either of the conjuncts.)

The rule for conjunction introduction tells us under what circumstances we are justified in writing a conjunction; namely, when we already know that both the conjuncts are true.

(10.3) Conjunction introduction
     1. p
     2. q
     3. $p \wedge q$ $\wedge$ Intro, 1,2
(10.4) $p, q \vdash p \wedge q$

Disjunction introduction is also very straightforward: if we have a proposition, p, then we can write $p \vee q$, for any proposition q we like. While this may not seem totally intuitive, it is easy to see that it is justified by the truth tables; if p is true, then any disjunction involving p is also true. We could equally write $q \vee p$, making p the right disjunct.

(10.5) Disjunction introduction
     1. p
     2. $p \vee q$ $\vee$ Intro, 1
(10.6) $p \vdash p \vee q$

The last rule that can be said to be really simple is implication elimination, which you have already met several times under the name of *modus ponendo ponens*.[8] It is an elimination rule because in proceeding from the premises to the conclusion, we have eliminated the implication.

(10.7) Implication elimination (*modus ponendo ponens* (MPP))
     1. $p \rightarrow q$
     2. p
     3. q $\rightarrow$Elim, 1,2
(10.8) $p \rightarrow q, p \vdash q$

Note that the justification for the step of elimination cites the lines 1 (for the major premise, the implication) and 2 (the minor premise, matching the antecedent of the implication) *in that order*. It may seem pedantic to insist on this detail, but the point of it will become clear later (Chapter 11).

The remaining rules are a little more difficult (and interesting). First a little exercise to consolidate.

EXERCISE 10.1.0.1

Prove the following by ND.

1. $p \wedge q \vdash p \vee r$
2. $p \rightarrow (q \rightarrow r), p, q \vdash r$
3. $p \rightarrow (q \rightarrow r), p \wedge q \vdash r$
4. $p \rightarrow (q \wedge r), r \rightarrow s, p \vdash s$
5. $p \rightarrow (q \rightarrow r) \vdash (p \wedge q) \rightarrow r$

The last of these is one half of the deduction equivalence (page 25).

Implication introduction is perhaps the most distinctive feature of ND, and is also the basis for the remaining connective rules. It is also something that many students have difficulty with at first, though it becomes clearer with practice. To understand what is going on, it is useful to have a look at the *other* half of the deduction equivalence:

(10.9) $(p \wedge q) \rightarrow r \vdash p \rightarrow (q \rightarrow r)$

Recall (from section 2.5) that if p and q are sufficient to prove r (left side), then if I have p, I cannot yet prove r, but I know that if I had q I could prove r. Suppose if I have bread and cheese I can make a sandwich. Then if I only have bread, I cannot yet make a sandwich, but I know that if I could supply some cheese from somewhere, I could make a sandwich.

The procedure to be followed here is, in effect, to imagine the cheese and show how you would use it to make a sandwich. So we are not given q, but we *assume* it, and use it to prove r. Suppose we succeed in doing this. What have we achieved? We have not proved r, because we have no right to rely on q. But we have proved that if we had q we could prove r, that is to say we have proved $q \rightarrow r$. So we now write the implication $q \rightarrow r$, using as justification our proof of r using q. Having done this, we must now withdraw or *discharge* our assumption of q, and anything depending on it. This is to avoid any subsequent proofs referring back to q, or any of the intermediate steps dependent on q, as if q were proved. In some styles of ND this is enforced by boxing off the whole subproof from the assumption of q to the proof of r (lines 3–5 in the example) in a little rectangle. Note that the assumption to be discharged is always the last undischarged assumption made. (If we are using the technique of boxing off subproofs, then the boxes will be nested.)

(10.10) Implication introduction

      1. p
      2. (...)
      3. q   Ass
      4. (...)
      5.   r (proved from p and q, by whatever means)
      6. $q \rightarrow r$ $\rightarrow$ Intro, 3, 5, discharging 3

(10.11) $p \vdash q \rightarrow r$

This method of introducing an assumption to prove a conclusion 'conditionally' is also known as **conditional proof** (CP). It reflects a very typical human way of reasoning, which is to make hypotheses and consider what follows if they are true. The desire to capture this 'hypothetical reasoning' was one of the reasons for the development of ND, and for the name given to it.

Note that q is not listed in the premises; we have assumed it in the course of the proof, and then discharged it. The premises, on the left of the turnstyle, consist only of assumptions that have *not* been discharged. This means that if all the assumptions are discharged during a proof (by steps of conditional proof / implication introduction), we can be left with a proof of a formula from *no premises at all*. This formula is therefore a **theorem** – something that is provable purely from the logic. These can be recognised by the occurrence of the turnstyle on the extreme left (there are no premises to put to the left of the turnstyle). This is parallel to the situation with the double turnstyle $\models$ and logical truths (Chapter 2), though those were read off the truth tables, not derived using a proof system.

Let us look at a very simple example of the proof of a theorem.

(10.12) Proof of a simple theorem

1.	p ∧ q	Ass
2.	p	∧ Elim, 1
3.	(p ∧ q) → p	→ Intro, 1,2, discharging 1

(10.13) ⊢ (p ∧ q) → p

The conjunction p ∧ q is assumed in line 1, and is used to prove the conclusion p (an easy proof in this case, just one step of conjunction elimination). The assumption is then discharged, and the whole implicational formula has been proved from no premises.

This strategy should be remembered as a rule of thumb which applies generally, however complicated the formulas involved:

(10.14) Conditional proof: when you have to prove an implicational formula, assume the antecedent and use it to prove the consequent.

EXERCISE 10.1.0.2

Prove the following. They all involve conditional proof – sometimes more than once! Some but not all of them are theorems.

1. p → r ⊢ (p ∧ q) → r
2. ⊢ (p → r) → ((p ∧ q) → r)
3. p → q ⊢ (r → p) → (r → q)
4. ⊢ (p → q) → ((r → p) → (r → q))

The remaining connective rules are all based on conditional proof in some way. Let's look first at disjunction elimination (also known as 'vel elimination', from the traditional name for ∨). The problem here is that in a disjunction p ∨ q we don't know which of the disjuncts is true, so we have to be careful not to rely on the truth of either one of them. However, if they both have a particular consequence, r, then it doesn't matter which of them is true; we can replace the whole disjunction by r. If we know that Wayne Rooney is either injured or suspended (or both), and we don't know which, but both have the consequence that he won't play, then we can just state that he won't play.

So the procedure to follow is like a double-barrelled version of conditional proof. Given a disjunction A ∨ B, we assume each of the disjuncts in turn and use them to prove (conditionally) a third formula C. We can then eliminate the original disjunction, and claim that we have proved C.

(10.15) Disjunction elimination
       1. p ∨ q
       2. p   Ass
       3. (. . .)
       4. r   (proved from p, by whatever means)
       5. q   Ass
       6. (. . .)
       7. r   (proved from q, by whatever means)
       8. r   ∨ Elim, 1,4,7
(10.16) p ∨ q ⊢ r

EXERCISE 10.1.0.3

Prove the following using disjunction elimination.

1. (p ∧ q) ∨ (p ∧ r) ⊢ p
2. p ∧ (q ∨ r) ⊢ (p ∧ q) ∨ (p ∧ r)

Finally we come to the treatment of negation, which is actually where the specifically intuitionistic aspects of this system come into play. First of all we need a symbol for contradiction, known as the **falsum** and written **f** or ⊥. The different symbols reflect a conceptual difference, which was mentioned in Chapter 2 (and will be discussed further in Chapter 11). The falsum can be taken in one of two ways:

1. An arbitrary logically false statement (or the disjunction of all logically false statements) – I will write this one as **f**.
2. The conjunction of all propositions whatsoever, which is false in any non-trivial logic (Chapter 8). This one will be written as ⊥.

With the falsum, we can now define negation in terms of implication: ¬p is defined as the implication p → **f**. In other words, if somebody now provided us with *p* as well, we would have a contradiction. We can now proceed using the connective rules we already have for implication, using **f**. Negation elimination will be a special case of implication elimination (*modus ponens*), and negation introduction a special case of implication introduction (conditional proof).

Because **f** and ⊥ are equivalent in intuitionistic logic, negation can equally be defined as p → ⊥, and this is, in fact, the more usual definition. The definition in terms of **f**, however, is more general, and will be valid in other logics where the two are not equivalent.

Negation elimination works by taking a proposition and its negation and deriving a contradiction. The connection with *modus ponens* is set out explicitly first.

(10.17) Negation elimination (I)
    1. p → **f**
    2. p
    3. **f**   → Elim, 1,2
(10.18) Negation elimination (II)
    1. ¬p
    2. p
    3. **f**   ¬ Elim, 1,2
(10.19) ¬p, p ⊢ **f**

Conversely, **negation introduction** proceeds by conditionally proving a contradiction from the assumption of *p*, which then licenses us to write ¬p. This is known as *reductio ad absurdum*, and is a well known technique in debating; if you can show that your opponent's proposition leads to an absurd conclusion (e.g. a contradiction), then you draw the conclusion that the proposition is false.

Here the parallelism with conditional proof is again set out first.

(10.20) Negation introduction (I)
    1. p   Ass
    2. (. . .)
    3. **f**   (proved from p, by whatever means)
    4. p → **f**   CP, 1, 3, discharging 1
(10.21) Negation introduction (II)
    1. p   Ass
    2. (. . .)
    3.   (proved from p, by whatever means)
    4. ¬p   ¬ Intro, 1, 3, discharging 1

This treatment of the negation connective (as implication plus **f**) gives an intuitive account of the basic meaning of negation. (There will be more on the subject in Chapter 11.) However, the rules given so far do not capture exactly the behaviour of negation in the truth tables. And so we come back to where this part of the book started off – the possible behaviours of negation. The account given so far in this section has to be augmented with supplementary rules, the choice of which determines the kind of negation that we will get.

The negation rules given in the last few paragraphs gives us a negation which is weaker than intuitionistic logic.[9] There are two main candidates for extensions to the system. One is double negation elimination or **DNE** (10.23). This corresponds to Aristotle's Law of the Excluded Middle (LEM), already discussed in Chapter 8; we have already seen that in the truth tables, ¬¬p ⊨ p.

The other is a traditional but at the same time controversial law of logic, to the effect that from a contradiction you can prove anything. We have already seen this rule in Chapter 8, under its Latin name, *e contradictione quodlibet* or **ECQ** (10.22). The intuitive problem is one of relevance: the conclusion you end up with may be unrelated to the premises that you started out with. However, ECQ is valid according to the truth tables of Chapter 2, and is also an important principle in intuitionistic logic.

(10.22) **ECQ**: ⊥ ⊢ p (for any p)
    1. ⊥
    2. p   ECQ, 1
(10.23) **DNE**: ¬¬p ⊢ p
    1. ¬¬p
    2. p   DNE, 1

Adding both of these rules gives the classical negation of the truth tables. Adding ECQ but not DNE gives **intuitionistic negation**, which is what we want in this chapter. Adding DNE together with ECQ is sufficient to prove LEM, which is valid in classical logic but not intuitionistic logic. It is also possible to do the opposite – to add DNE but not ECQ. This gives another kind of negation called **De Morgan negation**. Since it excludes ECQ it is a paraconsistent negation, which will be discussed in the next chapter.

Note that the rule of ECQ involves treating falsity as the bottom element of the propositional algebra (it implies any proposition). This is why, *in logics where ECQ is valid*, ¬φ can be appropriately defined as φ → ⊥ as an alternative to φ → **f**.

The relation between these negations is shown in Figure 10.1. Intuitionism, as it accepts ECQ but not LEM, is a **partial** but not a **paraconsistent** logic.

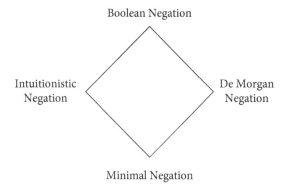

Figure 10.1 Four kinds of negation

As already mentioned, Aristotle seems not to have endorsed ECQ, despite his robust defence of the Law of Contradiction. ECQ became, however, a hot topic in medieval logic, and a classic defence was introduced into the literature by William of Soissons. I translate it here into roughly the format used in this chapter, with the addition of the rule of disjunctive syllogism; this is not one of the rules used in ND, but was mentioned in Chapter 2 as one of the valid modes of inference for propositional logic. It is repeated here as (10.25) for convenience. Paraconsistent logics, which reject ECQ as unintuitive, generally end up having to reject disjunctive syllogism as well. Since disjunctive syllogism is itself very intuitive, you see the dilemma.

(10.24) Proof of ECQ
     1. $p \land \neg p$
     2. p $\land$ Elim, 1
     3. $p \lor q$ $\lor$ Intro, 2
     4. $\neg p$ $\land$ Elim, 1
     5. q Disj syll, 3,4

(10.25) Disjunctive syllogism
     1. p or q
     2. not p
     3. (therefore) q

The problem of paraconsistent logics appearing to reject disjunctive syllogism will be discussed further in Chapter 11.

10.2 SYNTAX OF INTUITIONISTIC LOGIC

The syntax of intuitionistic logic is the same as that of classical logic. It is another 'deviant' logic, meaning that it uses the same logical language, but some of the symbols behave in a different way. It is the semantics that is different.

10.3 SEMANTICS OF INTUITIONISTIC LOGIC

There are many possible approaches to the semantics of intuitionistic logic. Heyting, who first showed that Brouwer's intuitionistic philosophy could be formalised as a logic, used an algebraic appoach, showing how the algebra of intuitionistic logic differs from Boolean algebra. The algebraic models he developed are known today as Heyting algebras. These are described briefly at the end of this chapter.

Another approach was developed by Kripke, based on his frame semantics for modal logics, discussed in Chapter 6. Many people find this the most intuitive semantics, and we will focus on it here, exploring some connections to relational semantics for other logics.[10]

10.3.1 KRIPKE FRAMES FOR INTUITIONISTIC LOGIC

Kripke's relational semantics for intuitionistic logic is derived from his semantics for modal logic – specifically S4 logic, with which it shares the notion of growth of information. An intuitionistic frame is, formally, a partially ordered set $\langle P, \sqsubseteq \rangle$, where P is a set of points (we can think of these as situations), and the partial ordering on them can be thought of either as analogous to an accessibility relation or as analogous to the inclusion relation in situation semantics; a situation can 'see' situations that are above it in the partial order, that is, larger situations of which it is a part. The partial ordering is a stricter condition than the conditions imposed on the accessibility relation in S4, which is only a preorder.

The points comprising P are often informally called 'worlds', but this can be misleading. Worlds, as used in classical and modal logic, are supposed to decide all propositions, so that in each world either the proposition or its negation is true. This is not true of the points used in intuitionistic frames. To underline this, I adopt the convention of using x, y and so on, rather than w, v and so on. Nonetheless they have much in common with worlds, and they appear on the left of the $\Vdash$ symbol in the semantic definitions.

As with modal logic, besides the frame we also have a valuation, which specifies which atomic propositions hold at each point x. If an atomic proposition is not given as true at x, however, we do not automatically write in that $\neg p$ is true at x; the conditions for $\neg p$ are slightly more complicated than in classical logic.

The whole set of propositions that are true at x is defined by what is called a **forcing** relation. This includes, first, the atomic propositions which are true at x by virtue of the valuation. The rules for complex formulae are in (10.26). With some connectives, there is a new element; they take account of information from situations further up the partial ordering. In this they have some similarity to a modal operators. They have, in fact, an 'intensional' quality, though in intuitionistic logic this intensionality is heavily limited by other factors. These remarks apply to implication and negation. The remaining connectives, $\wedge$ and $\vee$, remain purely 'extensional', in the sense that they only take into account the information in the current situation where they are evaluated.

Here are the definitions for the forcing relation for all the connectives. The symbol $\Vdash$ is read, in intuitionistic logic, as 'forces'.

(10.26) Forcing relation for intuitionistic logic:
1. $x \Vdash p$ iff $p \in V(x)$
2. $x \Vdash \phi \wedge \psi$ iff $x \Vdash \phi$ and $x \Vdash \psi$
3. $x \Vdash \phi \vee \psi$ iff $x \Vdash \phi$ or $x \Vdash \psi$
4. $x \Vdash \neg\phi$ iff, for no x' such that $x \sqsubseteq x'$, $x' \Vdash \phi$
5. $x \Vdash \phi \rightarrow \psi$ iff for every x' such that $x \sqsubseteq x'$, if $x' \Vdash \phi$ then $x' \Vdash \psi$.

This 'intensional quality' can be thought of in the following way. For intuitionists, $\neg p$ does not mean simply that we cannot assert p at the moment, but that we can exclude p (we know that no further addition of information will suddenly make p true). Similarly $p \rightarrow q$ means not just that there is no counterexample to the implication at the moment (remember a counterexample would be $p \wedge \neg q$), but that we can exclude such a counterexample. This is very close to saying that 'not' means 'necessarily not', or that 'implies' means 'necessarily implies', and so we are close here to modal language. This approach is saying, in effect, that we really *are* using modal notions (if not quite the language), and this can be captured in the semantics.

To model intuitionistic logic, the forcing relation is required to obey the conditions of **monotonicity** (information once obtained is never lost) and **consistency** (intuitionistic logic is not paraconsistent, so no point can force a contradiction). In fact these conditions are related. If x forces ϕ, then every point above x must force ϕ, so the conditions for x to force $\neg \phi$ cannot arise (refer to the definition just given for negation).

(10.27) **monotonicity**: if $x \sqsubseteq x'$ and x forces ϕ then x' forces ϕ.
(10.28) **consistency**: no point can force ϕ and $\neg \phi$.

What happens if we abandon these requirements of monotonicity and consistency? We might expect that the logic collapses into an inconsistent mess, but in fact all that happens is that we get some very interesting paraconsistent logics. These will be introduced in the last part of the book.

A formula is *valid* in intuitionistic logic iff it is true at all points in any intuitionistic Kripke models. However, there is a useful equivalent way of putting this: a formula is valid if it is forced at the bottom (root) node of a Kripke frame. Not all Kripke frames have a root (they are required to be partial orders, not trees); but a root node 0 can be added, which will force all (intuitionistic) logical truths, regardless of the valuation. (As a simple exercise, check that 0 will always force $p \rightarrow p$.)

A frame with a root 0, such that $0 \sqsubseteq p$ for every $p \in P$, is a 'rooted poset'. Generally 0 forces *only* logical truths, with contingent propositions (i.e. concrete information about the world) being added only further up the tree. Rooted frames are thus a way of capturing the difference between logic and information (Chapter 9). They will also be put to use in Chapter 11.

Kripke semantics can also be applied to intuitionistic predicate logic. Each point in the frame has a domain of individuals, as in the actualist semantics for quantified modal logic (Chapter 7). These are subject to the increasing domains condition, capturing the idea that as you proceed along a path in the frame, information can be added but not taken away. (Recall that the increasing domains requirement also applies to the actualist semantics for S4.)

(10.29) If $x \sqsubseteq x'$, then $D_x \subseteq D_x'$.

In such cases D_x' will be called an extension of D_x.

There is also a requirement that if a formula $P(a_1, \ldots a_n)$ is true at x, and $x \sqsubseteq y$, then $P(a_1, \ldots a_n)$ is true at y. This ensures that the denotation of any argument is fixed in all extensions of D_x.

The rules for interpreting quantified sentences are as follows:

(10.30) 1. x ⊩ ∃xφ iff for some d ∈ D$_x$,

      2. x ⊩ ∀xφ iff, for every x' such that x ⊑ x', for every d ∈ D$_x$', x' ⊩ φ.

Note that the rule for ∀, but not for ∃, refers to all domains that extend D$_x$.

Here are some further differences between intuitionistic and classical logic which are worth remembering (besides the absence of double negation elimination and LEM).

1. The De Morgan laws. One of these is not valid in intuitionistic logic: ¬(φ ∧ ψ) → (¬φ ∨ ¬ψ) – the one whose consequent has a disjunction as its main connective. In intuitionistic logic, a disjunction cannot be proved unless one of its disjuncts is proved.
2. Implication cannot be defined in terms of disjunction or conjunction.
3. The duality of the quantifiers does not apply; ∀ and ∃, like ∧ and ∨, are not inter-definable using negation.
4. The *reductio ad absurdum* argument schema cannot be used to prove a positive formula. If the original hypothesis was negative (¬φ), then *reductio* can be used to obtain ¬¬φ – but then we cannot conclude φ, because of the lack of double negation elimination.

One impression that might be given by this list is that the insights of intuitionism come at the price of much of the elegance and symmetry of classical logic. This point will be picked up in Chapter 12.

10.4 RELATION TO SITUATION SEMANTICS

Although situation semantics was not conceived as a logic, it does give rise to a number of logical or logic-like notions (section 9.5). In particular, as the **infon** is intended as a unit of information content, the relations between infons can be used to draw inferences. One infon, for example, may contain the information in another one, or two infons may be such that they cannot be supported by the same situation. Although situation semanticists classically speak of these relations using the more non-committal terms 'involvement' and 'incompatibility', it is also easy to think of them as entailment and contradiction.

As already discussed, these relationships and some others are analysed by Barwise and Etchemendy (1990). While declining to describe the results as a logic in the traditional sense (a formal language with an interpretation and a calculus of consequence), they develop an 'information-based theory of inference' which, they argue, shows the same structure as the semantics of intuitionistic logic.

Here are some of the points of contact.

1. Small situations are extended by larger situations which carry more information. This is like the relation of information extension between points in an intuitionistic Kripke frame.

2. The 'supports' relation between situations and infons is analogous to the forcing relation between points and formulae.

3. Given two infons distinguished by opposite polarity σ and σ^-, a situation does not have to support one or the other. However, it cannot support both. This is analogous to the failure of **LEM** and the validity of **LC** in intuitionistic logic.

The writers take the parallels further, arguing that infon algebras are Heyting algebras, which are also algebraic models for intuitionistic logic (see the end of this chapter).[11]

The similarities between intuitionistic logic and a 'logical' interpretation of situation semantics are very suggestive, and intuitions from situation semantics will be useful in this and later chapters in thinking about intuitionistic logic and its relatives. However, critics have pointed out some differences between the two. For example infons of negative polarity, like those of positive polarity, are simply supported or not supported in a given situation s without reference to its extensions; this is unlike intuitionistic negation, where all points above s in the informational ordering have to be taken into consideration when evaluating a negation. Another important difference is the infinite divisibility, in principle, of situations, whereas the points in an intuitionistic Kripke frame are given as a primitive set.

10.5 CONSTRUCTIVE PROOF AND LABELLED DEDUCTION

Mention has been made of the 'constructive' notion of proof used by intuitionists, and the consequences of this for the intuitionistic understanding of logical connectives. These notions are subtle and elusive, especially to people used to classical logic, and debate about them lasted for decades as the leading proponents of intuitionism, and those who engaged with them, tried to hammer out exactly what they meant. One of the important figures who had an influence on the outcome of these debates, was the Soviet mathematician Andrey Kolmogorov, who had developed a similar notion of a 'calculus of problems'.[12]

Out of these exchanges emerged a common understanding which is now referred to as 'the Brouwer-Heyting-Kolmogorov explication of intuitionistic truth' (or **BHK** for short!). According to BHK, to assert that a proposition is true means to provide a construction which demonstrates it. Each of the logical connectives can be thought of as a method of building complex constructions out of simpler constructions (or complex problems out of simpler problems).

This approach to truth and provability is one reason why intuitionistic logic has caught on in much wider circles than just the philosophy of mathematics. It has many applications in computer science, because provability can be understood as computability (recall the use of lambda calculus as a theory of computable functions).

Let's assume that atomic propositions come with some associated notion of proof, depending on the application. A term sometimes used is a 'realiser' – an object (perhaps a situation) that carries with it knowledge of the truth of the proposition. The task then for our compositional semantics is to think of reasonable interpretations of complex formulas involving connectives.

The simplest connectives are conjunction and disjunction. A conjunction $\phi \wedge \psi$ is interpreted as a *pair* of proofs, one of ϕ and one of ψ. Conjunction elimination consists of splitting the pair into its elements (a **projection function**). Taking the first element of the pair is like projecting a point onto the x axis, and taking the second element like projecting the point onto the y axis. These functions are called 'left projection' and 'right projection' respectively.

Since proofs are so important, it is useful to 'track' them by **labelling** them. We will use small letters from the beginning of the alphabet to serve as labels. Let's say that the label a represents a proof of p, and b represents a proof of q. Then the label $\langle a, b \rangle$ represents the proof of p $\wedge$ q. If we do conjunction elimination on p $\wedge$ q to get the left conjunct p, we will thereafter label p with a, the left projection of $\langle a, b \rangle$.

Similarly, if we perform conjunction introduction, we will label the resulting conjunction with an ordered pair containing the proof of the first conjunct and the proof of the second conjunct. This operation is called **pairing**.

The proof of a disjunction is not a pair of proofs (we do not have proofs of both disjuncts), but a proof of one of them. In the intuitionist system, this also requires that we know which one; p $\vee$ q is true if either we have a proof of p or we have a proof of q. If we have one of the two, we must know which it is. Supposing we are in Saudi Arabia, and I am only allowed to appear in public with two women if one of them is my wife. If I am stopped by the religious police, I have to show that one of them is my wife – it doesn't matter which, but which one I am married to is a question the policeman might reasonably ask me. From this point of view classical disjunction would be like vaguely claiming to be married to one of the two women without being married to either one of them specifically.

The labelling for proofs of disjunctions is slightly complicated, and since (unlike conjunction) it will not play a major role in what follows, we will not go into it in detail here. A brief outline will be given below, however.

Most of the interest in this approach resides in the treatment of implication. An implication p $\longrightarrow$ q is taken as a procedure which transforms a proof of p into a proof of q – which is to say, a function from proofs of p to proofs of q. Alternatively, as Kolmogorov's calculus of problems would put it, it reduces the problem q to the problem p. If you can solve p, then you have a solution to q. For example, the problem of calculating the median of an input can be reduced to the problem of sorting the input. The proof of this fact can be taken as a proof that a program for sorting an input gives you a program for computing the median.

Since the proof of p $\longrightarrow$ q is a function, it should behave as a function as we track steps of implication elimination and introduction. Implication elimination is straightforward. The implication is a function from proofs of p to proofs of q. The proof of p is therefore an *argument* of the proof of p $\longrightarrow$ q, and the result of applying the function to the argument is the proof of q. If we label the proof of p $\longrightarrow$ q as f and the proof of p as a, then the proof of q will be $f(a)$.

What about implication introduction? Recall that this involves making an assumption (the antecedent), using it to prove something (the consequent). and then discharging the assumption. In terms of proofs, we are trying to *make* a function. The argument to this function (the antecedent) is something we haven't proved, so we don't have a real proof term for it. Instead we can use a variable, say x, as a place-holder. The consequent is the result of some proof using x, in other words the value of some function f using x as its argument. If we ever got a real proof of the antecedent, we could slot that in in place of x to get the value according to the recipe given by f. If we take x as the argument and f as the recipe, then we have a ready-made notation for the function we are trying to construct: $\lambda x[f(x)]$. As a proof label for p → q, this can be read as 'if you were to give me a proof of p, then I am a procedure which shows you how to turn that proof into a proof of q'.

Note carefully the following correspondences from the discussion in the previous paragraph. An assumption is labelled by a free variable (x represents the assumption of p). The proof of q from p corresponds to applying a function to that variable. However, what we have so far is a proof from an assumption, not an implicational formula. We do not get an implication until we perform implication introduction, discharging the assumption; accordingly, we do not have a function until we have performed lambda abstraction, binding x. The lambda-bound variable no longer represents an undischarged assumption, but the antecedent of an implication.

In this section we have seen how ND formulas and derivations can be labelled with terms representing their proofs (the objects constructed in the process of proving them). The proof terms for conjunctions are pairs, while the proofs of implications are functions. Elimination and introduction rules are tracked by the natural operations on these constructions: projection and pairing in the case of pairs, application and lambda abstraction in the case of functions. A derivation where the formulas are labelled by proof terms using these rules is called a **labelled deduction**.

EXERCISE 10.5.0.1

1. Prove the following by ND and label the proofs. It will be convenient (for compatibility with conventions used elsewhere in this book) to write the labels to the left of the formulae. They may also be separated by a colon.
   (a) p ∧ q, q → r ⊢ p ∧ r
   (b) p, q, (p ∧ q) → r ⊢ r
   (c) ⊢ (p ∧ q) → q
   (d) p ⊢ (p → q) → q

10.6 INTERMEDIATE LOGICS AND THE S4–S5 SPECTRUM

The behaviour of a logic should reflect the notion of truth that it is intended to capture. For abstract, timeless notions of truth, there is a case for classical logic. Intuitionistic logic was developed hand in hand with the notion of truth as proof (previous section), and partial logic is also associated with notions of information and partial knowledge. To put it in the terms introduced in Chapter 6, the reasoning behind these logics is often as much epistemic as alethic.

This should bring to mind the modal systems discussed in Chapter 6, and in fact there is an intimate relationship between them. One of the first people to draw attention to the importance of S4 was Gödel, who was struck by the similarity between the epistemic interpretation of S4 and intuitionistic reasoning about truth in terms of proof. This in turn led Kripke to develop his well-known semantics for intuitionistic logic on the basis of his existing semantics for modal logics, especially S4. By contrast, there is a close relationship between classical logic and S5.

Further research by Gödel, Lemmon, Dummett and others revealed the existence of a whole range of logics between intuitionistic and classical logic. These are obtained by adding bits of classical logic to intuitionistic logic, in such a way as to extend intuitionistic logic without leading to full classical logic. These logics are usually known as **intermediate logics**, and will be so called here. (An alternative term is **superintuitionistic**.) Perhaps not surprisingly, in view of what has already been said, there are parallels between these intermediate logics and the S4–S5 spectrum of modal logics discussed in Chapter 6. This parallelism between the two spectra can be explored in a number of ways, of which we will focus on two: a translation between intermediate and modal logics, and similarities in the Kripke frame semantics for the different systems.

First the translation, the McKinsey–Tarski translation.[13] A basic proposition of intuitionistic logic is translated into modal logic as a necessity. The rules for the connectives $\rightarrow$ and $\neg$ introduce further necessity operators. As was seen earlier, the semantic rules for these connectives in intuitionistic logic involve evaluation on a whole set of branches, not just at one point, which is analogous to evaluation over an accessibility relation. The other propositional connectives do not have this property, and get translated without a necessity operator. The necessity operator in front of atomic propositions is because of the heredity constraint; once information is established, it cannot be lost. This is also a characteristic of necessities in S4 and its extensions (Chapter 6).

(10.31) 1. $T(p) = \Box p$
      2. $T(\neg\phi) = \Box \neg T(\phi)$
      3. $T(\phi \wedge \psi) = T(\phi) \wedge T(\psi)$
      4. $T(\phi \vee \psi) = T(\phi) \vee T(\psi)$
      5. $T(\phi \rightarrow \psi) = \Box(T(\phi) \rightarrow T(\psi))$

This translation relates classical logic to S5 and intuitionistic logic to S4. If a formula is provable in intuitionistic logic then its translation is provable in S4, and similarly for classical logic and S5. A modal logic which is related to a superintuitionistic logic by this translation is known as a **modal companion**. S4 is a modal companion of intuitionistic logic, S5 of classical logic, and other systems in the S4–S5 spectrum are modal companions of properly intermediate logics.

Let's look now at the characterisation by means of frames. Kripke frames for intuitionistic logic are partial orders, so they are by definition reflexive and transitive, properties which they have in common with S4 frames. For intermediate logics we put further restrictions on frames until we arrive at the limiting case of classical logic, which can be thought of as a Kripke frame with only one point (compare the modal system Triv in Chapter 6). In such a frame, if the single point does not force ϕ then it forces $\neg\phi$, as there are no further nodes at which ϕ can be true. Therefore $\phi \vee \neg\phi$ holds in such a frame. (This is also the case at an uppermost node in any intuitionistic frame; any such node similarly either forces ϕ or $\neg\phi$, for any ϕ.) The idea for intermediate logics is to introduce constraints on intuitionistic frames short of collapsing them into the one-point frame that would reduce it to classical logic.

The first intermediate systems explored by Dummett and Lemmon were those labelled by them as KC and LC. KC, the weaker of the two, is also known as Jankov's[14] logic, while LC is known as Dummett's or Gödel–Dummett logic.

The frame conditions for these two logics are immediately reminiscent of logics in the S4–S5 spectrum. In Dummett's logic (LC), the Kripke frame is constrained to be linear (like S4.3), while in Jankov's logic (KC) it is constrained to be finite and to have a single (top) endpoint, written $\top$. The latter is similar to the convergent frames of S4.2.

Here are the axioms added to intuitionistic PC to get these two systems:

KC: $\neg\phi \vee \neg\neg\phi$ (weak LEM[15])
LC: $(\phi \rightarrow \psi) \vee (\psi \rightarrow \phi)$ (pre-linearity)

The corresponding modal axioms are repeated here for convenience.

.2 (or C): $\Diamond\Box\phi \rightarrow \Box\Diamond\phi$
.3: $(\Box\phi < \psi) \vee (\Box\psi < \phi)$

The relationship of LC to the modal formula **.3** should be obvious, and the rationale – making the frame linear – is the same. It is straightforward to check that **.3** is the McKinsey–Tarski translation of **LC**.

Recall that LC is one of the 'paradoxes of material implication' in classical logic (Chapters 2 and 6). However, adding it to intuitionistic logic does not yet bring us back to classical logic, as it does not provide us with a proof of double negation elimination or **LEM**. In fact, you can easily construct a countermodel to **LEM** on a linear intuitionistic frame (with the same reasoning used above to show that **LEM** is valid at an endpoint).

LC logic may have a familiar ring to it, and in fact it has already been introduced – as the Gödel logic discussed in Chapter 8. The formula **LC** is known as the axiom of pre-linearity, which is included in the basic fuzzy logic BL and all its extensions. So LC belongs both to the family of fuzzy logics and to the family of intermediate logics; it is an extension both of BL and of intuitionistic logic. We will look at this again in Chapter 11.

The relationship between **KC** and **.2** is not so transparent, though in fact they too are linked by the McKinsey–Tarski translation. Axiom **KC** is known as 'weak LEM': although $\phi \vee \neg\phi$ is not valid, we always have either $\neg\phi$ or $\neg\neg\phi$.[16] This weak form of LEM is enough to give us De Morgan's laws, one of which is not valid in intuitionistic logic, as we have seen. (Consequently, KC is also sometimes known as De Morgan logic.)

The connection to S4.2 is perhaps more easily seen in the frame semantics. The characteristic principle of S4.2 is that if ϕ is established in one branch, we can never follow another branch which definitively rejects ϕ. Similarly in KC, either ϕ is rejected at all accessible points, in which case we have $\neg\phi$, or alternatively ϕ is established in some branch. In a KC frame, ϕ will then be true at $\top$ because of monotonicity, and consequently we cannot have $\neg\phi$ in any branch, so we have $\neg\neg\phi$. This is where the KC frame condition kicks in, because on an ordinary Kripke frame, without a top point, $\top$, we can have ϕ on one branch but not others, and neither $\neg\phi$ nor $\neg\neg\phi$ is forced.

The formula **KC** can be seen as giving an extra insight into the meaning of **.2**, despite or perhaps because of their apparent dissimilarity. It shows that **.2** requires either that definite confirmation of ϕ is excluded, or that its exclusion is excluded.

EXERCISE 10.6.0.1

1. The connection between KC and S4.2 was explained in the text using the frame semantics. Another approach is simply to translate the formula KC into its modal counterpart, using the McKinsey–Tarski translation. Perform this translation and show that, in S4, **.2** follows from this formula. You can use the fact (from the modality graph of S4, p. 108) that $\Box\Diamond\Box\,\phi$ entails $\Box\Diamond\phi$.

10.7 THE CURRY HOWARD ISOMORPHISM

The Curry Howard Isomorphism (CHI) is one of the most important concepts in logical approaches to language. An **isomorphism** (recall from Chapter 3) is a 1:1 correspondence between two different kinds of structure, which preserves relevant structure in both directions. In this case, the two structures concerned are propositional logic and the theory of functions. It therefore draws together two of the main themes of the book up to now – lambda expressions and their types, and logical formulas and their proofs. The CHI provides an essential tool for the remainder of the book.

10.7.1 LAMBDAS, TYPES, FORMULAS AND PROOFS

Chapter 5 introduced the simply typed lambda calculus as a translation language for meaningful expressions. This was convenient because most meanings are functions, and most compositional semantics proceeds by function application. To make sure that the right functions are applied to the right arguments, we introduced the system of typing, initially as a kind of bookkeeping. In effect, we ended up dealing with pairs, each pair consisting of an expression of the lambda calculus and its type. The pairs were written for convenience using the colon as a separator – *lambda expression : type*.

Clearly the type system plays a central part in holding this whole fabric together. For a start it mediates between the expressions and their intended meanings (domains of denotation). It is also involved in the key rules of function application and abstraction. It was pointed out that its behaviour in the first of these mirrors the logical rule of *modus ponens*. A functional type $\sigma \rightarrow \tau$ can be seen as saying 'give me something of type σ and I will give you back something of type τ. If you then feed it an argument of type σ, then the value it gives you is indeed of type τ.

We can now see that the typing conditions for the rule of functional abstraction similarly mirror conditional proof. If you abstract over an expression of type τ on a variable of type σ, then you have built a function of type $\sigma \longrightarrow \tau$, which looks for something of type σ as an argument and holds a slot for it as a variable.

One way of exploiting this parallelism is to treat types as logical formulas, and the $\longrightarrow$ connective used to form functional types as being the implication symbol. Of course, the selection of the symbol $\longrightarrow$ for this purpose rather than the various alternatives is intended to suggest precisely this. But it is more than a mere analogy; its behaviour is in fact exactly that of an implication connective. We have just seen a couple of simple examples of this in action.

Now consider the proof system that was set out earlier in this chapter, with its constructive interpretation. Complex formulas require complex proof labels, the rules for which are designed to capture the meaning and behaviour of the different connectives. This was seen in the rules for tracking elimination and introduction rules. Implications are modelled as functions, with implication eliminaton taking the form of function application and implication introduction taking the form of lambda abstraction. This works because (on the BHK interpretation) the proofs of implicational formulas really are functions.

These proof terms were introduced in the last chapter as an ancillary labelling system for tracking proofs. However, again we are able to think in terms of pairs, consisting of a logical formula and a proof term, written using the colon as separator – *proof term : logical formula.*

Whether we see the expressions on the left of the colon as primary and those on the right as ancillary bookkeeping (as in our original presentation of the simply typed lambda calculus), or the other way round (as in ND with its proof labels), the point to note is that the two systems always dovetail correctly. *Modus ponens* on the right corresponds to function application on the left, and conditional proof on the right corresponds to lambda abstraction on the left. The two systems are isomorphic – as far as we have seen. This correspondence between the lambda calculus and the ND proof theory (for intuitionistic logic) is the **Curry Howard Isomorphism**.[17]

Before reading on, it will help to think about the following points.

- What features of ND correspond to (i) function application, (ii) free variables, (iii) projection?
- What features of the lambda calculus correspond to (i) the consequent of an implication, (ii) conjunction, (iii) discharging an assumption?

In computational applications of the CHI, the proof terms are interpreted as computer programs (at a high level of abstraction). This is characteristic of **functional programming**, where programs and program segments are treated, in principle, as functions which return a value. The types of programs can be treated as formulas and manipulated using logical rules. Any formula that can be derived by these rules is guaranteed to have a corresponding program specification, for which it (the formula) gives the type.

It is possible to take a similar approach in linguistics. In Chapter 5, the lambda calculus was selected as a semantic translation language and lambda expressions were used to annotate the nodes of a syntactic tree. Rules were then given for computing the appropriate semantic expression at each node (especially the Rule of Function Application). The phrase structure tree was there as a convenient scaffolding, but it was noted that the real work was being done by the type system (the principle of 'type-driven translation'), and we also noted that what was going on at the level of types corresponds to *modus ponens*.

This suggests that the scaffolding of phrase structure trees was unnecessary. We can kick it away, use the types of the lambda expressions as formulas, and build up the structure by logical deduction instead. If we have a lambda expression of type $e \rightarrow t$ and another of type e, then we can perform *modus ponens* and write the new formula t. By the CHI the label of this formula will be a new lambda term, obtained by function application.[18] The result is the lambda expression for the sentence meaning.[19]

(10.32) Derivation of a sentence (type t) with meaning sing(mary).
    1. $\lambda x[sing(x)]$: $e \rightarrow t$ (Given)
    2. mary: e   (Given)
    3. $\lambda x[sing(x)](mary)$: t   MPP, 1,2
    $\mapsto_\beta$ sing(mary): t
(10.33) $\lambda x[\ sing(x)]$: $e \rightarrow t$, mary: $e \vdash$ sing(mary): t

Note that the lexical items (more precisely their types) perform the role of premises in this deduction, with the sentence type as the conclusion to be proved. In the process of proving it, the sentence meaning is computed from the meanings of the words.

The derivation of a transitive sentence is not much more complicated. The transitive verb expression (a curry function) combines with first the object and then the subject to give the sentence meaning. Notice that although we have done away with the tree structure, there is still something corresponding to the VP, namely line 4 of the derivation. This is a result of choosing to use curry functions rather than ordered pairs (see Chapter 5 for discussion).

(10.34) Derivation of a sentence (type t) with meaning speak(german)(mary).
    1. $\lambda x\lambda y[speak(x)(y)]$: $e \rightarrow (e \rightarrow t)$
    2. german: e
    3. mary: e
    4. $\lambda x\lambda y[speak(x)(y)](german)$: $e \rightarrow t$ $\rightarrow$ Elim, 1,2
    $\mapsto_\beta \lambda y[speak(german)(y)]$: $e \rightarrow t$
    5. $\lambda y[speak(german)(y)](mary)$: t $\rightarrow$ Elim, 4,3
    $\mapsto_\beta$ speak(german)(mary): t
(10.35) $\lambda x\lambda y[speak(x)(y)]$: $e \rightarrow (e \rightarrow t)$, german: e, mary: $e \vdash$ speak(german)(mary): t

These simple examples show how phrase structure trees can be replaced by logical derivations using the type system. Also, the structure of the proof is the same as the tree structures we were using earlier (one line of proof corresponds to each node of the tree). We are now using logic to do syntax as well as semantics. The general name often given to this approach to syntactic structure is **parsing as deduction**. The types of the words, together with the logical rules for performing deduction on these types, determine how the sentence is parsed.

This is the approach taken by categorial grammar, which will be explored in Chapter 12. However, we are not quite there yet. The rules of ND, as given in this chapter, will not tell us, for example, which of the NP premises to combine first with the transitive verb. There are a number of other things to be cleared up. For example, how many times can we use each of the premises? We do not yet have the tools in place for reasoning about syntax. These will be provided in the next chapter.

Let's tidy things up with a bit of formal terminology. We are now dealing with a system that combines two formal languages, a language Λ of the simply typed lambda calculus and a language J of intuitionistic propositional logic,[20] each with its own rules of derivation. If M is a wfe of Λ and ϕ is a wff of J, then an expression M: ϕ is called a **judgement**.[21] Depending whether we are taking the left side or the right side as primary, we can either refer to ϕ as the **type** of M, or M as the **label** of ϕ. We have a labelling discipline (a function from J to Λ which makes M the label of ϕ) and, in the other direction, a typing discipline (a function from Λ to ϕ which makes ϕ the type of M). This comes with rules for propagation of labels (tied to the derivation system of the logic, namely the proof theory), and rules for propagation of types tied to the derivation system of the lambda terms. (Examples of the latter are the rules of function application and abstraction in Chapter 5.)

The types in Chapter 5 can be seen as a (formalised) metalanguage for classifying lambda expressions, and the proof terms earlier in this chapter as a formalised metalanguage for tracking deduction. These are both perfectly valid perspectives, but we can also see judgements as complex object-language expressions, in which expressions from both systems are incorporated into an object language.[22]

10.7.2 PROOF NORMALISATION

The CHI is an isomorphism, so let's have a slightly closer look at what it is an isomorphism between. It is possible to list a number of things that correspond, and such a list is given in Table 10.1 at the end of the section. But there is one issue that has to be resolved to make the correspondence precise. It was stated earlier that a lambda expression records 'the' proof of a formula. However, in principle there can be many proofs of a formula from given premises. What is needed is some way of saying when these are, in some specifiable sense, the same proof. This was provided by Gentzen in the form of a technique for eliminating **detours** in proofs. Detours occur when an application of a rule is later undone by another rule, bringing us back to where we started. Eliminating them ensures that we can talk about *the* proof of a deduction meaning the shortest and most natural one, just as if I ask somebody for *the* way from London to Oxford I don't expect to be told that I can get there via Beijing.[23]

Suppose from some set of premises X we have proved ϕ and we have proved ψ. We can then write $\phi \wedge \psi$ by conjunction introduction, and then ϕ by conjunction elimination. Clearly we have achieved nothing by this manoeuvre; it is a detour. Similarly we

Table 10.1:   The Curry Howard Isomorphism

Lambda calculus	Natural deduction
function application	$\rightarrow$ elim (MPP)
lambda abstraction	$\rightarrow$ intro (CP)
free variable	assumption
projection	$\wedge$ elim
pairing	$\wedge$ intro
$\beta\eta$ normal form	normalised proof
inhabitation	provability

could start with $\phi \wedge \psi$ (from premises X), obtain ϕ and ψ separately by conjunction elimination, and then get back to $\phi \wedge \psi$ by conjunction introduction.

We want to be able to rewrite the proof without the detour, so that the result of the detour follows immediately from the premises X. For the instances just described, that is straightforward.

With implication there are also two types of detour. In the first, given premises X, we assume ϕ, prove ψ and thus obtain $\phi \rightarrow \psi$ by conditional proof; but then say we find we have ϕ anyway from X, and deduce ψ by *modus ponens*. Clearly the conditional proof step was a detour, elimating which leaves us with a proof of both ϕ and ψ from X. The second case arises when we have $\phi \rightarrow \psi$ from X, assume ϕ to obtain ψ and then discharge the assumption of ϕ to get $\phi \rightarrow \psi$ (which we already had). In this case removal of the detour leaves us with the original proof of $\phi \rightarrow \psi$ from X.

The first of these two cases is analogous to β reduction in the lambda calculus. The step of conditional proof gives us a proof term in the form of a lambda abstract, let's say $\lambda x.f(x)$, together with a constant a of the correct antecedent type ϕ. This is a β redex, and is reduced to the normal form f(a), labelling ψ. The second case is analogous to η reduction. We are given an implication, which we can label by the function f; the unnecessary step of conditional proof makes this into a lambda abstract $\lambda x.f(x)$. This is an η redex, which is reduced to the normal form f.

In this way the elimination of detours in ND proofs corresponds exactly to the normalisation of terms in the lambda calculus, and it is this that is the basis of the isomorphism. It will be useful to check the informal description I have just given with the definitions of normal form in Chapter 5. Proof normalisation also enjoys the Church–Rosser and strong normalisation properties of the simply typed lambda calculus.

The last entry in Table 10.1 refers to the fact that only formulae that are provable have proof terms. Looking at formulae as types, this means that a non-provable formula is not the type of any lambda expression; the type is said not to be **inhabited**. More on this in Chapter 13.

The CHI in its classic form includes only functional and product types (implications and conjunctions), and furthermore is confined to intuitionistic propositional logic. It can be extended in various ways: to classical logic by continuations,[24] and to predicate logic by record types.[25]

10.8 ALGEBRAIC BACKGROUND III

This brief section is a note on Heyting algebras, in connection with some of the ideas found in this part of the book. Heyting algebras are for intuitionistic logic what Boolean algebras are for classical logic.

A Heyting algebra is a bounded distributive lattice like a Boolean algebra (Chapter 3) – in fact a Boolean algebra is a special case of a Heyting algebra which is also complemented. Heyting algebras in general need not be complemented; that is, for an element x there is not required to be an element x' such that $x \wedge x' = 0$ and $x \vee x' = 1$. As you would expect given the absence of **LEM** from intuitionistic logic, it is the second of these that fails when Heyting algebras are used for intuitionistic logic. While not a true complement, x' is known as the **pseudocomplement** of x as it obeys $x \wedge x' = 0$.

Intuitionistic implication is modelled in a Heyting algebra by a **relative pseudo-complement**. The relative pseudocomplement of x with respect to y is the greatest element z such that $z \wedge x \leq y$. This z is written $x \longrightarrow y$. The conjunction $(x \longrightarrow y) \wedge x$ entails y (as in *modus ponens*). One definition of a Heyting algebra is a bounded lattice in which every pair of elements has a relative pseudocomplement.

The pseudocomplement x' is a particular case of a relative pseudocomplement; it is the greatest element whose conjunction with x gives 0, and it is therefore the relative pseudocomplement of x with respect to 0. It can be written $x \longrightarrow 0$, which, as explained in the text, is a standard way of looking at intuitionistic negation.

Heyting algebras can be used for many partial logics. These can be linear chains, such as the lattice of truth degrees $\{0, \frac{1}{2}, 1\}$, which are the simplest Heyting algebras (they are Boolean iff the number of elements is 2). In these lattices the relative pseudocomplement $x \longrightarrow y = y$ if x is greater than y, and 1 otherwise. This is the Gödel implication of Chapter 8.

A Heyting algebra can also be defined using the group-theoretic concepts of the previous chapter: it is a residuated monoid in which the multiplication operation $x \cdot y$ is the same as the **glb** $x \wedge y$. In other lattice-ordered monoids it merely has to be *compatible* with the partial order relation. In the discussion of fuzzy logics in Chapter 8, the monoid operator $\cdot$ corresponds to strong conjunction, while the lattice operator $\wedge$ is weak conjunction. In the case of Gödel–Dummett logic, strong conjunction and weak conjunction are the same thing, which is why that logic belongs to the (super-) intuitionistic family as well as the fuzzy family.

Given a Heyting algebra H, it is also possible to define a dual Heyting algebra H^{-1}, which is H with $\leq^{-1}$ instead of $\leq$ as its order relation. (A structure with both relations at the same time is a double Heyting algebra.) In a dual Heyting algebra $\vee$ and $\wedge$ change roles, as do 0 and 1 (the **glb** of $\leq$ is the **lub** of $\leq^{-1}$). An operator can also be defined which is dual to the relative pseudocomplement. This models the dual of the implication connective, is also called **co-implication**, and written variously as $/$, $-$ ('difference'), !, # or $\leftarrow$, but several of these are used in this book with a different meaning, so I will use $-$ here. The dual relative pseudocomplement of x with respect to y is the least element z such that $z \vee x \geq y$. This can be thought of as (roughly) the inhibition connective of Boolean logic ($\phi \wedge \neg\psi$). In dual intuitionistic logic it is usually known as subtraction.[26] The disjunction of a subtraction and the subtracted formula gives $(\phi - \psi) \vee \psi \geq \phi$, the dual of *modus ponens*.

(10.36) **Modus ponens**: $(x \longrightarrow y) \wedge x \leq y$
  Dual *modus ponens*: $x \vee (y - x) \leq^{-1} y$

Dual Heyting algebras are used to model a logic known as anti-intuitionistic (or dual intuitionistic) logic, which is paraconsistent as intuitionistic logic is partial. Related ideas of duality are used in fuzzy logic (e.g. the t-conorms mentioned in Chapter 8, and their dual residuals, which were not discussed). The notion of co-implication or difference has been used in some treatments of categorial grammar, and will make an appearance in Chapter 12.

10.9 EPILOGUE TO PART III

This part of the book has introduced a variety of approaches to partiality (and, in Chapter 8, a brief look at paraconsistency). They include generalisations of the classical truth tables (to truth degrees and truth combinations), an information based approach based on situations and, in this chapter, an approach based on constructive proof theory. The last of these included a relational semantics not unlike that of modal logic, including, for some connectives, evaluation at a range of information points.

The last few chapters of this book will develop the theme that implication and negation (in contrast to conjunction and disjunction as we know them) are at heart intensional connectives. Although we met them at first as truth functions, the discussion of intuitionistic ND, and the way they are evaluated on intuitionistic frames, gives us clues that this is not the whole story. In order to get at the nuts and bolts of these connectives, we will examine systems which are *weaker* than intuitionistic logic. By abandoning many of the assumptions made in classical logic about the meaning of connectives, we will find a new array of logical tools which have proved of great interest and use to linguists. Finally we will put the pieces together again, and see how these tools can be used to reconstruct the classical picture.

The Göttingen school

The Göttingen school is the name given to the exceptional concentration of logicians at the Georgia Augusta University of Göttingen between the world wars. The university already had a distinguished place in the history of logic, being associated with Leibniz, Frege and Husserl among others, but this 'golden period' was centred on the Hilbert programme – a research programme to establish the foundations of mathematics on a purely logical basis. The Göttingen school originally had a strong international dimension, attracting researchers, students and visitors from all over the world. However, this declined following the rise of Nazism (of which Göttingen was a major centre in northern Germany), and particularly after the expulsion of all Jewish professors in 1933. There is a story that some time after his retirement, Gödel was asked by a Nazi minister how mathematics in Göttingen was doing now that it had been purged of Jews. 'Mathematics?' replied Gödel. 'There really isn't any any more.'

David Hilbert

Hilbert's main work was in geometry and in the logical foundations of mathematics. The work of Frege and Russell seemed to open up the possibility of deriving the whole of mathematics from logical axioms, and as professor in Göttingen Hilbert twice launched a massive programme to accomplish this. His faced two main challenges, from rival conceptions of logic (notably the increasingly popular intuitionism, which attracted many of his students) and finally from Gödel's demonstration (by the incompleteness theorems) that his programme was impossible in the terms in which he had formulated it. Hilbert was quite a flamboyant and argumentative character, and fond of aphorisms. He is quoted as saying, when one of his students dropped out to study poetry, 'Good – he never had the imagination to be a mathematician.'

NOTES

1. Immanuel Kant, *Critique of Pure Reason*.
2. The name comes originally from Kant's use of 'intuition' to describe the conceptual framework with which humans organise their experience of the world, as in the quotation given.
3. Specifically, it does not allow a constructive proof, in which the mathematical object concerned is constructed and exhibited – see section 10.5 below.
4. Several early reactions to intuitionism tried to treat it as a three value logic along the lines explored in Chapter 8, but this was shown not to work. In particular Gödel showed that it could not be modelled using any finite set of truth values.
5. It was developed independently by the Polish logician Stanislaw Jaśkowski.
6. There are several ways of setting out an ND proof; a succinct history is given in Pelletier (2000). The style used in this chapter is usually called 'Lemmon style', though it goes back to Suppes and derives ultimately from the tradition of Jaśkowski. There is another layout based on numbered lines known as 'Fitch style'. Gentzen used a tree format, which we will see in action in later chapters. Restall comments that there is a geographical dimension here, with Fitch style being popular in the USA, Lemmon style in Britain and Gentzen style in Europe.
7. In Gentzen's words, 'The introductions represent . . . the definitions of the symbols concerned, and the eliminations are . . . the consequences of these definitions. This fact may be expressed as follows: In eliminating a symbol, we may use the formula with whose terminal symbol we are dealing only in the sense afforded it by the introduction of that symbol.' Gentzen (1934), quoted in von Plato (2014).
8. Yet another name for it is detachment; as mentioned in Chapter 6, the idea is that you 'detach' the consequent q from the implication, and can use it in further proof steps.
9. See Gamut (1990), Vol. I.
10. Other semantic interpretations that the reader might come across are Beth tableaux (somewhat similar to the tree method of Chapter 2), topological models and category theory. These are not covered here, but there are references in the Bibliography.
11. Barwise and Etchemendy focus, however, not on Kripke frames nor Heyting algebras but on topological models, which are not covered in this book; see Vickers 1990.
12. Roughly, propositions represent problems and constructions are their solutions.
13. There is also a Gödel translation, which is similar.
14. Jankov's name is also transcribed as Yankov.
15. Note that this name is sometimes used in other ways.

16. The latter does not give ϕ, because we do not have double negation elimination. Note also the difference between weak LEM and the formula $\neg\neg\,(\phi \vee \neg\,\phi)$, which is valid in intuitionistic logic.
17. The original isomorphism was later extended by William Howard. Curry's work did not actually involve the lambda calculus, which was invented by Church a little later, but rather an equivalent system called combinatory logic, discussed in Chapter 13. The form of the isomorphism used here, and commonly in linguistics, is due to Howard.
18. In the example, this is then normalised by β reduction. Note that this is only necessary because we chose to spell out the translation of 'sing' as a lambda abstract. We could equally have translated it by the constant *sing* of type e $\longrightarrow$ t, and the step of reduction would not be needed.
19. Van Benthem (1983).
20. Intuitionistic logic is often notated as J, from the older German style of writing capital I as $\mathcal{J}$.
21. Another term is 'declarative unit'.
22. The distinction between object language and labels is relative. Generally speaking, it is the object language that we are trying to explicate by means of the metalanguage, which should ideally be something that we understand better, and which gives a connection to the intended model. For example lambda expressions are given types which connect them to their domains of denotation (Chapter 5), while ND formulae are labelled with lambda terms which may be connected to some programming implementation.
23. The idea of eliminating detours goes back to Gentzen, but was only implemented for his consecution calculus (Chapter 12). It was worked out for ND by Prawitz in the 1960s (Prawitz 1965). This was the background to Howard's statement of the CHI in the form we know (Howard 1980).
24. Barker (2002), de Groote (2001).
25. Ranta (1994), Cooper (2005, 2011).
26. Crolard (2004).

PART IV

SUBSTRUCTURAL LOGICS AND CATEGORIAL GRAMMAR

CHAPTER 11

RELEVANCE, RESOURCES AND ORDER

Material implication is no more a kind of implication than a blunderbuss is a kind of bus. (Anderson and Belnap 1975)

11.1 STRUCTURAL RULES

It is now time to look again at some basic assumptions we have been making about the behaviour of connectives. For example, it is assumed in all the logics discussed up to now that in a conjunction the order of the subformulae does not matter. However, it is not always possible to flip the order of two conjuncts, *salva veritate*. Examples where this is not possible include sequences of actions,[1] and also certain statements about syntax.

(11.1) 1. (a) We will qualify for the Champions League and buy some better players.
      (b) We will buy some better players and qualify for the Champions League.
   2. (a) A sentence comprises an NP and a VP.
      (b) A sentence comprises a VP and an NP.

The first pair of sentences is naturally understood as describing two different plans for aspiring football clubs. It is natural to take the second pair too with an implicit 'in that order'; the first one would be a good description of a grammatical sentence in English, whereas the second would be appropriate for Malagasy.

If we are concerned with general truths, then it makes sense to follow classical logic in assuming that conjunction is **commutative** (conjuncts can always be flipped). However, reasoning in different contexts may require different logical tools.

While considerations like these affect all connectives, the focus in this final part of the book will be on conjunction and implication. These go closely together, as can be seen from the deduction equivalence (p. 25). In classical logic, this looks like (11.2). When a whole lot of premises are involved, it can be put in a more general form as (11.3).

(11.2) $\phi \wedge \psi \vdash \chi$ iff $\phi \vdash \psi \rightarrow \chi$
(11.3) $X, \phi \vdash \psi$ iff $X \vdash \phi \rightarrow \psi$

X represents a combination of premises, which it is natural at first blush to take as a set. (This can be the empty set, in which case $\phi \rightarrow \psi$ is a theorem.) The comma in the first half of the consecution X, $\phi \vdash \psi$ indicates the combination of X with a further premise, the single formula ϕ. The consecution means that ψ is provable from the combination of X *and* ϕ. This comma therefore has some relationship to conjunction; it combines X and ϕ into a single body of information.

In (11.3), however, X and the comma are not formulas or connectives of the logical language; they are a way of expressing combinations of formulas, in a kind of meta-language. Note that it is not committal about X being a set, or about the comma being conjunction as we know it.

Let's be more precise about this metalanguage which is used to build consecutions, as we need to reason about it. It consists of premise structures (X, Y, Z etc.), punctuation marks (in this case the comma), and the turnstyle symbol, $\vdash$. Any formula of a logical language is a premise structure, and if X and Y are premise structures then so is (X, Y) – but outermost brackets will be left out as usual. If X is a premise structure and ϕ is a formula, then X $\vdash \phi$ is a consecution.[2]

Why is the right-hand side of the consecution limited to a single formula? In fact it can be generalised to allow structures rather than just single formulae, but to the right of the turnstyle the interpretation of stuctures is different: they are analogous to disjunctions rather than conjunctions. We will come back to this, but single-formula conclusions will do for now, as the natural deduction proofs we have been using have single formulae as their conclusions.

In natural deduction proofs, we have been taking a number of liberties with premise structures. Since these liberties are rather natural, they were allowed to go unremarked at the time. The first example is that we allowed ourselves to take the premises in any order; in other words, we assumed that the combination of premises was **commutative**, in just the same way that classical conjunction is commutative. But as the examples above show, there are some applications where we may need to tighten up our proofs.

Natural deduction was presented in Chapter 10 in terms of **connective rules**, which capture the basic meaning of connectives. The 'liberties' we have been taking in rearranging or manipulating the premises are known as **structural rules**. The one we have just been discussing is the structural rule of Permutation,[3] which allows us to change the order of premises. Without it, we have to stick to the order of premises as given. This will affect the proofs that can be made.

What other structural rules are there? There are four structural rules of basic importance, Permutation being one of them.

A second liberty we have been taking is to use premises as many times as we want. Again, this seems natural in the contexts we have been considering up to now. If a statement is true, then it doesn't matter how many times we use it; it won't go away, and is still there to refer to again whenever necessary. But suppose we are not reasoning about philosophical truths, but for example about a computation. Just because we can use some information once doesn't mean that we can rely on it any time we want to. Just using it might modify it in some way. The same applies when reasoning about money. If I have the information that there is a sum of money in my account, and I draw the conclusion that I can afford a new camera, then that is fine, but I cannot go on assuming that the money is still there. Parsing a string in language is another application where, generally speaking, an expression is going to appear in the parsed structure once and once only. There may be certain exceptions to that, but normally once a constituent is accounted for we would expect to tick it off and move on. The structural rule that gives us free rein to reuse premises is called Contraction.

A third structural rule concerns the bracketing of premises – the idea that some premises belong more closely together than others. In the consecutions used up to now, premises have been listed without brackets, so that if we have premises X, Y, Z, we are free to combine X with Y first or Y with Z first, at our convenience. That, too, seemed perfectly natural. However, if we are thinking of words as premises (or more accurately, categories as premises), we know from basic syntax that some groups of words combine closely together. They are called **constituents** (and are usually represented using trees, although bracketing serves the same purpose). To allow sequences of words to be strung together without brackets amounts to allowing rebracketing at will. The structural rule that allows this is called Associativity. This says that a combination of premises X, (Y, Z) can be treated as (X, Y), Z. Since the bracketing is no longer fixed, it serves no purpose and is often not written at all.

The final structural rule to be considered here allows us to introduce any new premises we want. This may seem strange, but in fact it is an important feature of standard logics. If a conclusion follows from a set of premises, then it also follows if you add more premises. The extra premises will not detract from the truth of the conclusion (although they may be irrelevant to it). So any set of premises X can be replaced by X, ϕ (where ϕ can be any formula); because if X is sufficient to prove a conclusion, then X and ϕ together are more than sufficient. To say that the conclusion follows from X and ϕ together is a weaker claim than to say that it follows from X on its own; accordingly, this structural rule is called Weakening. Weakening seems, on the one hand, motivated by considerations of monotonicity,[4] but it is also responsible for a lot of features of classical logic that seem unintuitive.

Example (11.4) gives a summary of the four structural rules, with X, Y and Z representing any premises or combinations of premises.

(11.4) Structural rules
1. Associativity (**B**): X, (Y, Z) can be rewritten as (X, Y), Z
2. Permutation (**C**): (X, Y), Z can be rewritten as (X, Z), Y
3. Contraction (**W**): (X, Y), Y can be rewritten as X, Y
4. Weakening (**K**): X can be rewritten as X, Y (for any Y).

The rules are traditionally given the labels in brackets, though they are now pretty meaningless. They are derived from combinatorial logic (Chapter 13).[5] For now, note that **C** is Permutation not Contraction and **W** is Contraction not Weakening.

Before going on, let's look again at some of the natural deduction proofs from Chapter 10, paying attention to the structural rules in action. The following are some important consecutions. Some of them should already be familar from previous exercises.

(11.5) 1. $p \rightarrow (q{\rightarrow}r) \vdash q \rightarrow (p \rightarrow r)$
      2. $p \rightarrow q \vdash (r{\rightarrow}p) \rightarrow (r \rightarrow q)$
      3. $p \rightarrow q \vdash (q{\rightarrow}r) \rightarrow (p \rightarrow r)$
      4. $p \rightarrow (p \rightarrow q) \vdash p \rightarrow q$
      5. $p, p \rightarrow q \vdash q$
      6. $p \vdash (q {\rightarrow} p)$ (possibly difficult)

EXERCISE 11.1.0.1

Prove the consecutions in (11.5). For each proof, make a note of which of the following have occurred:

1. A premise has been used more than once in the derivation.
2. The order of premises has been changed (*modus ponens* has been applied to lines whose numbers are not in ascending order).
3. The minor premise of a step of *modus ponens* has itself been derived using *modus ponens*.
4. A premise has been introduced without being used to prove anything new.
   Which structural rules do you think are involved in each case?

11.1.1 SUBSTRUCTURAL LOGICS

It should already be clear that changing the structural rules has quite a drastic effect on the behaviour of the logic. In fact by selecting from among the structural rules, we can define a whole family of related logics. The four structural rules in (11.4) above, together, give the correct behaviour for intuitionistic logic. Logics which select a *subset* of these structural rules are known as **substructural** or **subintuitionistic** logics.

In principle a large number of logics can be formed by selecting structural rules. Some of the better known ones are shown in Table 11.1.

There is also a non-associative version of the Lambek Calculus, which dispenses with the structural rule **B**. Unless stated otherwise, Lambek Calculus will here refer to the version with associativity.

The **axiom of identity**, $\phi \rightarrow \phi$, is usually assumed along with whatever structural rules are adopted.

Table 11.1:   Some of the main substructural logics

Name	Structural rules
Intuitionistic logic	B, C, K, W
Relevance logic (R)	B, C, W
BCK or affine logic	B, C, K
Linear logic (LL)	B, C
Ticket entailment (T)	B, W
Lambek Calculus (L)	B

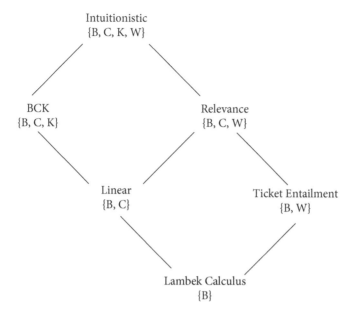

Figure 11.1   Part of the lattice of substructural logics

These logics can be arranged in a lattice, with the strongest at the top and the weakest at the bottom (Figure 11.1).

There are, of course, other possible combinations which are not included here, as well as several intermediate options. Even among those logics included in the diagram, not all are equally important for linguistics, though they may have other uses.

Above intuitionistic logic in this lattice lies classical logic. However, the difference between classical and intuitionistic logic is not a matter of structural rules; as far as structural rules are concerned, they both have the full set. I will often refer to both collectively as 'standard logic' (meaning just this property of having the full complement of structural rules). The familiar behaviour of standard logics is the result of all these structural rules working together. Taking one or more away leads to surprising and sometimes unintuitive behaviour. Logics with only one or two of the normal structural rules can look very unfamiliar; just as when white light is split, or chemical compounds decomposed, the results do not look at all like what we started out with. In this part of the book standard logic is taken apart in a similar way to have a look at the nuts and bolts of which it is composed.

The rest of this section will take a preliminary look at a series of logics starting from the top of the lattice and dropping one structural rule at a time until we get to the Lambek Calculus. This will include the substructural logics most widely discussed in linguistics. As usual, there will be a more detailed 'second pass' after the formal syntactic and semantic definitions have been introduced.

11.1.2 CHARACTERISTICS OF SUBSTRUCTURAL LOGICS

As should be clear from the deduction equivalence (11.3), the liberties we take with premise combination will affect, first of all, the conjunction and implication connectives. The structural rules used, and those omitted, determine the meaning of the metalinguistic symbols, X, ',' and ⊢, and these in turn affect the meaning of the connectives which mirror them in the logical language.

Relevance logic

In previous chapters (Chapters 2 and 6), mention was made several times of certain counter-intuitive consequences of material implication (often referred to as 'paradoxes', though there is nothing self-contradictory about them). It has often been suggested that an adequate notion of implication should include not only preservation of truth but also the ideas of necessity and relevance. Necessity was addressed by modal logic, but relevance was not: even with strict implication, there are cases where the antecedent has nothing to do with the consequent. This can arise whenever the antecedent is a contradiction or the consequent is a tautology. For example $(p \wedge \neg p) \prec (q \vee \neg q)$. Mary being pregnant and not pregnant 'strictly implies' that the moon either is or isn't made of green cheese.

The key idea behind relevance logic is that such cases can be excluded by dropping Weakening (**K**). The paradigmatic example of an *irrelevant* implication is $\phi \rightarrow (\psi \rightarrow \phi)$, which is valid in standard logic. If you did the earlier exercise, you will have noted that the proof of this formula requires Weakening. The proof is set out here in Lemmon style. The assumption q is made at line 2 and discharged vacuously at line 4, without being used to prove p in the subproof from lines 2 to 4 (the conclusion p is obtained independently of q).

(11.6) 1. p   Ass
       2. q   Ass
       3. p   Reiteration, 1
       4. $q \rightarrow p$ CP, discharging 2
       5. $p \rightarrow (q \rightarrow p)$ CP, discharging 1
(11.7) ⊢ $p \rightarrow (q \rightarrow p)$

Such vacuous discharging of assumptions is not against the rules of natural deduction as given in Chapter 10, though it leaves many people feeling as if they have been taken in by some kind of trick. Such tricks are prohibited in relevance logic, with far-reaching consequences. First, an implication is no longer true simply because the consequent is true. This means that the implication connective is no longer material implication. It requires that the antecedent and consequent share something in common (this notion can be made precise), and is therefore called **relevant implication**. It also follows that this relevant implication is not a truth function. If you look at the formula proved in (11.6), it holds precisely because a true statement (p by assumption) is implied by anything. It epitomises the truth-functional nature of material implication. Making implication non-truth-functional is a fundamental change to the logic.

The absence of Weakening also has an effect on the notion of premise combination, and hence conjunction. The kind of combination represented by the comma is now stricter than just conjunction, because it means that the premises must *interact* to give the conclusion. Premises that are just standing around have no business to be there. This stronger notion of combination is known in relevance logic as **fusion**. In fact, we now end up with two conjunction-like connectives: ordinary conjunction and fusion. Fusion should be read not simply as 'and', but as 'taken together with', or 'in combination with'. In relevance logic it is this fusion connective, not ordinary conjunction, that corresponds to the meaning of the comma in the deduction equivalence.

There is also a knock-on effect on the other connectives, negation and disjunction. One result of implication not being truth-functional is that ECQ is not valid, in other words relevance logic is **paraconsistent** (Chapter 8). ECQ is the mirror image of Weakening, as its characteristic formula, $\neg\, \phi \rightarrow (\phi \rightarrow \psi)$, depends on the falsity of ϕ to prove the implication $\phi \rightarrow \psi$. Both Weakening and ECQ commit what are traditionally described as 'fallacies of relevance'. Recall from the discussion of negation in Chapter 10 that one negation connective which excludes ECQ is De Morgan negation. This is the negation connective used in relevance logic.

Disjunction, like conjunction, splits into two: ordinary disjunction and a relevant disjunction which captures a notion of 'relevant alternatives'. The relevant version is known, by analogy with fusion, as **fission**. More on this later.

So much for relevance logic for the time being. The reader may have the impression that the debate about relevance is more philosophical than linguistic, and it is true that relevance logic has not been extensively used in linguistics *as such*.[6] However, the properties of relevance logic that result from the exclusion of Weakening are also inherited by the logics beneath it in the hierarchy of substructural logics, which include most of the substructural logics used in linguistics. I will describe all such logics as 'relevance-sensitive'.

Linear logic

Linear logic excludes not only Weakening but also Contraction – the right to reuse premises as often as you want to. As has already been discussed, there are several applications that involve keeping track of the premises we have used, and checking them off. This kind of close control over premises can be desirable not only when reasoning about computer programs but also when reasoning about syntax (as discussed in more detail in Chapter 12). The intuition here is that the use of premises is kept track of like use of expendable assets, and logics which exclude Contraction are commonly known as **resource-sensitive** logics,[7] or resource logics for short. The strongest resource logic is BCK, which is simply intuitionistic logic without Contraction. (BCK is also popular in computer science for that reason.) Linear logic is both resource-sensitive and relevance-sensitive, as will be clear from Figure 11.1.

Let's see how Contraction works, to get a better idea of what it means to exclude it. It can be seen in its purest form in the proof of the formula $(p \rightarrow (p \rightarrow q)) \rightarrow (p \rightarrow q)$. The premise p, though assumed only once (line 2), has to be available for use twice (lines 3 and 4).

(11.8) 1. $p \rightarrow (p \rightarrow q)$ Ass
      2. p Ass
      3. $p \rightarrow q$ MPP, lines 1, 2
      4. q MPP lines 3, 2
      5. $p \rightarrow q$ CP, discharging line 2
      6. $(p \rightarrow (p \rightarrow q)) \rightarrow (p \rightarrow q)$ CP, discharging line 1
(11.9) $\vdash (p \rightarrow (p \rightarrow q)) \rightarrow (p \rightarrow q)$

Inference in linear logic can be thought of as a procedure for converting the premises into the conclusion. The conclusion *replaces* the premises. Linear implication can be thought of as a procedure for making omelettes – as the saying goes, it involves breaking eggs. In linear deduction *p* is 'consumed' in the process of producing *q*. (In fact so is the other premise p→q, which is rather like smashing up the kitchen as well as breaking the eggs.)

Like relevance logic, linear logic has two sets of conjunction and disjunction connectives. One conjunction goes with implication, in the sense that it mirrors the behaviour of the comma in the deduction equivalence (11.3). This connective is the linear version of fusion; in the linear logic tradition it is usually called **tensor**.

The other forms of linear conjunction and disjunction will be discussed later in the chapter, along with negation. They are not entirely easy to understand intuitively in terms of the classical connectives; as we have already dropped 50 per cent of the structural rules of standard logic, it is not surprising that we are quite a long way away from it.

Lambek Calculus (associative)

Proceeding further down the hierarchy, the next structural rule to go is Permutation, which allows premises to be swapped round. This means that the comma for combining premises is no longer commutative, so the order of premises becomes important. The same applies to the fusion connective which mirrors the behaviour of the comma. In one application, one of great interest to linguists, it can be thought of as a concatenation operator; the concatenation of strings is not commutative.

There are plenty of other applications in which fusion is not commutative. As already noted, reasoning about actions and sequences of actions is not commutative: doing X and then Y is not the same as doing Y and then X. Another example is the logic of function composition: the sum of the square of two sides is not the same as the square of the sum; $f \circ g \neq g \circ f$.

Perhaps the most spectacular feature of non-commutative logics is that the implication connective is split into two. In natural deduction, *modus ponens* combines the major premise and the minor premise *in that order*. This did not matter a lot when premises could be taken in any order, but now suppose that the minor premise precedes the major premise, and we cannot change the order. To do *modus ponens* another implication connective is needed, which combines the premises in reverse order. To bring across the idea of reverse directionality, this extra connective can be written ←. So the deduction equivalence now has two clauses:

(11.10) 1. $X, \phi \vdash \psi$ iff $X \vdash \phi \rightarrow \psi$
      2. $\phi, X \vdash \psi$ iff $X \vdash \psi \leftarrow \phi$

In linguistic applications, the two implication symbols are normally written as forward and backward slashes. One looks to combine with something to its right, the other with something to its left. This will be the main theme of the next chapter.

The only structural rule left is Associativity, which allows the rebracketing of premises. If this liberty too is clamped down on, then we get to a logic in which the bracketing of premises is fixed. Thinking in terms of syntax, bracketing can be thought of as breaking up strings into constituents, and we therefore have something very much like fixed phrase structure. Dropping Permutation makes the logic order-sensitive; dropping Associativity can be said to make it constituency-sensitive.

Premise structures

This brief introduction has looked at the change in meaning of the turnstyle and comma as successive structural rules are dropped, and at the implication and fusion connectives which, respectively, mirror them inside the object language. What about the other element in the deduction equivalence, the X which I described, with a certain amount of hand waving, as a kind of combination of premises? In standard logic, it is reasonable to think of it as a *set* of premises. The order of elements does not matter, duplicate elements are written only once, and there is no internal grouping of elements corresponding to bracketing. More subtly, membership amounts to 'being there', whether or not the element is interacting in the consecution.

In the properly substructural logics, this picture of X as a set breaks down. In relevance logic, the elements of X are required to contribute to the deduction, so that it is not just a set but a combination. Just as in chess you would not talk of a combination of pieces if one of them was standing on the other side of the board doing nothing, a combination in relevance logic consists of premises that are contributing to the conclusion. Other formulas are not part of it just because they happen to be around too. I will refer to this notion of X as a 'combination' or a 'relevant set' – no bold type because they are not established technical terms (many terms have been used in the literature).

Dropping Contraction means that the number of times an element occurs becomes important. Duplicates are listed twice, not just once as they would be in a set. This is called a **multiset**, or 'bag'. In BCK, premise structures are multisets. In linear logic they are also multisets, but remember that linear logic also excludes Weakening, so I will call them 'relevant multisets'. (It is usual, however, just to talk of multisets.)

In a multiset, although the number of times an element is counted is important, the order is not. When Permutation is dropped, order becomes important; a premise structure is an ordered **list** or sequence of premises, and the comma can be seen as a 'list constructor'. In a list, both the order and number of occurrences is important. This description assumes the absence of Contraction as well as Permutation; in a logic without Permutation but with Contraction (which substructural logic is this?), X would represent a list with duplicates removed. As the Lambek Calculus also rejects Weakening, its premise structures can be described as 'relevant lists'; they exclude any elements which do not contribute to the conclusion.

Without Associativity constituent structure is important, so X can be thought of as a tree, and the comma as something which merges constituents (subtrees).

11.1.3 INTERPRETING SUBSTRUCTURAL LOGICS

Like modal logics, substructural logics were studied for some time without a clear idea of their semantics. Over the past few decades this has changed, and there are several approaches not just to individual logics but to substructural logics in general. This makes it easier to see them as a family, to compare them, and to 'tweak' them so as to get exactly what is needed for different applications. At least this is the case for propositional substructural logic. The semantics of quantified substructural logics has not reached the same degree of stability, and they will not figure here at all, though references are given for further reading.

The main part of this chapter will adopt a **relational semantics** (frame semantics) for substructural logics. Let's start by having another look at the notion of 'worlds'.

In classical logic and modal logic (Chapters 3 and 6), a world is a totality which decides, for all propositions, whether they are true or false. With Boolean negation this is a simple matter: some atomic formulae are listed as true according to a valuation, and the rest are therefore false. Modal logic uses the same set-up, but takes a plurality of worlds into consideration, and allows some connectives (the modal operators) to be evaluated 'intensionally' in different worlds. (The classical connectives, by contrast, are all evaluated 'extensionally' in the current world.)

Similar ideas were applied by Kripke to intuitionistic and intermediate logics (Chapter 10). Because these are not classical but partial logics, certain changes have to be made. The first is that the points of evaluation are not strictly speaking worlds, because they do not decide all formulae as true or false (they are not **total**). If a formula is not listed by the valuation as true at a point in the frame, it does not follow that its negation is true, as negation is evaluated by a more complicated rule. So points of evaluation in an intuitionistic frame are analogous to worlds, but partial. It is useful to think of them as situations, though as we may want to consider situations which are not actual, it may be better to talk of 'possible situations'. However, all possible situations have to at least be consistent; intuitionistic logic is not paraconsistent.

The frame semantics for intuitionistic logic includes a partial ordering $\sqsubseteq$ on the set of situations. This is in some ways analogous to the accessibility relation of modal logic. (The similarity is the basis of the McKinsey–Tarski translation.) In fact it does two jobs. First, it enforces **heredity**, so that propositions which are true in a situation s remain true in all situations above s in the partial ordering. The second job it does can be understood by looking at negation, which is evaluated by considering all possible situations above s in the $\sqsubseteq$ ordering. In effect, we are considering all situations *compatible* with the information in s. If there is no situation compatible with s where ϕ is true, then we conclude that $\neg \phi$ is true. We can call this a **compatibility relation** on situations. In intuitionistic logic this compatibility relation is the same as the $\sqsubseteq$ relation, which means that negation cannot be paraconsistent. If ϕ is true at s, then there is no way that $\neg\phi$ can be true at s.

For paraconsistent logics, we have to move from partial worlds (situations) to worlds that can include contradictory information. These are a long way from the worlds of classical modal logic: if we still want to think of them as worlds, they are not possible worlds so much as (potentially) **impossible worlds**. Some people prefer to avoid the term 'worlds' all together, reserving the term for total worlds. The formal definitions here will be non-committal and replace worlds with a set P of **points**. They can be understood as points of evaluation or information states. Whether they are possible worlds or possible situations, or neither, depends on the logic being interpreted – classical, partial or paraconsistent.

In relational semantics, the semantic conditions for intensional connectives refer to more than one world. The modal operators of Chapter 6 are prototypical examples. In substructural logcs, however, modal operators are not the only intensional connectives. Negation and implication are intensional in all the logics that reject Weakening. Conjunction and disjunction normally split, so that we have the normal extensional versions ∧ and ∨, and the intensional connectives fusion and fission. Of these intensional connectives, the modalities (including negation) are unary, and the remainder binary.

Unary intensional connectives involve two points or worlds – the current world where the whole formula (say $\Box \phi$) is evaluated, and a world where the formula ϕ in its **scope** is evaluated (or generally a range of such worlds). The same is true for negation (as described a few paragraphs ago); it is based on the evaluation of the negand ϕ in all compatible situations. So a one-place intensional connective needs a two-place accessibility relation.

What about two-place intensional connectives? The subformulae joined by the connective may themselves be evaluated at different points (worlds). So two points are needed to evaluate the two subformulae, plus a third point to evaluate the whole compound formula. So two-place connectives need a three-place accessibility relation.

In the case of implication, it is important that the antecedent and consequent can be evaluated at different points. If they are evaluated in the same world, as in modal or intuitionistic logics, the implication always ends up as a truth function. Separating the evaluation of the antecedent and consequent is the only way to model the non-truth-functional implication needed for most substructural logics.

The key to a relational semantics for substructural logics is therefore a **ternary accessibility relation** on the set of points P. This was worked out by Routley and Meyer (1972), and is often known as the Routley–Meyer semantics. Formal details will be given in the semantics section.

Some people find this semantics exotic, but we have seen something similar in Chapter 9, while discussing **constraints** (the analogue of implication in situation semantics). A constraint is supported by a relation between two situations, known as a **channel**. The antecedent holds in one of the two situations and the consequent in the other. But implications themselves do not in general hold everywhere, and we have to specify which channels support them. If the channel is regarded as a third situation, then we have, in essence, the same idea of a ternary relation over situations, as pointed out by Barwise (1993).

Besides the relational semantics there is also an algebraic approach to the semantics of substructural logics, which will be discussed briefly at the end of this chapter.

11.2 SYNTAX OF SUBSTRUCTURAL LOGICS

As with partial logics, the logics in this chapter do not involve new syntax as such, but the familiar connectives behave in such a variety of ways that it is often convenient to introduce new symbols for them.[8] This section will therefore be largely about symbols. The inductive rules for introducing them follow the same pattern seen in previous chapters, and rather than repeat the same rules for all the variants, I will just focus on the symbols.

Although the substructural logics form a family, many of them have also separate traditions of study. The resulting variation in terminology and notation can be confusing. You will get to know the main occupants of this exotic zoo a bit better in the rest of this chapter and the next one.

The first thing to note is variation in the names of the logics! From the point of view of relevance logic, the logics described in this chapter are all 'weak relevance logics' (relevance logic minus further structural rules). This is correct, in the sense that they all exclude the structural rule of Weakening which is responsible for irrelevance. At the other end of the scale, linguists working with the Lambek Calculus L are apt to describe all the other substructural logics as 'extensions of L' – that is, L with various structural rules added back in again. This is, again, a perfectly correct perspective. Afficionados of linear logic (LL), for their part, often take some form of linear logic as basic, and try to annex the other logics above and below as extensions or weakenings of it. In this book, the various substructural logics will be named according to the lattice presented on page 227, which also specifies their composition in terms of structural rules.

For each connective, I will identify one variant as being 'generic' for most substructural logics, and try to use it throughout the discussion in this chapter; for example, I will normally use → for implication, as it is possible to infer from the context whether it is relevant implication, linear implication or whatever.

Implication symbols are shown in Figure 11.2. The general symbols for implication and entailment are → and ⇒. Material implication is often written ⊃. Similarly, the strict implication of modal logic is written <. In relevance logic, → and ⇒ are reserved for relevant implication and its modal version **entailment**, which combines relevance and necessity. Linear implication is written as a lollipop symbol ⊸, while the split implications of the Lambek Calculus are usually written as forward and backward slashes, especially in categorial grammar.

In the absence of Weakening, conjunction and disjunction split into two pairs

1. → – implication in general / relevant implication
2. ⇒ – entailment in general / relevant implication combined with modality
3. ⊃ – material implication
4. < – strict (modal) implication
5. ⊸ – linear implication
6. →, ← – split implication for non-commutative logics
7. /, \ – the same, especially in categorial grammar

Figure 11.2   Implication symbols

1. ∧, ∨ – extensional conjunction and disjunction (lattice **glb** and **lub**)
2. × or ∘, + – fusion and fission (especially in relevance logic)
3. ⊗, ⊕ – the same; also multiplicative conjunction and additive disjunction in linear logic
4. &, ⅋ (or |) – additive conjunction and multiplicative disjunction in linear logic
5. · or ∘ – multiplicative conjunction or concatenation
6. (simple juxtaposition) – the same, especially in categorial grammar

Figure 11.3   Conjunction and disjunction symbols

1. ~ – negation in general / relevant (De Morgan) negation
2. ¬ – Boolean or intuitionistic negation
3. (.)⊥ – linear negation
4. ~, −, ¬ – split negations for non-commutative logics

Figure 11.4   Negation symbols

1. ⊤ – trivial truth (disjunction of all propositions, top element of a propositional lattice)
2. ⊥ – trivial falsity (conjunction of all propositions, bottom element of a propositional lattice)
3. **t** – logical truth (conjunction of all tautologies)
4. **f** – logical falsity (disjunction of all contradictions)
5. **1, 0** – truth constant symbols in linear logic (logical truth and trivial falsity – while ⊥ is used for logical falsity)

Figure 11.5   Truth constant symbols

(Figure 11.3): the familiar extensional connectives and a pair of intensional connectives which go with implication. The intensional versions are usually written in a way that suggests multiplication (for conjunction) and addition (for disjunction).

In the linear logic notation of Girard (1987), multiplication and addition symbols are used for intensional conjunction but for *extensional* disjunction, which may be confusing at first. In Girard's system, the intensional connectives are known as multiplicative and the extensional ones as additive.

The ¬ symbol (Figure 11.4) has been used up to now for classical and intuitionistic negation. A more general symbol for negation is ~, which will be used by default for the paraconsistent negation of most substructural logics. Some of the logics also have their own notation.

It is often useful to include constants for truth (Figure 11.5) and falsity in the logical language. These can be thought of as nullary (0-place) connectives. Two possible ways of defining them were introduced in Chapters 3 and 10: as the top and bottom elements of a Lindenbaum propositional lattice, and in terms of tautologies and contradictions. In standard logic the two definitions coincide, but now they too

1. □, ◊ – necessity and possibility
2. !, ? – exponentials (linear logic)
3. Δ – restricted permutation
4. ◊, □↓ – extraction operators
5. ↓, ⊙, ↑ – discontinuity operators

Figure 11.6   Modal operators

have to be split. The *logical* truth constants are sometimes called the Ackermann constants, and the lattice-based ones Church constants. (Note that the notation used in linear logic is once again unexpected given these definitions.)

Finally, modal operators can be added to substructural logics. In the stronger substructural logics, such as relevance logic, they have their familiar meaning (and notation). However, they also have another use in substructural logics, which is to regain access, under controlled conditions, to structural rules that have been dropped. This is particularly important in type logical grammar (based on the Lambek Calculus); they will be discussed in the next chapter, but the list in Figure 11.6 will give some idea of their uses.

11.3 SEMANTICS OF SUBSTRUCTURAL LOGICS

This section outlines the Routley–Meyer **relational semantics** for substructural logics.[9]

A frame $\langle P, R, 0 \rangle$ for a language $\mathcal{L}$ of a substructural logic comprises:

P a point set
R⊆**P**^{3} a *ternary* accessibility relation
0∈**P** a distinguished point where logical truths in $\mathcal{L}$ hold
($0 \Vdash \phi$ iff $\vdash_{\mathcal{L}} \phi$)

There are also a number of binary accessibility relations, but the ternary relation R is the 'master relation' in terms of which all the others can be defined. It is, first and foremost, the relation used to evaluate implication and fusion.

In the notation used here, the first co-ordinate is for the implicational formula, the second is for the antecedent and the third for the consequent. The first argument is therefore a **channel** between the second and third. There is something to be said for a more iconic notation which puts the channel in the middle. Barwise, for example, often represents the relation which I am writing R(x, y, z) as y $\underset{\rightarrow}{x}$ z. The notation used in this book follows Restall and the references cited.

The distinguished 'logic world' 0 was introduced in Chapter 10; it has a similar role here. Sometimes it is replaced by a set of worlds T (a **truth set**), but in many of the applications considered here, T = {0}.

Here are the three binary relations. They can be defined on the basis of R, by setting one of the three arguments to 0. Alternatively they can be added independently, in which case they ought to be added to the definition of a frame (above).

⊑ **(heredity relation)**: $x \sqsubseteq y$ iff $R(0, x, y)$.
S (positive accessibility relation): $S(x, y)$ iff $R(x, 0, y)$.
C (compatibility relation): $C(x, y)$ iff $R(x, y, 0)$.

It may be helpful here to remember that $\Box \phi$ is often equivalent to $\mathbf{t} \rightarrow \phi$, and $\sim \phi$ to $\phi \rightarrow \mathbf{f}$.

The ⊑ relation is a partial order representing increasing information, as in intuitionistic Kripke frames, and 0 is its root. However, crucially, there is no requirement that all points be connected to 0 by ⊑. The positive accessibility relation S is used for positive modal operators, and the compatibility relation C for negation.

The conditions relating ⊑ to R are:

1. If $R(x, y, z)$ and $x' \sqsubseteq x$, then $R(x', y, z)$.
2. If $R(x, y, z)$ and $y' \sqsubseteq y$, then $R(x, y', z)$.
3. If $R(x, y, z)$ and $z \sqsubseteq z'$, then $R(x, y, z')$.

Note that the direction of monotonicity varies for the different co-ordinates. The reason is that x will be used to evaluate implications, y to evaluate antecedents and z consequents. It was pointed out in connection with channel theory (Chapter 9) that implications are downward entailing (antitone) on their antecedents and upward entailing (isotone) on their consequents. Implications themselves are antitone. (If an implication p→q holds at x, then it still holds at any point x' where information is taken away, but might not hold at a point where information is added.)

If the points are total worlds, then there is no relation of information growth, and the ⊑ relation holds only between each world and itself ($x \sqsubseteq x$), and amounts to identity ($x = x$). This is called a **flat point set**.

A **model** for $\mathcal{L}$ is a frame $\langle P, R, 0 \rangle$ plus a valuation V which assigns a set V_x of propositional letters of $\mathcal{L}$ to each point x; $x \Vdash p$ iff $p \in V_x$. Here are the rules for non-atomic formulae:

(11.11) If ϕ and ψ are wffs of $\mathcal{L}$, then:
1. $z \Vdash \phi \times \psi$ iff, for some x and y such that $R(x, y, z)$, $x \Vdash \phi$ and $y \vdash \psi$.
2. $x \Vdash \phi \rightarrow \psi$ iff, for every y and z such that $R(x, y, z)$, if $y \Vdash \phi$ then $z \Vdash \psi$.
3. $x \Vdash \psi \leftarrow \phi$ iff, for every y and z such that $R(y, x, z)$, if $y \Vdash \phi$ then $z \Vdash \psi$.
4. $x \Vdash \phi \wedge \psi$ iff $x \Vdash \phi$ and $x \Vdash \psi$.
5. $x \Vdash \phi \vee \psi$ iff $x \Vdash \phi$ or $x \Vdash \psi$.
6. $x \Vdash \Box \phi$ iff, for every y such that $S(x, y)$, $y \Vdash \phi$
7. $x \Vdash \Diamond \phi$ iff, for some y such that $S(x, y)$, $y \Vdash \phi$
8. $x \Vdash \sim \phi$ iff, for every y such that $C(x, y)$, $y \nVdash \phi$
9. $x \Vdash - \phi$ iff, for every y such that $C(y, x)$, $y \nVdash \phi$

The first three clauses relate to the intensional binary connectives, fusion and its two residuals. The next two cover extensional connectives, the next two modal operators, and the last two negations. The second implication clause (3) and the second negation clause (9) are needed for logics without Permutation.

11.4 FRAME CONDITIONS

In a relational semantics for modal logic, conditions on frames such as reflexivity or transitivity capture the distinctive content of different modal systems. The relational semantics for substructural logics works in the same way. The different logics in the substructural family can be captured by frame conditions corresponding to structural rules. (This chapter uses structural rules rather than axioms, but there is a close relationship between the two; in fact structural rules can be replaced by axioms, an approach that will be seen in Chapter 13.) As before, conditions on a frame amount to conditions on its accessibility relations. Conditions on R determine the behaviour of fusion and implication; conditions on S determine the behaviour of the modal component if there is one; and conditions on C determine the behaviour of negation. Many of these conditions are quite perspicuous, once it is clear what is going on, and familiar notions such as reflexivity and symmetry reappear in various forms.

It will be helpful to think of $R(x, y, z)$ in two ways, adopting whichever is most intuitive. One is x as a channel between y and z. The other is to think of z as a combination of x and y. The perspectives are justified by the rules for implication and fusion respectively. Note that the second approach involves, in principle, treating R as a binary function from x and y to z. This is not always strictly accurate, but often makes understanding easier.[10]

Let's start with the conditions on R for the structural rules. I will start with modified ('weak') versions of Permutation and Contraction, as they are transparently ternary versions of symmetry and reflexivity.

Weak Permutation: If $R(x, y, z)$ then $R(y, x, z)$.
Weak Contraction: $R(x, x, x)$ for all x.
Weakening: $R(0, 0, x)$ or $0 \sqsubseteq x$.

Weak Permutation does what one would expect; it swaps the first and second arguments of R. Thinking in terms of implication, it swaps the major and minor premises, so that we can do *modus ponens* with premises in any order.

The condition for Weak Contraction means, first, that the antecedents and consequents of an implication can always be interpreted in the current world (worlds are 'closed under *modus ponens*'). One result is that premises do not go away after they have been used, so that they can be used again.

The condition for Weakening implies that all points in P are related to 0 by the partial ordering $\sqsubseteq$. (The condition is often given, equivalently, as $0 \sqsubseteq x$ for all x.) For implication, it means that any information in the world where the antecedent is evaluated is carried over into the world where the consequent is evaluated. (Recall that 0 contains all logical truths, which include $\phi \rightarrow \phi$.) The result is that implication is truth-functional.

The conditions for Associativity, along with (full) Permutation and Contraction, make use of an auxiliary definition (11.12). They can be understood by thinking of the points related by R in terms of premise structures, and the various rules as being parallel to the operations on those structures that we have already seen: replication, permutation and rebracketing. The operations just look more complicated when expressed as ternary relations.

(11.12) 1. R^2(a, b, c, d) iff for some x, R(a, b, x) and R(x, c, d).
      2. R^2(a, (b, c), d) iff for some x, R(b, c, x) and R(a, x, d)

Here are the rules in full. Many people do not find them intuitive at first, in which case the best policy may be to move on and refer back to them as needed. I have included, for convenience, one or two structural rules which have not yet been discussed.[11]

Contraction (W): R(x, y, z) → R_2(x, y, y, z)
Permutation (C): R_2(x, z, y, w) → R_2(x, y, z, w)
Associativity (B): R_2(x, y, z, w) → R_2(x, (y, z), w)
Twisted Associativity (B′): R_2(y, x, z, w) → R_2(x, (y, z), w)
Mingle (M): R(x, x, y) → x ⊑ y

Positive modalities □ and ◊ are interpreted using the binary positive accessibility relation S, just as in Chapter 6. The usual modal system used with relevance logic is S4, so that S is reflexive and transitive. The modalities used with weaker substructural logics will be discussed separately.

That leaves negation. This is interpreted using the binary compatibility relation C, which is related to ⊑ in the following way:

(11.13) If C(x, y), x′ ⊑ x and y′ ⊑ y, then C(x′,y′).

That is, if two situations are compatible, and one or both of them have information taken away, there will be nothing there to make them incompatible (whereas information that is added might make them incompatible).

C is usually assumed to be symmetric: if x is compatible with y, then y is compatible with x. This seems reasonable. However, it is not true for logics without Permutation. Such logics, as already noted, have split negation as well as split implication. In the semantic definitions of the previous section, C was not assumed to be symmetric, and the two halves of the split negation are evaluated using C in different directions. We will look at some ways of making intuitive sense of split negation later in this chapter.

Assuming that C is symmetric, negation is simple rather than split, and the evaluation condition boils down to:

(11.14) x ⊩ ~ϕ iff, for all y, if C(x, y) then y ⊮ ϕ.

This is reminiscent of the condition for intuitionistic negation. Unlike intuitionistic logic, however, there is nothing here that says that a point cannot force both ϕ and ~ϕ, so negation may be paraconsistent. To prevent a point from supporting contradictions would require a particular condition on the compatibility relation.

- What condition on C would prevent a point from supporting ~ϕ if it supports ϕ?

It is also plausible to require that each point has at least one point with which it is compatible (compare seriality in modal logic). In the exercises, you are asked to show why this condition is needed.

The normal negation for relevance logic (and linear logic) is De Morgan negation, which obeys the De Morgan laws and double negation elimination.

For the De Morgan laws, there needs to be a maximal world compatible with x. This is notated x^* – the 'Routley star'[12] – and is defined by the condition that for all y, if $C(x, y)$ then $y \sqsubseteq x^*$. In other words, the set of points compatible with x is **convergent**. As Restall (1995) puts it, x^* is a state which 'collects together everything consistent with x'. It is also required that if $x \sqsubseteq y$, then $y^* \sqsubseteq x^*$.

To see this in action, let's look at the rule $\sim (\phi \wedge \psi) \vdash \sim \phi \vee \sim \psi$, which is one of the De Morgan laws.[13] If $\sim(\phi \wedge \psi)$ holds in the current world x, then there are no worlds compatible with x that support both ϕ and ψ. Therefore every world compatible with x supports only ϕ, only ψ, or neither. From this alone, however, we cannot conclude either $\sim\phi$ or $\sim\psi$, as there might be a compatible world y which supports ϕ and another compatible world z which supports ψ. However, with the Routley star operation, there is a world x^* which is an extension of both y and z, which would support both ϕ and ψ. However, this contradicts the premise we started out with. Therefore if we have $\sim (\phi \wedge \psi)$ then either ϕ or ψ must be absent from all compatible worlds, so $\sim\phi \vee \sim\psi$.

For double negation elimination we need the further condition that $x^{**}= x$ (the maximal point compatible with x^* is x itself). Then if $x \Vdash \sim \sim \phi$, $x^* \nVdash \sim\phi$, which can only happen if $x^{**} \Vdash \phi$, that is, $x \Vdash \phi$.

As with modal and intuitionistic frames, quite simple conditions can be imposed on C to get us back to standard logic.

If C is required to be reflexive, then each world is compatible with itself and therefore negation is no longer paraconsistent. (This is the case with intuitionistic logic, where x cannot force $\neg \phi$ if it forces ϕ.)

Finally, if $x^* = x$ (the maximal point consistent with x is x itself), then x is a total world, and negation is Boolean negation. It also follows that $x \sqsubseteq y$ only if $y = x$, in other words x is itself a maximal point or endpoint in the heredity ordering. It was shown in Chapter 10 that maximal points in an intuitionistic Kripke frame behave like classical worlds.

EXERCISE 11.4.0.1

1. Construct a model in which $x \Vdash \phi \rightarrow \psi$ and $x \Vdash \phi$ but $x \nVdash \psi$. Think of x as the belief state of an agent. What would this mean about the beliefs that can be attributed to the agent? Show that such a countermodel cannot be constructed if the frame condition for Contraction is satisfied.

2. Show from the definitions in the semantics section that in the absence of Permutation, the compatibility relation C is not symmetric. (Use the definition given for weak Permutation.)

3. What would the behaviour of negation be like if C were not required to be serial? (Hint: think of the modal system **Ver** in Chapter 6.)

11.5 CHARACTERISATION OF PROOF TERMS

Chapter 10 showed how formulas can be labelled with expressions from the λ-calculus recording their proofs by natural deduction. For intuitionistic logic, this relationship is a 1:1 correspondence or isomorphism – the Curry Howard Isomorphism or CHI.

What about substructural logics? The correspondence was defined for each of the *connective* rules of natural deduction. The structural rules were left implicit. However, it is possible to keep track of the use of structural rules in a proof; in fact it is possible to tell, just by looking at a λ expression, what structural rules have been used to prove a formula. This is helpful to an intuitive understanding of the different substructural logics.

Before continuing, I will streamline the notation for λ expressions with some conventions which will make them easier to read, and which will be used in the rest of this book. First, function application will be notated by simple juxtaposition without brackets: fx instead of f(x). This is assumed to be left-associative, so that fxy means that fx is evaluated first and then the result is applied to y. Brackets are used only when the opposite result is intended, so f(gx) means that gx is evaluated and f is applied to the result (as in function composition).

For abstraction, lambda operators are assumed to be right-associative, so that $\lambda x.\lambda y.\alpha$ means $\lambda x(\lambda y.\alpha)$ – which is the only sensible way of reading it anyway. As a further abbreviation, repeated lambdas can be missed out, so the same expression will be written $\lambda xy.\alpha$.

So, back to structural rules. As often, Permutation is an intuitive place to start. Permutation allows us to use premises regardless of the order in which they are given, or, if they are assumptions, the order in which they have been assumed and discharged. Here is a labelled proof of the formula $(\phi \rightarrow (\psi \rightarrow \chi)) \rightarrow (\psi \rightarrow (\phi \rightarrow \chi))$. You might already suspect from the shape of this formula, with ϕ and ψ swapping places, that Permutation is going to be involved, and this is a healthy kind of suspicion to develop. The proof proceeds by conditional proof according to the recipe seen many times in Chapter 10. (The justifications on the right are not necessary given the labelling, but are included for extra clarity.)

(11.15) 1. $x : \phi \rightarrow (\psi \rightarrow \chi)$ Ass
        2. $y : \psi$ Ass
        3. $z : \phi$ Ass
        4. $xz : \psi \rightarrow \chi$ MPP 1,2
        5. $xzy : \chi$ MPP 4,3
        6. $\lambda z.xzy : \phi \rightarrow \chi$ CP, discharging 3
        7. $\lambda yz.xzy : \psi \rightarrow (\phi \rightarrow \chi)$ CP, discharging 2
        8. $\lambda xyz.xzy : (\phi \rightarrow (\psi \rightarrow \chi)) \rightarrow (\psi \rightarrow (\phi \rightarrow \chi))$ CP, discharging 1

In the subproof of χ, the assumptions ϕ and ψ are used in the 'wrong' order (not the order in which they are assumed). Inspecting the proof term, this shows up as a mismatch between the order in which the variables y and z are λ-bound and the order in which they are used in the body of the term. This order mismatch is the fingerprint that gives away the use of Permutation in the proof. We can further conclude that the formula proved in this example is a theorem of any logic which includes Permutation, but not, for example, of the Lambek Calculus.

Contraction is also easy to spot. The point of Contraction is that a premise which is given (or assumed) once can be used more than once. So the corresponding proof term will have a variable appearing more than once in the body of the term, recording the times it has been used. A typical example is $\lambda xy.xyy$. If you do a labelled natural deduction proof of the formula $(\phi \to (\phi \to \psi)) \to (\phi \to \psi)$, you should get this as the proof term. This is an easy but useful exercise.

The trademark of Weakening is **vacuous abstraction**. We have already seen how the proof of $\phi \to (\psi \to \phi)$ involves introducing ψ and then discharging it without actually using it. The proof term therefore has a lambda-bound variable which, as it is never used, does not appear in the body of the term: $\lambda xy.x$. All logics which exclude Weakening exclude vacuous abstraction: any lambda-bound variable must also appear in the body of the term.

Finally there is Associativity, which can be seen in the proof of $(\phi \to \psi) \to ((\chi \to \phi) \to (\chi \to \psi))$. If you inspect this formula before proving it, it illustrates the transitivity of implication. If $\phi \to \psi$, then anything that implies ϕ also implies ψ.

(11.16) 1. $x : \phi \to \psi$ Ass
      2. $y : \chi \to \phi$ Ass
      3. $z : \chi$ Ass
      4. $yz : \phi$ MPP lines 2, 3
      5. $x(yz) : \psi$ MPP lines 1, 4
      6. $\lambda z.x(yz) : \chi \to \psi$ CP discharging 3
      7. $\lambda yz.x(yz) : (\chi \to \phi) \to (\chi \to \psi)$ CP discharging 2
      8. $\lambda xyz.x(yz) : (\phi \to \psi) \to ((\chi \to \phi) \to (\chi \to \psi))$ CP discharging 1

Associativity here arises because the result of applying y to z has to be fed in as an argument to the function x. Using the notational convention introduced in this section, it is easy to spot Associativity: it is present whenever there is explicit bracketing in the body of the term.

The proof here shows the connection between rebracketing of premises, function composition (in the proof term on the left) and transitivity of implication (in the formulas on the right). These are important principles but not universal: a weak substructural logic without Associativity does not have them, and in such a logic the formula proved here is not a theorem.

To sum up this section, the use of structural rules can be seen in the shape of the proof terms when proofs are labelled. The various substructural logics will admit proofs of certain shapes, and will include as theorems exactly those formulae whose proofs give rise to terms of the right shapes. This can be proved by induction (essentially a formalisation of the arguments given informally in this section).

(11.17) **Weakening**: There are lambda-bound variables which do not appear in the body of the lambda expression.

Contraction: There are lambda-bound variables which appear more than once in the body of the lambda expression.

Permutation: Variables appear in the body of the lambda expression in a different order from that in which they are bound.

Associativity: Application in the body of the lambda expression is not uniformly left-associative. Using the notation introduced in this section, this is signalled by any explicit bracketing.

As the formulas proved in this section are all theorems (proved from no premises and with no undischarged assumptions), the proof terms also exhibit another important property, repeated from Chapter 5 (p. 85). They include nothing except lambda-bound variables (corresponding to discharged assumptions).

(11.18) 1. A λ expression with no constants is said to be **pure**.
        2. A λ expression with no unbound variables is said to be **closed**.
        3. A pure, closed λ expression is a **combinatorial term**.

Combinatorial lambda terms include no content apart from the way they rearrange their arguments, which is exactly what structural rules do to premises. It is quite common to see them referred to simply as **combinators**, which will be the topic of Chapter 13. Since the correspondence between combinators and combinatorial terms is exact, this terminology possibly does no real harm, but it will be avoided here.

Each of the substructural logics from this chapter can be characterised by the shape of the proof terms corresponding to the theorems of that logic.

(11.19) The term characterisation theorem (Restall (2000), p. 135).
        If $\Gamma \vdash$ M:A (M a λ term, A a formula), then:

Relevance logic: Each lambda binds at least one variable, and every variable in Γ is free in M.[14]

BCK: Each lambda binds at most one variable, and every variable in Γ is free at most once in M.

Linear logic: Each lambda binds exactly one variable, and every variable in Γ is free exactly once in M.

In the case where A is a theorem, this gives a characterisation of relevant, BCK (affine) and linear combinatorial terms. More generally, it gives a characterisation of relevant, affine and linear functions.

Similar results can be shown for logics without Permutation, but in this case we need to distinguish between left and right application and left and right abstraction, a distinction which is not available in our usual notation. Adding these operations gives the **directional lambda calculus**, which will be important in the next chapter.

(11.20) **Right application**: If M is a term of type $\sigma \rightarrow \tau$ and N is a term of type σ, then
        M $\rangle$ N is a term of type τ.

Right abstraction: If N is a term of type τ and x is a variable of type σ, then $\lambda \rangle$ x.M is a term of type $\sigma \rightarrow \tau$.

Left application: If M is a term of type $\tau \leftarrow \sigma$ and N is a term of type σ, then M $\langle$ N is a term of type τ.

Left abstraction: If N is a term of type τ and x is a variable of type σ, then $\lambda \langle$ x.M is a term of type $\tau \leftarrow \sigma$.

Although these results are helpful for an intuitive understanding of the substructural logics, note that they hold only for implicational logic (the terms for which include application and abstraction but not, for example, product types). The business of term characterisation becomes more complicated when other connectives besides implication are involved.

Finally, it will be very useful to remember the formulae used in this section to derive the characteristic proof terms for different structural rules. By the Curry Howard Isomorphism, these formulas can be thought of as the **types** of combinatorial terms. The ones used for the structural rules in this chapter are listed here for reference, using their traditional abbreviations (I is for identity). More of these will be introduced in Chapter 13.

(11.21) **I:** $\lambda x.x : \phi \rightarrow \phi$

$\quad\quad$ **K:** $\lambda xy.x : \phi \rightarrow (\psi \rightarrow \phi)$

$\quad\quad$ **W:** $\lambda xy.xyy : (\phi \rightarrow (\phi \rightarrow \psi)) \rightarrow (\phi \rightarrow \psi)$

$\quad\quad$ **C:** $\lambda xyz.xzy : (\phi \rightarrow (\psi \rightarrow \chi)) \rightarrow (\psi \rightarrow (\phi \rightarrow \chi))$

$\quad\quad$ **B:** $\lambda xyz.x(yz) : (\phi \rightarrow \psi) \rightarrow ((\chi \rightarrow \phi) \rightarrow (\chi \rightarrow \psi))$

11.6 CONNECTIVES IN SUBSTRUCTURAL LOGICS

A variety of connective symbols were introduced in section 11.2. This section explores a bit further the behaviour of these creatures in various logical habitats, primarily relevance logic and linear logic. The Lambek Calculus has the following chapter to itself, so only a few basic points will be drawn out here.

11.6.1 RELEVANCE LOGIC (R)

The main motivation of relevance logic was to dispense with truth-functional implication and its counter-intuitive consequences. Specifically, it is based on the principle that ϕ only implies ψ if it shares some content with ψ. In propositional logic, this can be made precise by saying that ϕ and ψ must share propositional atoms, with certain constraints on their distribution: this will be referred to as the **relevance property**. Note, however, that relevant implication does not involve the idea of necessity. If Maria leaving Kostas implies that Kostas is upset, the antecedent is certainly relevant to the consequent; but this is a contingent fact, not a necessary truth. There are possible worlds in which Kostas might actually be quite relieved. The combination of relevance and necessity is what is known in the relevance logic literature as entailment, and denoted $\Rightarrow$.

Relevance logic was first extensively explored and advocated by Anderson and Belnap (1975), though they acknowledge a number of predecessors.[15] They investigated more than one system, but the idea is shown in its simplest form in their system **R**, shown in the lattice in Figure 11.1, which is just standard logic without Weakening.[16] The **relevant implication** connective in **R** includes relevance but not necessity.

There are a number of reasons why relevance logic might be of interest to linguists. In the first place, it continues the theme of trying to model intensionality, which is one of the fundamental problems of any linguistic theory that tries to use logic for semantics. There are many other approaches, including modal logic, but no single approach seems to have won universal approval.[17] In the second place, its focus on implication makes it a candidate for semantic interpretations of conditional constructions, and it has been used for counterfactual conditionals. Perhaps most important, the weaker logics used in reasoning about syntax are all relevance-sensitive logics in the sense defined in section 11.1. There is something to be said for understanding the properties of relevance-sensitive connectives first in a logic where they are close enough to their classical equivalents for their intended meaning to be intuitive.

Besides relevant implication, relevance logic has intensional versions of conjunction and disjunction, **fusion** and **fission**. These are also characteristic of the weaker relevance-sensitive logics. Fusion has the following properties of conjunction if the appropriate structural rules are included. Note in particular that projection requires Weakening (in which case fusion behaves like conjunction), and therefore does not apply in **R**.

(11.22) Associativity: $(p \times q) \times r \vdash p \times (q \times r)$
(11.23) Commutativity: $p \times q \vdash q \times p$
(11.24) Idempotence: $p \vdash p \times p$
(11.25) Projection: $p \times q \vdash p, p \times q \vdash q$

The familiar extensional conjunction and disjunction are often included as well as fusion, but this has to be done carefully or there is a danger of compromising the 'relevant' character of the logic. The following problem will serve as a useful illustration of several points. The standard rule for conjunction introduction in Chapter 10 – $\phi, \psi \vdash \phi \wedge \psi$, also known as the rule of **adjunction** – looks unobjectionable, but in relevance logic it leads to problems. It follows that $\phi \rightarrow (\psi \rightarrow (\phi \wedge \psi))$; but then $\phi \wedge \psi \vdash \phi$ (by conjunction elimination), and then, by the transitivity of implication, $\phi \rightarrow (\psi \rightarrow \phi)$. In other words, we have the trademark formula of Weakening reintroduced by the back door, without doing anything obviously wrong.

This particular problem can be resolved by keeping track of where the original ϕ and ψ come from. The correct rule makes sure that they are derived from the same premises: if $X \vdash \phi$ and $X \vdash \psi$, then $X \vdash \phi \wedge \psi$. What we get as a result is not $\phi \rightarrow (\psi \rightarrow \phi)$, but only $((\chi \rightarrow \phi) \wedge (\chi \rightarrow \psi)) \rightarrow (\chi \rightarrow (\phi \wedge \psi))$. Fusion, by contrast, is introduced by different sets of premises: if $X \vdash \phi$ and $Y \vdash \psi$, then $X, Y \vdash \phi \times \psi$. Since fusion, unlike conjunction, does not allow you to discard one of its subformulas by projection, this does not lead to the reintroduction of Weakening.

This discussion illustrates another important principle. Suppose we define relevance logic with relevant implication alone (the 'implicational fragment' of relevance logic, or **R→**). Obviously, this does not include $\phi \rightarrow (\psi \rightarrow \phi)$ as a theorem. However, by adding a new connective ∧ to the logic – and doing so without due care – we can end up with an unsatisfactory situation: a purely implicational formula, which is not included in the implicational fragment, can be reached by a detour involving ∧. If that was the case, then ∧ would not be a **conservative extension** of the implicational fragment of R; it distorts it in extending it. One concern in adding connectives to a core logic with certain properties, is whether the extensions change the character of the original logic.

This is an important concern when it comes to selecting modalities for R. Different modal systems and different types of negation (negative modality) have been studied independently, and it is a question of which fits best with a given substructural logic. A natural requirement is for the connective to be a conservative extension. For reasons to be discussed shortly, the modal system usually added to relevance logic is S4. The negation is De Morgan negation, as already discussed.

The **fission** connective stands for intensional or relevant disjunction. Let's look again at the example used above for relevant implication: Maria leaving implies that Kostas will be upset. We can say that the two states of affairs, Maria staying and Kostas being upset, are **relevant alternatives**: Maria's presence and Kostas' state of mind have a bearing on each other (or, if not, there was no justification for calling it a relevant implication). So we can re-express the relevant implication $\phi \rightarrow \psi$ as $\sim \phi + \psi$. This means that implication and disjunction are interdefinable, provided that disjunction means *relevant* disjunction.

That extensional disjunction (∨) does not have this relevant quality can be seen from the rule of ∨ introduction. If ϕ is true then $\phi \lor \psi$ is true for any ψ whatsoever: if Maria stays, then it follows that either Maria stays or there is life on the moons of Jupiter. Such an introduction rule is only plausible if there is no connection required between the two.

This has a bearing on the question of ECQ and disjunctive syllogism. As pointed out in Chapter 10, rejection of the first (as in relevance logic) is normally taken to involve rejection of the second, which is often seen as a problem. The proof of this on page 202, however, involves ∨, the extensional version of disjunction. We know this because it crucially involves ∨ introduction. So the rejection of disjunctive syllogism really applies to *extensional* disjunction. What about relevant disjunction? Because this is interdefinable with relevant implication, $\sim \phi + \psi$ amounts to $\phi \rightarrow \psi$, and so ψ does follow from $\phi + \psi$ together with $\sim \phi$, if ϕ and ψ were relevant alternatives.[18]

R is the classic 'relevance logic', but not the only one. The space just above and below it in Figure 11.1 has been investigated as well. It is worth saying just a few things about one logic that is slightly weaker and one that is slightly stronger.

The logic of entailment E

The holy grail in early relevance logic was a logic which captured necessity and relevance at the same time – a complete logic of entailment. The idea of a necessary proposition involves one that is entailed by 'truth', let's say $t \rightarrow \phi$. But to be a *relevant* entailment, **t** must share content with ϕ. The obvious candidate for a logical truth that fulfils this condition is $\phi \rightarrow \phi$. So $\Box \phi$ was recast in relevance logic as $(\phi \rightarrow \phi) \rightarrow \phi$.

From this definition the modal axioms **T** and **4** can be proved, giving a version of S4.[19] However, there is a snag. One theorem of relevance logic is $\phi \rightarrow ((\phi \rightarrow \psi) \rightarrow \psi)$ (known as Assertion). Proving it by natural deduction will show that it is indeed a relevant combinatorial term (there is no vacuous abstraction), and also that its proof involves Permutation. Nothing wrong with that, as **R** contains Permutation. However, substituting ϕ for ψ gives $\phi \rightarrow ((\phi \rightarrow \phi) \rightarrow \phi)$. In other words, $\phi \rightarrow \Box \phi$. In modal logic, this principle characterises the system **Triv**, in which all modality collapses (all propositions that are true are necessary).

To avoid this problem, the logic of relevant entailment was formalised with a restriction on Permutation so that it can only apply when the antecedent is itself in the form of an implication. This has the desired effect of stopping an ordinary contingent proposition from entailing a necessity. The logic obtained by restricting Permutation in this way is called **E**, for entailment. In Figure 11.1, it is between **R** and **T** (which does not allow Permutation at all). In **E**, the implication connective $\rightarrow$ behaves as entailment, combining both relevance and necessity.

However, the modal part of this elegant system turned out not to be exactly equivalent to S4. This has resulted in a shift of attention to another approach: using a standard modal operator $\Box$ independently of the relevant implication connective. We then need a separate modal accessibility relation S, which is required to be reflexive and transitive. This is analogous to the usual treatment of negation in relevance logic; it is constrained to behave as De Morgan negation by putting the appropriate requirements on the compatibiity relation C. Relevance logic with these arrangements for modality is known as **R4**. Since the relevant implication connective does not have to do the work of an entailment connective (entailment is done by combining it with the necessity operator), there is no need for the restriction on Permutation.

Relevance with Mingle

The licence to add any extra premises whatsoever would be Weakening, which leads immediately to the destruction of relevance. However, what if you just allow the duplication of premises you already have? This is, in a sense, the reverse of Contraction, and for this reason is sometimes known as Expansion. The usual name for it, however, is Mingle. The structural rule is given here together with two equivalent characteristic formulae which can be proved from it.

(11.26) 1. X can be rewritten as X, X
      2. $\phi \vdash \phi \rightarrow \phi$
      3. $(\phi \times \phi) \rightarrow \phi$

Relevance logic with Mingle added is called **RM**. Like the intermediate logics of Chapter 10, much of the interest lies in how far you can go without the system collapsing into standard logic. For example in RM with negation, we can get pre-linearity, $(\phi \rightarrow \psi) \vee (\psi \rightarrow \phi)$, a theorem of classical logic and **LC** (Chapter 10), but not intuitionistic logic. It does not, at first sight, sit well with relevance logic, as the idea that of any two propositions one must imply the other is often regarded as a fallacy of relevance. However, RM still does not collapse into classical logic because it does not include Weakening or ECQ.

An application of RM will be discussed at the end of the chapter.

11.6.2 LINEAR LOGIC

If we take relevance logic and drop **W**, the result is linear logic, a system which currently enjoys great popularity both in computer science and in linguistics. The main reason is that if premises can only be used once, we have greater control over derivations. This is important whether we are reasoning about computation or about grammar. Linear logic became popular through the work of Girard (1987), to which the connective symbols currently used go back. Meredith and Prior (1963), developing Curry's work on combinators, had already explored it under the name BCI (together with BCK, which they also named). It was also investigated by several people researching extensions to the Lambek Calculus, for example Grishin (1983) and Van Benthem (1986), who called it LP (Lambek Calculus with Permutation).

The important point in linear logic is its resource sensitive nature: premises are resources. By the 'omelette principle' (section 11.1), premises are 'used up' when they are used, and are no longer available. So we can read a linear implication $p \rightarrow q$ as a process which consumes p to produce q. More exactly, it consumes one instance of p to produce one instance of q (we may have other copies of p lying around).

This 'resource' interpretation of linear logic can be applied to other connectives as well. Negation, for example, amounts to the destruction of a resource (it fuses with the resource to produce nothing, like matter and anti-matter).

With conjunction and disjunction things become slightly complicated. Remember that we now have two versions of 'conjunction', one of which we are calling 'fusion'. The behaviour of fusion in each logic mirrors the structural rules that are allowed, so in linear logic fusion will have properties (11.22) and (11.23), but not (11.24) or (11.25). What this amounts to is that resources are available in any order; however, they do not multiply (as in (11.24)) or disappear (as in (11.25)). Fusion in linear logic is usually called **tensor** and written as $\otimes$. (Note the connection with multiplication.)

The connectives in linear logic are not immediately intuitive, so let's pause to take a look round. There is a tradition in linear logic tutorials of presenting them in terms of the menu in a restaurant. Recall that implication involves using up the premises to get the conclusion. Let's say that the premises are five dollars, and the conclusion is a meal; if you pay your dollars you get your meal (but no longer have your dollars). Fusion is like the 'and' in 'meat and vegetables' – they come together, and you can eat them in any order. You can even save one till later if you want to. But your portion of meat will not suddenly become two portions of meat. Equally (unlike in most restaurants, but perhaps at some family lunches) you cannot decide to leave one of them.

Implication and fusion (tensor) are the only connectives normally used in linguistic applications. Confining linear logic to these connectives gives us what is known as the 'tensor fragment'. A linguistic application of this fragment will be considered later in the chapter.

The remaining connectives have slightly different behaviours. I will summarise them here partly because they are fun, and partly because they are a good illustration of the 'resource' perspective of linear logic. Both conjunction and disjunction split into intensional and extensional versions, which are known in linear logic as 'multiplicative' and 'additive'. Multiplicative conjunction is tensor (fusion), which we have seen. The additive conjunction ∧ (read as 'with') gives you a choice, as in a choice between 'fruit and cheese'. Intuitively, this sounds more like disjunction; however, the point is that both are available. However, when you have chosen one, you no longer have the possibility of the other. The rationale is that whatever resources produced the one you chose are used up in producing it; although they *could have* equally well produced the other alternative, they can't now. When you dig your potatoes, it is no use wishing you had used the plot for beans instead.

There are also two disjunctions. Additive disjunction ∨ presents two alternatives, but this time there is no choice; you are given one or the other. The restaurant example might be soup of the day, where lobster and leftover cabbage are both on the menu but the restaurant decides which to serve.

The other binary connective is multiplicative disjunction, written ⅋ (or more simply |) and read as **par**. This is the equivalent of relevance logic's fission connective – the sense of disjunction in which a relevant implication $\phi \longrightarrow \psi$ can be defined as $\sim\!\phi + \psi$. However, here it is linear implication and linear negation, so the sense of $\phi \,⅋\, \psi$ is more like 'give something which destroys a ϕ to get a ψ'. For example when Dick Whittington was offered money for his cat to clear a ship of mice, the captain could have made his proposal in linear logic as 'mouse ⅋ money'. (Unfortunately in linear logic the cat also would never be seen again.)

This last option is not available in the best restaurants, but the other connectives will be summarised in the little menu (11.9). First, however, a note on the standard linear logic notation and nomenclature for these connectives, which is derived from Girard. The symbols ⊗ and ⊕ are used for multiplicative conjunction and *additive* disjunction. The ampersand symbol is used for additive conjunction ('with') and (inverted) for multiplicative disjunction ('par'). These notations are used in the menu, as they are part of the 'feel' of linear logic, and much of the literature will not be accessible without them. Elsewhere in the text, however, I will continue to use the symbols from the general substructural literature (e.g. Restall). Table 11.2 provides a translation of the symbols.

Table 11.2:   Linear connective symbols

General name	General notation	Girard name	Girard notation
Fusion	×	Tensor	⊗
Conjunction	∧	With	&
Fission	+	Par	⅋ or |
Disjunction	∨	Plus	⊕

Source: Girard (1987).

Table 11.3:   A linear logic menu

𝕾𝕰𝕿 𝔐𝕰𝔑𝔲	
Only $5	$\$ \otimes \$ \otimes \$ \otimes \$ \otimes \$$
	$\multimap$
Soup of the day	
(Onion or tomato)	$((\text{onion-soup} \oplus \text{tomato-soup})$
	$\otimes$
Fish with chips or salad	$((\text{fish} \otimes (\text{chips \& salad})$
or	&
Chicken madras with rice	$(\text{curry} \otimes \text{rice}))$
	$\otimes$
Unlimited coffee	$!\text{coffee})$

Linear logic with these multiplicative and additive connectives forms a system known as MALL. Full linear logic (since Girard) comes equipped with two 'modal' operators, written ! and ? and called **exponentials**. These allow you to multiply or delete resources at will. The first was used in Table 11.3 for the complimentary coffee, but another popular example is money. Let's say that the formula $ means a dollar in an ordinary bank account; once you have used it, it is no longer there. On the other hand !$ could be used for a licence to print as many dollars as you like, like a central bank. More precisely it allows you 'as many as you need' for a particular deduction, so a better analogy might be an expense account, or a construction grant, where you have to show that the resources have been used. ?$, by contrast, would represent dollars disappearing into some financial black hole.

Since the point of linear logic is that these operations are not generally allowed, you might wonder what is going on here. In fact these modal operators represent the reintroduction of Contraction and Weakening, in specified contexts. The argument goes that it is occasionally necessary to take these 'liberties', and that by using special 'permissions' for them, at least we are tracking and to some degree controlling their use in a derivation.

The idea behind calling these devices modalities[20] is that although we may not want to allow structural rules for ordinary formulae, they may still be applicable to modalised formulae. Although an ordinary premise may be consumed in use, a modalised premise might behave more like a 'necessary truth' and stick around to be used again. In fact the rules governing ! in linear logic follow the principles for $\square$ in S4 modal logic.

(11.27)	$!A \vdash A$	**T**	$\square \phi \to \phi$
	$!A \vdash !!A$	**4**	$\square \phi \to \square \square \phi$
	$!(A \to B), !A \vdash !B$	**K**	$\square (\phi \to \psi) \to (\square \phi \to \square \psi)$

This idea is used a lot in the weaker substructural logics; modal operators are used rather like diacritics which discriminate between contexts where structural rules are allowed and where they are not.

Table 11.4:   Linear negation as duality

General notation		Girard notation	
Positive	Negative	Positive	Negative
ϕ	$\sim\phi$	ϕ	$\phi^\perp$
$\phi \times \psi$	$\sim\phi + \sim\psi$	$\phi \otimes \psi$	$\phi^\perp \mid \psi^\perp$
$\phi \wedge \psi$	$\sim\phi \vee \sim\psi$	$\phi \mathbin{\&} \psi$	$\phi^\perp \oplus \psi^\perp$
$\phi + \psi$	$\sim\phi \times \sim\psi$	$\phi \mid \psi$	$\phi^\perp \otimes \psi^\perp$
$\phi \vee \psi$	$\sim\phi \wedge \sim\psi$	$\phi \oplus \psi$	$\phi^\perp \mathbin{\&} \psi^\perp$

The linear negation operator is usually written $\phi^\perp$, which looks like a notational variant of the intuitionistic $\phi \to \perp$. However, as $\perp$ in linear logic means a kind of shredder for destroying resources, linear negation is better thought of as a recipe for destroying the resource ϕ. Double negation ensures that ϕ is also a destroyer of $\phi^\perp$.

In another way, linear negation is not like more standard negations at all, but more like a polarity marker. It occurs only with atomic propositions (or also with their negation, flipping the polarity back to positive). Double negation elimination is thus included in the logic, and so are the De Morgan laws, which operate, however, in an exotic form. Since negation does not occur on the outside of a composite formula, certain formula are simply listed as being duals. These dualities (Table 11.4) correspond to the De Morgan laws in classical logic. A compound formula (any conjunction or disjunction) is negated by being transformed into its dual in the negative column, which will automatically drive the negation inward onto the two juncts.

The Girard translation
Girard (1987) includes a translation from intuitionistic logic to linear logic with exponentiation, showing how the entire content of the former can be expressed in the latter. Intuitionistic implications, conjunctions and disjunctions are translated into linear implications, additive conjunctions and additive disjunctions respectively, with the exponential ! in some cases to allow reuse. Whole proofs are translated in the same way as implications, with the premises exponentiated.

(11.28)   1. $T(A \to B) = {!}T(A) \multimap T(B)$
         2. $T(A \wedge B) = T(A) \mathbin{\&} T(B)$
         3. $T(A \vee B) = {!}T(A) \oplus {!}T(B)$
(11.29) $T(A_1, \ldots A_n \vdash_J B) = {!}T(A_1), \ldots {!}T(A_n) \vdash_{LL} T(B)$

11.6.3 THE LAMBEK CALCULUS

In the Lambek Calculus (L) the structural rule of Permutation (C) is dropped, leaving a logic that is sensitive to the order of premises. When premises are words, this means sensitive to word order (Chapter 12). Here we look briefly at some properties of order-sensitive logic in general.

The only structural rule remaining in L is Associativity (**B**). The non-associative version of the Lambek calculus drops even that, leaving no structural rules whatsoever.

The absence of Permutation affects, first of all, the fusion operator, the implication connective and *modus ponens*. Attention has to be paid now to whether an implication looks to match its antecedent with a minor premise before or after it. Since the order of premises cannot be changed, we need two distinct implication connectives, with a separate elimination rule for each. The 'normal' implication symbol → behaves exactly as before, combining with a minor premise after it. The 'backward' implication symbol ← combines with a minor premise before it.

(11.30) $p \rightarrow q, p \vdash q$ → Elim
(11.31) $p, q \leftarrow p \vdash q$ ← Elim

In order-sensitive logics, negation splits as well as implication. A split negation is a pair, $\langle \sim, - \rangle$ in the notation used here.[21] An ordinary negation (**simple negation**) can be defined as $\langle \sim, \sim \rangle$ – a split negation whose halves are identical. Simple negation obeys the law of contraposition (11.32); with split negation, the two 'halves' of negation are related by (11.33).

(11.32) $\phi \vdash \sim\psi$ iff $\psi \vdash \sim\phi$.
(11.33) $\phi \vdash \sim\psi$ iff $\psi \vdash -\phi$.

How can we make sense of this? One interpretation of contraposition, in general, is prohibition. If falsity is interpreted as some undesirable or excluded state, then we can say that if ϕ entails ψ, and you don't want ψ, then don't do ϕ.

One application for order-sensitive logic is the logic of action, in which actions are sequential. Doing X and then Y is not the same as doing Y and then X. Here the split negations can refer to unacceptable consequences before and after respectively. So we can say that the two conditions in (11.34) are equivalent.

(11.34) 1. If you want ϕ, then don't do ψ afterwards
        2. If you want ψ, then don't do ϕ first.

An intuitive example of a split prohibition might be drinking and driving. We can give the action 'drink' the type 'don't drive after me', and give 'drive' the type 'don't drink before me'. Then with split negation:

(11.35) 1. Drink $\vdash \sim$Drive
        2. Drive $\vdash -$Drink

The identity element (truth constant) for this logic of actions will be the 'empty action' of doing nothing (in the literal sense of spending no time on anything, not as a euphemism for being lazy). For concatenation it is the empty string, and for function composition, the identity function.

(11.36) 1. $e \cdot x = x \cdot e = x$
   2. do nothing and then do X = do X and then do nothing = do X
   3. ('' concatenated with X) = (X concatenated with '') = X
   4. id $\circ$ f = f $\circ$ id = f

11.7 A FEW WORDS ABOUT QUANTIFIERS

In general, these last few chapters of the book deal only with propositional logic. However, it is interesting to see how the interpretation of quantifiers, especially the universal quantifier, also changes as you descend through the lattice of substructural logics. Essentially, these changes follow the modifications in the behaviour of conjunction and implication.

The classical and intuitionistic universal quantifier includes all the objects in its restriction set, if there are any. The latter is an important qualification. If there are no objects answering to the description, then we have the situation of vacuous quantification, as mentioned in Chapter 4. If the set denoted by P is empty, then $\forall x(P(x) \to Q(x))$ is vacuously true; $\forall x(P(x) \to Q(x))$ is equally true, and in fact P(x) implies anything, as the empty set is a subset of every set.

In relevance logic, vacuous quantification is not allowed, just as vacuous or bogus implications are not allowed. The 'vacuity' is due to the rule of Weakening. When relevance logic is applied to set theory (forming 'relevant set theory'), the subset relation requires that the two sets share some content, and the empty set is thus not a 'relevant subset' of anything.

In linear logic, besides inheriting this property of relevance, the dropping of contraction means that 'every' no longer means that all objects quantified over are simultaneously available, but rather that you can choose any one you like. Compare the behaviour of & in linear logic, which has the same meaning for the same reasons.

If you drop permutation, then the behaviour of the universal quantifier becomes even less intuitive; as order now matters, you are allowed to choose only the first object presented to you, rather like in a Soviet election.

To compare these substructural quantifiers, consider a situation in which a child is told 'you can have all the cakes'. What can she expect from the different logics?

(11.37) **Classical**: She can have all the cakes if there are any cakes. If not, that is tough luck.

   Relevant: She can have all the cakes, and if there aren't any she is entitled to feel cheated.

   Linear: She has a choice of all the cakes there are (and there are bound to be some), but once she has chosen one, the rest are taken away.

   Lambek Calculus: She can choose whichever cake she likes, as long as she chooses the first one that is offered to her.

11.8 APPLICATIONS OUTSIDE CATEGORIAL GRAMMAR

11.8.1 LINEAR LOGIC AS A 'GLUE LANGUAGE'

In linguistics syllabi, logic is often boxed in the semantics component, but it can have many other areas of application; one of these is the syntax–semantics interface. Many syntactic frameworks find themselves addressing the question of how to relate their syntactic representations to the logical forms which drive semantic interpretation. This task is approached in a variety of different ways.

In Chapter 5, a naïve phrase-stucture approach to syntax was adopted, for expository purposes. The mismatch between this structure, in which any direct object is inside a VP which excludes the subject, and the flat structure of binary predicates in first order logic, was one of the motivations for adopting a higher order logic in which binary relations can be curried, mimicking the preferred syntactic structure. This was the approach of Montague; Montague himself did not use phrase structure grammar, but used a form of categorial grammar which in this respect is equivalent. (More on categorial grammar in the next two chapters.)

However, not all natural languages follow this pattern in which subject and object are distinguished by their stuctural position inside or outside the VP. At least, they do not do so as far as the immediate surface grammar of the language is concerned, though there are theories in which they conform to this pattern at some non-obvious abstract level. Alternatively, one can abandon the attempt to force all languages into the same syntactic mould. In one such approach, the grammatical relations in a sentence are simply labelled (Subj, Obj etc.) rather than defined by structural position. This approach was pioneered, within modern linguistics, in Relational Grammar[22] and Arc Pair Grammar,[23] and is also adopted by Lexical Functional Grammar (LFG).[24]

In LFG, the most important level of syntactic representation is the functional structure (f-structure), which lists the predicate and other main grammatical relations (or grammatical functions) of the sentence, usually in the form of a matrix (11.38). This f-structure is built up by algorithms (which do not concern us here) from lexical information and the surface syntax and morphology of the language.

$$(11.38)\ f-structure: \begin{bmatrix} \text{PRED } '\lambda x \lambda y.\text{love}(x)(y)' : h \rightarrow (g \rightarrow f) \\ \text{SUBJ } [\text{PRED' john': g}] \\ \text{OBJ } [\text{PRED 'mary': h}] \end{bmatrix}$$

Suppose we want to proceed from here to build up a semantic representation and eventually interpret the sentence. The suggestion is to use logic as a **glue language** to guide the process of moving from f-structure to semantic structure. A glue language is an instruction language for co-ordinating or sequencing applications; shell scripts in Unix are a good example. Typically they are relatively simple in relation to the components they invoke. Here, too, the task of a glue language is simply to provide a mapping between two rather more complex components, the functional structure which in LFG is at the heart of syntax, and the semantics. The glue language should be distinguished from the logical language used for the semantics, known as the **meaning language** (what we have been calling the 'logical translation language'). The meaning language is chosen independently – and there are plenty to choose from. Originally in LFG it was often first order logic, but this example uses the simply typed lambda calculus (Chapter 5).[25]

Dalrymple (2001) presents linear logic as a glue language for LFG. Each f-structure provides one or more **meaning constructors**, which map PRED values to formulas of linear logic, and the construction of the semantic representation proceeds according to linear deduction. The point of linear logic is that each of the premises (the bits of information provided by the lexical entries and the grammar) must be used once and once only. The problem with classical logic is that premises can be dropped (by Weakening) so that they do not contribute to the semantic representation, or they can be duplicated (by Contraction) so that they can kick in more than once. In effect, linear logic comes with its own built-in theta theory, or in LFG terminology the criteria of **completeness** (every role must be assigned to an argument) and **coherence** (arguments are only allowed if they are assigned a role).

The amount of linear logic needed for this task is very small: just the 'tensor fragment', comprising linear implication, multiplicative conjunction (tensor) and the (linear) universal quantifier. The lexical entries associate a logical form in the meaning language with a formula in the glue language (known as a **type** – because of the Curry Howard Isomorphism it is both the type of the λ expression and a formula which can be used in a deduction). Note that the implication symbol $\rightarrow$ in these formulae represents *linear* implication.

The conclusion love(mary)(john) : f can be derived by just two steps of *modus ponens* (last chapter). The use of linear logic ensures that all the premises are used (consumed) exactly once. This conclusion will then be fed into the semantic interpretation.

11.8.2 FUZZY LOGICS REVISITED

This section takes a brief look at how the substructural family and the fuzzy logic family of Chapter 8 are related. One obvious difference between the two is that the former are truth-functional, while the latter (at least those focused on in this chapter) are relevance-sensitive and non-truth-functional. This does not apply to substructural logics which contain Weakening, such as BCK.

On the other hand BCK, like most fuzzy logics, excludes Contraction. It was noted in Chapter 8 that strong conjunction is not **idempotent** in fuzzy logic, with the exception of Gödel logic. In substructural terms, that means it does not allow Contraction or its converse, Mingle, each of which captures one half of idempotence.

(11.39) **Contraction**: X, X $\mapsto$ X (upper semi-idempotent)
        Mingle: X $\mapsto$ X, X (lower semi-idempotent)

While fuzzy logics generally exclude Contraction, they have additional conditions which do not figure in substructural logics, notably **divisibility** and **pre-linearity**. Pre-linearity is not valid even in intuitionistic logic.

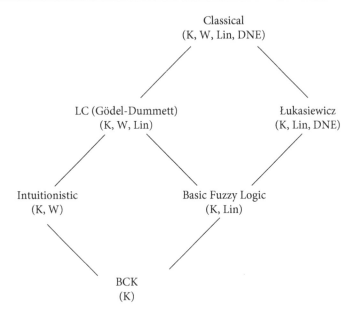

Figure 11.7: Lattice of some substructural and fuzzy logics

(11.40) **Divisibility**: $(\phi \wedge \psi) \rightarrow (\phi \times (\phi \wedge \psi))$
Pre-linearity: $(\phi \rightarrow \psi) \vee (\psi \rightarrow \psi)$

Fuzzy logics are therefore weaker than intuitionistic logic in some respects (lack of Contraction) and stronger in others (inclusion of pre-linearity). In the case of Gödel's fuzzy logic, which does include Contraction, the result is LC, which we have already encountered among the intermediate logics (between intuitionistic and classical) in Chapter 10. Łukasiewicz logic, by contrast, does not include Contraction but does include another feature of classical logic, namely double negation elimination (DNE). Figure 11.7 shows an outline map of the relevant territory, ordered by inclusion of logics. (Lin is pre-linearity, DNE is double negation elimination, W is Contraction, and the structural rules B and C are assumed.)[26]

What about logics which exclude Weakening? They cannot exactly be fuzzy logics as defined, because their fusion connective is not a t-norm. But there is one logic that comes close, which is RM (R plus Mingle). As noted above, one consequence of Mingle (with negation) is the principle of pre-linearity, $(\phi \rightarrow \psi) \vee (\psi \rightarrow \phi)$. This does not help its credentials as a relevance logic (this formula is regarded as one of the 'paradoxes of material implication'), but it brings it closer to a fuzzy logic. In fact there is only one t-norm condition that RM does not satisfy: the requirement that truth degrees be upper bounded by 1. In RM, as with all logics without Weakening, there is a distinction between logical truth and the top element of the propositional lattice, and logical truth (**t** or 1) ends up somewhere within the lattice, not at the top.

In fact a model for RM was considered in Chapter 8, in the exercises on Belnap's logic. Belnap's logical lattice BN4 can be split into two, one with the values {F, N, T} and the other with the values {F, B, T}, both with the appropriate subparts of the connective tables for BN4. The first of these is partial and corresponds to $Ł_3$, as was seen in Chapter 8. The second is paraconsistent and is a model for RM with three values, or RM_3. However, these values are not mapped to the interval [0,1]. Instead, T is taken as 1, F as -1 and B as 0. This can be extended to more values, from $-n$ to $+n$, to get the logic RM $_{2n+1}$. The model for an infinite valued version would be the set Z of all integers. The middle value, 0, always represents B – true and false combined. This construction is called a Sugihara model.[27]

What is a good way to make sense of this? One way, taking the five valued Sugihara model (n = 2) as example, would be as follows. The extreme values 2 and -2 represent clear truth and clear falsity; of the intermediate values 1 represents 'true but also a bit false', and vice versa for -1; and 0 represents the presence of truth and falsity to equal degrees. One could think of a trial in which the case may be clear-cut in favour of the prosecution or in favour of the defence, or there might be good arguments for both to varying degrees, up to the limit of equally cogent arguments on both sides.

Negation is simply arithmetical $-$. Fusion and implication are interpreted as follows:

(11.41) $V(\phi \otimes \psi) =$
     1. $\min(V(\phi), V(\psi))$ if $V(\phi) \leq V(\sim \psi)$
     2. $\max(V(\phi), V(\psi))$ if $V(f) > V(\sim \psi)$
(11.42) $V(\phi \rightarrow \psi) =$
     1. $\max(V(\phi), V(\sim \psi))$ if $V(\phi) \leq V(\psi)$
     2. $\min(V(\phi), V(\sim \psi))$ if $V(\phi) > V(\psi)$

In the exercises, you are asked to play with these definitions and show that ECQ and Weakening are not valid in these models.

EXERCISE 11.8.2.1

1. Prove the following formulae using labelled deduction. Are they theorems of (i) relevance logic, (ii) linear logic, (iii) the associative Lambek Calculus?
   (a) $p \rightarrow ((p \rightarrow q) \rightarrow q)$
   (b) $p \rightarrow (q \rightarrow q)$
   (c) $(p \rightarrow (q \rightarrow r)) \rightarrow ((p \rightarrow q) \rightarrow (p \rightarrow r))$
2. (a) For the five valued Sugihara model (above), evaluate the implication $p \rightarrow q$ when (i) $V(p) = 2$ and $V(q) = 0$; (ii) $V(p) = 0$ and $V(q) = -2$; (iii) $V(p) = -1$ and $V(q) = 1$.
   (b) Assume that all the non-negative numbers are **designated values**. Show that ECQ is not valid (there are valuations in which it does not have a designated value).
   (c) Do the same for $p \rightarrow (q \rightarrow p)$.

(d) Show from the truth conditions for implication that $(p \rightarrow q) \vee (q \rightarrow p)$ always has a designated value.

NOTES

1. This seems to depend on verbal aspect; telic event structure and perfective aspect favour the 'and then' interpretation of 'and'. There are also arguments that this 'and then' reading is a pragmatic implicature rather than a true semantic entailment. The present discussion is about how to handle these readings, however they arise.

2. Much more formal detail can be found in Restall (2000), Chapter 2.

3. I will generally use capital letters for the names of structural rules.

4. This is the idea that if a consecution is true, it cannot be made untrue by adding more information.

5. In Chapter 13 they will be given names, originating with Smullyan (1962): the Bluebird, Cardinal, Warbler and Kestrel.

6. See, however, Morrill and Carpenter (1990) and Gregory (2002).

7. This is a metaphor which may at times seem stretched; another suggestion is 'occurrence-sensitive' (Morrill 2011a).

8. This is a common phenomenon: logics setting out to change the behaviour of standard connectives find it convenient to add connective symbols to standard logic, and so end up as extensions as well as deviations.

9. Routley and Meyer (1972).

10. Historically, this interpretation precedes the ternary relation semantics; it is known as the 'operational semantics', treating the combination of x and y as a binary operation like fusion. In the language models of the next chapter, it also happens that the operational understanding of R is accurate: fusion is concatenation of strings, which is functional.

11. Restall (2000), p. 250.

12. Routley and Routley (1972).

13. This is the most 'difficult' of the De Morgan laws; for example, it is the one that is not valid in intuitionistic logic. The other three hold for almost any definition of negation.

14. As a historical note, Church's original formulation of the λ calculus did not include vacuous abstraction, so it was a model for relevance logic. Later he found it useful to include vacuous abstraction. The original 'weaker' system (which excludes Weakening) is known as the λI calculus, and the full system with vacuous abstraction is called the λK calculus.

15. As mentioned in the previous section, Church originally assumed a form of relevance logic. Other precursors include Orlov and Ackermann. At risk of being anachronistic, one could claim Aristotle himself as a relevance logician, as he rejected certain paradoxes associated with modern classical logic.

16. We are concerned at the moment primarily with implication. Some adjustments to other connectives are also involved, some of which will be discussed shortly.

17. See the survey by Pollard (2008c).

18. This at least is one way in which relevance logicians address the problem of disjunctive syllogism. It is based on Anderson and Belnap (1975).

19. The concern with S4 in relevance logic goes back to Ackermann, whose logic of entailment was originally a weakening of Lewis's S4 (Restall 2006).

20. In linear logic they are usually called exponentials.

21. It is common to see $\neg$ rather than $-$.

22. Perlmutter and Postal, see Perlmutter (1983) and Perlmutter and Rosen (1984).

23. Johnson and Postal (1980).

24. Bresnan (1982).

25. Crouch and van Genabith (2000).
26. Adapted from Dubois. DNE implies pre-linearity in classical logic, so the latter is redundant.
27. RM3 was advocated as a paraconsistent logic by Priest (1979), and is sometimes known as Priest's logic or LP.

CHAPTER 12

GRAMMAR AS LOGIC

There is in my opinion no important theoretical difference between natural languages and the artificial languages of logicians; indeed, I consider it possible to comprehend the syntax and semantics of both kinds of language within a single natural and mathematically precise theory. On this point I differ from a number of philosophers, but agree, I believe, with Chomsky and his associates.[1]

In this chapter the logical techniques introduced in previous chapters are applied to syntax.

Chapter 5 introduced the simply typed lambda calculus as a logical translation language. This was pegged, for expository purposes, to a syntactic scaffolding in the form of a naïve phrase structure grammar or tree. We also saw, however, how the process of syntactic composition (merging of constituents) was mirrored by operations on the types of lambda expressions (the rules of function application and abstraction) which correspond to familiar operations on logical formulas. In Chapter 10, this 'type logic' was used to guide the derivation of lambda expressions, rather than relying on rules tied to the phrase structure – the principle of **type driven translation**. By the Curry Howard Isomorphism, the types of lambda expressions correspond to formulae of a logical language, while the lambda expressions themselves correspond to proofs in the logical calculus.

It is possible to go further and use the type logic directly for syntactic structure, dispensing with the phrase-structural scaffolding used earlier. When types are used for syntax rather than semantics they are normally called categories, and the approach to syntax based on type logic is therefore usually called **categorial grammar** (though type logical grammar is a well represented alternative).[2]

Simple categorial grammars were first introduced by the Polish logician Ajdukiewicz. After the Second World War they were developed by Bar-Hillel, as part of an early attempt to develop a framework for machine translation. They thus predate generative grammar (phrase structure and transformational) by several decades. These early versions are known as 'Ajdukiewicz–Bar-Hillel categorial grammars', often abbreviated to AB categorial grammars.

It was proved by Bar-Hillel et al. (1964) that AB grammars are equivalent to context free phrase structure grammars, that is, trees. Chapter 5 showed how this equivalence works in practice, for simple cases. Montague Grammar, as the syntactic framework actually employed by Montague became known, was such an AB grammar. As a theory of syntax it was not very interesting, though it achieved some popularity in the 1970s when transformational grammar was going through problems.

However, more interesting treatments of categorial grammars *as logic* were already available, especially Lambek (1958) and Geach (1972). In the 1980s Van Benthem and others showed how the Curry Howard Isomorphism can be used to derive lambda-based logical translations as the proof terms of categorial grammar deductions.[3] This all contributed to a resurgence of interest in categorial grammars and related approaches. One date that is often taken as a milestone is the Tucson conference of 1985, which was seminal for many significant modern trends in formal grammar.[4]

12.1 BASIC ISSUES

12.1.1 MULTIPLICATION AND DIVISION

The formalism of the original categorial grammars was based on fractions. The basic categories are taken to be NP and S (sentence), corresponding to the logical types e and t[5]. A VP or intransitive verb is a function from NPs to Ss, so its category is written $\frac{S}{NP}$. This fraction notation represents a functional type, with the input type (domain) as denominator and the output type (range) as numerator.[6]

Since functional types are implications, the denominator can be seen as the antecedent and the numerator as the consequent of an implication, with the division sign corresponding to the implication connective.

The other basic notions we need are **strings** and **concatenation**. A string is simply a sequence of symbols. A single symbol is a string, and strings can be concatenated ('strung together') to form larger strings. In syntax the symbols are normally taken as being words, which are concatenated to form phrases and sentences. For example 'mary sings' is the concatenation of 'mary' and 'sings'. The operation of concatenation is often left without an explicit symbol (as in English orthography, though we could say that it is represented by the space between words). It can be written explicitly as a dot (·), so the concatenation of 'mary' and 'sings' can be written as 'mary' · 'sings'. Similarly, 'the cat ate the fish' is the concatenation 'the cat' · 'ate the fish' (among other possibilities). It is also often written as plain juxtaposition of symbols without any special symbol. These notations (including juxtaposition) suggest multiplication in algebra.[7]

As seen in Chapter 11, concatenation is one application of the fusion connective (×) in substructural logics, for which · and juxtaposition are notational variants.

When fusion (multiplication) and implication (division) are combined, we get *modus ponens*, corresponding to fraction cancellation (12.1). In this example an NP is concatenated with an adjacent VP, and fraction cancellation gives the result S. This was Ajdukiewicz's original idea.

$$(12.1) \quad NP \times \frac{S}{NP} = S$$

The connection between division, as seen in this set-up, and implication, is that both are **residuals**: implication is the residual of fusion (Chapter 8), and division is the residual of multiplication. A fraction can be seen as the numerator with the denominator 'missing' (divided out). If you combine it (by multiplication) with something equal to the denominator, you get the numerator back again.

Back to the example – what happens with a transitive sentence? The category of a transitive verb is something that combines with an NP to give a VP – the syntactic equivalent of type e→(e→t). This means it will have the VP category – itself a fraction – as its numerator, and NP as its denominator. Combining with an NP will give the VP by cancellation. This then combines with the other NP to give S by cancellation, as in the previous example.

$$(12.2) \quad NP \times \left(\frac{\left(\dfrac{S}{NP} \right)}{NP} \times NP \right) = NP \times \frac{S}{NP} = S$$

There are two things to note here. The first is that the expression for the transitive verb is already beginning to look unwieldy – and as we have seen, types (or categories, as we are now calling them) can get considerably more complex than transitive verbs. We need some other notation here. As in arithmetic $\frac{a}{b}$ can be written a/b, it is common to adopt the same solution, using brackets when needed. So the VP category can written s/np, and so on. The / symbol is usually referred to as **slash**. From now on, this slash will be our notation for the division symbol in forming fractions (i.e. functional or implicational categories).[8]

The second thing is that no account has yet been given of which NP the transitive verb combines with first. I have bracketed it together with the second NP (the object), to show what conventionally happens (combination first with the object NP to form a VP). But there is no particular reason, from what has been said so far, *why* things should happen in that order. Now that we are dealing with syntax, we have to look carefully at how syntactic ideas of word order and order of combination relate to the logic.

The solution most widely adopted in categorial grammar is to split the slash connective into a rightward-looking slash, /, which combines with an argument on its right, and a leftward-looking slash, \. These are exactly the split implication connectives of the previous chapter. A transitive verb (in English) can be written (np\s)/np, requiring it to combine first with its object to the right and then with its subject to the left:

$$(12.3) \quad NP \times (NP\backslash S)/NP \times NP$$
$$= NP \times NP\backslash S$$
$$= S$$

The notation of categorial grammar can be recast as natural deduction consecutions, which in turn can be arranged in derivation trees.[9] The combination of a fraction (implication) with something matching its denominator (antecedent), to give the numerator (consequent) as result, is equivalent to *modus ponens*. The slash connective corresponds to implication, concatenation to fusion (or in this case the comma which is its metalinguistic correlate).

(12.4) 1. $\text{NP} \times \dfrac{S}{NP} = S$ (fraction notation)

   2. S/NP, NP ⊢ S (logical notation, using /)
   3. NP→S, NP ⊢ S (logical notation, using →)

S is the conclusion of the derivation; to think again in tree terms, the logical derivations are working 'bottom up' to derive the category S at the root. (However, in categorial grammar these derivation trees are usually written with the root node at the bottom.) The premises are the daughters. Ultimately the premises for the whole derivation are the words (or, rather, their categories, which correspond to pre-terminals in a phrase structure tree). It is useful to remember these equivalences for orientation purposes: lexical categories are premises, sentences are conclusions – and syntactic derivations are logical proofs.

12.1.2 WHICH LOGIC?

The substructural logics of the previous chapter provide many of the tools needed for reasoning about syntax. At one end of the scale, AB grammars do not allow any structural rules at all, and the resulting derivations are much like phrase structure trees. To see why properly substructural logics are needed, rather than standard logic, it is worth thinking about what each of the structural rules means when doing grammar as logic.

Associativity would give the ability to rebracket words, changing the constituent structure of the sentence. This would break the correspondence between derivations and conventional phrase structure, which was used in Chapter 5. The bracketing representing constituency is then meaningless and might as well be left out (the logic is not constituent-sensitive). Lambek considered two systems, with and without Associativity. The Associative Lambek Calculus (**L** in the lattice on page 226) has proved more influential.

Permutation would allow the order of words or constituents to be changed at will (in contrast to **L** which is order-sensitive). With Permutation, if 'john speaks german' can be derived as a grammatical sentence, then so can 'speaks german john'. This might seem a strange thing to want to do, given the importance of word order in languages such as English, in which changes in word order are possible but very constrained. Accordingly, Lambek Calculus (in both versions) is an order-sensitive logic, rejecting Permutation.

   Another appeoach to this question was suggested by Curry (1961): to analyse syntax at a more abstract combinatoric level which does not involve word order, and leave word order to be dealt with by some other component. In Curry's terminology, the more abstract level of syntax, which does not deal with word order, is **tectogrammar**, and the more superficial level where word order kicks in is **phenogrammar**. A tectogrammatical statement about top-level sentence structure might read, 'A sentence is composed of an NP and a VP, and the order between them is somebody else's problem (namely that of the phenogrammar for each language).' On this view, the logical analysis of syntax is best done at the level of tectogrammar, while word order is a language-specific phenomenon to be sorted out by the phenogrammar. Such a separation of linear order from structure is found in a number of syntactic frameworks.

Most categorial grammar frameworks have followed Lambek in exploring the possibilities of order-sensitive logics.[10] However, there are a number of related approaches, such as Convergent Grammar (CVG)[11] Lambda Grammar (λG)[12] and Abstract Categorial Grammar (ACG), which adopt Curry's distinction.

Contraction would allow premises to be used more than once each in a derivation. For example if 'martha likes martha' is grammatical it would also be possible to derive a transitive sentence from 'martha likes', understanding 'martha' twice, once as subject and once as object. This would play havoc with θ theory, which generally requires that a grammatical constituent play only one role in the building up of a sentence.

Sometimes, however, the ability to state an expression only once but understand it (or use it) again on another occasion does seem to be important in language. Control is one example (its alternate name, equi-subject deletion, reflects the idea that the second occurrence somehow ought to be there and is missing). Another is parasitic gaps, where the dislocated element appears to be linked to two roles. And with certain verbs which can have an intrinsic reflexive reading, like 'shower' or 'shave', even the simple reuse of the subject NP can make sense.

Some categorial grammarians have explored the possibilities of using Contraction for such phenomena. However, its global presence in the logic would be disruptive.

Weakening would mean that words can be introduced into a sentence without playing any part in the syntactic structure. If a sentence can be derived from 'john likes mary', then it can equally be derived from 'john rhubarb likes mary rhubarb rhubarb'. This results from the fact that, in logics with Weakening, premises can 'just be there' without participating in the derivation of the conclusion. The idea that constituents of a sentence have to play some role in the sentence which licenses them to be there breaks down. Therefore, a suitable logic for grammatical connexity must be relevance-sensitive (must exclude Weakening).[13]

Even so, candidates have been suggested to support the use of Weakening. Expletives, for example, do not play a semantic role in a sentence, and yet are grammatical in the surface string. However, such cases do not seem to be parallel to the example with rhubarb, and some other explanation should be sought.[14] Other candidates include resumptive pronouns, such as 'baggins we hate it' (or 'hates' in Gollum's idiolect). One thing to note here is that such elements co-refer with some other item in the sentence. If they were to be analysed as a case of Weakening, it would have to be confined to the redundant repetition of something already in the sentence, rather than the introduction of arbitrary redundant material. This restricted form of Weakening is in fact the Mingle rule (usually known in categorial grammar contexts as Expansion, the opposite of Contraction).

So we end up with a hierarchy of possible categorial grammars, according to the structural rules they allow. The associative Lambek calculus will be assumed as the default case – some of the reasons for admitting Associativity are discussed in the next section. Cases can be made for adding Permutation and Contraction or Mingle, possibilities explored by van Benthem (1983) and Moortgat (1988).

12.1.3 CATEGORIAL GRAMMAR AND LOGIC

AB grammars derive sentences from lexical premises using fraction cancellation or *modus ponens*. If the connection with logic is taken seriously, however, one can do a lot more than just *modus ponens*. Here are some more basic ideas which have become the stock in trade of categorial grammarians.

It is common to find semantically sentential modifiers appearing in the syntax as VP adverbials. These include negation, but also modal and temporal operators such as 'always' or 'definitely'. The following rule (the Geach rule) allows sentence adverbials to function as VP adverbials.

(12.5) $S/S = (S/NP)/(S/NP)$

The expression on the right is the category of a VP modifier (semantic type $(e \rightarrow t)$ $\rightarrow (e \rightarrow t)$). The validity of this transition is clear whether we think in terms of fractions (12.6) or implications (12.7). The first divides the numerator and the denominator by the same value (NP). The second is an instance of the logical rule of the transitivity of implication (Chapter 11).

$$(12.6) \quad \frac{S_2}{S_1} = \frac{\left(\dfrac{S_2}{NP}\right)}{\left(\dfrac{S_1}{NP}\right)}$$

(12.7) $S_1 \rightarrow S_2 \equiv (NP \rightarrow S_1) \rightarrow (NP \rightarrow S_2)$

Another operation based on Associativity is composition. If two adjacent categories are a/b and b/c, it is possible to cancel the middle term b and derive a category a/c. Again this can be seen in terms of division or implication.[15]

$$(12.8) \quad \frac{a}{b} \times \frac{b}{c} = \frac{a}{c}$$

(12.9) $f : a \rightarrow b, g : b \rightarrow c \vdash \lambda x.f(gx) : a \rightarrow c$

The formulas in (12.9) have been labelled with lambda terms to show how this operation involves the composition of two functions f and g. (See Chapter 10 and also section 12.8 below.)

One application of composition is to form verb groups consisting of auxiliaries and a main verb. Auxiliaries have the category (np\s)/(np\s). Let's say the verb is (mono)transitive and has the category (np\s)/np. In an AB grammar, the transitive verb would combine with an NP to its right by application, and then the auxiliary would combine with the resulting VP, again by application. This derivation would correspond exactly to the normal (right-branching) tree for such a structure in a phrase structure grammar. However, if composition is available, the middle category np\s cancels, resulting in the composed category (of an auxiliated verb, or verb group) (np\s)/np, looking for an object NP to its right.

Why is this useful? Although the auxiliary and verb do not form a conventional constituent, they still seem to belong together as a single intelligible idea. In many languages the combination of a verb and modal auxiliary can be lexicalised, just as with tense auxilaries in English (did go = went). Moreover it can participate in non-constituent co-ordination structures, as in 'Howard [loves but can't speak] Thai'.

A similar account was proposed for raising verbs by Jacobson (1990). A raising verb such as 'seems' has the semantic type t $\longrightarrow$ t, and thus would be expected to have the category s/s. In the syntax, however, it takes as its arguments an NP and a VP whose subject has been 'raised' to be the matrix subject. Composing 'seems' (s/s) with the lower predicate P, which we can take to be of category s/np, gives the combined category s/np with the semantics $\lambda x.\text{seems}(P(x))$. (Any extra arguments of the lower predicate can be incorporated with minor adjustments – see Chapter 13.)

Another use of composition to obtain an incremental left-to-right build-up of structure, rather than the typically right-branching derivations of an AB grammar,[16] will be introduced in the next chapter.

Once the categorial system is treated as a full logic, rather than just a few rules, there are many resources available. One of these is conditional proof, with lambda abstraction.[17] This can be used for unbounded dependencies. The missing category at the foot of the dependency is introduced as an assumption (labelled by a free variable). This is passed up until it is discharged at the top of the dependency by a rule of implication introduction (and the free variable labelling it is lambda bound).[18]

Another important rule is type lifting.[19] This was used by Montague to obtain a uniform type for NPs as generalised quantifiers (type $(e \longrightarrow t) \longrightarrow t$). In categorial grammar it is often used to distinguish between subject and object NPs. (This difference is lexically marked for pronouns in English, and NPs in general in many other languages.) The subject NP takes a VP to its right as argument, while the object NP takes a transitive verb to its left. Note that reversing the functor-argument relation in this way is a form of Permutation.

(12.10) **Subject NP**: S/(NP\S)
         Object NP: ((NP\S)/NP)\(NP\S)

The combination of lifting and composition can be used to obtain a left-branching structure reflecting the incrementality of sentence processing.[20] This will be seen in Chapter 13.

These brief hints indicate that the Lambek Calculus offers a powerful and flexible set of resources for going beyond rule-based systems such as AB grammars. In principle, anything that can be derived as a theorem in L is a potential grammatical rule. Not all categorial grammarians are comfortable with availing themselves of the full power of this logical approach, especially lambda abstraction.[21] The next chapter will look at another approach based on combinatory logic, which uses only a controlled subset of these resources.[22]

12.2 LOGICAL SYNTAX OF CATEGORIAL GRAMMAR

The *basic* syntax of categorial grammar is that of the substructural logics of the previous chapter, specifically the Lambek calculus L. In the simplest case it is confined to the implicational fragment of L, usually with fusion.

The basic categories are *np* and *s*. However, it is common to use abbreviations for some compound categories, such as *vp*, *pp* and *cn* (common noun). They can also be subscripted with features, for example for verb form, case, preposition type, or agreement.

As in the last chapter, this section is mainly about connectives. The actual symbols used vary in the literature.

× or · – fusion, which in L represents concatenation. (It can be replaced by juxtaposition.)
/ – right division
\ – left division

Note that there are two different versions of the slash notation. In the Lambek notation, the argument is written 'under' the slash, whichever way it leans, and the value or result is on top. (X\Y is read as 'X under Y', and Y/X as 'Y over X', the two representing the same function with different directionality.) This represents somewhat iconically the direction in which the argument will be, but in complex formulas it can be difficult to spot the main functor. In Steedman notation, by contrast, formulas are written with the result invariably on the left of the slash and the argument on the right. The direction of the slash still indicates on which side it combines with the argument, but not quite so intuitively. On the other hand, it is immediately clear where the main functor is.

In these chapters Lambek notation will be used throughout, even when discussing work written in Steedman notation. Practice in rewriting from one notation to the other is provided in the exercises.

Other standard logical connectives can be added. Conjunction is added for product types in syntactic approaches which do not assume binary branching (currying); and conjunction and disjunction can be used to create polymorphic categories.[23] A variety of extra symbols are needed by particular proposals, for example those in sections 12.5 and 12.7.

EXERCISE 12.2.0.1

1. Rewrite these formulas from Steedman to Lambek notation.
   (a) ((S\NP)/NP)/PP
   (b) (S\NP)/(S\NP)
   (c) NP/(S\NP)
2. Rewrite these formulas from Lambek to Steedman notation.
   (a) (NP\S)/NP
   (b) (NP\S)/(NP\S)
   (c) S/(S\NP)

In each case, state what syntactic category the formula represents.

12.3 SEMANTICS OF CATEGORIAL GRAMMAR

There are several approaches to the semantics of categorial grammar, but the relational semantics for substructural logics described in the last chapter works perfectly well for the Lambek Calculus as a particular case. It is also a particularly *easy* case to understand intuitively, for reasons which will be mentioned as we come to them.

This book started with applications of logic to semantics, and this has remained its main, though not exclusive, focus. This chapter is different in that it applies logic explicitly to the *syntax* of natural language. So giving a semantics for this application calls for some clarification. First, we might want to give a semantics for the natural language for which we are giving a syntactic analysis. This is what we have been doing in much of this book, and it appears again, from a categorial grammar perspective, in section 12.8. In this section, however, something different is intended: a formal semantic interpretation of the use of logic for natural language syntax ('the semantics of syntax').

As the syntax is provided by the type logic (logic of categories), a suitable model is the strings of any natural language, or usually a restricted fragment of such a language. That, after all, is what the categorial grammar is describing. This is called a **language model**. To give a more complete account, we should not talk simply about strings but rather about **signs**, the multidimensional bundles of information of which language is composed. However, since we are concerned here with their concatenation and related operations, strings, or 'signs as strings', will be an acceptable approximation.

In the semantics for this application, the frames and models of Chapter 11 are understood as follows. First the frame $\mathcal{F} = \langle P, R, \{0\} \rangle$ such that:

- P is the set of strings of a language.
- $R \subseteq P^3$ is a relation such that $R(x, y, z)$ iff $x \cdot y = z$.
- $0 = e$ (the empty string)

Note that R is the relational encoding of the binary function of concatenation (which makes the conditions for structural rules easier to follow than in the general ternary relation semantics). Also the truth set consists of only one element, the empty string.

A model $\mathcal{M} = \langle \mathcal{F}, V \rangle$, where V assigns each basic category in $\mathcal{L}$ a subset of P. As usual when doing relational semantics we write this using the $\Vdash$ notation. The following are the rules of interpretation for composite types:

1. $x \Vdash a/b$ iff, for every y and z such that $R(x, y, z)$, if $y \Vdash b$ then $z \Vdash a$.
2. $y \Vdash b \setminus a$ iff, for every x and z such that $R(x, y, z)$, if $x \Vdash b$ then $z \Vdash a$.
3. $z \Vdash a \cdot b$ iff, for some x and y such that $R(x, y, z)$, $x \Vdash a$ and $y \Vdash b$.

This is a subset of the rules given in the previous chapter. The $\cdot$ operator is the equivalent of fusion; it is understood here as concatenation, reflecting the understanding of R as the concatenation of strings.

Frame conditions are introduced for whatever structural rules are required. They are the same as in Chapter 11 (section 11.4, p. 238f). A frame for the associative Lambek Calculus **L** will use condition B. (From what has been said in the introduction to this chapter, no versions of categorial grammar will be expected to use K.)

12.4 THE GENTZEN CALCULUS

12.4.1 A DECISION PROCEDURE

Natural deduction proofs have good intuitive properties, but they have one drawback: there is no sure way of showing that a formula can or cannot be proved. The proofs used in the last few chapters rely on intuition and rules of thumb. Dissatisfaction with this led its inventor, Gentzen, to devise another proof system which comes with a guaranteed decision procedure. I will call this the Gentzen consecution calculus, though it is more commonly known as the sequent calculus.[24]

The Gentzen system was adopted by Lambek, and since then has been almost universal in categorial grammar. In part this is due to its computational attractions. But it is also because categorial grammar, besides being a logical system, is also a formal grammar, that is, a procedure for deciding between grammatical and ungrammatical strings, just like other grammar formalisms such as context free grammars or unification grammars. As such, questions of complexity and decidability are a core theoretical interest as well as being useful for implementations.[25]

To understand Gentzen systems, it is best to think backwards, from the conclusion of a derivation to the premises. Natural deduction can also be done like this, so let's think for the moment in terms of natural deduction, as in the first part of this chapter. We want to be sure that we can derive the conclusion at the root of the tree from the premises at the leaves, and do so in a finite number of steps.

If you think back to the construction trees of Chapter 2, the guarantee that we could parse a formula of propositional logic lay in the fact that, at each step, the formula is broken down into subformulas which are strictly shorter, until we get to atomic formulae. This is the **subformula property**. In natural deduction, the same applies to introduction rules. If we are working back from conclusion to premises,

$$\frac{\Gamma_1 \vdash \phi_1 \qquad\qquad \Gamma_2 \vdash \phi_2 \qquad \textbf{(Premises)}}{\Gamma_3 \vdash \phi_3 \qquad\qquad\qquad \textbf{(Conclusion)}} \textbf{Rule}$$

Figure 12.1   Notation for Gentzen rules

then meeting an introduction rule will take us from a composite formula back to the subformulae of which it is composed. If the proof somehow consisted only of introduction rules, we would have a ready-made decision procedure. Unfortunately, this is not what we find in categorial grammar, where derivations consist mainly of *elimination* rules. What is needed is some way of rearranging things so that elimination rules also have the subformula property.

The solution discovered by Gentzen is to think in terms of consecutions rather than just formulae. Rules of the calculus operate on whole consecutions, not just on formulae. The **premises**, or imput to the rule, are one or more consecutions written above the line, and the consecution below the line is the **conclusion** or output of the rule (Figure 12.1). Since we are accustomed to thinking of consecutions themselves as proofs, a rule in the Gentzen Calculus can be thought of as a proof about proofs.

Each connective rule will change a formula either before the turnstyle or after it. Applying an introduction rule will introduce a composite formula to the right of the turnstyle. Applying an elimination rule will have a composite formula on the *left* of the turnstyle. We can take it back to a consecution above the line where that composite formula does not appear, only its constituent parts. In this system, the introduction-like rules are called **right rules** and the elimination-like rules are **left rules**.[26]

As usual, conjunction is an easy place to start. For the left rules we need an extension to our semi-formal notation for premise structures: X(Y) denotes a structure X in which Y (which may be a single formula) occurs as a distinguished substructure.[27]

(12.11) $\wedge \mathbf{R} \dfrac{\Gamma \vdash \phi \quad \Gamma \vdash \psi}{\Gamma \vdash \phi \wedge \psi}$

$\wedge \mathbf{L} \dfrac{\Gamma(\phi) \vdash \chi}{\Gamma(\phi \wedge \psi) \vdash \chi}$

The first rule corresponds to $\wedge$ introduction; the second to $\wedge$ elimination. The reasoning behind the left rule is that if you prove from $\phi \wedge \psi$ something which relies only on ϕ, then you must have obtained ϕ from the conjunction in the process.

Now, working backwards from conclusion to premises, the composite formulae in the conclusion are broken up in the premises. This is true for left rules as much as right rules. This is the guarantee we were looking for that all formulae will be broken down into atoms in a finite number of steps.

Let's now look at implication and fusion, which are the most important connec-tives for the applications in this chapter. As in natural deduction, the rules for these connectives are based on the deduction equivalence.

$$(12.12) \quad \times \mathbf{R} \, \frac{\Gamma \vdash \phi \quad \Delta \vdash \psi}{\Gamma, \Delta \vdash \phi \times \psi}$$

$$\times \mathbf{L} \, \frac{\Gamma((\phi, \psi)) \vdash \chi}{\Gamma(\phi \times \psi) \vdash \chi}$$

$$\rightarrow \mathbf{R} \, \frac{\Gamma, \phi \vdash \psi}{\Gamma \vdash \phi \rightarrow \psi}$$

$$\rightarrow \mathbf{L} \, \frac{\Gamma \vdash \phi \quad \Delta (\psi) \vdash \chi}{\Delta ((\phi \rightarrow \psi, \Gamma)) \vdash \chi}$$

As we are using a non-commutative logic, implication for present purposes splits into the two slashes, each of which has its own left and right rules. (Don't confuse the terminology of left and right rules with left and right implications or slashes.)

$$(12.13) \quad /\mathbf{R} \, \frac{\Gamma, \phi \vdash \psi}{\Gamma \vdash \psi / \phi}$$

$$\backslash \mathbf{R} \, \frac{\phi, \Gamma \vdash \psi}{\Gamma \vdash \phi \backslash \psi}$$

$$/\mathbf{L} \, \frac{\Gamma \vdash \phi \quad \Delta (\psi) \vdash \chi}{\Delta ((\psi \rightarrow \phi, \Gamma)) \vdash \chi}$$

$$\backslash \mathbf{L} \, \frac{\Gamma \vdash \phi \quad \Delta (\psi) \vdash \chi}{\Delta ((\Gamma, \phi \backslash \psi)) \vdash \chi}$$

Here are the rules for disjunction and negation (12.14). (In the right rule for dis-junction I omit the symmetrical case of introducing a left disjunct.) The left rule is very similar to the natural deduction elimination rule – and possibly, for once, a bit clearer.

In the negation rules we see for the first time consecutions with empty consequents. These can be thought of as another way of representing logical falsity, in the same way as the empty premise structure before the turnstyle represents logical truth. If we also understand $\sim \phi$ as $\phi \rightarrow \mathbf{f}$, then the rules for negation boil down to implication rules.

$$(12.14) \quad \vee \mathbf{R} \, \frac{\Gamma \vdash \phi}{\Gamma \vdash \phi \vee \psi}$$

$$\sim \mathbf{R} \, \frac{\Gamma, \phi \vdash}{\Gamma \vdash \sim \phi}$$

$$\sim \mathbf{L} \ \frac{\Gamma \vdash \phi}{\Gamma, \sim\phi \vdash}$$

$$\vee \mathbf{R} \ \frac{\Gamma \vdash (\phi)\chi \quad \Gamma(\psi) \vdash \chi}{\Gamma(\phi \vee \psi) \vdash \chi}$$

This is all for the connective rules. We need to consider two other types of rule: structural rules, which are essentially the same as in natural deduction, and the Cut rule, which is specific to Gentzen systems and about which something has to be said (section 12.4.2).

The structural rules for Associativity (**B**) and (Weak) Permutation (**CI**) are:[28]

$$(12.15) \ \mathbf{B} \ \frac{X((\Gamma,\Delta),E) \vdash \phi}{X(\Gamma,(\Delta,E)) \vdash \phi}$$

$$\mathbf{CI} \ \frac{X(\Gamma,\Delta) \vdash \phi}{X(\Delta,\Gamma) \vdash \phi}$$

What about the termination of the proof procedure? With construction trees, the process comes to a halt when you get to an atomic proposition. In Gentzen systems the process is grounded by instances of the identity axiom, which sit at the leaves of the derivation tree. Because it is an axiom, the line above (where the premises should be) is left blank.

$$(12.16) \ \frac{}{p \vdash p} \ \textbf{Axiom.}$$

The p in this example will be an atomic formula (a basic category in the case of categorial grammar). The consecutions are so arranged so that the premises computed will be the simplest categories involved in the derivation. Figure 12.2 shows a very simple example. Note that the formulas have been labelled in the same way as they would be in labelled natural deduction.

The final consecution (the conclusion, in Gentzen Calculus terminology) gives in summary form the entire derivation of the sentence s from np plus vp (or np\s), what in a natural deduction derivation would be termed the premises. In the Gentzen system the ultimate 'premises' are obtained by breaking down any composite categories (in this case np\s) into the basic categories np and s, which are then grounded by instances of the identity axiom.

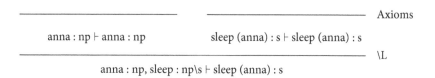

		Axioms
anna : np ⊦ anna : np	sleep (anna) : s ⊦ sleep (anna) : s	
anna : np, sleep : np\s ⊦ sleep (anna) : s		\L

Figure 12.2   A Gentzen Calculus derivation

12.4.2 CUT ELIMINATION

There is one other rule in Gentzen systems: the **Cut** rule. The idea of this is that if you have a proof of ϕ, plus a proof of ψ from ϕ, then you can assert ψ on the basis of whatever premises gave you ϕ and the proof of ψ. The ϕ itself, which was the intermediary in the proof, is 'cut'. The formula ϕ can be thought of as a **lemma**, a formula whose proof is a useful intermediate stage in the proof of the final conclusion; it can be used in any subsequent step in the proof and then discarded. In some cases the use of such lemmas can make a huge difference to the length and complexity of a proof.

$$(12.17) \quad \textbf{Cut} \quad \frac{\Gamma \vdash \phi \quad \Delta\,(\phi) \vdash \psi}{\Delta(\Gamma) \vdash \psi}$$

This is not a connective rule, so there are no left and right versions. More importantly, you will see that it does not have the subformula property. Back-chaining from conclusion to premises, we do not get less complicated formulas or fewer formulas: we actually get one more formula, namely the ϕ which has been 'cut'. It might seem that such a rule completely undermines the Gentzen decision procedure. However, Gentzen showed (and regarded this as the key to the whole system, the '*Hauptsatz*'), that Cut does not change the properties of the system. This is known as **Cut elimination**.[29]

The proof of this has two parts. First, it is possible to show that for any given logic $\mathcal{L}$, the formulation of $\mathcal{L}$ in a Gentzen system with Cut is equivalent to the natural deduction formulation of $\mathcal{L}$ (this can be shown by a translation). Then the Cut elimination theorem itself shows that Cut is redundant within the Gentzen system. The essence of the proof is that a Cut in one part of the deduction can always be converted to a Cut further back in the deduction (further up the tree), until it reaches the leaves. Since the formulas at the leaves are instances of the identity axiom, the Cut is shown to be redundant as the conclusion is identical with one of the premises. Eliminating the redundant Cut can be considered a form of proof normalisation (Chapter 10).

$$(12.18) \quad \frac{\Gamma \vdash p \quad p \vdash p}{\Gamma \vdash p} \ \ \textbf{Cut}$$

Gerhard Gentzen

A researcher with Hilbert in Göttingen, where he became known for his study of proof theory, inventing first natural deduction and then the system now known after him as the Gentzen sequent calculus (or consecution calculus). Unless appearances are deceptive, he was also a committed Nazi. In the Second World War he became a professor in occupied Prague. On the surrender of the German forces there he was identified by the Czech resistance as a leading Nazi, interned by the Soviet authorities in a prison camp and left to die of starvation.

12.5 MULTI-MODAL CATEGORIAL GRAMMAR

The Lambek Calculus either admits no structural rules at all, or only Associativity. Which structural rules do you think are required for the following?

1. To analyse a string as a left branching tree, when the lexical categories indicate a right-branching one.
2. To lift the type of an individual to a functor over predicates of individuals.
3. To allow a non-subject assumption (trace) to be bound off by a dislocated constituent.
4. Inversion of arguments, as in passivisation.
5. Binding of two assumptions by a single dislocated constituent.

It seems that for certain purposes the introduction of structural rules beyond just Associativity is desirable, although to reintroduce them across the board (globally) would surrender the fine-grained control provided by weak substructural logics. One way to effect this is to allow structural rules to apply in specified 'modal' contexts. Recall that this idea was used in linear logic, where the rules of Weakening and Contraction can be recovered using modal operators called 'exponentials'. The same idea has been adapted to type logical grammar,[30] and more recently used in combinatorial categorial grammar.[31]

A multimodal logic for categorial grammar generally employs one of two devices. The first is to replace fusion by a family of indexed fusion connectives $\times_i$, each with its own accessibility relation R_i and residuated by slashes $/_i$ and $\backslash_i$. As with the multimodal logics in Chapter 6, the behaviour of different connectives can be varied as they have different accessibility relations.

Alternatively, unary modal operators $\square$ and $\lozenge$ can be used,[32] with a binary accessibility relation S. Note that the duality between the two is that between *substructural* rather than classical modal operators: for the former the order of worlds is reversed in the interpretation rule for $\lozenge$ (12.19).[33]

(12.19) 1. $x \vdash \lozenge\phi$ iff for some y, S(y, x) and $y \vdash \phi$
            2. $x \vdash \square \phi$ iff for every y, if S(x, y) then $y \vdash \phi$

The two operators are related by (12.20), which is a form of residuation. To see this, recall the relationship between $\square\phi$ and $t \rightarrow \phi$. There is a similar relation between possibility and fusion: $\lozenge\phi$ corresponds to $t \times \phi$. Using the deduction equivalence (12.21) gives the relationship in (12.20).

(12.20) $\lozenge \phi \vdash \psi$ iff $\phi \vdash \square\psi$
(12.21) $\phi \times t \vdash \psi$ iff $\phi \vdash t \rightarrow \psi$

- Show using (12.20) and modal axiom **4** that $\lozenge\square\phi \vdash \phi$, and $\phi \vdash \square\lozenge\phi$. Which modal principle would this be in normal modal logic?

These equivalences allow us to introduce and eliminate modalised formulas. ◊ (possibility) can be thought of as licensing the use of extra structural rules, while □ is used for blocking them.

One application can be found in the treatment of gaps, for example in relative clauses. These unbounded dependencies are an issue in categorial grammar, for the following reason. It is natural to give the subject relative pronoun the category (cn\cn)/(np\s), and the non-subject relative pronoun the category (cn\cn)/(s/np). The latter, however, will only work if the NP gap is at the end of the gapped sentence (right-peripheral). In a sentence like 'the book which$_i$ Mary read t$_i$ yesterday', the gap is non-peripheral and there is no way, simply using **L**, of bringing the gap to the medial position where it needs to be. This is known as the problem of medial extraction.

Using modal operators, the (non-subject) relative pronoun can be given the category (cn\cn)/(s/◊□np), subcategorising as before for a slashed sentence. The modal operators on the dislocated NP mean that it can be manipulated by structural rules, such as Permutation, which are so written as to accept only modal categories. Using these, the modalised NP can be manoeuvred to a medial position adjacent to the verb which subcategorises for it at the foot of the dependency. This verb subcategorises for an ordinary (non-modal) NP; however, this can be satisfied because of the inference ◊□np ⊢ np.

12.6 DISCONTINUITY

Phenomena involving discontinuty are expected to be a problem for a logic based on concatenation. In general, either some material is missing from a constituent (**extraction**), or some extraneous material appears within it (**infixation**). Besides medial extraction, here are a few more examples in English (not an exhaustive list):

Discontinuous idioms: give [X] the cold shoulder.
Separable phrasal verbs: put [X] down (or optionally put down [X]).
Quantifier scope: sometimes involves a mismatch between the position where a quantifier is expressed and where it is interpreted.
Parentheticals: 'Logic involves, I think, too much hard work.'

One proposal for directly reasoning about discontinuity involves connectives with precisely the meanings 'extraction' ↑ and 'infixation' ↓ [34]. These are the two residuals of a binary operator called discontinuous product or 'wrap', ⊙. Whereas concatenation and its residuals give a logic of continuous strings, ⊙ is the basis of a logic of split strings – the Discontinuous Lambek Calculus or **DL**. A split string has one or more 'split points'; if there is more than one, then there is an element of non-determinism as to where the infixed material can land (cf. the example of phrasal verbs).

The split points are marked with a distinguished element in the string called a separator, which is manipulated using the two unary operators ^ (bridge) and ˅ (split). Categories are sorted according to the number of split points, so that a constituent with two potential sites for intrusive material is said to be of sort 2.

To give a very simple example, in **DL** a phrasal verb like 'put down' would have the category $^\vee(np\backslash s)\uparrow np$. It would also be of sort 2, with two split points, medial and right-peripheral. Combining the object NP by $\uparrow$ elimination (not the normal slash elimination) results in it being inserted in one of these positions. Then a unary rule of $^\vee$ elimination removes the remaining split point, to give the category $np\backslash s$ for the VP.

The next section looks at another approach to discontinuity, using the substructural fission connective.

12.7 SYMMETRIC LOGIC

At the beginning of Chapter 11 there was a semi-formal discussion of the premise structures which form part of consecutions. Some of the points noted were the correspondence between the comma and the object-language fusion connective, and also the asymmetry between the use of structures before the turnstyle and the restriction of the field after the turnstyle to a single formula.

It is possible to do away with this restriction and allow structures after the turnstyle as well as before it. The difference is that after the turnstyle, structures are interpreted disjunctively rather than conjunctively, and the comma will correspond to a kind of disjunction connective. The 'kind of disjunction connective' depends on the structural rules present. In classical logic it is $\vee$, in relevance logic it is **fission**, in linear logic it is the multiplicative disjunction known as **par**, and we will discuss the equivalent in the Lambek Calculus shortly. I will refer to the connective generically as **fission**; another general term for it is **coproduct**.

The other connective that is greatly affected by this change is negation. One way of expressing falsity, as we saw earlier in this chapter, is through a consecution with nothing after the turnstyle. This is equivalent, however, to negating a premise and moving it to the right of the turnstyle. To take the simple case of a single formula, if ϕ is logically false, then $\sim\phi$ is a theorem and so can appear after the turnstyle with no premises.

(12.22) 1. $\phi \vdash$
        2. $\vdash \sim\phi$

Now consider the identity proof, $\phi \vdash \phi$. If we move the premise over the turnstyle, negating it in the process, we obtain $\vdash \sim\phi, \phi$. But the comma to the right of the turnstyle is understood as a disjunction. If conjunction and disjunction are the standard $\wedge$ and $\vee$, this gives us $\phi \vee \neg\phi$ as a theorem – which is LEM.

It was mentioned in the last chapter that the difference between classical and intuitionistic logic was not a matter of structural rules. Rather, the difference is precisely that intuitionistic logic only allows a single formula after the turnstyle, and so LEM is not provable in this way. Allowing structures to the right of the turnstyle is the standard way of getting classical logic in Gentzen Calculus.

At least, we get classical logic if all the structural rules are present. If not, we have some substructural logic, but we have to say now that substructural logics each come in two flavours, 'classical' or 'intuitionistic', depending on whether or not multiple consequents are allowed. Classical is a potentially misleading term here; another term used in the literature, which is perhaps preferable, is **symmetric** logics. Classical logic is the symmetric version (and intuitionistic logic the asymmetric version) of the logic with all structural rules present.[35]

Probably the best known of these symmetric logics is symmetric linear logic. As Girard (1987) says, it combines the control over derivations of a resource logic with the symmetry and simplicity of classical logic. However, symmetric logics have also been applied to categorial grammar, based on the work of Grishin (1983).[36] We will look at this shortly.

Here are the main connective rules for a symmetric consecution calculus, based on symmetric linear logic. They include the nullary connectives **t** and **f**, for which the new nullary punctuation mark 0 is used to designate the empty structure (denoting truth before the turnstyle and falsity after it).

(12.23) **Negation:** $\dfrac{\Gamma \vdash \phi, \Delta}{\Gamma, \sim\phi \vdash \Delta}$ ~L $\quad \dfrac{\Gamma \vdash \phi \vdash \Delta}{\Gamma, \vdash\sim\phi, \Delta}$ ~R

Fusion: $\dfrac{\Gamma(\phi, \psi) \vdash \Delta}{\Gamma(\phi\times\psi) \vdash \Delta}$ ×L $\quad \dfrac{\Gamma \vdash \Delta, \phi;\ \Gamma' \vdash \psi, \Delta'}{\Gamma, \Gamma' \vdash (\Delta, \phi\times\psi), \Delta'}$ ×R

Fission: $\dfrac{\Gamma, \phi \vdash \Delta;\ \psi, \Gamma' \vdash \Delta'}{(\Gamma, \phi+\psi), \Gamma' \vdash \Delta, \Delta'}$ + $\quad \dfrac{\Gamma \vdash \Delta(\phi, \psi)}{\Gamma \vdash \Delta(\phi+\psi)}$ +R

Implication: $\dfrac{\Gamma, \vdash\Delta(\phi);\ \Gamma'(\psi) \vdash \Delta'}{\Gamma'(\Gamma, \phi\rightarrow\psi) \vdash\Delta(\Delta')}$ →L $\quad \dfrac{\Gamma, \phi, \vdash\psi, \Delta}{\Gamma\vdash\phi\rightarrow\psi, \Delta}$ →R

True: $\dfrac{\Gamma(0) \vdash \Delta}{\Gamma(t) \vdash \Delta}$ tL $\quad \dfrac{}{0\vdash t}$ tR

False: $\dfrac{f \vdash 0}{}$ fL $\quad \dfrac{\Gamma \vdash \Delta(0)}{\Gamma \vdash \Delta(f)}$ fR

Note the symmetry between the fusion and fission rules, and between the rules for **t** and **f**.

Symmetric logic also opens up the possibility of **dual logic**. This is like doing logic 'in reverse' – reading down the entailment ordering on propositions, rather than, as normal, up it. (In place of ≤, the ordering relation is ≤⁻¹, or ≥.) In dual logic, disjunction takes on the role normally played by conjunction (as the glb). But what about a dual of implication? In the discussion of Boolean logic in Chapter 2, it was mentioned that there is a mirror image of material implication ($\neg \phi \vee \psi$) in the form of the **inhibition** connective (ϕ but not ψ):

- Draw the truth table for $\phi \wedge \neg\psi$, and check that it is (i) the complement of $\phi \rightarrow \psi$, and (ii) the dual of $\psi \rightarrow \phi$ – that is, they are interdefinable by negation, as in the De Morgan laws. (Hint: rewrite the formulae using conjunction or disjunction.)

Recall that in the discussion of Heyting algebras (Chapter 10) we mentioned the possibility of defining a dual Heying algebra with a pseudocomplement operation $\sim$ which respects $\phi \vee \sim\phi = 1$ but $\phi \wedge \sim\phi$ may not be 0. Then inhibition (also called subtraction in dual intuitionistic logic) is a (dual) relative pseudocomplement operation, just as implication is a relative pseudocomplement in a straight Heyting algebra.

In the substructural logics we are dealing with, the disjunction connective is fission. By analogy with the deduction theorem, we want a (dual) residual of fission, just as implication is the residual of fusion. The residual of fission is called **difference**. As a matter of notation, inhibition in standard logic is often notated with the slash (a / b = a $\wedge$ ¬b), or by the minus sign, but in symmetric categorial grammar difference is written $\oslash$. As the logic does not contain Permutation, this difference connective splits into left and right directional versions, $\oslash$ (right difference) and $\ominus$ (left difference). $\phi \oslash \psi$ and $\psi \ominus \phi$ both have the meaning 'ϕ excluding ψ' (or ϕ but not ψ). (They are both read with the result on top, as in Lambek notation for slashes.)

Left and right difference are related to fission by the following rules. Note the similarity with residuation and fusion: they are the co-residuals of fission.

(12.24) 1. $\chi \vdash \phi + \psi$ iff $\chi \oslash \psi \vdash \phi$
        2. $\chi \vdash \phi + \psi$ iff $\phi \ominus \chi \vdash \psi$

That is, χ entails the relevant alternatives ϕ or ψ iff χ excluding ψ entails ϕ, and similarly if χ excluding ϕ entails ψ – the directionality of the difference symbol tracking whether the left disjunct or the right disjunct is to be excluded.

We now have two families of (co-)residuated triples, centred on fusion and fission. We need to know how they interact. Take any consecution with formulas before the turnstyle joined by fusion and those after the turnstyle by fission: $\phi \times \psi \vdash \chi + \xi$. Suppose we now add an inhibition to ϕ so as to exclude the left disjunct of the conclusion; if we then had ψ to the right, we would have the right disjunct of the conclusion: that is, (12.25).[37]

(12.25) 1. $\dfrac{\phi \times \psi \vdash \chi + \xi}{\chi \ominus \phi \vdash \xi / \psi}$

       2. $\dfrac{\phi \times \psi \vdash \chi + \xi}{\psi \oslash \xi \vdash \phi \backslash \chi}$

Either of the premises and either of the alternatives from the conclusion can be selected for the initial difference, leaving the others to form the implication formula; it is then a matter of selecting the right directionality for each case. The fact that this extension does respect the order-sensitivity of the calculus we started with is clearly important for linguistic applications; the purpose of making the logic symmetric is not to reintroduce structural rules by the back door.[38]

The rules in (12.25) give two of four possible conclusions of this form derivable from the same premises. The four together are called the **Grishin interactions**. You are asked to work out the remaining two in the exercises.

The fission and difference connectives allow alternative derivations from given premises, other than those based purely on concatenation. They therefore offer another resource for dealing with discontinuity.

12.8 ADDING SEMANTICS

The focus of this chapter has been on the logic of syntax, and it has discussed a number of ways in which the non-directional substructural logic **L** can be enriched to reason about grammar. It is not an introduction to categorial grammar as such; the intention is to introduce some of the logical tools available to categorial grammarians.

Wansing (1982) and Van Benthem (1983) showed how labelling the categories (as formulas) with expressions of the lambda calculus as a semantic translation language leads to correct semantic results for the Lambek Calculus, as for intuitionistic logic. The characterisation of lambda terms for substructural logics has already been discussed in section 11.5, p. 241ff. It is worth looking again at the lambda terms corresponding to the most commonly used structural rules.

(12.26) **B** $f : a/b, g : b/c \vdash \lambda x.f(gx) : a/c$

　　　　　CI $f : a \vdash \lambda p.pf : a/(b \backslash a)$

It is a worthwhile exercise to prove these consecutions by labelled natural deduction and see how the lambda terms fall out. (They are not just stipulated.) In the exercises you are asked to practise these rules in some of the derivations.

While lambda terms derived in the combinatorial process have to be linear (in categorial grammars excluding Contraction and Expansion), there is no such constraint on lexical items. Lambda expressions involving multiple binding have been suggested for lexical items such as reflexive pronouns and equi (control) verbs.

- Derive the following sentences with the appropriate semantics:
  1. Newcastle will beat Barcelona. (With and without composition of 'will' and 'beat'; treat the NPs simply as category NP and type e.)
  2. Politics sucks. (With the type of the subject NP lifted.)
  3. Polyphemus admires himself. (The semantics of the VP node should be $\lambda x.admire(x)(x)$.)

It is possible to label categories not only with lambda expressions for a semantic translation language, but also with other sets of labels. One candidate for this is a set of labels for phonological (or **prosodic**) information.

To see why this is advantageous, it is worth revisiting Saussure's sign-based architecture for language (Chapter 1). In this, sound (signifier) is paired with meaning (signified) at the lexical level (lexical signs) and also at the supralexical level (phrasal or sentential signs), the latter being produced by a combinatorial system which is syntax. The set-up we have been using does not quite reflect this, in that the categories / logical formulas are doing the work both of the combinatorial system and implicitly of signifiers. Providing another component to take care of the prosodic dimension of language can remove from the syntax logic not only phonology, intonation and morphology, but also some of the more superficial aspects of syntax, such as word order. The reasoning here follows Curry's (1961) distinction between tectogrammar and phenogrammar, introduced earlier in this chapter, and frameworks which take this approach sometimes refer to prosody as the phenogrammatical dimension.[39] Phenomena such as discontinuity can also be treated as phenogrammatical.[40]

CVG[41] adds a further dimension of *syntactic* terms, including syntactic functional terms which record grammatical relations such as subject and object; the implication connectives in the categorial logic also come in flavours labelled by grammatical relations. This architecture enables grammatical relations to be treated as syntactic primitives, as in Relational Grammar or LFG, which can be reasoned about without directly referring to either word order or semantics.

EXERCISE 12.8.0.1

1. (a) Derive the following sentences using either natural deduction or the Gentzen Calculus, and labelling them with semantic lambda terms.
     i.   Victoria gave Wilhelm Kilimanjaro
     ii. Emily seems amused.
     iii. Tom is a scholar and a gentleman.
     iv. The man who David saw loves Helen. (Take the relative clause as an intersective modifier.)
   (b) In (12.25), you were given two of the four Grishin interaction rules. State the other two, using the same premise ($\phi \times \psi \vdash \chi + \xi$) and paying attention to the directionality of the difference and implication connectives.

NOTES

1. Richard Montague (1974a).
2. Historically, the term 'categorial' came from Husserl's concept of meaning categories and the principles governing their combination (*Bedeutungsgestalt*). Husserl's notion influenced the Polish School through Twardowski.
3. Van Benthem (1983).
4. The proceedings were published as Oehrle et al. (1988).

5. It is usual to use N rather than NP for the syntactic category denoting individuals. I use NP to avoid confusion with common nouns. Note, however, that this is just a mnemonic and has no connotations of a 'phrase' in the sense of phrase structure grammar.

6. Wood (1993) is a very good general introduction to categorial grammar. More advanced, but still very accessible, is Moortgat (1988).

7. In programming languages, concatenation is often written as +. However, the connection with multiplication is more useful for present purposes.

8. The 'slash' terminology also occurs in Generalized Phrase Structure Grammar (GPSG) and HPSG, though no longer written with a slash. This was inspired by the categorial grammar notion, though it is not the same, and is used for a different purpose (non-local dependencies, rather than subcategorisation as here). They share the idea, however, of a category with 'something missing'. A closer parallel to GPSG's 'slash' in categorial grammar would be the extraction operator ↑.

9. Trees were the format for natural deduction originally used by Gentzen.

10. See Moortgat (2012) for discussion.

11. See Pollard (2008a), de Groote et al. (2009).

12. Muskens (2007).

13. Derivations with Weakening are technically connex, but the notion of connexity would be trivialised.

14. Morrill (2011a) treats expletives as identity functions, which are semantically vacuous but do not involve vacuous abstraction in the syntax.

15. In some of the literature, the fusion or concatenation operator is also referred to as 'composition'. In this chapter, composition refers only to the operation described here, which is a form of function composition.

16. Ades and Steedman (1982).

17. The terminology used here is from phrase structure grammar.

18. This still leaves many issues in the treatment of unbounded dependencies, some of which we will come back to after the formal definitions in the next section.

19. Also known as Raising, but I avoid that terminology here.

20. Ades and Steedman (1982).

21. '..the quintessence of logical categorial grammar' (Morrill (2011a)).

22. The power of the Lambek Calculus was an unresolved question for many decades, but it was proved by Pentus (1993) that, like AB grammar, it is context free. It is, however, NP complete.

23. See, for example, Carpenter (1998), Morrill (2011a).

24. Gentzen used the word '*Sequenz*' for these structures, for which the English translation 'sequent', as a noun, was suggested by Kleene and has become established in the literature. The alternative 'consecution' was suggested by Anderson and Belnap (1975), as combining the idea of sequence ('consecutive') with that of consequence, in particular getting away from the idea of premises as simply whatever bits of information happen to be standing around. 'Consecution' is adopted by Restall (2000) and this book follows suit, though the reader should be aware that it is not the most common usage.

25. See Moortgat (2012).

26. While the right rules are simply the introduction rules, left rules are often less transparent. This is natural, as the latter are the 'elimination' rules which were causing the difficulty, and a certain amount of juggling has had to take place to get left rules with the subformula property. This was part of Gentzen's ingenuity.

27. As usual I omit the symmetric rule where conjunction elimination gives ψ rather than ϕ. For the importance of both conjuncts being derived from the same premise context Γ, see the discussion of relevance logic in Chapter 11.

28. In Gentzen systems, structural rules are explicitly set out as rules rather than left implicit as in the Lemmon style natural deduction proofs we were using. (They are explicit, however, in the style of ND proof used by Gentzen; the difference is, therefore, not one between ND and Gentzen systems as such.)

29. Gentzen proved it for intuitionistic logic, and later for classical logic. It can also be proved for the substructural logics discussed in the last chapter.
30. Morrill (1994), Moortgat (2012).
31. Baldridge (2002).
32. Morrill (1994) is the best reference for this approach. There is a brief summary in Moortgat (2012).
33. Restall (2000), Chapter 2. It is common to use a different symbol for ◊ to indicate that it is not the standard possibility operator.
34. Moortgat (1988), Morrill (2011a).
35. However, the terms 'classical linear logic' and 'intuitionistic linear logic' are very common in the literature.
36. Grishin's work was rediscovered by Lambek (1993) and developed in a number of papers by Moortgat, e.g. Moortgat (2009).
37. The presentation given here is based on Moortgat (2012).
38. It is also a fact that making a constituency-sensitive logic symmetric will not reintroduce Associativity. See Moortgat (2009).
39. The implementation of this idea in categorial grammar goes back to Oehrle's (1988, 1994) theory of multidimensional compositional functions. Every item is an n-tuple and composite functions are defined over these tuples which operate differently on the different components of their arguments.
40. Mansfield et al. (2009).
41. Pollard (2008a).

CHAPTER 13

COMBINATORS

Then feed on thoughts, that voluntarie move
Harmonious numbers; as the wakeful Bird
Sings darkling, and in shadiest Covert hid
Tunes her nocturnal note.[1]

13.1 INTRODUCTION TO COMBINATORS

13.1.1 SOME FAMILIAR EXAMPLES

In the course of this book a number of lambda expressions have been encountered which seem to do nothing except (re)arrange their arguments.

The first of these were copulas or certain auxiliaries in Chapter 5. These take two arguments, a VP denotation and an individual (the grammatical subject), and apply the first to the second to get a sentence denotation. Sometimes auxiliaries also add semantic content, usually of an abstract nature such as tense, modality or negation, but we will ignore that here.

These auxiliaries were given the semantic translation $\lambda x.\lambda y.x(y)$, or, using the more streamlined notation introduced in Chapter 11, $\lambda xy.\, xy$. The β reductions work as follows, with the predicate argument ending up applied to the subject argument.

(13.1) $(\lambda xy.xy)\,(\lambda z.\text{asleep}(z))\,(\text{anna})$
   $\mapsto_\beta (\lambda y.\,(\lambda z.\text{asleep}(z))\,(y))\,(\text{anna})$
   $\mapsto_\beta (\lambda z.\text{asleep}(z))\,(\text{anna})$

If you are not sure about the machinery of the lambda calculus, it might be good to reread the relevant parts of Chapters 5, 10 and 11.

Such an expression consists only of lambda-bound variables. Abstracting away from any extra semantic content it may provide (that is to say, ignoring any constants such as negation or modality), it simply combines its arguments and manipulates them in some way – in this case, feeding them as functor and argument to a step of function application. Such an expression, consisting only of lambda-bound variables, is a **combinatorial term** (Chapter 11). We could hide the internal structure, with its lambdas and variables, and simply write it with the letter A (for Apply), specifying that its effect on its arguments is to apply the first to the second. As we are now writing function application as simple juxtaposition, the rule will be:

(13.2)   Axy = xy

The effect of applying A to x and then y is just the same as the expression xy (x applied to y).

By doing this, we have made the lambda expression (a combinatorial lambda term) into a **combinator**. This is a predefined function, whose behaviour is specified by a rule called an **axiom**. Example (13.2) is the axiom for the combinator called A. Otherwise it does what a combinatorial lambda term does – it rearranges its arguments and nothing else.

Like lambda expressions, combinators may be typed. The type of A, in our example where it repesents an auxiliary, is $(e \rightarrow t) \rightarrow (e \rightarrow t)$. But the pattern is not confined to individual constants and unary predicates, so we will write it more generally as $(a \rightarrow b) \rightarrow (a \rightarrow b)$, without caring what a and b stand for. (In principle this is now a **type schema** rather than a type.) Not all combinators have (finite) types, just as the typed lambda calculus is not the only way of doing lambda calculus. But as the simply typed lambda calculus is usual for linguistic applications, and is also important for the characterisation of substructural logics, the focus here will be on combinators which are simply typed.

Let's have a look at a few more combinators. A slightly more interesting operation than A would be to take two arguments and flip them round, so that the second one applies to the first. In Montague semantics, there is a type-raising operation which, instead of applying the VP to an individual, turns the individual into a function which applies to the VP. I will call this combinator CI, and its behaviour is defined by the following axiom:

(13.3)   CIxy = yx

The type-raising operation takes (for example) an individual of type e and turns it into a function of type $(e \rightarrow t) \rightarrow t$. More generally, we will give CI the type schema $a \rightarrow ((a \rightarrow b) \rightarrow b)$.

The type raising combinator for individuals is not expressed by a lexical item in English in the same way that A can be expressed by an auxiliary. However, type raising is not confined to individuals. Keenan and Faltz (1985) treat sentential complements in the same way – an inflection phrase (IP) denotes a proposition (type t), but a CP denotes a set of properties of propositions (type $(t \rightarrow t) \rightarrow t$). In this case the type raising combinator is lexicalised as the complementiser 'that'.

Another thing we can do to functions is compose them. Some important linguistic applications for this were seen in the previous chapter. The pattern for composition is that one function f applies to the output of a second function g for an input x. So the composition operation takes three objects f, g and x and rearranges them into the pattern f(gx). I will call the combinator that does that B, and here is its axiom:

(13.4)   Bxyz = x(yz)

Note as a rule of thumb how rebracketing the second and third arguments corresponds to composing the first argument with the second.

Before pausing to take stock, let's have another look at the currying operation of Chapter 5. This takes a predicate with an ordered pair of arguments and rearranges it into a higher order function which takes the arguments one at a time. We can also specify an *uncurrying* operation, which does exactly the reverse. Angled brackets are used, as usual, for a pair of arguments.

(13.5) $(\text{CURRY})xyz = x \langle y, z \rangle$

(13.6) $(\text{UNCURRY})x \langle y, z \rangle = xyz$

It is easy to get these formulations the wrong way round. CURRY *takes* its arguments one by one and *uses* the second and third as an ordered pair. UNCURRY does the opposite.

These operations enable us to move between relations of any arity and higher order unary functions at our convenience.

13.1.2 AXIOMS AND STRUCTURAL RULES

Combinators were discovered by Schönfinkel as part of a programme he initiated at the University of Göttingen to eliminate bound variables from first order logic. His procedure for doing so involved rearranging formulae until they are in a form which can be interpreted unambiguously without the use of bound variables. Combinators were originally devices to effect this rearranging. Formulae might be curried (as we now call it) into unary functions, which would then be permuted, rebracketed, duplicated or generally mangled by other combinators until the desired form was reached. In the process a great many important discoveries were made about the most basic building blocks of logic, and computability of functions.

Schönfinkel's work was developed in different directions by two eminent American logicians who spent time in Göttingen at about the same time: Curry and Church. Curry and his students built on Schönfinkel's combinatory logic, and also brought it to a wider audience in the United States and elsewhere. Church developed the lambda calculus, which looks very different – in particular, it is not squeamish about bound variables. However, as has already been seen from these simple examples, it is possible to translate from one into the other, and the two approaches are in an important sense equivalent. When it comes to function application there is little to choose between them. However, it is not obvious how to do abstraction with combinators. This is one of the main differences between the two approaches, and in fact the reason why the lambda calculus needs so many bound variables is because of abstraction, this being the only rule that introduces lambdas and variables. However, this does not mean that the lambda calculus is more powerful than the combinatorial approach; the latter does not *need* abstraction. We will look now at the equivalence between the two.

Another set of operations we have seen whose purpose is to rearrange things are the structural rules in natural deduction. It was also seen in Chapter 11 that these structural rules correspond to particular families of combinatorial terms (by the term characterisation theorem). Recall that in labelled natural deduction, lambda abstraction corresponds to conditional proof, and as proof of theorems proceeds through the making and discharging of assumptions, the corresponding proof terms end up composed entirely of lambda-bound variables, that is, combinatorial terms. In this way, the central place of conditional proof in natural deduction corresponds exactly, through the Curry Howard Isomorphism, to the prevalence of lambda-bound variables in the proof terms.

Combinators, on the other hand, correspond to axiomatic or Hilbert systems (introduced briefly in Chapters 1 and 6). As an axiomatic proof proceeds entirely by *modus ponens* (and substitution of variables), its proof terms use only function application. There are no steps of lambda abstraction because there is no conditional proof. Nonetheless they are equivalent (that is, for a given logic, the same theorems are provable using either method). The same expressiveness which in natural deduction is provided by rules (connective rules and structural rules together) is provided in Hilbert systems in another way: it is contained within the axioms.

Many of the axioms of classical propositional logic correspond in an obvious way to connective rules. Here are a few easy examples: which connective rules do these axioms correspond to?

(13.7) 1. $(\phi \wedge \psi) \rightarrow \phi$
      2. $\phi \rightarrow (\phi \vee \psi)$
      3. $(\phi \rightarrow \neg\phi) \rightarrow \neg\phi$

However, the axioms corresponding to structural rules are not so obvious. They can be found on page 244, where they are listed as the types of combinatorial terms characterising each of the structural rules. Here they are again for convenience. Each is the type of a combinator, whose axioms are also given.[2]

(13.8)	Name	Axiom	Type
	K	$Kxy = x$	$a \rightarrow (b \rightarrow a)$
	W	$Wxy = xyy$	$(a \rightarrow (a \rightarrow b)) \rightarrow (a \rightarrow b)$
	C	$Cxyz = xzy$	$(a \rightarrow (b \rightarrow c)) \rightarrow (b \rightarrow (a \rightarrow c))$
	B	$Bxyz = x(yz)$	$(a \rightarrow b) \rightarrow ((c \rightarrow a) \rightarrow (c \rightarrow b))$
	I	$Ix = x$	$a \rightarrow a$

The axioms of these combinators correspond to the actions of structural rules: K deletes or 'cancels' its second argument (or if you see its arguments as a pair, it projects the first); W duplicates its second argument; C permutes its second and third arguments, and B rebrackets its second and third arguments (or, equivalently, performs function composition on its first and second arguments).

As noted before (Chapter 6), there is more than one way of selecting a set of axioms for a logic, and often the choice involves a trade-off between concision and perspicuity. Similarly with combinators, there are different possible choices for a **basis** (a set of **basic combinators** from which all others can be derived). The set used here is Curry's basis, and is selected because of its transparent correspondence to structural rules (together with the identity axiom **I**).

Another important combinator, which was used as a basic combinator by Schönfinkel, is known as S or 'strong composition'. Its axiom is given here together with its type schema (a formula known in propositional logic as the axiom of self-distribution).

(13.9) Sxyz = xz(yz): $(a \rightarrow (b \rightarrow c)) \rightarrow ((a \rightarrow b) \rightarrow (a \rightarrow c))$

- Prove this formula by labelled natural deduction. The proof term obtained should be the combinatorial lambda term corresponding to S.
- What structural rules are present? Of which substructural logics is the formula a theorem?

In terms of functions, S composes two functions (x and y in the example), both separately applied to the same argument z (which can be termed the 'environment'). Szabolcsi describes it as a 'forked' combinator, which takes the last argument z on both of its prongs. Another way of looking at it is as a combination of Permutation and Composition. If we drop the second occurence of z, then we would simply have C; if we dropped the first occurrence of z, we would have B.

Schönfinkel showed that S and K on their own are a sufficient basis for the whole of combinatorial logic. (Even I is not needed, as it can be defined using them.) By the same reasoning, the types of these two combinators can serve on their own as a set of axioms for the whole of the implicational fragment of intuitionistic logic.

It is a useful exercise to see how this works, so we will use the derivation of I as an example. The first example shows the derivation of I from S and K; we are trying to show that SKKx = Ix (= x). The second shows the derivation of the identity formula a $\rightarrow$ a from the type schema of S applied to that of K in two successive steps of *modus ponens*.

(13.10) SKKx
$\qquad \mapsto$ Kx(Kx)
$\qquad \mapsto$ x

(13.11) 1. $(a \rightarrow (b \rightarrow c)) \rightarrow ((a \rightarrow b) \rightarrow (a \rightarrow c))$ Axiom S
$\qquad$ 2. $d \rightarrow (e \rightarrow d)$ Axiom K
$\qquad$ 3. $(d \rightarrow (e \rightarrow d)) \rightarrow ((d \rightarrow e) \rightarrow (d \rightarrow d))$

Line 1, substituting d for a, e for b, d for c

$\qquad$ 4. $(d \rightarrow e) \rightarrow (d \rightarrow d)$ MPP, lines 3, 2
$\qquad$ 5. $(d \rightarrow (f \rightarrow d)) \rightarrow (d \rightarrow d)$

Line 4, substituting f $\rightarrow$ d for e

$\qquad$ 6. $d \rightarrow (f \rightarrow d)$ Axiom K
$\qquad$ 7. $d \rightarrow d$ MPP, lines 5, 6

The steps of substitution are assumed to find the simplest substitution which will match the shape of the minor premise with the shape of the antecedent of the major premise, in order to enable *modus ponens* (detachment) to be performed. The requirement that it be 'the simplest' is needed to prevent long detours, as in general several substitutions can be found, some of them very long. This matching operation is a form of unification, and the substitution selected is the most general unifier.

These examples show how the system works, but they may also give rise to a suspicion that proofs in this system are a laborious process. If this much work is needed just to derive the identity axiom, one can imagine what it is like for other combinators, whose expressions in terms of S and K may be extremely long. So the bases used in practice often include other predefined combinators as a concession to human weakness. I, at least, is normally included, giving the (easily remembered) SKI basis. The Curry basis has already been introduced, and will be assumed in what remains of this book, unless otherwise specified. There is also the Church basis, which is the Curry basis but with S in place of W.

Human weakness is not the only reason for expanding the basic set of combinators. Another is computational efficiency. In the functional programming paradigm, procedures are modelled as functions, which are given appropriate variables as arguments and return a specified value. The classic functional programming languages Lisp and Haskell are based on the lambda calculus (untyped and typed respectively). However, it was argued by Turner (1979) that combinators offer the possibility of using a set of predefined and precompiled functions representing particularly common operations, with a gain in efficiency. The result of this was the programming language Miranda, based on a selection of combinators known as the Turner set. This set includes a number of combinators which are not 'basic' in the sense described above, but which are chosen for their computational usefulness. These non-basic precompiled combinators are known as **supercombinators**; we will meet a few of Turner's supercombinators later in the chapter.[3]

Steedman[4] has argued for the recasting of categorial grammar into a combinatorial framework, for a somewhat similar reason: sets of combinators such as the Turner set allow for simple and constrained derivations. He further argues that this is preferable from a *psycholinguistic* view, as there is no evidence for the psychological reality of variables or abstraction in language processing. In fact Steedman makes linguistic use of the Turner set itself, though in principle linguists following this line of research could define their own supercombinators if they were linguistically motivated. Steedman's framework of Combinatory Categorial Grammar (CCG) is the main linguistic application of the ideas in this chapter.

13.1.3 COMBINATORS AS BIRDS

In one of Raymond Smullyan's popular books of logic puzzles, *To Mock a Mockingbird*,[5] combinators are treated as songbirds. Songs are made up of the names of birds, and each bird rearranges any song that it hears according to its own rule. The response of a bird X to a song Y is written XY, and corresponds to function application. Not only is the sustained metaphor engaging, but the puzzles based on it go deep into the foundations of logic and computation.

Thanks to Smullyan, the obscure abbreviations we have been using for combinators (and structural rules) become more memorable. Here they are in their new role as songbirds, along with the identity combinator I. The latter, as it just repeats whatever song it hears, is unkindly known as the Idiot Bird.

(13.12)

	Bird name	Hears	Responds
K	Kestrel	X, Y	X
W	Warbler	X, Y	XYY
C	Cardinal	X, Y, Z	XZY
B	Bluebird	X, Y, Z	X(YZ)
S	Starling	X, Y, Z	XZ(YZ)
I	Idiot	X	X

Let's go back briefly to the combinators introduced as motivating examples at the beginning of this chapter. The type raising combinator was given the double-barrelled name CI because it can be derived by applying C to I. The type of CI is a formula known as Assertion, $a \rightarrow ((a \rightarrow b) \rightarrow b)$. This formula was discussed in Chapter 11, where it was pointed out that it is an instance of Permutation.

(13.13) $CIxy \mapsto Iyx \mapsto yx$

Some other important combinators can be obtained by applying basic combinators to I. Applying K to I gives us a combinator KI which projects its second argument instead of its first. If we apply W to I, we get a combinator WI which simply duplicates its argument.

(13.14) $KIxy \mapsto Iy \mapsto y$
(13.15) $WIx \mapsto Ixx \mapsto xx$

In the literature, CI and WI are known As Weak Permutation and Weak Contraction. (KI should presumably be weak weakening, but that sounds odd.) In the ornithological approach to combinators they are given new names. I give them here, as I will sometimes do for others in the chapter, with their abbreviations, axioms, types and also a corresponding lambda expression, for those who find it more natural to think in lambdas.

(13.16)

	Name	Axiom		Type
KI	Kite	$KIxy = y$	$\lambda xy.y$	$a \rightarrow (b \rightarrow b)$
T (= CI)	Thrush	$Txy = yx$	$\lambda xy.yx$	$a \rightarrow ((a \rightarrow b) \rightarrow b)$
M (= WI)	Mockingbird	$Mx = xx$	$\lambda x.xx$	recursive

Note that the last of these does not have any finite type, as it replicates itself infinitely. It therefore does not correspond to anything in the simply typed lambda calculus, though it is of great importance for the theory of computable functions (and is the eponymous hero of Smullyan's book).

The Apply combinator belongs to the family of identity combinators. Whereas the Idiot Bird I takes just one argument and returns it, the Apply combinator takes two and returns them, with the effect of applying the first to the second. It is known as the Idiot Bird once removed, notated I'. The Idiot Bird twice removed, I'', takes three arguments (Ixyz = xyz); it will feature in section 13.6 as the IF-THEN-ELSE function.

The combinators Curry and Uncurry do not normally have bird names. (For what it's worth, I call the first the Spice Bird.)

It is time now for the usual formal syntactic and semantic definitions.

Moses Ilyich Schönfinkel

A Ukrainian Jew by origin, Schönfinkel came to Göttingen to work under Hilbert. He was unhappy about the use of bound variables in logic, and launched his own research project to do away with them. In the process he discovered combinators – originally devices for rewriting formulas until they can be interpreted without variables. In 1924 Schönfinkel opted to return to what was now the Soviet Union. However, the experience of living under Stalin's purges seems to have had a deep psychological effect on him; he was confined to a sanatorium for some time, and never published any further work. He died in the midst of hardships caused by the German advance on Moscow, his remaining manuscripts being burnt by neighbours for fuel. Several discoveries of his became influential in the English-speaking world through Curry, who came to Göttingen to study Schönfinkel's work and, on his return to the United States, enjoyed a more prosperous career.

13.2 COMBINATOR SYNTAX

The syntax of combinatory logic is quite simple. The vocabulary is: (i) a set Con of constants[6] representing named combinators, and (ii) a set Var of 'variables', usually taken from the end of the alphabet, which can stand for anything, including combinators. In principle Con = {S, K}, but, as already discussed, other combinators can be included in the base for various reasons. Assuming the Curry basis, Con = {K, W, C, B, I}. In this book variables are written in lower case to avoid ambiguity. This is not usually needed when the set of named combinators is small – it is common to see KXY where I have written Kxy – but here there will be some situations where ambiguity could arise.

The wfes of combinatory logic are called terms, and are understood as functions; compound terms are formed using a binary concatenation operation which is understood as function application (and is written simply as juxtaposition). There are a number of possible extensions, of which I include here an angled-bracket notation for ordered pairs. The inductive definition goes as follows:

(13.17) 1. If A ∈ Con, then A is a term.
         2. If x ∈ Var, then x is a term.
         3. If M and N are terms, then so is (MN).
         4. If M and N are terms, then so is ⟨M, N⟩.
         5. Nothing else is a term.

Application is left associative, as in the convention followed since Chapter 11, and also outermost brackets are omitted.

Expressions formed by the fourth clause (the pairing operation) will not be considered further, as pairs and all other n-ary relations are assumed to be curried into higher order unary functions. Later in the chapter we will see how to mimic the effect of pairs or lists using a unary combinator. However, it is important to be aware that this is a design decision, not a necessary part of combinatorial logic. It is perfectly possible to define combinators that operate on ordered n-tuples to give other ordered n-tuples (see Carpenter (1998), Chapter 2, for examples). Quine, who famously did not believe in higher order logic, devised a whole combinatory system on this basis.[7]

CL comes with a calculus of term reduction which should be compared carefully with that of the lambda calculus (Chapter 5). A term in the form $CM_1M_2 \ldots M_n$, where C stands for some combinator and the M_i are metavariables standing for anything, is called a **redex** and C is its **head**. The arity n of the combinator can be read from its axiom. The term that results from applying the combinator is a **reduct**.

The axioms of combinators specify a single step of reduction. The relation of **weak reduction**, written $\geq$, is the reflexive transitive closure of this single-step reduction. Its axioms include, besides those of the combinators being used, the axioms of reflexivity and transitivity and also a monotononicity requirement which ensures that subterms which are themselves redexes can be reduced irrespective of context:

Reexivity: $M \geq M$
Transitivity: If $M \geq N$ and $N \geq P$, then $M \geq P$
Monotonicity: If $M \geq N$, then $PM \geq PN$ and $MP \geq NP$

Like $\beta\eta$ reduction in the lambda calculus, weak reduction has the Church–Rosser property.

Terms may, but need not, be typed. If they do have a type, then that type (or more correctly **type schema**, as pointed out in the introduction) is a theorem of intuitionistic logic. If so, then the term records the proof of that theorem. Propositional formulas which are not intuitionistic theorems do not have any corresponding combinators; as types, they are said not to be **inhabited**.

The focus in this chapter, as in the chapters on the lambda calculus, will be on terms that are simply typed, which includes the combinators used for substructural logics.

Basic types are written with lower case letters taken from the beginning of the alphabet. Compound type schemata are defined as follows. The typing system can be extended to include other logical connectives. Here just conjunctive or product types (Chapter 5) are included.

(13.18) 1. If σ and τ are types, then so is $(\sigma \rightarrow \tau)$.
      2. If σ and τ are types, then so is $(\sigma \times \tau)$.
      3. Nothing else is a type.

The type schemas of the basic combinators are specified, and those of other combinators are usually derived by deduction. It is possible to derive even the types for basic combinators from their axioms in CL, by specifying $\rightarrow$ as the residual of function application, and interpreting reduction as the $\vdash$ relation. A few very simple examples:

(13.19) 1. (a) $Ix \vdash x$
         (b) $I \vdash x \rightarrow x$
    2. (a) $Kxy \vdash x$
         (b) $Kx \vdash y \rightarrow x$
         (c) $K \vdash x \rightarrow (y \rightarrow x)$

13.3 COMBINATOR SEMANTICS

As combinatorial logic is equivalent to the lambda calculus, this time it is the semantics section that is relatively short. The relational semantics introduced in Chapter 11 applies here too, the intended interpretations being functional models (for CL in general) and language models (for categorial grammar). In a functional model the first co-ordinate of the ternary relation R is used for functions, the second for the domain and the third the range. For language models, the first co-ordinate supports the type schema of the functor daughter of a constituent, the second that of the argument daughter, and the third that of the mother (the whole connex string).

The frame definition includes the point set P, ternary relation R and designated 'logic world' 0 from the previous chapter, but also other designated 'worlds' for each basic combinator. Thus for a language of CL using the {S, K} base, the frame $\mathcal{F} = \langle P, R, 0, S, K \rangle$, where S and K are points corresponding to their homonymous combinators.

For the Curry base, the worlds for the basic combinators enforce the same conditions on R imposed by structural rules in Chapter 11. Similar remarks apply when a subset of these combinators is selected, in which case we will get the appropriate behaviour for a substructural logic.

13.4 COMBINATORY CATEGORIAL GRAMMAR

Categorial grammars were introduced in the previous chapter, and some motivations for using a combinatorial approach were discussed at the beginning of this one. This section introduces a selection of the linguistic phenomena which have been described using combinators.

13.4.1 NON-STANDARD CONSTITUENTS

The use of composition to form auxiliary–verb combinations was noted in the previous chapter. Instead of using application, which would give a lower VP excluding the auxiliary, the combinator B is used to give a composed verb group which then takes the arguments of the verb as its arguments.

(13.20) Wigan might beat Barcelona
        $np \otimes (np\backslash s)/(np\backslash s) \otimes (np\backslash s)/np \otimes np$
        $np \otimes (np\backslash s)/np \otimes np$ **B**

At this stage of the (incomplete) derivation, we have the composed verb group might · beat, of type (np\s)/np. Recall from the last chapter that the semantic term for the output of this composition was $\lambda xy.\text{might}(\text{beat}(x))y$. The explicit bracketing in the body of the term signals the presence of function composition.

Now consider almost the same situation but with a ditransitive verb, 'give'. The combinatorial rule B will give the wrong results in this case.

(13.21) $\text{np} \otimes (\text{np} \setminus \text{s}) / (np \setminus s) \otimes ((np \setminus s) / np) / \text{np} \otimes \text{np} \otimes \text{np}$

Cancelling the elements in italics will no longer match the composition rule, so a modified rule is needed:

(13.22) $\text{a/b, (b/c)/d} \vdash \text{(a/c)/d}$

Is this a valid instance of composition? It does not look as obvious as the basic composition rule, but if it is written out with implications, it is easy to prove that it is a theorem in a logic with Associativity. Just inspecting it shows that it is another instance of the transitivity of implication.

(13.23) $(a \rightarrow b) \rightarrow ((c \rightarrow (d \rightarrow a)) \rightarrow (c \rightarrow (d \rightarrow b)))$

- Prove (13.23) using natural deduction, and label the formulas with lambda terms.

Labelling the proof should give the lambda expression $\lambda wxyz.w(xyz)$, and substituting *might* and *give* for w and x produces: $\lambda yz.\text{might}(\text{give}(y)(z))$.

But what does the formula in (13.23) mean? The type substitution in (13.24) shows that it combines the type of the auxiliary with the type of the ditransitive verb to give another ditransitive verb with the same NP arguments.

(13.24)

Formula	Type
a	$e \rightarrow t$
b	$e \rightarrow t$
c	e
d	e

What has this shown? We saw that the story about composing auxiliaries and (mono)transitive verbs using B does not work straightforwardly for ditransitive cases, and it is necessary to extend B to a family of combinators. In CCG the combinator we have just created is called B^2, and in Smullyan it is the Blackbird (notated B_1). In principle this extends to B^n (for small n if we are only interested in natural language) to compose auxiliaries with any kind of main verb. These all belong to the family of **composing combinators**. Although in this system they are distinct combinators, the little exercise you have just done illustrates how they are all derivable as theorems in **L**.

- In combinatorial logic, the Blackbird can be defined as BBB (three bluebirds acting in tandem). Normalise the expression BBBwxyz and check that it gives the correct result.

13.4.2 REBRACKETING AND INCREMENTALITY

Phrase structure grammars, and categorial grammars using only application, give a predominantly right-branching analysis for most English sentences. However, there is evidence for the building up of partial structures incrementally during processing, which is better captured by a left-branching analysis.

In CCG this is effected by a combination of type lifting and composition (CI and B), which were seen in action separately in the previous chapter.[8] For example the sentence 'David sent flowers' might be given a left-branching analysis as in Figure 13.1.

This derivation makes 'David sent' into a connex substring. Why would anybody want to do that, when it is not usually regarded as a constituent? There are several possible reasons, besides the desire to model incremental processing.

1. Non-constituent co-ordination. This was mentioned in Chapter 12.
2. Right-node raising: 'David sent, but Natasha didn't accept, flowers.'
3. Parentheticals: 'David sent, I think, flowers.'
4. Intonational phrases: 'David sent *flowers* (not a triffid).'

The argument from non-constituent co-ordination is independent of left-branching structures, and the CI and B combinators can apply to the left as well as to the right. For example, it is proposed to account for 'argument cluster co-ordination'[9] (also treatable as a form of ellipsis). Figure 13.2 shows a derivaton for the complex VP 'gave Mary flowers and Rosa chocolates', in which [Mary flowers] and [Rosa chocolates] are both derived as connex. (Note v_{dt} is an abbreviation for $((np\backslash s)/np)/np$, and v_t for $(np\backslash s)/np$.) In the second line all the non-subject NPs are type-lifted to different types which in line 3 combine by leftward composition.

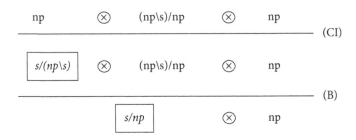

Figure 13.1   Left branching in CCG

Figure 13.2   Argument cluster co-ordination

• What semantic types are involved in lifting (i) direct object and (ii) indirect object NPs from type *e* to the types used in Figure 13.2? Prove the formulas by labelled natural deduction and show that they are both instances of CI.

13.4.3 EXTRACTION AND PARASITIC GAPS

The need for replicating combinators (the equivalent of Contraction) is controversial.

• The following lambda terms are both non-linear, as they involve Contraction. What types of lexical items might they be used for?
  1. λxy.xyy
  2. λxyz.x(yz)z

As long as Contraction is confined to lexical items, it might seem that it is not problematic. The need for it in syntax, however, is suggested by the existence of parasitic gaps. Example (13.25) is from Szabolcsi (1987).

(13.25) He is a man who$_i$ everybody who knows [t$_j$] ends up liking [t$_i$].

Let's give 'everybody who knows [t$_j$]' the category np/np, and 'ends up liking [t$_i$]' vp/np. They have to combine to form the category s/np. What is needed is a rule of the form (a/b)/c, b/c ⊢ a/c, or c → (b → a), c → b ⊢ c → a. Such a rule is provided by the combinator S, whose type schema corresponds to the formula known as self-distribution (13.26).

(13.26) (a → (b → c)) → ((a → b) → (a → c))

You have already met this in example (13.9) on page 287, and the lambda term for it is λxyz.xy(xz). By substituting *like* for *x* and *knower-of* for *y* (and ignoring the quantifier, which is irrelevant to the point at hand) we get λz. like(z)(knower-of(z)), which seems correct for the gapped sentence in the example.

13.5 MORE COMBINATORS

A number of basic combinators were introduced in section 13.1, and some non-basic 'supercombinators' later on. It is useful to look at how more complicated combinators can be constructed, even if most linguistic work at present revolves around a few basic ones. Smullyan is a fertile source of non-basic combinators, and his avian names for them have become quite well entrenched in the literature. This section is intended to be suggestive only, not to be a complete inventory.

Using Curry's base, I wil classify combinators which show the characteristic actions of K, W, C and B as cancellators, replicators, permutators and associators (or composers) respectively. The usefulness of thinking in such 'families' was exemplified in section 13.4.1.

Another important dimension of classification is the number of arguments on which a combinator operates. A combinator can appear at the head of a term of any length, but its arity is taken as extending only to the last argument on which it has an effect. For example the Thrush can be followed by three variables, with the effect $Txyz = yxz$, but its arity is still only two, the z being there just for the ride. All the combinators considered so far have had a maximum arity of three.

Let's start by completing the inventory of permutators with arity up to three, as we have so far missed some important ones. In principle the number of permutations of three arguments is $3! = 6$. Of these, one is to leave the arguments in the same order, so that is another identity combinator (the Idiot Bird twice removed, or I^{**}). The combinator which flips its first two arguments and leaves the third alone is just a version of the Thrush, T, as just discussed; and we have also seen the Cardinal, C, which flips its last two arguments. The three other permutations are given here (without types because some of them are in the exercises).

(13.27)

	Name	Axiom		Type
R	Robin	$Rxyz = yzx$	$\lambda xyz.yzx$	?
V	Vireo	$Vxyz = zxy$	$\lambda xyz.zxy$	?
F	Finch	$Fxyz = zyx$	$\lambda xyz.zyx$	?

The Vireo is important because it mimics the effect of ordered pairs (an alternative to uncurrying). It makes its first two arguments x and y the arguments of z. For example applying the Vireo to John and Mary (and a third argument z) gives the result $z(john)(mary)$, a curried ordered pair.

We can then manipulate this pair by using K and KI as projection functions. Recall that K cancels its second argument (i.e. projects the first), while KI does the opposite. So K(john)(mary) will project John, while KI(john)(mary) projects Mary. This idea will play an important role in section 13.6 at the end of this chapter.

Another family of three-argument combinators combines permutation and composition. The head of the family is the combinator Q (the Queer Bird). This corresponds to a structural rule called Twisted Associativity, which allows premises to be commuted when being composed (though not in other contexts). Its type schema is known in propositional logic as the axiom of Suffixing. Like the type of B, which is the axiom of Prefixing, it represents the transitivity of implication, but the proof term obtained also involves a 'twist' in the first two arguments. In terms of function composition, it represents composing Y with X instead of composing X with Y.

The whole family, all of which have equally curious names, is given here. They have the same general shape but each inflicts a different twist.

(13.28)

	Name	Axiom		Type
Q	Queer	$Qxyz = y(xz)$	$\lambda xyz.y(xz)$	$(a \to b) \to ((b \to c) \to (a \to c))$
Q_1	Quixotic	$Q_1xyz = x(zy)$	$\lambda xyz.x(zy)$	
Q_2	Quizzical	$Q_2xyz = y(zx)$	$\lambda xyz.y(zx)$	
Q_3	Quirky	$Q_3xyz = z(xy)$	$\lambda xyz.z(xy)$	
Q_4	Quacky	$Q_4xyz = z(yx)$	$\lambda xyz.z(yx)$	

The only non-trivial composing operation on three arguments is the Bluebird. With four or more there is more variety. In general, the number of composing operations possible with n arguments is the same as the number of full binary trees with n leaves, which is given by the series of Catalan numbers: $\{1, 1, 2, 5, 14, 42 \ldots\}$.[10] We will have a quick look at the ones with four arguments, and a few with five.

With four arguments there are four non-trivial operations, one of which is just the Bluebird. There is also the Blackbird, which you met in section 13.4.1. The other new ones are the Dove, which performs composition like the Bluebird but at a 'distance', and the Becard, which performs a double composition $f \circ g \circ h$. The Becard is a member of the Turner set.

(13.29)

	Name	Axiom	Type
D	Dove	$Dwxyz = wx(yz)$	
B_1	Blackbird	$B_1wxyz = w(xyz)$	
B_3	Becard	$B_3wxyz = w(x(yz))$	

- Compare the axiom for the Becard with that of the Blackbird. Can you think of a linguistic application of the Becard to verb groups?

Here are a few with four arguments which both compose and permute, but do not replicate or cancel: in other words they are linear combinators. In fact the first, the Goldfinch (G), can be used together with I as a **basis** from which all linear combinators[11] can be derived. The second is a member of the Turner set, though not of Smullyan's aviary.

(13.30)

	Name	Axiom	Type
G	Goldfinch	$Gwxyz = wz(xy)$	
C'	(none)	$C'wxyz = w(xz)y$	

Replicating combinators are often not typable, as there are many configurations in which one of the arguments ends up applying to itself. These untyped combinators are tangential to the purposes of this book, though important to the theory of recursive functions. Here are a few of both varieties (typed and untyped). In which cases will the type schema be recursive (a function is applied to itself)?

(13.31)

Name	Axiom	Type
L	Lark	$Lxy = x(yy)$	
O	Owl	$Oxy = y(xy)$	
U	Turing's Bird	$Uxy = y(xxy)$	
H	Hummingbird	$Hxyz = xyzy$	

13.6 PAIRING AND TRUTH FUNCTIONS

The last three chapters have been largely about taking classical logic apart and looking at the elements that make it up. In particular, they have focused on logics without K, as this has to be rejected for the linguistic applications under discussion. This final section of the book looks at how to put things back together again, and do classical truth table logic using combinators. As you might expect for truth functions, a crucial role is played by the cancellator combinators which are associated with Weakening.

As already indicated, it is possible to emulate ordered pairs using just higher order unary combinators. The key combinator here is the Vireo (V), which makes its first two arguments x and y into the arguments of a curried binary relation, for which z can be thought of as a place holder. V thus acts as a pairing operation. It is then possible to extract either element of the pair by using the Kestrel (K) or Kite (KI) respectively, which act as projection functions.

(13.32) 1. $Vxyz = zxy$
        2. $VxyK = Kxy = x$
        3. $Vxy(KI) = KIxy = y$

An important application of pairing is to represent the set of truth values $\{0, 1\}$. As remarked in Chapter 2, it does not matter what we call the two elements, as long as they behave in a suitable way. For this application, it is convenient to call K (the projection of the first element) *true* and KI (the projection of the second element) *false*.

First of all, note what happens with a sequence xyz when x can be either K or KI. If it is K, then y is returned (projected), and if it is KI then z is returned. This can be thought of as the ternary IF-THEN-ELSE connective, read as 'If x then y, else z'.[12]

The familiar propositional connectives can then be defined as follows.

As the logical connectives will be encoded using only function application, it is best to think of them in prefix notation, with the connective first and then its arguments (which in the case of binary connectives will be curried). You might want to refer back to Chapter 2 for prefix notation and Chapter 5 for the treatment of Boolean connectives as curry functions.

Let's look at conjunction first, which we will write as $\wedge \, \phi \, \psi$. As propositions, ϕ and ψ will both end up represented by their truth values, K or KI. We now want a combinator for $\wedge$ which will give the right result, namely that if ϕ is false, then the conjunction is immediately false, while if ϕ is true, then the truth value of the conjunction is the truth value of ψ. The $\wedge$ combinator must therefore inspect ϕ, go straight to *false* if ϕ is false, and otherwise return the value of ψ. So what we need now is for the next argument after ψ to be *false*. Then if ϕ is false (KI) then it will cancel ψ and skip to *false*, while if it is true (K) then it will move to ψ (and cancel the extra *false* that we have put after it).

So we need a combinator C which will encode $\wedge$ ϕ ψ as $\phi\psi$(KI). The combinator which will do this is the Robin (R), the three-place permuting combinator which pushes its first argument (KI) to the end. If we give it KI as its first argument we get the desired result, and therefore the encoding for $\wedge$ is R(KI). You might like to check the four possible values of ϕ and ψ and verify that in all cases R(KI)$\phi\psi$ gives the right truth value for the conjunction.

Now let's try negation. Here we simply want to inspect ϕ, return false if it is true, and return true if it is false. So we want a combinator C which encodes $\neg\phi$ as ϕ *false true*. If ϕ is true (K) then it will return the first argument (*false*), cancelling the second, and vice versa if ϕ is false. The combinator which will do this for us is the Vireo, which pushes the pair KI and K to after ϕ. The encoding for negation is thus V(KI)K.

For disjunction, we want the same approach as for conjunction, but this time ϕ, if true, must return *true* for the conjunction, and if ϕ is false move on to ψ and return its value. So this time we need to insert a *true* in between the disjuncts, which will be returned if ϕ is true (K) and passed over if ϕ is false (KI).

- Which combinator, when fed the arguments *true*, ϕ and ψ will give the required result?

These definitions can be stated more economically as follows, though they are not very transparent at first. Note that the *true* or *false* in these definitions will be the same as the value of at least one of ϕ and ψ. The connectives can then be defined as follows:

(13.33) 1. $\wedge xy = xyx$
      2. $\vee xy = xxy$

It is possible to do something similar with negation:

(13.34) $\neg xyz = xzy$

This reverses the effect x will have on its own arguments y and z, so that if x is K it will act like KI and vice versa.

This encoding of ordered pairs and of Boolean truth values and truth functions is known as the Church encoding. (Church actually formulated them in the lambda calculus, and one of the exercises will be to convert them.) Church encodings also exist for lists and Peano numerals, which allow the expected list operations and arithmetic operations. The demonstration that this is possible was what convinced

Church that the lambda calculus is a suitable formalism for expressing all computable functions.

EXERCISE 13.6.0.1

1. Derive the following sentences using the ideas from CCG discussed in the text.
   (a) Sally sent David to Otago and Jeremy to Tromso.
   (b) Igor promised and may have given surprises to Katia.
   (c) The book which you reviewed without reading is awful.
2. Select from the following terms which are definitions of (i) B, (ii) D, (iii) R, (iv) A (I'), (v) M (WI).
   (a) BB
   (b) BBT
   (c) SII
   (d) S(KS)K
   (e) S(SK)
3. Prove the following formulas by labelled natural deduction. They are all type schemas inhabited by combinators in this chapter. Decide, by inspecting the lambda terms, which combinators they correspond to.
   (a) $(a \to (b \to c)) \to (a \to ((d \to b) \to (d \to c)))$
   (b) $a \to (b \to ((a \to (b \to c)) \to c))$
   (c) $(a \to b) \to ((c \to a) \to ((d \to c) \to (d \to b)))$
   (d) $(a \to (b \to a)) \to (a \to (b \to b))$
   (e) $(a \to (b \to c)) \to ((d \to b) \to (d \to (a \to c)))$
4. (a) Convert the combinatorial encodings given in the last section for $\wedge$, $\vee$ and $\neg$ into lambda terms.
   (b) Work out combinatorial encodings for implication (easy) and exclusive or (difficult).

NOTES

1. Milton, *Paradise Lost*, III 37–40.
2. Note that the word **axiom** is being used here in two different senses. The rule describing the behaviour of each combinator is called an axiom (of combinatorial logic). The type schema of a combinator, considered as a formula, is an axiom of propositional logic.
3. Another programming language based on combinators is Unlambda, which uses the SKI basis.
4. Steedman (1986) and much subsequent work.
5. Smullyan (1962).
6. These are usually Roman capital letters, but other symbols and diacritics may be thrown in.
7. Quine (1981); see also Gamut (1990), section 5.6.
8. Or as Steedman (2000) puts it, a thrush and a bluebird operating in tandem. (The thrush is Smullyan's name for CI.)
9. Based on Dowty (1988), cf. Steedman and Baldridge (2011). Dowty proposes this operation for ditransitive VPs in general.

10. The formula is $C_n = \dfrac{(2n)!}{(n+1)!\, n!}$. For a term of length n the number of composing opera-
    tions is C_{n-1}. The restriction to *full* binary trees is to exclude non-branching non-terminal
    nodes.

11. Recall that linear combinatorial terms are those in which each variable is bound exactly
    once. A linear combinator can permute and rebracket, but not replicate or cancel.

12. In this context – that is, provided that its first argument ends up as either K or KI – the
    Idiot Bird twice removed (I^{**}) can serve as the IF-THEN-ELSE connective: Ixyz = xyz. The
    first argument x is the condition, the second one the THEN, and the third one the ELSE.

BIBLIOGRAPHY

Ades, A. and M. Steedman (1982), 'On the order of words' in *Linguistics and Philosophy* 4, pp. 517–58.

Ajdukiewicz, Kazimierz (1967), 'Die syntaktische Konnexität'. Translation in S. McCall (ed.), *Polish Logic, 1920–39*, Oxford: Oxford University Press.

Anderson, Alan Ross and Nuel Belnap (1975), *Entailment: The Logic of Relevance and Necessity*, Vol. 1. Princeton: Princeton University Press.

Anderson, Alan Ross, Nuel Belnap and J. Michael Dunn (1992), *Entailment: The Logic of Relevance and Necessity*, Vol. 2. Princeton: Princeton University Press.

Bach, E. (1981), 'Discontinuous constituents in generalized categorial grammars' in V. Burke and J. Pustejovsky (eds), *Proceedings of the 11th Annual Meeting of the Northeastern Linguistics Society*. Amherst: University of Massachusetts, pp. 1–12.

Baldridge, Jason (2002), *Lexically Specified Derivational Control in Combinatory Categorial Grammar*. PhD dissertation, University of Edinburgh.

Barcan, R. (1946), 'A functional calculus of first order based on strict implication' in *Journal of Symbolic Logic* 11 (1), p. 116.

Bar-Hillel, J. (1953), 'A quasi-arithmetical notation for syntactic description' in *Language* 29, pp. 47–58.

Bar-Hillel, J., C. Gaifman and E. Shamir (1964), 'On categorial and phrase structure grammars' in J. Bar-Hillel (ed.), *Language and Information*. Boston: Addison-Wesley, pp. 99–105.

Barker, C. (2002), 'Continuations and the nature of quantification' in *Natural Language Semantics* 10 (3), pp. 211–42.

Barker, C. (2004), 'Continuations in natural language' in H. Thielecke (ed.), *CW04: Proceedings of the 4th ACM SIGPLAN Continuations Workshop*, Tech. Rep. CSR-04-1: 1–11. Birmingham, 2004.

Barwise, J. (1993), 'Constraints, channels and the flow of information' in P. Aczel, D. Israel, V. Katagiri and S. Peters (eds), *Situation Theory and Its Applications*, Vol. 3. Stanford: Center for the Study of Language and Information.

Barwise, Jon and Robin Cooper (1981), 'Generalized quantifiers and natural language' in *Linguistics and Philosophy* 4 (2), pp. 159–219.

Barwise, Jon and John Perry (1983), *Situations and Attitudes*. Cambridge, MA: MIT Press.

Barwise, J. and J. Etchemendy (1990), 'Information, infons and inference' in Robin Cooper, Kuniaki Mukai and Jon Barwise (eds), *Situation Theory and Its Applications*, Vol. 2. Stanford: Center for the Study of Language and Information.

Barwise, J. and J. Etchemendy (1995), 'Heterogeneous logic' in J. Glasgow, H. Narayanan and B. Chandrasekaran (eds), *Diagrammatic Reasoning: Cognitive and Computational Perspectives*. Cambridge, MA: MIT Press, pp. 209–32.

Barwise, Jon and Jerry Seligman (1997), *Information Flow: The Logic of Distributed Systems*.

Cambridge Tracts in Theoretical Computer Science, Cambridge: Cambridge University Press.

Bayes, Thomas (1763), 'An essay towards solving a problem in the doctrine of chances' in *Philosophical Transactions of the Royal Society of London* 53, pp. 370–418.

Beaver, D. (1997), 'Presupposition' in J. van Benthem and A. ter Meulen (eds), *The Handbook of Logic and Language*. Amsterdam: North Holland Press.

Belnap, N. D. (1977), 'A useful four-valued logic' in J. M. Dunn and G. Epstein (eds), *Modern Uses of Multiple-Valued Logics*. Dordrecht: D. Reidel Publishing, pp. 8–37.

Bobzien, S. (2014), 'Ancient logic' in E. N. Zalta (ed.), *The Stanford Encyclopedia of Philosophy*, Spring. URL = http://plato.stanford.edu/archives/spr2013/entries/logic-ancient/

Boole, George (1854), *An Investigation of the Laws of Thought, on Which are Founded the Mathematical Theories of Logic and Probability*. London: Macmillan.

Bresnan, Joan (ed.) (1982), *The Mental Representation of Grammatical Relations*. Cambridge, MA: MIT Press.

Cann, Ronnie (1993), *Formal Semantics: An Introduction*. Cambridge: Cambridge University Press.

Cann, Ronnie, Ruth Kempson and Eleni Grigoromichelaki (2009), *Semantics: An Approach to Meaning in Language*. Cambridge: Cambridge University Press.

Carnap, Rudolf (1947), *Meaning and Necessity: A Study in Semantics and Modal Logic*. Chicago: University of Chicago Press.

Carpenter, R. (1998), *Type Logical Semantics*. Cambridge, MA: MIT Press.

Chierchia, Gennaro and Sally McConnell-Ginet (1990). *Meaning and Grammar*. Cambridge, MA: MIT Press.

Chierchia, Gennaro and Sally McConnell-Ginet (2000), *Meaning and Grammar - 2nd edition: An Introduction to Semantics*. Cambridge, MA: MIT Press.

Chomsky, Noam (1957), *Syntactic Structures*. The Hague: Mouton.

Chomsky, Noam (1966), *Cartesian Linguistics: A Chapter in the History of Rationalist Thought*. New York: Harper & Row.

Church, A. (1932), 'A set of postulates for the foundation of logic', in *Annals of Mathematics*, Series 2, 33: 346–66.

Church, A. (1940), 'A formulation of the simple theory of types' in *Journal of Symbolic Logic* 5.

Cooper, Richard (1990), 'Persistence and structural determination' in Robin Cooper, Kuniaki Mukai and Jon Barwise (eds), *Situation Theory and Its Applications*, Vol. 2. Stanford: Center for the Study of Language and Information, pp. 295–310.

Cooper, Robin (1996), 'The role of situations in generalized quantifiers' in S. Lappin (ed.), *Handbook of Contemporary Semantic Theory*. London: Blackwell, pp. 65–86.

Cooper, Robin (1997), 'Austinian propositions, Davidsonian events and perception complements' in J. Ginzburg, Z. Khasidashvili, J.-J. Levy and E. Vallduvi (eds), *The Tbilisi Symposium on Language, Logic and Computation: Selected Papers*. Stanford: Center for the Study of Language and Information, pp. 19–34.

Cooper, Robin (2005), 'Records and record types in semantic theory' in *Journal of Logic and Computation* 15 (2), pp. 99–112.

Cooper, Robin (2011), 'Type theory and semantics in flux' in R. Kempson, T. Fernando and N. Asher (eds), *Handbook of the Philosophy of Science*. Vol. 14: Philosophy of Linguistics. Amsterdam: Elsevier.

Cornell, T. (2004), 'Lambek calculus for transformational grammar' in *Research on Language and Computation* 2, pp. 105–26.

Crolard, T. (2004), 'A formula-as-types interpretation of subtractive logic' in *Logic and Computation* 14 (4), pp. 529–70.

Crouch, Dick and Josef van Genabith (2000), *Linear Logic for Linguists*, Introductory Course, European Summer School in Logic, Language and Information.

Curry, H. (1961), 'Some logical aspects of grammatical structure' in R. Jakobson (ed.), *Structure of Language in its Mathematical Aspects*. Providence: American Mathematical Society, pp. 56–68.

Curry, Haskell and Robert Feys (1958), *Combinatory Logic*, Amsterdam: North-Holland Publishing Company.

Dalrymple, Mary (2001), *Lexical Functional Grammar*, Syntax and Semantics 34. Bingley: Emerald Group Publishing.

Davidson, D. (1967), 'Truth and meaning' in *Synthèse 17*.

De Groote, P. (2001), 'Type raising, continuations, and classical logic' in *Proceedings of the 13th Amsterdam Colloquium*, pp. 97–101.

De Groote, P., S. Pogodalla and C. Pollard (2009), 'On the syntax-semantics interface: from convergent grammar to abstract categorial grammar', Inria.

De Saussure, Ferdinand (1915), *Cours de Linguistique Générale*. Ed. Charles Bailly and Albert Sechehey. Geneva.

Devlin, Keith (1991), *Logic and Information*. Cambridge: Cambridge University Press.

Donnellan, K. (1966), 'Reference and definite descriptions' in *Philosophical Review*, 77: 281–304.

Dowty, D. (1988), 'Type-raising, functional composition and nonconstituent coordination' in R. Oehrle, E. Bach and D. Wheeler (eds), *Categorial Grammars and Natural Language Structures*. Dordrecht: D. Reidel Publishing.

Dummett, Michael (1977), *Elements of Intuitionism*. Oxford: Oxford University Press.

Dunn, J. M. (1995), 'Positive modal logic' in *Studia Logica* 55, pp. 301–17.

Dunn, J. M. and G. Restall (2003), 'Relevance logic' in D. Gabbay and F. Günthner (eds), *Handbook of Philosophical Logic*, Vol. 10 London: Kluwer, pp. 1–128.

Fenstad, J. E., P. K. Halvorsen, T. Langholm and J. van Benthem (1985), *Situations, Language and Logic*, Vol. 34 of Studies in Linguistics and Philosophy. Dordrecht: D. Reidel Publishing.

Fox, Chris and Shalom Lappin (2005), *Foundations of Intensional Semantics*. London: Blackwell.

Frege, Gottlob (1879), *Begriffsschrift, eine der arithmetischen nachgebildete Formelsprache des reinen Denkens*. Halle: Louis Nebert.

Frege, G. (1892), 'Über Sinn und Bedeutung', in *Zeitschrift für Philosophie und philosophische Kritik* 100, p. 2550.

Gabbay, Dov (1996), *Labelled Deductive Systems*. Oxford: Oxford University Press.

Gabbay, D. and Ruth Kempson (1991), 'Natural language content: a proof-theoretic perspective' in *Proceedings of the Eighth Amsterdam Colloquium*. Amsterdam: Institute for Logic, Language and Computation, pp. 173–96.

Gabbay, Dov and Nicola Olivetti (2000), *Goal-Directed Proof Theory*. Dordrecht: Springer.

Gaines, B. (1978), 'Fuzzy and probability uncertainty logics' in *Information and Control* 38, pp. 154–69.

Gallin, Daniel (1975), *Intensional and Higher Order Modal Logic*. Amsterdam: North Holland Press.

Gamut, L. T. F. (1990), *Language, Logic and Meaning*. 2 Vols. Chicago: University of Chicago Press.

Garson, J. (2013), 'Modal logic' in E. N. Zalta (ed.), *The Stanford Encyclopedia of Philosophy*, Spring. URL = http://plato.stanford.edu/archives/spr2013/entries/logic-modal/

Geach, Peter (1972). 'A program for syntax', in D. Davidson and G. Harman (eds), *Semantics of Natural Language*, pp. 483–97. Dordrecht: Reidel.

Gentzen, G. (1934), 'Untersuchungen über das logische Schliessen', in *Mathematische Zeitschrift*

39, pp. 176–219 and pp. 405–31. Translation in M. E. Szabo (ed.) (1969), *The Collected Papers of Gerhard Gentzen*. Amsterdam: North-Holland Publishing Company.

Ginzburg, Jonathan and Ivan Sag (2000), *Interrogative Investigations: The Form, Meaning and Use of English Interrogatives*. Stanford: Center for the Study of Language and Information.

Girard, J.-Y. (1987), 'Linear logic' in *Theoretical Computer Science*, 50, pp. 1–102.

Gregory, H. (2002), 'Relevance logic and natural language semantics' in *Proceedings of the Conference on Formal Grammar*, Trento.

Grishin, V. N. (1983), 'On a generalization of the Ajdukiewicz-Lambek system' in A. Mikhailov (ed.), *Studies in Nonclassical Logics and Formal Systems*. Moscow: Nauka, pp. 315–34.

Haack, Susan (1978), *Philosophy of Logics*. Cambridge: Cambridge University Press.

Hájek, A. (2001), 'Probability, logic and probability logic' in L. Goble (ed.), *The Blackwell Companion to Philosophical Logic*, pp. 362–84.

Hájek, Petr (1998), *Metamathematics of Fuzzy Logic*. London: Kluwer.

Hájek, P. (2010), 'Fuzzy logic' in E. N. Zalta (ed.), *The Stanford Encyclopedia of Philosophy*, Fall. URL = http://plato.stanford.edu/archives/fall2010/entries/logic-fuzzy/

Hamblin, C. L. (1971), 'Instants and intervals' in *Studium Generale* 24, pp. 127–34.

Heim, Irene and Angelika Kratzer (1998), *Semantics in Generative Grammar*. London: Blackwell.

Helman, G. (1992), 'Relevant predication and relevant functions', in A. R. Anderson, N. D. Belnap and J. M. Dunn *Entailment: the Logic of Relevance and Necessity*, Princeton: Princeton University Press.

Hendricks, V. and J. Symons (2014), 'Epistemic logic' in E. N. Zalta (ed.), *The Stanford Encyclopedia of Philosophy*, Spring. URL = http://plato.stanford.edu/archives/spr2013/entries/logic-epistemic/

Heyting, A. (1930), 'Die formalen Regeln der intuitionistischen Logik' in *Sitzungsberichte der Preussischen Akademie der Wissenschaften*, pp. 42–71 and pp. 158–69.

Hintikka, Jaakko (1962), *Knowledge and Belief: An Introduction to the Logic of the Two Notions*. Ithaca: Cornell University Press.

Horn, Lawrence (1989), *A Natural History of Negation*. Chicago: University of Chicago Press.

Howard, W. (1980), 'The formulae-as-types notion of construction' in J. P. Seldin and J. R. Hindley (eds), *To H.B. Curry: Essays on Combinatory Logic, Lambda Calculus and Formalism*. London: Academic Press, pp. 479–90 (original manuscript 1969).

Hughes, George and Max Cresswell (1996), *A New Introduction to Modal Logic*. London: Taylor and Francis.

Israel, David and John Perry (1990), 'What is information?' in P. Hanson (ed.), *Information, Language and Cognition*. Vancouver: University of British Columbia Press, pp. 1–19.

Jacobson, P. (1990), 'Raising as function composition' in *Linguistics and Philosophy* 13, pp. 423–76.

Jacobson, P. (1999), 'Towards a variable-free semantics' in *Linguistics and Philosophy* 22, pp. 117–84.

Johnson, David and Paul Postal (1980), *Arc Pair Grammar*. Princeton: Princeton University Press.

Kahneman, Daniel (2011), *Thinking, Fast and Slow*. New York: Farrar, Straus and Giraux.

Kamp, Hans (1968), *Tense Logic and the Theory of Linear Order*. PhD dissertation, University of California, Los Angeles.

Karttunen, L. (1973), 'Presuppositions of compound sentences', in *Linguistic Inquiry* 4, pp. 168–93.

Keenan, E. (1996), 'The semantics of determiners' in S. Lappin (ed.), *Handbook of Contemporary Semantic Theory*. London: Blackwell.

Keenan, Edward and Leonard Faltz (1985), *Boolean Semantics for Natural Language*. Dordrecht: Springer.

Keenan, E. and Jonathan Stavi (1986), 'A semantic characterization of natural language determiners' in *Linguistics and Philosophy* 9 (3), pp. 253–326.

Kempson, Ruth (1975), *Presupposition and the Delimitation of Semantics*. Cambridge: Cambridge University Press.

Klima, Gyula (tr.) (2001), *John Buridan: Summulae de Dialectica*, Yale Library of Medieval Philosophy. New Haven: Yale University Press.

Kripke, S. (1963), 'Semantical analysis of modal logic I: normal modal propositional calculi', in *Zeitschrift für mathematische Logik und Grundlagen der Mathematik* 9, pp. 67–96.

Kripke, S. (1980), *Naming and Necessity*. Oxford: Blackwell.

Lagerlund, H. (2012), 'Medieval theories of the syllogism' in E. N. Zalta (ed.), *The Stanford Encyclopedia of Philosophy*, Winter. URL = http://plato.stanford.edu/archives/win2012/entries/medieval-syllogism/

Lambek, J. (1958), 'The mathematics of sentence structure' in *American Mathematical Monthly* 65, pp. 154–70.

Lambek, J. (1993), 'From categorial to bilinear logic' in Kosta Došen and Peter Schroeder-Heister (eds), *Substructural Logics*, Oxford: Oxford University Press, pp. 207–37.

Landman, Fred (1991), *Structures for Semantics*, Studies in Linguistics and Philosophy. Dordrecht: Springer.

Lappin, Shalom (ed.) (1996), *Handbook of Contemporary Semantic Theory*. London: Blackwell.

Lemmon, Edward John and Dana Scott (1977), *An Introduction to Modal Logic*. London: Blackwell.

Lemon, O. and Ian Pratt (1998), 'On the insufficiency of linear diagrams for syllogisms' in *Notre Dame Journal of Formal Logic* 39 (4), pp. 573–80.

Levin, Beth and Malka Rappaport Hovav (1995), *Unaccusativity: At the Syntax-lexical Semantics Interface*. Cambridge, MA: MIT Press.

Lewis, Clarence Irvine and Cooper H. Langford (1932), *Symbolic Logic*. London: Dover.

Lewis, D. (1970), 'General semantics' in *Synthèse* 22, pp. 18–67.

Lewis, David (1986), *On the Plurality of Worlds*. London: Blackwell.

Łukasiewicz, Jan (1920), 'On 3-valued logic' in *Ruch Filozoficzny* 5.

Lyons, John (1981), *Language, Meaning and Context*. London: Fontana.

Mansfield, L., S. Martin, C. Pollard and C. Worth (2009), 'Phenogrammatical labelling in convergent grammar: the case of wrap', Ohio State University.

Mares, E. (1997), 'Relevant logic and the theory of information' in *Synthese* 109, pp. 345–60.

Meinong, Alexius (1915), *Über Möglichkeit und Wahrscheinlichkeit: Beiträge zur Gegenstandstheorie und Erkenntnistheorie*. Leipzig: J. A. Barth.

Meredith, C. and Arthur Prior (1963), 'Notes on the axiomatics of the propositional calculus' in *Notre Dame Journal of Formal Logic* 4 (3), pp. 171–87.

Montague, R. (1974a), 'English as a formal language' [EFL] in R. Thomason (ed.), *Formal Philosophy. Selected Papers of Richard Montague*. New Haven: Yale University Press.

Montague, R. (1974b), 'Universal grammar' [UG] in R. Thomason (ed.), *Formal Philosophy. Selected Papers of Richard Montague*. New Haven: Yale University Press.

Montague, R. (1974c), 'The proper treatment of quantification in ordinary English' [PTQ] in R. Thomason (ed.), *Formal Philosophy. Selected Papers of Richard Montague*. New Haven: Yale University Press.

Moortgat, Michael (1988), *Categorical Investigations: Logical and Linguistic Aspects of the Lambek Calculus*. Berlin: de Gruyter.

Moortgat, M. (2009), 'Symmetric categorial grammar' in *Journal of Philosophical Logic* 38 (6), pp. 681–710.

Moortgat, M. (2012), 'Typelogical grammar' in E. N. Zalta (ed.), *The Stanford Encyclopedia of Philosophy*, Winter. URL http://plato.stanford.edu/archives/win2012/entries/typelogical-grammar/

Moot, Richard and Christian Retoré (2012), *The Logic of Categorial Grammars*. Heidelberg: Springer.

Morrill, Glyn (1994), *Type Logical Grammar: Categorial Logic of Signs*. Dordrecht, London: Kluwer.

Morrill, Glyn (2011a), *Categorial Grammar: Logical Syntax, Semantics, and Processing*. Oxford: Oxford University Press.

Morrill, G. (2011b), 'Logical grammar' in R. Kempson, T. Fernando and N. Asher (eds), *Handbook of the Philosophy of Science, Vol. 14: Philosophy of Linguistics*. Amsterdam: Elsevier.

Morrill, G. and R. Carpenter (1990), 'Compositionality, implicational logics, and theories of grammar' in *Linguistics and Philosophy* 13 (4), pp. 383–92.

Muskens, Reinhart (1996), *Meaning and Partiality*, Studies in Logic, Language and Information. Stanford: Center for the Study of Language and Information and FoLLI.

Muskens, R. (2007), 'Separating syntax and combinatorics in categorial grammar'in *Research on Language and Computation* 5 (3), pp. 267–85.

Nguyen, H. T., M. Mukaidono and V. Kreinovich (2002), 'Probability of implication, logical version of Bayes' Theorem and fuzzy logic operations', Departmental Technical Report, University of Texas at El Paso.

Oehrle, R. (1988), 'Multi-dimensional compositional functions as a basis for grammatical analysis' in R. Oehrle, E. Bach and D. Wheeler (eds), *Categorial Grammars and Natural Language Structures*. Dordrecht: D. Reidel Publishing, pp. 349–89.

Oehrle, R. (1994), 'Term-labelled categorial type systems' in *Linguistics and Philosophy* 17, pp. 633–78.

Oehrle, Richard, Emmon Bach and Deirdre Wheeler (eds) (1988), *Categorial Grammars and Natural Language Structures*. Dordrecht: D. Reidel Publishing (Proceedings of the Conference on Categorial Grammar, Tucson AZ, 1985).

Partee, Barbara, Alice Ter Meulen and Robert Wall (1990), *Mathematical Methods in Linguistics*. Dordrecht, London: Kluwer.

Peirce, C. S. (1870), 'Description of a notation for the logic of relatives, resulting from an amplification of the conceptions of Boole's calculus of logic' in *Memoirs of the American Academy of Science* 9, pp. 317–78.

Pelletier, F. (2000), 'A history of natural deduction and elementary logic textbooks' in J. Woods and B. Brown (eds), *Logical Consequence: Rival Approaches*, Vol. 1. Oxford: Hermes Science Publications, pp. 105–38.

Pentus, M. (1993), 'Lambek grammars are context-free' in *Proceedings of the IEEE Symposium on Logic in Computer Science*, Montreal, pp. 429–33.

Perlmutter, David (ed.) (1983), *Studies in Relational Grammar*, Vol. I. Chicago: Chicago University Press.

Perlmutter, David and Carol Rosen (eds) (1984), *Studies in Relational Grammar*, Vol. II. Chicago: Chicago University Press.

Perry, J. (1986), 'From worlds to situations' in *Journal of Philosophical Logic* 15, pp. 83–107.

Pinker, Steven (1989), *Learnability and Cognition: The Acquisition of Argument Structure*. Cambridge, MA: MIT Press.

Pollard, C. (2004), 'Type-logcal HPSG' in *Proceedings of the 9th Conference on Formal Grammar*, Nancy.

Pollard, C. (2008a), 'A parallel derivational architecture for the syntax-semantics interface', ESSLLI.

Pollard, C. (2008b), 'Hyperintensions' in *Journal of Logic and Computation* 18 (2), pp. 257–82.

Pollard, C. (2008c), 'Hyperintensional questions' in D. Hodges and R. de Queiroz (eds), *Logic, Language, Information and Computation*. Edinburgh: Proceedings of the 15th International Workshop, WoLLIC.

Pollard, Carl and Ivan Sag (1987), *Information-Based Syntax and Semantics*, Vol. 1: Fundamentals. Stanford: Center for the Study of Language and Information Lecture Notes No. 9.

Pollard, Carl and Ivan Sag (1994), *Head-Driven Phrase Structure Grammar*. Chicago: University of Chicago Press.

Prawitz, Dag (1965), *Natural Deduction: A Proof-Theoretical Study*. Stockholm: Almqvist and Wiksell.

Priest, G. (1979), 'Logic of paradox' in *Journal of Philosophical Logic* 8 (1), pp. 219–41.

Priest, G., K. Tanaka and Z. Weber (2013), 'Paraconsistent logic' in E. N. Zalta (ed.), *The Stanford Encyclopedia of Philosophy*, Fall. URL = http://plato.stanford.edu/archives/fall2013/entries/logic-paraconsistent/

Prior, Arthur (1957), *Time and Modality*. Oxford: Oxford University Press.

Quine, W. van Orman (1956), 'Quantifiers and propositional attitudes' in *Journal of Philosophy* 53.

Quine, W. van Orman (1970), *The Philosophy of Logic*. Cambridge, MA: Harvard University Press, 2nd edition.

Quine, W. van Orman (1981), 'Predicate functors revisited' in *Journal of Symbolic Logic* 46, pp. 649–52.

Ranta, Arne (1994), *Type-Theoretical Grammar*. Oxford: Oxford University Press.

Restall, Greg (1995), *Negation in Relevant Logics (How I Stopped Worrying and Learned to Love the Routley Star)*, Technical Report TR-ARP-3-95. Canberra: Australian National University.

Restall, G. (1996), 'Information flow and relevant logics', in J. Seligman and D. Westerstahl (eds), *Logic, Language and Computation*, Vol. 1. Stanford: Center for the Study of Language and Information, pp. 463–78.

Restall, Greg (2000), *An Introduction to Substructural Logics*. London: Routledge.

Restall, Greg (2006), 'Relevant and substructural logics' in Dov Gabbay and John Woods (eds), *The Handbook of Philosophical Logic*, Vol. 7. Berlin: Springer, pp. 289–398.

Routley, R. and R. K. Meyer (1972), 'Semantics of entailment' (Parts II, III) in *Journal of Philosophical Logic* 1.

Routley, R. and V. Routley (1972), 'Semantics of first-degree entailment' in *Nous* 3, pp. 335–59.

Russell, B. (1905), 'On denoting' in *Mind* 14, pp. 479–93.

Schönfinkel, M. (1924) 'Über die Bausteine der mathematischen Logik'. Talk given in the University of Göttingen, December 1920. Edited version in *Mathematische Annalen* 92, pp. 305–16.

Shannon, C. (1948), 'A mathematical theory of communication' in *Bell Systems Technical Journal* 27, pp. 379–423 and pp. 623–56.

Smullyan, Raymond (1962), *To Mock a Mockingbird*. Oxford: Oxford University Press.

Stalnaker, Robert (1984), *Inquiry*. Cambridge, MA: MIT Press.

Steedman, Mark (1986), *Combinatory Grammars and Human Language Processing*. Edinburgh: University of Edinburgh.

Steedman, M. (1988), 'Combinators and grammars' in R. Oehrle, E. Bach and D. Wheeler (eds), *Categorial Grammars and Natural Language Structures*. Dordrecht: D. Reidel Publishing.

Steedman, Mark (2000), *The Syntactic Process*. Cambridge, MA: MIT Press.

Steedman, M. and J. Baldridge (2011), 'Combinatory categorial grammar' in R. Borsley and K. Borjars (eds), *Non-Transformational Syntax: Formal and Explicit Models of Grammar*. London: Wiley-Blackwell.

Stenning, K. and O. Lemon (2001), 'Aligning logical and psychological perspectives on diagrammatic reasoning' in *Artificial Intelligence Review* 15 (12), pp. 29–62.

Strawson, P. (1950), 'On referring' in *Mind* 59, pp. 320–34.

Szabolcsi, A. (1987), 'Bound variables in syntax - are there any?' in *Proceedings of the 6th Amsterdam Linguistic Colloquium*.

Szabolcsi, A. (1992), 'Combinatory grammar and projection from the lexicon' in I. Sag and A. Szabolcsi (eds), *Lexical Matters*. Stanford: Center for the Study of Language and Information, pp. 241–69.

Tarski, A. (1935), 'Der Wahrheitsbegriff in den formalisierten Sprachen' in *Studia Philosophica* 1, pp. 261–405 (Polish original 1933).

Thomason, R. (ed.) (1974), *Formal Philosophy. Selected Papers of Richard Montague*. New Haven: Yale University Press.

Thouless, Robert (1953), *Straight and Crooked Thinking*. London: Pan Books.

Troelstra, Anne (1992), *Lectures on Linear Logic*. Stanford: Center for the Study of Language and Information.

Turing, A. (1937), 'Computability and λ-definability' in *The Journal of Symbolic Logic* 2 (4), pp. 153–63.

Turner, D. (1979), 'Another algorithm for bracket abstraction' in *Journal of Symbolic Logic* 44 (2), pp. 267–70.

Van Benthem, J. (1983), 'The semantics of variety in categorial grammar'. Technical Report 83–29, Simon Fraser University. Revised version in W. Buszkowski, W. Marciszewski and J. van Benthem (eds), *Categorial Grammar*, Philadelphia: John Benjamin Publishing.

Van Benthem, Johann (1986), *Essays in Logical Semantics*, Dordrecht: D. Reidel Publishing.

Van Benthem, J. (1988), 'The Lambek Calculus', in R. Oehrle, E. Bach and D. Wheeler (eds), *Categorial Grammars and Natural Language Structures*. Dordrecht: D. Reidel Publishing.

Vickers, Steven (1990), *Topology Via Logic*, Number 5 of Cambridge Tracts in Theoretical Computer Science. Cambridge: Cambridge University Press.

Von Plato, J. (2014), 'The development of proof theory' in Edward Zalta (ed.), *The Stanford Encyclopedia of Philosophy*, 2014. URL = http://plato.stanford.edu/archives/spr2014/entries/proof-theory-development/

Von Wright, G. H. (1951), 'Deontic logic' in *Mind* 60, p. 115.

Wansing, H. (1982), 'Formulas-as-types for a hierarchy of sublogics of intuitionistic propositional logic' in D. Peirce and H. Wansing (eds), *Nonclassical Logics and Information Processing*. Dordrecht: Springer-Verlag, pp. 125–45.

Wittgenstein, Ludwig (1922), *Tractatus Logico-Philosophicus*. English translation by C. K. Ogden. London: Routledge and Kegan Paul.

Wood, Mary McGee (1993), *Categorial Grammar*. London: Routledge.

Zadeh, L. (1965), 'Fuzzy sets' in *Information and Control* 8, pp. 338–53.

Zalta, E. (1990), 'A theory of situations' in Robin Cooper, Kuniaki Mukai and Jon Barwise (eds), *Situation Theory and Its Applications*, Vol. 2. Stanford: Center for the Study of Language and Information, pp. 81–112.

Zeman, J. J. (1973), *Modal Logic, the Lewis Modal Systems*. Oxford: Oxford University Press.

INDEX